ARGUING WITH GOD

ARGUING WITH GOD
A Jewish Tradition

ANSON LAYTNER

Jason Aronson Inc.
Northvale, New Jersey
London

For credits, see page 308.

10 9 8 7 6 5 4 3 2 1

Library of Congress Cataloging-in-Publication Data

Laytner, Anson.
  Arguing with God: a Jewish tradition / Anson Laytner.
    p. cm.
  Includes bibliographical references.
  ISBN 0-87668-817-2 :
  1. God (Judaism)—History of doctrines. 2. Covenants (Jewish theology)—History of doctrines. 3. Providence and government of God—History of doctrines. 4. Prayer—Judaism. I. Title.
BM610.L39 1990
296.3′11—dc 20   89-28654
                                                           CIP

Manufactured in the United States of America. Jason Aronson Inc. offers books and cassettes. For information and catalog write to Jason Aronson Inc., 230 Livingston Street, Northvale, New Jersey 07647.

To my wife Merrily, with love and gratitude

Proverbs 31:26 and Ecclesiastes 9:9

Contents

PART II

Acknowledgment

This book would not have been possible without the help and encouragement of many people. First and foremost, my teachers. At York University: Sydney Eisen, Peter Mitchell, Richard Schneider, Shu-Ying Tsau, Sol Tanenzapf, and Jordan Paper. At Hebrew Union College: Jakob Petuchowski and Alexander Guttmann, among others. In the working world: Jordan Pearlson, Yitz Greenberg, and Arthur Lagawier. Life also has been my teacher, and here I must acknowledge the profound impact my year of study in each of both China and Israel has had upon the development of my thinking.

A special thanks goes to my former secretary, Jette Rhodes, for motivating me to return to my manuscript and for her many hours of typing and editing. Thanks also to Arthur Kurzweil, Jane Andrassi, and the staff of Jason Aronson for their encouragement and assistance in seeing this work through to publication.

My family has been a great source of support and inspiration— so, to my parents, Bernard and Ray Laytner; to my wife, Merrily; and my children, Amy, Anna, and Miriam; to my brother and sister, my aunts, uncles, in-laws, cousins, and friends, I say "yasher cohachem" and thanks.

The Law-Court Pattern of Prayer: An Introduction and an Overview

BIBLICAL ROOTS

The patriarch Jacob was a most extraordinary fellow, truly worthy of the name "Israel," one who struggled with God. In Genesis 28, Jacob received a vision and a promise afforded to few other mortals. In his dream, Jacob saw a ladder stretching from the earth to the Heavens, and at the very top stood YHVH (the Lord) God. Then Jacob heard God swear to him: "Behold, I am with you. I will protect you wherever you go and I will bring you back to this land" (Genesis 28:15). Yet on the morrow, when the bright Middle Eastern sun penetrated into the dream-enchanted corners of his mind, Jacob vowed the following vow: "If God be with me, if He protects me on this journey that I am making, and gives me bread to eat and clothing to wear, and if I return safely to my father's house—then the Lord shall be my God" (Genesis 28:20–21). Most unusual! First God promises Jacob divine protection, and then Jacob proceeds to put a qualifier on God's word. "IF God does thus and so for me, then the Lord shall be my God and I will serve Him."

This juxtaposition of God's promise and Jacob's vow troubled rabbinic exegetes of all ages, as the following story shows:

Two rabbis, Rabbi Abahu and Rabbi Yohanan, disagreed on the interpretation of Jacob's vow. On the one hand, Rabbi Abahu said: "The story requires chronological rearrangement, for the events did not occur in the order in which they were written. First Jacob prayed, 'If God will be with me,' and afterwards the word of the Lord came to him in his dream: 'Behold I am with you.' For could it be that Jacob would have uttered such a vow after God had already promised to protect him?"

On the other hand, Rabbi Yohanan said: "The text requires no rearrangement. For this is what Jacob meant: 'If all the conditions that God promised me—to be with me and to protect me—are fulfilled; then I will keep my vow.'"[1]

This second Jacob, Rabbi Yohanan's Jacob, knew something about this God who spoke in dreams in the night. No doubt he had heard something from father Isaac's lips about a near-sacrifice at this God's command. Jacob wasn't about to entrust his future well-being to words spoken in some dark dream. The arrangement had to be tied up but good! YHVH, if He was to be Jacob's God, had to prove Himself worthy. He had to earn Jacob's respect if Jacob was to take the Lord as his God.

As the story of Jacob illustrates, the Jewish relationship with God has, almost from the very beginning, been expressed in terms of a mutually beneficial contract. Before Jacob would enter into a Covenant with God, he had to be shown that God would indeed *act* as his God. Only after God had demonstrated His reliability was Jacob willing to give the Lord a shot at a steady job as the God of Israel. Jacob may have been young, but he was wily. He knew how to get what he wanted—even from God. By binding God to a clear-cut contract, Jacob provided an excellent model upon which to build.

But what happened with the generation of the Exodus? Slowly, and not without a good deal of cajoling and a great number of miracles, Israel came to accept the Lord as their God. God had to prove Himself worthy of Israel's devotion. It took some doing, but God performed admirably and, on account of this, Jewish people still sing His praises several times every day, not to mention dedicating an entire holiday to commemorate the occasion of His giving the Torah to Israel.

Unfortunately, the Israelites were so overwhelmed at finally being delivered from Egyptian bondage that they strayed from Jacob's example when it came to renegotiating their contract with God. First, they pledged themselves and their descendants to an eternal Covenant, which gave God free rein (or reign) to do as He pleased. Second, and most significant for later generations, in a moment of panic, they asked never directly to see or hear God again. From that moment, God, it would seem to many, grew lax about fulfilling His side of the bargain. From that time onward, the course of Jewish history was totally different.

Indeed, in many generations, God has not acted toward His people as a God should act. And His people have known it. The Jewish literary heritage is replete with laments and dirges, complaints and arguments, all protesting God's mistreatment of His people. In every period of the people's suffering, a cry of outrage and injustice rose alongside the words of those who continually prayed: "U'mipnei hata'einu,"—"on account of our sins are we punished." Such was the case with the generations that endured the Roman persecutions. Such was the case with the generations that suffered during the Crusades, with those tortured and killed in Spain during the Inquisition, and with those butchered by Chmielnitski's hordes. And the cry of protest has also been heard in our century: witness the pogroms in Russia from the 1880s to the 1920s, and, of course, the Holocaust.

This history of suffering has given rise to a unique literature of argument prayers, which is the subject of this book. Argument with God—called the "law-court" pattern of prayer by scholars—is a particularly (and perhaps uniquely) Jewish response to the problem of theodicy. The law-court argument prayer is an authentic Jewish form of prayer that, though rooted in deep faith, nevertheless calls God to task for His lapses of duty which result in suffering and injustice. It is the Jewish mode of appealing to God the Chief Justice of the Supreme Court against God the Partner, and records of such protest/appeals may be found in the literature of practically every period of Jewish history—from the Bible to rabbinic texts, from medieval liturgical poetry to the hasidic tale, from Yiddish folksongs to post-Holocaust poetry and literature.

THE COVENANTAL RELATIONSHIP

At the heart of this form of prayer lies an unusual God–concept, one that has persisted for centuries, as if in defiance of the alliance made between mainstream Muslim, Jewish, and Christian theologians on the one hand and Greek philosophy on the other. A God with whom one can argue is an emotive God; a God with personality; a changing and changeable God; an omnipotent but simultaneously self-limiting God, ruler over all yet accessible to all who call out.

The "Jewish" God is a unique God, unique because, in the Jewish religious imagination, He has bound Himself by means of a Covenant (*brit*) with the Jewish people. In classical Jewish imagery, the covenantal relationship culminates as an act of betrothal and marriage at Mount Sinai although it had begun long before with Abraham. The Covenant idea remains the single most important factor in the whole range of Jewish responses to the Jewish God. It is the basic definition of the Jewish relationship with God. Yet even so, the parameters of the relationship are broad.

On the other hand, following standard religious terminology, God is our Father, our King; we are His children, His flock, His servants. God creates, plans and acts; we are rewarded, chastised, forgiven. The Covenant, in this form, closely resembles a fealty oath offered by a vassal to a powerful lord. Prayer is the standard means of communication between man and God; as God commands, we pray. But prayer, in this context, is always submissive; our requests always cloaked in a garment of praise and humility. This form of relationship is central, not only to Judaism, but also to Christianity and Islam.

Yet, on the other hand, there has existed alongside this mainstream tradition another expression of the covenantal relationship. According to this view, the relationship with God is more one of contractual equals, of partnership. According to this view of the Covenant, it is as though God and the Jewish people grew up together and so treat each other with the familiarity common to old friends or lovers. (Marriage would be a good analogy were it not for the fact that from ancient times, marriage has been the symbol of an unequal power relationship and not a binding together of two equal human beings.) In the Jewish cultural context, the sort of communication this second sort of covenantal relationship sometimes requires is called "acting with nerve [*hutzpah*] against Heaven," after the Aramaic expression, *hutzpah k'lapei shemaya*.[2] In this alternate view of the covenantal relationship, the Covenant can serve as the tool by which an individual can challenge or even defy the will of God. Erich Fromm, himself building upon this tradition, rightly identifies the radical nature of this version of the covenantal relationship:

> With the conclusion of the covenant, God ceases to be the absolute ruler. He and man have become partners in a treaty. God is transformed from an "absolute" into a "constitutional" monarch. He is bound, as man is bound, to the conditions of the constitution. God has lost his freedom to be arbitrary, and man has gained the freedom of being able to challenge God in the name of God's own promises, of the principles laid down in the covenant.[3]

THE LAW-COURT PATTERN
OF PRAYER

The most basic word for prayer in Hebrew is *tefillah*, which comes from the verb root *palal*.[4] In the Bible, *palal* was one of three verb roots originally associated with the concept of sacrifice. All three came to mean "prayer" in the sense of offering something to God in exchange for His granting one's request—an arrangement based on the quid pro quo principle, which one scholar called "the bargaining spirit of early oriental prayer."[5]

But the root *palal*—which is the basis for *tefillah*—had a second sense of meaning, one manifesting "a bargaining spirit" in a legal, or law-court, context. According to one scholar, the root also meant "to adjudicate,"[6] while another saw the root meaning "to arbitrate."[7] This second understanding of *palal* corresponds to the use of other legal terms to describe varied aspects of the divine–human relationship generally associated with the concept of "prayer." Chief among them was *riv*, a legal case or controversy, which was also applied to the divine–human relationship. The imagery of the law-court in fact gave rise to a biblical form of prayer called "the rîb pattern," by B. Gemser, and the "law-court pattern" by S. Blank.[8] J. Heinemann also categorized a form of rabbinic prayer as "the law-court pattern" of prayer.[9]

In the Bible and rabbinic literature, this law-court pattern is used in three situations: in the human court, in the heavenly court, and in human–divine controversies. The first can be dismissed: it is not prayer. The second describes controversies either between God and the angels or, as is often the case in the prophetic texts, between God and a personified Israel, in which God summons and accuses Israel of faithlessness and then issues a verdict.[10] But the third usage depicts situations in which an individual (or Israel) brings a charge against God Himself. The appeal thus is both against God yet also to God, making Him, paradoxically, both judge and defendant. In this third usage, the human–divine controversies, "the petitioner–worshiper addresses God as a judge before whom he presents his case, setting all of the 'facts' in order to 'defend' himself, and concluding with a plea that the Divine Judge may uphold his cause and vindicate him in judgement."[11]

These are the components—or structure—of the law-court pattern of prayer:

1. An address to God the judge

2. A presentation of the facts of the case; the complaint and petition brought against God and to God

3. A concluding petition or request made by the individual (or Israel)

In certain cases, an additional component may follow:

4. A divine response to the petition[12]

THE UNIQUENESS OF HEBREW PRAYER

Scholars recognize that biblical prayer, and specifically its law-court pattern, was greatly influenced by more ancient Near Eastern models.[13] However, the Hebrew law-court pattern of prayer also represented a marked departure from the older pagan models. First and foremost, only in the Israelite version of the law-court pattern were complaints and charges allowable against God Himself. Second, use of the law-court pattern indicated a certain frame of mind that manifested a highly personalized approach to the problem of the individual's and the nation's fate. Third, the legal controversy between man and God had its basis in an active and personalistic relationship, which in turn was based upon a radically monotheistic faith. (In polytheism, objections to one's fate could easily be rationalized by attributing one's misfortune to the power of another god.) Fourth, the use of the law-court pattern revealed a decidedly ethical, normative conception of God and His relationship with humankind based upon the assumption of a divinely-instituted moral order in the world. *Tzedakah*, justice, was the name given to this order and it remains the fundamental concept of the Jewish ethicoreligious world-view. Only in this context could the individual appeal to God to set things right because it presupposed that there is an order of things to which even God must adhere in His relationship with the individual, the nation, and the world.[14]

A COMPARISON WITH THE GREEKS

A number of scholars have seen a Promethean element in the prayers and stories that employ the law-court motif.[15] Certainly there is no similarity between the Hebrew stories and Hesiod's story of Prometheus. In the latter, Prometheus is humankind's emissary to the gods, while the gods, and Zeus in particular, are malevolent figures who harbor hostile intentions toward humankind. The Hebrew stories, on the other hand, presuppose that God is good and that creation (and the creation of people) is good. Even Aeschylus' version of the Prometheus myth does not approach the Hebrew view of the relationship between people and God. Zeus remains a hostile and malevolent force, vehemently opposed to the advancement of humankind. Perhaps the only thread of similarity between Aeschylus' Prometheus and the Hebrew heroes lies in Prometheus' unbounded love and devotion to humankind, which led him to risk everything for its sake, just as the Hebrew heroes also risked their very lives in order to call God

to account. But despite this, there remains a significant difference between the Greek and Hebrew figures. Though the Hebrew
heroes do confront and challenge God, they do so knowing that
God is good, that He is benevolent. Whatever their complaint, the
basis of their complaint rests upon the assumption that God is
just and that He rules the world with *tzedakah*, with justice. Each
story begins with the presupposition of God's justice and concludes with an affirmation of God's justice. One of the purposes
then of each story was as a "didactic device, designed to spread
the truth that God cannot be unjust."[16] But injustice did exist.
God could be "sued" and justice demanded. This, as we shall see,
was a message as necessary to affirm throughout the centuries as
it was in the biblical period.

THE LAW-COURT PATTERN
THROUGHOUT JEWISH HISTORY

Different generations of Jews have made use of the "argument
with God" form of prayer to address their own unique problems
and needs. In the Bible, the arguments have a didactic intent: to
reinforce the teachings of monotheism, to refute the dual or
multi-divinity religions of the ancient Near East, or to emphasize
specific attributes of the Jewish God. Thus, for example, in order
to stress that God is truly just and merciful, Abraham argues with
God over the fate of Sodom and Gomorrah and "convinces" God to
spare the cities for the sake of ten righteous individuals. Moses,
Elijah, Jeremiah, and Job are but a few of the other biblical figures
who also took God to task, while the psalms of lament and Lamentations depict argument with God as a form of prayer.

In the rabbinic period, argument with God is found primarily in
the stories that the Rabbis created to clarify biblical arguments.
The didactic intent is even more pronounced here. Through the
words they placed in the mouths of biblical figures, the Rabbis
sought not only to counter the competing claims of Gnosticism
and Christianity, but also to advance their own interpretations of
Judaism. The argument with God form was used to comfort and
reassure the people in an age of statelessness and powerlessness;
it was used to voice existential discontent with the human condi-

tion—from the problem of human nature itself to childlessness to the problems of suffering and death. The rabbis also used this form of forceful prayer in a personal intercessory mode, in times of communal emergency and distress.

The liturgical poetry of the medieval period and the hasidic stories utilize the "arguing with God" motif primarily as a means of coping with life in the Exile. Here questions and doubts can be hurled at God, even while remaining within the faith community, in part because the poems and tales were meant to complement the "submissive" theology of the prayerbook. In these works, God is called to account and charged, at the very least, with indifference. If God is not acting unjustly, He is, at any rate, permitting injustice and suffering to flourish. However, at the same time, just by raising the issue in a liturgical or worship context, the belief in God as a just and humane Judge is reaffirmed and the people comforted by having their anger and questions aired. The demand for redemption—an end to the Exile, together with the concomitant vindication of Israel and the punishment of the wicked—stands as the paramount petition during this dark era.

The situation is radically different in the post-Holocaust age. I believe that this age represents the breaking point in the Jewish people's attitude toward suffering and toward God. Many Jewish people hunger for God, but are disillusioned with Him, and this disillusionment leads to doubt. Other generations may have doubted, but only today has this doubt reached epidemic proportions. The answers of times past no longer satisfy all the doubts of today. One thing is clear to many: the God of Abraham, Isaac, and Jacob, the God of the Bible and of the Rabbis, appears no longer to be personally and actively involved in the course of history. The "old" God of the Jewish people was an active god, yet for centuries Jews have not experienced God's activity as related in Scripture. Our miracleless present stands in conflict with the accounts of our miraculous past. Everything we do is but an attempt to answer this question: What has become of the God of our ancestors? As Raba once stated so well: "Master of the Universe! O God! We have heard with our ears; our fathers have told us what deeds You did perform in their days, in the days of old—but as for us, with our own eyes we have not seen [it]!"[17] This challenge is the focus of this book's final chapter, which deals with post-Holocaust Yiddish poetry and the works of Elie Wiesel.

These responses may or may not satisfy, but at least they attempt to address the problem. Many people today remain deeply troubled by the God–concept presented in the liturgy and in mainstream Jewish theology. Much of the current interest in mysticism derives from a dissatisfaction with the answers of traditional (that is, rational) theology and philosophy. Thinkers like Wiesel and Glatstein simultaneously are links in the chain of the arguing with God tradition and pioneers, breaking new ground as they search for meaningful responses to the latest tragedy and the oldest contradiction.

Their endeavor is shared by this author. It is the ultimate purpose of this book. By tracing the argument with God motif through the ages, I hope that contemporary Jews not only will learn of the continuous heritage of doubt and protest and acquire a vocabulary through which to express the present mood, but will also gain a sense of reassurance that the present spiritual crisis, far from being unique in history, has analogies and precedents in other times and in other places of Jewish history. Beyond this, knowledge of the motif may help to reawaken or reanimate a sense of the potential dynamism of prayer by revitalizing and reevaluating the divine–human relationship. This, especially after the confrontation with the Holocaust, is the motif's strength and beauty. The challenge is how to use it to heal.

PART I

1

ARGUING WITH GOD IN THE BIBLE

INTRODUCTION

In the Bible, individuals argue with God in times of crisis through use of the law-court pattern of prayer. Certain outstanding individuals, Abraham or Moses for example, employ it on behalf of a third party under the cloud of divine judgment; others, a Jeremiah or a Job, utilize it in arguing their own personal cases before God; and it is used by the anonymous authors of the petitionary psalms and Lamentations when pleading for salvation and redemption. Over all, there is a dramatic increase both in the usage of the arguing with God motif and the law-court pattern of prayer. They appear occasionally in the stories of Genesis, become more frequent in Moses' addresses, and quite prevalent in the works written around the time of the Babylonian Exile. The Book of Job, both in content and structure, represents the climax of the Bible's use and development of the arguing with God motif and the law-court pattern of prayer.

ABRAHAM

There are a number of examples of the arguing motif and the law-court pattern in the Book of Genesis,[1] but perhaps the most dramatic usage of the motif is found in the story of Abraham's argument with God over the fate of the people of Sodom and Gomorrah (Genesis 18:23–32). Because the argument takes the form of a dialogue, the structure of the law court pattern is obscured. But even so, all its components—address, argument, peti-

3

tion—are present. This is how Abraham argues his case before God:

> (23) Abraham came forward and said, "Will You sweep away the innocent along with the guilty? (24) What if there should be fifty innocent within the city; will You then wipe out the place and not forgive it for the sake of the innocent fifty who are in it?
> (25) Far be it from You to do such a thing, to bring death upon the innocent as well as the guilty, so that innocent and guilty fare alike. Far be it from You! Shall not the Judge of all the earth deal justly?" (26) And the Lord answered, "If I find within the city of Sodom fifty innocent ones, I will forgive the whole place for their sake." (27) Abraham spoke up, saying, "Here I venture to speak to my Lord, I who am but dust and ashes: (28) What if the fifty innocent should lack five? Will you destroy the whole city for want of the five?" And He answered, "I will not destroy it if I find forty-five there." (29) But he spoke to Him again, and said, "What if forty should be found there?" And He answered, "I will not do it, for the sake of the forty." (30) And he said, "Let not my Lord be angry if I go on: What if thirty should be found there?" (31) And He answered, "I will not do it if I find thirty there." And he said, "I venture again to speak to my Lord: What if twenty should be found there?" And He answered, "I will not destroy, for the twenty." (32) And he said, "Let not my Lord be angry if I speak but this last time: What if ten should be found there?" And He answered, "I will not destroy, for the sake of the ten."

Abraham builds his case upon two important premises. He appeals to both God's (presumed) moral nature and a universal moral order by which even God is expected to abide (verse 25). Having forced God's acknowledgment of these premises, Abraham is then able to bargain with God as to what constitutes a saving remnant. But what precedes and follows the argument only affirms that this is precisely what God wanted Abraham to do.

What is the intent of this dialogue? Scholars have suggested two apparently contradictory interpretations. Either the dialogue shows that God may, on occasion, be unjust and therefore in need of the human direction and instruction that Abraham's argument provides,[2] or—the alternative—the dialogue teaches, by means of Abraham's questioning, that God is truly just and that all His deeds are likewise just.[3] But the two perspectives need not be mutually exclusive.

In verses 20–21, God Himself decides to investigate whether Sodom and Gomorrah are indeed as sinful as the outcry (*za'akah* and *tza'akah*) against them suggests. Here God is acting as a judge investigating the justice of a complaint that has reached his court.[4] God also decides to share His judgment of the cities with Abraham "since Abraham is to become a great and populous nation and all the nations of the earth are to bless themselves by him. For I have singled him out, that he may instruct his children . . . to keep the way of the Lord by doing what is just and right" (verses 17–19). The reason is clear: God has chosen Abraham and his line and charged them with keeping "the way of the Lord"; therefore God wishes to show Abraham that what He intends to do to the cities is, in fact, totally warranted and justified. Abraham is to serve as the witness of God's justice to later generations, giving testimony through his argument that God is truly just.

God all but invites Abraham to question His justice, and Abraham responds by asking the basic questions that any member of the faith community would ask were he in Abraham's place: "Is God just if He destroys the righteous with the wicked so that the end of the righteous is as that of the wicked?" Abraham's questions are meant to affirm rather than cast doubt upon God's justice; they are rhetorical questions. This point is confirmed by the conclusion of the story. First of all, by accepting Abraham's argument, God implicitly confirms Abraham's belief that God should act justly. Second, there is the matter of Abraham's choice of the number ten. Why does Abraham settle on the saving number of ten righteous men? Why does he not bargain still further? Abraham's choice of numbers is yet another means to teach about God's justice.

God agrees to spare the cities if ten righteous men can be found in their midst. But ten righteous men cannot be found there. Moreover, God's messengers, His "detectives," receive firsthand experience of the inhabitants' sinfulness (Genesis 19:1–11). God now knows the truth of the complaint that has been brought to His court and He passes sentence against them. But even as this verdict is reached, God's messengers simultaneously act to save the lives of the few comparatively righteous people who dwell there, namely Lot and his family (Genesis 19:12–13). In the end, justice is meted out in full measure against the wicked (Genesis 19:24–25), but toward the righteous, even the partially righteous (Lot and his family), God shows abundant mercy and spares them (Genesis 19:16 and 29). Thus the story as a whole stresses the completeness of God's justice. Abraham's argument with God serves as a didactic and dramatic device within the story, heightening the impact of this fundamental doctrine.

The biblical narrative is meant to relate both history and theology. It must provide the drama of the historical encounter (that is, the human perspective) and also the "true facts" of the story, its theology, by placing the dialogue within a wider context (the perspective of the author[s] or God). To Abraham, and to the hearers of the tale, it would appear that God stood on the brink of acting unjustly and that therefore He had to be brought around to acting in a more becoming (and godly) manner—an awesome and terrifying task for anyone to undertake (hence Genesis 19:27). But in the author's (and God's) mind, there was never any doubt about the veracity of God's justice. This double perspective invests the biblical account with its dramatic tension even as it presents its theological message. Both aspects are necessary for a complete sense and feeling of the story.

Since Abraham's argument with God is the first major one of its kind—and certainly the first "Jewish" one—a number of observations are in order. First, what gives Abraham the right to question God's judgment? It is the Covenant (*brit*) that bestows this privilege. The Covenant, the contract into which Abraham entered at God's behest, unites Abraham and his seed in a unique relationship with God. Abraham's line is bound to keep the commandments of the Lord (the first of which is circumcision), but it is also understood that God has His obligations to uphold (Genesis 17:1–14). Furthermore, both parties are bound to pursue justice and righteousness, these things being both the God-given charge to Abraham and his descendants and "the way of the Lord" by which God Himself is obligated.

This concept of Covenant has a number of implications that set the ground rules for the arguing motif and the law-court pattern of prayer. The Covenant, in that it sets forth the concrete and the moral responsibilities of both parties, gives Abraham and his descendants the right to dissent and even protest against any

apparent abrogation of its terms by God. And God has a similar
right to protest against Israel's failure to observe its side of the
Covenant (something that, in the Bible, God has greater occasion to do than does Israel!). The contractual nature of the Covenant accounts for the prevalence of a legalistic form of address—
the law-court pattern—which both God (as judge) and Israel (as
plaintiff) use to call the transgressing party to accounts. By
means of the Covenant, Israel becomes a partner with God; by
means of the arguing motif and the law-court pattern of prayer,
Israel asserts not only its moral equality with God, but also its
"revolutionary faith in God's responsiveness to the call of justice."[5]

A second observation, of great importance for later arguments:
Lot is saved because he acted righteously toward the angels
(Genesis 19:1–3,4–9) and because God is merciful (verses 12–16).
But at the conclusion of the story, we are offered a third reason for
Lot's salvation. God spares Lot because "God remembered Abraham" (Genesis 19:29). Here we see the beginnings of the concept
of the doctrine of merit, *zekhut.* Abraham's righteousness (his
merit) not only enables him to challenge God, it also has a protect-
ing and redeeming quality for those associated with him. In succeeding generations, less emphasis was placed on personal merit
and more emphasis on the merit of the ancestors, the *zekhut
avot.* But both forms of the concept were used in later law-court
arguments.[6]

Finally, the story continues the biblical struggle against the
influence of the neighboring pagan religions, refuting fundamental pagan religious concepts and advancing alternative monotheistic religious concepts. In broad terms, the story sets the belief in
a single, universal God against the belief in a pantheon of gods. It
advances the belief in God's justice and mercy, and in a divinely
ordained moral order, over either the belief in the powers of a
multitude of competing gods or the possibility that the one God
could be capricious in the exercise of His power. It affirms the role
of justice as the key relational concept between God and the world,
as something expected of and received from God, as well as something obligatory upon humankind (and upon Israel especially)
under a divinely ordained system of reward and punishment (the
moral order). And last, the story teaches that God is personally

involved in the affairs of the world and that He may be engaged in dialogue and appealed to, by an Abraham at least, on the basis of the presumed moral order and the presumed divine nature.

The Torah depicts Abraham as the consummate man of faith. When commanded by God to remove himself and his family from Ur, Abraham does not ask, "Who speaks?" or, "To where am I being sent?" or, "Why should I go?" He simply packs up and leaves. When commanded to sacrifice Isaac, his beloved son, Abraham does not protest; he simply obeys. But his relationship with God has depth beyond simple obedience. When Abraham does argue with God over the fate of Sodom and Gomorrah, it is largely without any of the dread or doubt that one might expect a person to feel in such a circumstance. The relationship between the Patriarch and God was unique in its wholeness from the start. Not so with Moses.

MOSES

God had told Abraham that his descendants would be enslaved for 400 years. During that time, according to one biblical/rabbinic tradition, Israel became assimilated and forgot their God.[7] The text of Exodus bears this out, for when Israel was oppressed it says "they cried out" and "their cry rose up to God." Note that the text does not say "they cried out to God," only that "they cried out and their cry rose up to God" as a simple matter of injustice. (The verb used for "cry out" is the same as that used to depict the outcry from Sodom and Gomorrah.) Only then did God look upon the Israelites and take notice of them; only then did He remember His covenant with Abraham, Isaac, and Jacob. There could be no remembering on God's part if there was no forgetting by Israel.

Moses typifies Israel's feelings as an abandoned and Godless people. His response to God's call—a running dialogue of doubts and questions—epitomizes Israel's loss of faith and knowledge of God. Five times in chapters 3–4 Moses attempts to refuse his mission (Exodus 3:11,13; 4:1,10,13); five times God answers Moses' doubts until His anger is provoked (Exodus 4:14). Finally forced to go confront Pharaoh and failing miserably in his first attempt to free the people, Moses confronts God with a defiant complaint (Exodus 5:22–23).

The crux of Moses' reluctance lies in his lack of faith in God, his lack of knowledge of God, and his lack of direct experience of God's power. When commanded to appear before Pharaoh, Moses does not ask, "How will Pharaoh know You?" but, "When I come to the Israelites," they will ask, "What is His name?" Moses needs to know the answer as much as do the people in whose name he presumes to ask. Despite God's assurance of help, Moses still hides behind his people's doubts. In Exodus 3:18 God assures Moses, "They will listen to you," but in 4:1 Moses responds, "They will not believe me, nor will they listen to me"—a rather daring contradiction considering with whom Moses is talking. Nonetheless, God provides Moses with proofs of His power, which Moses in turn can use to educate the Israelites and Pharaoh. Henceforth Moses believes in this God of the talking bush even though he remains opposed to his mission and skeptical of its success, no doubt, in part, because God has already twice told him that He will harden Pharaoh's heart so that Pharaoh will not accede readily (Exodus 3:19; 4:21). The plagues are meant as much to convince Israel of her God's power and reality as they are to convince the Egyptians. After all, it is hard to make amends for ignoring One's own people while they suffer in bondage for 400 years!

Moses' initial efforts meet with success. He convinces first Aaron, then Israel, of God's existence and designs. Pharaoh, on the other hand, is more like his adversary Moses. "Who is YHVH that I should heed Him and let Israel go?" he asks. "I do not know YHVH, nor will I let Israel go" (Exodus 5:2). His response to Moses' demand is to increase the travails of Israel, with the result that Moses and Aaron are cursed (in the name of their rediscovered God YHVH!) by the Israelite foremen. Moses then turns and confronts God with an understandably strong protest (Exodus 5:22–23):

> **Address:** O Lord!
> **Presentation:** Why did You bring harm upon this people? Why did you send me? Ever since I came to Pharaoh to speak in Your name, he has dealt worse with this people;
> **Petition:** But You have not delivered Your people at all!

Although God responds with a rousing recapitulation of His plans, His covenant with the Patriarchs, His names, and His promises ("Now you will see what I will do to Pharaoh . . ." [Exodus 6:1–8]), first Israel (6:9) and then Moses (6:12) remain skeptical. It is the beginning of the most unique relationship a God ever had with His people.[8]

The survival of this relationship was nowhere more tenuous than when Israel chose to worship the Golden Calf. On that occasion, as on many others, Moses utilizes a law-court argument prayer to intercede on Israel's behalf, to turn God from His decision to destroy the Israelites (Exodus 32:9–14):

> (9) The Lord further said to Moses, "I see that this is a stiff-necked people. (10) Now, let Me be, that My anger may blaze forth against them and that I may destroy them, and make of you a great nation." (11) But Moses implored the Lord his God, saying, "Let not Your anger, O Lord, blaze forth against Your people, whom You delivered from the land of Egypt with great power and with a mighty hand. (12) Let not the Egyptians say, 'It was with evil intent that He delivered them, only to kill them off in the mountains and annihilate them from the face of the earth.' Turn from Your blazing anger, and renounce the plan to punish Your people. (13) Remember Your servants, Abraham, Isaac, and Jacob, how You swore to them by Your Self and said to them: 'I will make your offspring as numerous as the stars of heaven, and I will give to your offspring this whole land of which I spoke, to possess forever.'" (14) And the Lord renounced the punishment He had planned to bring upon His people.

Here is manifest an example of a complete law-court argument prayer: an opening address (verse 11), a defense argument (verses 12a, 13), a plea (or petition) (verse 12b), and a divine response (indirect) (verse 14). But the threat of destruction is not ended. Although God relents of His plan (verse 14), He still requires further appeasement if Israel's annihilation is to be avoided. Moses, therefore, intercedes a second time (Exodus 32:30–35):

> (30) The next day Moses said to the people, "You have been guilty of a great sin. Yet I will now go up to the Lord; perhaps I may win forgiveness for your sin." (31) Moses went back to the Lord and said, "Alas, this people is guilty of a great sin in making for themselves a god of gold. (32) Now, if You will forgive their sin (well and good); but if not, erase me from the

record which You have written!" (33) But the Lord said to
Moses, "He who has sinned against Me, him only will I erase
from My record. (34) Go now, lead the people where I told you.
See, My angel shall go before you. But when I make an accounting, I will bring them to account for their sins." (35) Then the
Lord sent a plague upon the people, for what they did with the
calf that Aaron made.

This second argument should be considered as a continuation
of the first, although structurally each can stand alone. First of all,
it pursues the same line of argumentation as does the first. Second, it provides the real conclusion to the story (that is, God's
actual sentence and its execution [verses 33–35]). Third, Moses'
ultimatum, "erase me,"seems to be a direct response to God's offer
in verse 10 to make of Moses a great nation. Fourth, Moses'
recounting of the event, in Deuteronomy 9:26–29, blends the two
arguments of the Exodus story into a single unit.[9] Finally, both
arguments are needed to save the people fully.

Taken together, Moses' prayers advance five reasons in order to
convince God to spare the Israelites. First, he alludes to God's
great activities during the Exodus, and indirectly questions God's
intention to destroy the very people He has just saved (Exodus
32:11–12b). Second, Moses strengthens this argument by stating
that God's own name would be besmirched (God would be considered malicious) were He to destroy His people (12a). Third, such
an act would contradict and deny God's promise to the Patriarchs
and make of God a liar. Moses asks God not only to recall the
eternal promise made to those three (which Moses quotes verba-
tim), but also to remember them—as though to say, "Let the
memory of their merit and the recollection of the promise made to
them be entered into the records."

Continuing with the second argument, Moses next acknowledges the sin (crime) committed by the people (Exodus 32:31).
Such a confession alone would have left Israel at the mercy of the
judge (God). Moses, however, now offers his final and most dramatic argument. Putting his prestige (merit) on the line, he links
his personal fate with the fate of the people (verse 32). In order to
understand the strength and daring of Moses' fifth argument, one
must realize that it has the form of an oath. Moses, in fact, is
saying something on the order of "if I am truly Your chosen

prophet, then You will forgive their sin and I too shall live; but if You don't pardon them then You must kill me as well." Were Moses not entirely sure of his merit in the eyes of God, such an oath could have ended in total disaster both for Israel and for himself. The oath, in its complete form (which this is not), is an open and direct invitation for divine intervention into human affairs. But the oath is also part of the law-court procedure and is frequently used by biblical characters in situations where they are dependent on the mercy of divine help.[10]

Moses' two prayers result in a near-perfect law-court structure and a very powerful argument.

Address and introductory petition:	verse 11a
Defense argument:	verse 11b—recitation of God's acts
	verse 12—for Your Name's sake
	(verse 12b—intermediate petition)
	verse 13—the Covenant and the Merit of the Ancestors
	verse 31—the confession of guilt
	verse 32b—Moses' personal merit
Petition:	verse 32—a combined oath and petition
Divine response/verdict:	verses 33–34—only the sinners will be punished
Execution and sentence:	verse 35—a plague

The episode of the Golden Calf is very nearly a disastrous crisis for the Israelites. However, as in the story of Sodom and Gomorrah, the crisis around the Golden Calf must be considered in its wider context. Its true importance lies in its leading to another, even greater event: the revelation of "God's glory" to Moses. After the crisis, Moses asks for and receives a divine revelation of incomparable quality (Exodus 33:13,17–23; 34:5–8), following which he again petitions God to remain in Israel's midst (Exodus 34:8–9). God then reaffirms His covenant with Israel and issues its new terms (Exodus 34:10–27), which Moses, in turn, relates to all Israel (Exodus 34:29–35). God's revelation to Moses, in which He reveals the nature and the exercise of the divine justice (Exodus 33:13,19–23; 34:5–7), also provides the theological underpinning to the story of the Golden Calf.

On one level, it would seem that Moses convinces God to change His mind; on a deeper level, the story teaches that God is truly merciful and gracious in overabundance. No sooner had God established the first covenant with Israel at Sinai, than Israel abrogated its primary clause by worshiping the Golden Calf. God would have been justified in destroying them for this act alone. Yet He pardoned them then as well as on many subsequent occasions. Thus the story of the Golden Calf teaches something further about the nature of God: that His justice is tempered with a great abundance of mercy, as it says (Exodus 34:6-7):

> The Lord! The Lord! a God compassionate and gracious, slow to anger, abounding in kindness and faithfulness, extending kindness to the thousandth generation, forgiving iniquity, transgression and sin; yet He does not remit all punishment, but visits the iniquity of fathers upon children and children's children, upon the third and fourth generations.

Perhaps the Golden Calf arguments were divided to emphasize this teaching. After the first argument, God repents of the total destruction of Israel which He had planned. Moses nonetheless then attempts to purge the sin from the midst of Israel (Exodus 32:25-29). Having done so, he argues again, acknowledging the guilt of the people and pleading for their pardon (Exodus 32:30-32). But God knows who has sinned and, in His own time, sends a plague to punish the guilty ones that remain (Exodus 32:33-35).[11] In His exercise of justice, God is wholly just, merciful beyond bounds to those even remotely deserving, yet duly punishing those guilty of sin. This is the didactic message of the Golden Calf story.

The episode describing the crisis that followed the report of the spies builds upon several of the motifs used by Moses at the time of the Golden Calf. Upon hearing the disheartening report of the spies, the people rebel against God, and God judges them harshly (Numbers 14:11-12). Moses then intercedes in fine fashion (Numbers 14:13-19):

> (11) And the Lord said to Moses, "How long will this people spurn Me, and how long will they have no faith in Me despite all the signs that I have performed in their midst? (12) I will strike

them with pestilence and disown them, and I will make of you a
nation far more numerous than they!" (13) But Moses said to
the Lord, "When the Egyptians, from whose midst You brought
them in Your might, hear the news, (14) they will tell it to the
inhabitants of that land. Now they have heard that You, O Lord,
are in the midst of this people; that You, O Lord, appear in plain
sight when Your cloud rests over them and when You go before
them in a pillar of cloud by day and in a pillar of fire by night.
(15) If then You slay this people to a man, the nations who have
heard your fame will say, (16) 'It must be because the Lord was
powerless to bring that people into the land which He had
promised them on oath that He slaughtered them in wilderness.' (17) Therefore, I pray, let my Lord's forbearance be great,
as You have declared, saying, (18) 'The Lord! slow to anger and
abounding in kindness; forgiving iniquity and transgression;
yet not remitting all punishment, but visiting the iniquity of the
fathers upon children, upon the third and fourth generations.'
(19) Pardon, I pray, the iniquity of this people according to Your
great kindness, as You have forgiven this people ever since
Egypt."

Again the law-court pattern: the address is implicit in verse 12a;
verses 13b–16 constitute one argument containing several motifs
centering around the theme of "for His name's sake," that is, that
God should not do what He was considering because of the implications such a deed would have on His name—His "international
reputation."[12] Verses 17–18 provide Moses' second argument, in
which he quotes God's own words back to Him, "forcing" God to
remain constant. Verse 19 concludes the prayer with a petition for
mercy based upon an appeal to God's nature and to His merciful
decisions in the past. Verses 20–35 represent the divine response
and the subsequent execution of God's verdict.

This prayer builds upon several of the motifs used at the time of
Moses' intercession with God over the Golden Calf. First is the
argument "for His name's sake." The two passages (Exodus
32:11–12 and Numbers 14:13–16) are quite similar, but in the
story of the spies, Moses brings in not only the Egyptians, but also
the Canaanites, who by then had also heard of God's great deeds
on behalf of Israel. Here God is not threatened by being considered
as an evil God by His witnesses, the Egyptians, but by being
"universally" considered as a weak or limited God who must

destroy His people because He cannot fulfill His promise to them.[13] Second is the agument based on "quoting God's own word back to Him." At the time of the Golden Calf, Moses used the technique that referred in that instance to the promise made to the Patriarchs. Here, Moses quotes the words of God's own panegyric uttered on Mount Sinai back to Him, and asks God to be true to His own word and pardon them. The prayer as a whole sums up the character of the God of the ancient Hebrews. God is considered to be greatly concerned with His reputation in the world, because it is through the knowledge (and the experience) of God's deeds that all people will learn of His powers and come to acknowledge that the Lord is God. Furthermore, God is considered wholly just. But God's justice does not denote severity. God's justice implies consistency and constancy, both in His love and, as repeated examples illustrate, in His mercy.

ELIJAH

Almost as close to God as Moses was and facing a people as faithless as Moses ever had, Elijah also argued with God, producing spectacular effects but negligible results. In fact, Elijah comes to argument from the opposite perspective of Moses. Moses argues with God on behalf of Israel, even if sinful; but Elijah is Israel's prosecuting attorney. When he argues with God, it is to prove himself (and God) right and Israel wrong.

Elijah's most impressive "argument" was his confrontation with the priests of Baal on Mount Carmel. In a desperate effort to win the Israelites back to God, Elijah challenges the priests to a contest: let both sides prepare a sacrifice and whichever god answers the prayer with fire from heaven, that god is God. As Elijah says to Israel: "How long will you leap between two branches [waiver between two opinions]? If the Lord is God, follow Him; but if Baal, follow him" (1 Kings 18:21).

The priests prepared their sacrifices and prayed from morning to noon; they danced and cried and cut themselves and prophesied until evening, all to no effect. Elijah then took the stage. First he rebuilt the Lord's altar, then he prepared the wood and the bullock. Next came the dramatic moment. Elijah called for twelve jars of water to be cast over the sacrifice and the wood, and more water in the ditch around the altar, so that everything was soaked. Then Elijah prayed:

> Lord God of Abraham, Isaac and Israel, let it be known this day that You are God in Israel and that I am Your servant and that I have done all these things at Your word. Answer me, Lord, answer me, that this people will know that You, Lord, are God and that You have turned their hearts back again. [1 Kings 18:36–37]

The Lord, of course, answered with the necessary fire, which spectacularly consumed everything, even the water. Elijah "forced" God to demonstrate His reality, to prove His presence. For Israel, it was like a second Sinai; the people fell to the ground and proclaimed: "The Lord is God, the Lord is God!" At Elijah's command, the priests of Baal were slaughtered. Then the drought was ended. At this point, Elijah was triumphant. But soon after, his life was once again threatened by Jezebel and he was forced to flee first to the wilderness of Judah and then to Horev, the Mountain of God. There God asked him twice: "What are you doing *here* Elijah?," and Elijah responded both times with a condemnation of Israel and a vindication of himself. Later, the rabbis would see in God's questions an opportunity to defend Israel, something that Elijah twice failed to do. Having forced God to manifest His power in order to convince Israel once and for all that the Lord alone is God, Elijah had no more love for his people. Perhaps the "still, small voice" was a form of rebuke. God was no longer to be found in the spectacular (as at Sinai or on Carmel) but inside, in that still, small voice. Having twice condemned Israel, Elijah was told by God to annoint his prophetic successor. Elijah's own career as a prophet ended when he no longer cared to defend his people.

JEREMIAH

Although the prophets make much use of law-court argument prayers, they do so usually to represent God's lawsuit against Israel or the nations. There are, however, certain occasions when a prophet challenges God either for his own sake or on behalf of the people.[14] Jeremiah, in particular, is celebrated for his personal dialogues with God, commonly known as his "confessions." In fact, they represent nothing startlingly new. Their source lies in the argument prayers of Moses. Moses, like Jeremiah, was an unwilling prophet; he too cried out demanding relief from the burden of his office; he too "took God to task" for acting (or planning to act) in an unworthy manner. However, what characterizes Jeremiah's confessions is that Jeremiah argues primarily for his own benefit. In tone and content, the confessions prefigure the personalistic outlook and problems of Job and the petitionary psalms.

While scholars disagree on the exact verses comprising Jeremiah's confessions, they are in general agreement that the form of the confessions is that of the law-court pattern of prayer[15] (see Table 1). Appropriate to his use of this motif, Jeremiah frequently resorts to legal terminology: God is a "Righteous Judge" (*shofet tzedek*) (Jeremiah 11:20) before whom Jeremiah appeals his lawsuit or case (*riv*) (Jeremiah 11:20; 20:12). Elsewhere Jeremiah disputes with God, laying certain cases before Him, as would a lawyer: "You will win [be in the right], O Lord, if I enter suit against You, yet I shall present charges [or points of judgment] against You" (Jeremiah 12:1). In another instance Jeremiah appears as a plaintiff: "Listen to me, O Lord, and hear what those who contend with me say. Shall good be repaid with evil?" (Jeremiah 18:19–20). In two of the confessions, God is clearly the judge to whom Jeremiah appeals for justice, that is, the punishment of his enemies (Jeremiah 11:18–23; 18:19–23). In the other four, God still serves as judge, but also is indicted as a co-defendant along with Jeremiah's enemies. It is in these cases that Jeremiah saves his harshest words for God: "You will [no doubt] win, O Lord, if I enter suit against You" (Jeremiah 12:1); "Will You be to me like a deceitful brook, like waters that fail?" (Jeremiah 15:18); "Be not a terror to me" (Jeremiah 17:17), "O Lord, You have deceived me and I was deceived; You are stronger than I and You have prevailed" (Jeremiah 20:7).

Yet even as Jeremiah accuses God of complicity, he appeals to God for justice. God knows the truth of each situation; Jeremiah merely recites the facts to call them to God's attention. The questions and accusations Jeremiah makes are rhetorical. In each case the anticipated answer implies a refutation of Jeremiah's words. God is expected to confirm the justice of Jeremiah's cases

	Jer. 11:18-23	Jer. 12:1-6	Jer. 15:15-21	Jer. 17:14-18	Jer. 18:19-23	Jer. 20:7-12
Address	v. 20a: "O Lord of Hosts who . . .	v. 1: "Righteous are You, O Lord. . . ."	v. 15a: "O Lord, You know . . ."	v. 14: "Heal me, O Lord. . . ."	v. 19: "Give heed to me, O Lord. . . ."	v. 7: "O Lord. . . ."
Object of Address	Against the wicked: God as judge	God (and wicked) as defendants; God as judge	God (and wicked) as defendants; God as judge	Wicked (and God) as defendants; God as judge (with emphasis on latter)	Against the wicked; God as judge	God (and wicked) as defendants, with a transition to God as true and faithful judge
Argument	1. v. 18: "The Lord has given me knowledge of it. . . . You showed me their doings." 2. v. 19: accusation against his enemies: "I was like a gentle lamb brought to the slaughter. . . .	1. v. 1b: "Why does the way of the wicked prosper? . . ." 2. v. 21: accusation "You have planted them. . . ." 3. v. 2b: the hypocrisy of the wicked 4. v. 3a: Jeremiah's integrity (his innocence) 5. v. 4: "How long. . . ."	1. v. 15b: "Know that for Your sake I have suffered insult." 2. v. 6: "I served You willingly. . . ." 3. v. 17: more self-justification and accusation: "You have filled me with indignation." 4. v. 18: "Why? . . ." accusations: "Will You be to me like a deceitful stream."	1. v. 15: mockery of the wicked 2. v. 16: self-justification 3. v. 17: indirect accusation against God and confession of trust: "Be not a terror to me: You are my hope in the day of evil."	1. v. 20: accusation against the wicked and self-justification: "Shall evil be recompensed for good? Remember that I stood before them to speak good for them. . . ." 2. v. 22b: evil deeds of Jeremiah's persecutors	1. v. 7a: accusations against God: "You have deceived me and I was deceived, You are stronger than me, and You have prevailed" 2. v. 7b-8: depiction of Jeremiah's misery 3. v. 9: self-justification 4. v. 10: Jeremiah's plight and the plotting of his enemies 5. v. 11: expression of trust in the Lord

Petition/Plea	v. 20: "But, O Lord of hosts, who judges righteously ... let me see Your vengeance on them...."	v. 3b: "But You, O Lord, know me ... pull them out...."	v. 15a: "O Lord ... remember me ... and revenge me of my persecutors."	v. 18: two-fold petition: "Let them be ... but let me not be...."	v. 21, 22a: "Therefore, deliver up ... pour out their blood ... let...." v. 23: "Yet, O Lord, You know ... forgive not their iniquity ... let them be ... deal thus with them."	v. 12: "But, O Lord of hosts ... let me see Your vengeance on them."
Divine Response	v. 21–23: "Behold, I will punish them...."	v. 5–6: "Why aren't you stronger? Don't believe your enemies' deceiving words."	v. 19–21: "If you make an effort, I will strengthen you and deliver you."	none	none	(expression of trust v. 11 replaces divine response); possibly v. 13 follows divine response

Table 1

(although Jeremiah does not always receive the answer for which he had hoped).

The dual role ascribed to God is especially pronounced in the sixth confession, in which God is suddenly switched from the role of co-defendant to that of judge. In the sixth confession, Jeremiah begins with accusations against God, but suddenly switches to an expression of trust: "But the Lord is with me as a dread warrior; therefore my persecutors will stumble, they will not overcome me" (Jeremiah 20:11). This sudden switch is nothing more than an articulation of the answer to the rhetorical questions and accusations found in the other examples. God is just, He knows the truth of the matter at hand; He will not forget His servant nor let the wicked go unpunished. And Jeremiah now feels this. In form and content, the sixth confession is very much like the psalms of individual lament.

The problem of theodicy lies at the heart of Jeremiah's complaints. While he knows God to be a just judge, and expects to see a just and favorable verdict handed down (why else would he even bother to appeal to God?), he is nonetheless impatient. God may be just, but His justice is too long in coming for Jeremiah to wait in silent expectation, thus his urgent and repeated complaint, "Why does the way of the wicked prosper? Why do all who are treacherous thrive?" (Jeremiah 12:1). While God tarries (or deliberates), Jeremiah suffers physical and psychological abuse at the hands of his enemies. This makes Jeremiah's confessions also remarkably similar to the Book of Job. Like Job, Jeremiah appeals to God for a just judgment of his case. Like Job, Jeremiah is absolutely convinced of his innocence. The confessions are replete with statements of self-justification and appeals to God as the One who knows the heart and mind of His creatures. Like Job, and like Moses when confronted by Korah, Jeremiah asserts his innocence by inviting God to judge his case. If Jeremiah has not sinned, if he is blameless, then his suffering is unwarranted; hence there must be some other reason for his having to endure such tribulations. This raises some fundamental questions regarding Jeremiah's confessions: Why are these personal prayers included among his prophecies? Are they intended, perhaps, to serve some larger purpose beyond that of merely recording Jeremiah's individual anguish?

Unlike Job, Jeremiah is clearly a real person forced to endure real suffering. What is a theological problem for the Book of Job is, for Jeremiah, something very real. Does Jeremiah's example have something in it that makes it of benefit to others? Blank, in his article "The Prophet as Paradigm," follows Buber's thinking in positing that the confessions were included among Jeremiah's prophecies to make the prophet serve as a paradigm for the people.[16] Many prophets—Hosea, Jeremiah, Ezekiel, and Deutero-Isaiah, to name a few—engaged in symbolic activities in order to instruct the people. Blank sees Jeremiah's confessions serving a similar function. Because many of Jeremiah's prayers (the confessions) were met with a divine response, they therefore had a suprapersonal significance. Thus, according to Blank, Jeremiah's experience of suffering serves as a step in the development of the concept of the "personification of the people Israel, as a prophet after the manner of Jeremiah," that is, the people of Israel personified as the "suffering servant" of God. Jeremiah's experience, like those of Hosea before him and Ezekiel after him, becomes paradigmatic of the people's experience.[17] This is an unlikely reason for their inclusion.

The central problem with this view goes right to the heart of the nature of prophecy itself. Did Jeremiah (or Barukh) record these confessions with the knowledge (which was surely prophetic) that they would, in the not too distant future, hold a profound message for the soon-to-be-conquered Israel? Or were Jeremiah's words ignored, as his message had been during his active mission, their worth recognized only later, once Israel had indeed suffered what Jeremiah had prophesied would befall it? For who knew whether Jeremiah was a true prophet except after the event: "If the prophet speaks in the name of the Lord and the oracle does not come true, that oracle was not spoken by the Lord; the prophet has uttered it presumptuously; do not stand in dread of him" (Deuteronomy 18:22).

Jeremiah's teachings, the message he obtained through his sufferings, only acquired meaning in the succeeding period of the Babylonian Exile; perhaps it was only then that his words were collected and written down. Jeremiah was a prophet, not for his own age, but for the later generations. What, then, is the message of Jeremiah's confessions? They teach that:

> [God's] growing incomprehensibility is mitigated and even com-
> pensated by His becoming the God of the sufferers and by

> suffering becoming a door of approach to Him, as is already
> clear from the life of Jeremiah where the way of martyrdom
> leads to an ever purer and deeper fellowship with YHVH. Be-
> tween God and suffering a mysterious connection is opened. In
> every generation God's emissaries not only worked and fought
> by His order, they also bore suffering in the course of their work
> and fighting. But hitherto these sufferings were only something
> incidental, having no intrinsic import of their own. Hencefor-
> ward the sufferings themselves began to rise into prominence.[18]

But Blank would rightly add to this that Jeremiah's confessions
gain suprapersonal meaning because they were actually met with
a divine response.[19] In other words, Jeremiah's suffering did not
go unnoticed by God—an important message for the generation of
the Babylonian Exile.[20] Jeremiah's words later help Israel cope
with the national disaster and to interpret its implications for
their covenantal world view.

Speaking as they do about the undeserved suffering of the
righteous and the prosperity and success of the wicked, the confessions voice the concerns of the generation of the Babylonian
Exile. Though written before the Exile, Jeremiah's teaching about
the meaning of suffering gains currency about the same period as
the psalms of national lament, the Book of Lamentations, and the
Book of Job were written. All deal with one crucial problem: how to
reconcile the belief in the God of justice and history with the fact
of undeserved (or disproportionate) suffering on the part of His
chosen people (or His servant, in the case of Job). This problem is
taken up in these later works.

PSALMS OF PETITION AND
THE BOOK OF LAMENTATIONS

Scholars advocating the form-critical method of Bible study have
divided the Book of Psalms into a number of different types. One
major category is identified as the psalms of petition (or lament),
which in turn breaks down into two subcategories, the lament of
the individual and the lament of the nation. In origin, the lament
of the individual type, like the confessions of Jeremiah, may have

been based on the lament forms of Babylon and Ugarit, and share their frequent application of legal terminology.[21] These psalms of petition closely follow the form and tone of the law-court prayers as expressed in the confessions of Jeremiah.[22] The Book of Lamentations, as a collection of laments, also follows the same pattern and echoes many of the same themes found in the petitionary psalms and the confessions of Jeremiah. Consider two examples of the national lament, Psalm 44 and Psalm 80.[23]

Address and/or Introductory Petition

Psalm 44:2
"O God" and use of second person singular to address
God throughout
Psalm 80:2–4
Give ear, O shepherd of Israel
. . . Appear, . . .
Rouse Your might and come to our help!
Restore us, O God;
show Your favor that we may be delivered.

Argument

LAMENT/COMPLAINT/ACCUSATIONS

Psalm 44:10–17
Yet You have rejected and disgraced us . . .
You make us retreat before our foe . . .
You let them devour us like sheep . . .
You sell Your people for no fortune . . .
You make us the butt of our neighbors . . .
You make us a byword among the nations,
a laughingstock among the peoples.
I am always aware of my disgrace;
I am wholly covered with shame
at the sound of taunting revilers,
in the presence of the vengeful foe.
Psalm 80:5–8
O Lord, God of hosts,
how long will You be wrathful
toward the prayers of Your people?

You have fed them tears as their daily bread,
. . . our enemies mock us at will.

RECOLLECTION OF GOD'S PAST DEEDS

Psalm 44:2–4
> We have heard, O God,
> our fathers have told us the
> days of old.
> With Your hand You planted them,
> displacing nations . . .
> It was not by their sword that they took the land,
> their arm did not give them victory,
> but Your right hand . . .
> for You favored them. . . .

Psalm 80:9–12
> You plucked up a vine from Egypt;
> You expelled nations and planted it.
> . . . Its branches reached the sea,
> its shoots, the river.

EXPRESSION OF TRUST AND
FAITHFULNESS/ASSERTION OF INNOCENCE

Psalm 44:5–9
> You are my king, O God;
> . . . I do not trust in my bow
> . . . You give us victory . . .
> In God we glory . . .
> and praise Your name. . . .

Psalm 44:18–23
> All this has come upon us,
> yet we have not forgotten You,
> or been false to Your covenant.
> . . . If we forgot the name of our God
> and spread forth our hands to a foreign god,
> God would surely search it out.
> . . . It is for Your sake that we are slain all day long . . .

Psalm 80:13–14
> Why did You breach its wall
> so that every passerby plucks its fruit . . . ?
> (assertion of innocence by accusatory question).

Psalm 80:19
> We will never turn away from You;
> preserve our life that we may invoke Your name.

PETITION/SUPPLICATION

Psalm 44:24–27

> Rouse Yourself; why do You sleep, O Lord?
> Awaken, do not reject us forever!
> Why do You hide Your face,
> ignoring our affliction and distress?
> We lie prostrate in the dust;
> our body clings to the ground.
> Arise and help us,
> redeem us, for the sake of Your faithfulness.

Psalm 80:4,8,20

> O God of hosts, restore us;
> show Your favour that we may be delivered.
> [a refrain]
> [verses 15–20]
> O God of hosts, turn again,
> look down from heaven and see;
> take note of that vine, . . .
> For it is burned by fire and cut down,
> perishing before Your angry blast.
> Grant Your help to . . .
> the one You have taken as Your own.
> . . . restore us. . . .

There are numerous examples of the individual lament in Psalms, of which Psalm 22 is typical.[24]

Address and/or Introductory Petition

[verses 2–4] My God, my God, why have You abandoned me; why so far from delivering me and from my anguished roaring? My God, I cry by day—You answer not; by night, and have no respite.

Argument

LAMENT/COMPLAINT ACCUSATIONS

[verses 7–9] I am a worm, less than human; scorned by men. . . . All who see me mock me . . . "Let him commit himself to the Lord; Let Him rescue him, let Him save him. . . ."

[verses 13–19] Many bulls surround me . . . they open their mouths at me like tearing, roaring lions. I am poured out like water. . . . You commit me to the dust of death. . . . Dogs surround me; a pack of evil ones. . . . I take the count of all my bones while they look on and gloat. . . .

RECOLLECTION OF GOD'S PAST DEEDS

[verses 4–6] But You are the Holy One. . . . In You our fathers trusted, they trusted and You rescued them. . . . In You they trusted and were not disappointed.

EXPRESSION OF TRUST

[verses 10–12] You drew me from the womb, . . . I became Your charge at birth; from my mother's womb You have been my God. Do not be far from me, for trouble is near, and there is none to help.

PETITION/SUPPLICATION

[verses 20–22] But You, O Lord, be not far off; my strength, hasten to my aid. . . . Save my life from the sword. . . . Deliver me from a lion's mouth . . . answer me.

VOW OF PRAISE

[verses 23–32] Then I will proclaim Your fame to my brethren, praise You in the congregation. You who fear the Lord, praise Him! . . . For He did not scorn, he did not spurn the plea of the lowly; He did not hide his face from him; when he cried out to Him, He listened. Let all the ends of the earth pay heed and turn to the Lord . . . for kingship is the Lord's . . . they shall tell of His beneficence to people yet to be born, for He has acted.

As in the confessions of Jeremiah, God, in both kinds of the lament, figures sometimes as judge and sometimes as both judge and defendant. This was not the case in the Torah where God was appealed to solely as judge. However, what differentiates the structure of the laments from that of Jeremiah's confessions is the expression of trust. Conversely—and herein lies the solution—

what differentiates Jeremiah's confessions from the laments is the divine response that follows most of his complaints. Jeremiah, as God's chosen prophet, is in direct communication with God, just as Abraham and Moses were before him. Jeremiah knows that his petition is heard because he receives an immediate (although not always favorable) response. In the case of the individual or the community, however, the situation is quite different. They are not on the same level of chosenness as is God's prophet. Thus, in the lament, the confession of trust that God will hear and answer their petition replaces the actual divine response granted the prophet. This expectation is not unwarranted. Just as the prophet is God's chosen messenger, so too Israel is God's chosen people, something about which God is reminded in almost every lament. The role of faith is central to the laments. Faith—the expectation that God will respond—provides the laments with that quality we usually associate with prayer. Faith, of course, speaks of nothing other than the trust and hope in God's justice. God can be asked to regard the plight of His afflicted, He can be admonished to change His attitude, if and only if there exists the expectation that He is a just and compassionate judge.

This expectation has its roots in the great deeds ascribed to God in ages past, primarily in the accounts of the Exodus and the Conquest of the Land. This appeal to and protest against God is, as was already noted with regard to Abraham, possible only within the context of the concept of the Covenant established between God and His people Israel. The lament functions as an appeal to God because it occurs within "the context of the account of deliverance, which became the basis of Israel's relationship with God; it is thus related to the saving acts of God."[25] This explains why so many of the laments include among their arguments specific mention of God's former acts of salvation and contrasts these with the present state of misery. The hope is that God will recognize the justice of the people's complaint and intervene on their behalf.

This hope expresses itself in a very dynamic way in both the national lament and the lament of the individual, when the psalmist turns from addressing God to invoke the "congregation" in support of his petition. In the national lament, this takes the form of a communal "expression of faithfulness and an assertion of innocence." In Psalm 44, after reiterating his case, the psalmist cries out: "All this has come upon us, yet we have not forgotten You. . . . If we forgot the name of our God . . . God would surely search it out" (18–23). In Psalm 80, the psalmist asserts: "We will not turn away from You, preserve our life that we may invoke your name" (19). One can almost hear the congregation respond with assorted affirmations. In the lament of the individual, the congregation is encouraged to participate in the "vow of praise" with an appropriate response: "You who fear the Lord, praise Him! Be in dread of Him, all you offspring of Jacob" (Psalm 22:24). In both types of lament, the use of the congregation gives added weight and a dynamic quality to the psalmist's complaint and petition. This participatory role, as will be seen, takes on a new and strident urgency in Deutero-Isaiah and Lamentations.

Unlike the national lament, the lament of the individual includes a vow of praise in addition to the expression of trust. This may be in response either to a favorable oracle (if indeed the individual laments were cultic ceremonies), or to a sudden inner perception that the individual's petition has been heard and accepted on high.[26] In either case, the vow is but a further expression of trust; it represents an abiding faith that God will indeed deliver the afflicted. "The cry to God is never one-dimensional, without tension. It is always somewhere in the middle between petition and praise. By nature it cannot be *mere* petition or lament, but is always underway from supplication to praise."[27]

The psalms of petition share a number of basic motifs. Common to all, of course, is the appeal for justice. And concomitant with this appeal for justice is some allusion to the recollection of God's mighty deeds of old, in creation or in history; to His steadfast love (*hesed*) (Psalms 6, 13, 22, 25, 26, 44, 51, 69, 80); to the covenant (Psalms 74, 89); or to His righteousness (Psalms 31, 35). Often the appeal has a twofold thrust: "give us our due and give our enemies theirs." This vindictive element frequently occupies a significant portion of the petition. The petitioner has two attitudes, either of which, or sometimes both of which, are used to form the basis of his argument. The lament can be penitential in tone (Psalms 25, 38, 51, 106, 130, 143; Lamentations 1:20–22), or it can be a protestation of one's innocence (Psalms 7, 17, 26, 44, 74, 83). In many cases, the protestation of innocence contains an admission of guilt along with the demurral that the punishment

received is greatly out of proportion to the sin committed
(Psalms 38, 60, 79, 85, 89, 90; Lamentations 3:42–45; 4:6, chap. 5;
Isaiah 64). In both of the latter cases, this in turn leads to harsh
accusations against God (Psalms 44, 74, 79, 80, 89; Lamentations
2:20–22; Isaiah 63:15–17).

God's self-interest is appealed to in a number of ways. First,
there are those reminders of His past promises and acts of salvation with the implication that God must remain true to His word
and constant in His behavior. Second, the descriptions of His
ruined city and/or the sacked Temple are meant to reflect negatively upon God's glory and prestige here on earth. By allowing
these calamities to happen, God gives the nations cause to mock
Israel's faith in God and, by implication, God Himself. Third,
explicit reference is made urging God to act "for His name's sake"
(Psalms 25:11, 79:9; Jeremiah 14:7; and in many other places), an
argument Moses had used with great effectiveness (Exodus 32:12;
Numbers 14:15). Fourth, appeal is made to God because He needs
the praise of the living: "Will the dust praise You? Will it tell of
Your faithfulness?" (Psalm 30:10; also Psalms 6:6; 88:11–13). A
similar sentiment is voiced when God is urged to rebuild Zion and
the Temple so that Israel may offer praise and sacrifices once
again. Fifth, questions such as "Why?" and "How long?" are
hurled at God in almost every lament. God is accused of being
unheeding or rejecting, of sleeping or hiding His face. Similarly,
God is commanded "Arise!," "Awake!," "Rouse Yourself!," "Behold!" Such appeals, uttered in the conviction that God will indeed do as requested, directly parallel Elijah's mocking comments
addressed to the priests of Baal on Mount Carmel (1 Kings
18:27).[28] But when God is estranged from Israel, it becomes a
most urgent matter. Thus, in Isaiah 62:1–7 (and paralleled in
Habakkuk 2:1 and Lamentations 3:49–50), a desperate task is
undertaken:

> For Zion's sake I will not hold my peace,
> And for the sake of Jerusalem I will not be still,
> Until her righteousness goes forth like radiance,
> And her salvation like a burning torch . . .
> I have set watchmen upon your walls, O Jerusalem,
> Who shall never hold their peace day or night:

You that make mention of the Lord, take no rest,
And give Him no rest till He establishes,
And till He makes Jerusalem a praise in the earth.

It is hoped that persistence will be rewarded—a concept that leads us directly into the Books of Lamentations and Job.

The Book of Lamentations is a collection of laments, partial laments, and laments within laments, parts of which are addressed to a general audience (Lamentations 1:1–19; 2:1–19, chapter 4) while other parts are addressed to God (Lamentations 1:20–22; 2:20–22; 3:41–66; chapter 5). The relation of Lamentations to the psalms of petition and the relation of both these works to the Book of Job is of interest. Structurally, the laments in Lamentations (Lamentations 1:20–22; 2:20–22; chapter 5) follow the law-court pattern of prayer in the same manner as do the psalms of petition. Lamentations, as a single work, includes both individual and national laments (Lamentations 1:20–22; chapter 3; and Lamentations 2:20–22; 3:42–47; chapter 5, respectively). How are the two intended to blend? The answer lies in the central chapter, chapter 3, which very nearly functions as "the expression of trust" for the whole book when considered as a single lament.[29]

Chapter 3 of Lamentations provides the message of the book, which concerns the proper attitude one should have toward suffering. But it imparts this by means of an ingenious technique, moving the listener/reader from the experience of one individual's suffering to the suffering of the nation. Certain psalms of lament, Psalms 51, 94, 123, and 130 for example, similarly run the individual and national laments together. This merging is also evident in Lamentations 1:9b–11. Chapter 3 continues and amplifies this motif. It begins with an individual's recitation of the suffering he has endured under the wrath of God (1–17). His suffering is such that he despairs of God (18–20). But then, in the depths of despair, hope is born (21–24) and understanding gained (25–27). Suffering comes as divine chastisement for sins committed. But with repentance there is an end to suffering, and God will turn in forgiveness to save the afflicted. This understanding is then passed on to the people (28–40) and a new posture of prayer is proposed (41–45). Then, precipitously, the individual returns with a renewed lament (46–48, 51, 52–54) coupled with a certain defiance similar to the passage in Isaiah cited above (62:1–7): "My eye runs down with rivers of water for the breach of the daughter of my people. My eye trickles down, and ceases not, without any intermission, till the Lord looks down, and beholds from heaven" (Lamentations 3:48–50). The individual concludes with a praise of God that closely parallels the form of an actual lament, except that here God has answered each and every complaint (55–63). His case having been heard and his cause championed by God, the individual closes, confidently predicting the downfall of his enemies at the hand of God (64–66).

Is there something new in all this? While at first glance it appears to confirm the Deuteronomic view of retributive justice, that suffering is divine punishment for sins committed, there is something here that marks a significant departure from this older attitude. This something is the new posture of prayer:

> Let us lift up our heart with our hands to God in the heavens.
> We have transgressed and rebelled; but You have not pardoned.
> You have covered with anger, and pursued us; You have slain,
> You have not pitied. You have covered Yourself with a cloud, so
> that prayer should not pass through. [Lamentations 3:41–44]

This is echoed elsewhere as accusations against the enormity of the punishment (2:20–22; 4:6), protestations of innocence (5:7), and a defiant persistence to force God back into action (3:48–50). The similarity in tone of Lamentations, the petitionary psalms, and portions of Deutero-Isaiah is striking. All are attempting to cope with a changed reality—the reality of the destruction of the Temple and the exile to Babylon. And the response these works suggest is also similar. All are based on the law-court pattern and all make use of the arguing with God motif. All affirm Israel's case against God through a variety of similar arguments. All hurl the question at God: "How long will You hide Your face? How long will You withhold Your justice?"

It is also not surprising to find in each of these works the presence of a mysterious individual whose fate is intimately linked with that of the nation. Who is this person? He is the speaker of Lamentations 3, he is the petitioner of those psalms that combine the individual and national laments, he is Isaiah's suffering servant. He is the Jeremiah of the confessions, he is the prophet as paradigm, he is Job. But who is Job?

THE BOOK OF JOB

Job continues the development of the law-court pattern and the arguing with God motif. He builds upon them with such intensity that he has been regarded as the apex of the law-court form.[30] The legal dispute is the basic image of Job (chapters 9, 13, 23, 31), and legal terms and allusions abound throughout the book. The central problem in the Book of Job is the suffering of the innocent. In other words, it is the question of God's justice.[31]

The story begins with a heavenly wager between God and Satan concerning the nature of Job's faithfulness (1:6-12; 2:1-6). Job then is put to two tests in which he suffers loss of his wealth, children, and health (1:13-22; 2:7-10). Job's friends come to comfort him and, after sitting together in silence for seven days, Job begins to lament bitterly (chapter 3). His friends each respond in turn, urging Job to live according to the convictions he had formerly espoused, namely, to rely on God because sufferings are, in one way or another, instruction from the Lord (chapter 4f). Job, however, refuses to admit the justice of his sufferings, his friends repeat their arguments with increasing harshness, and Job likewise responds vehemently (chapters 6-7; 9-10; 12-14; 16-17; 19; 21; 23-24; 26-31) against the traditionalist views his friends espouse. The friends urge Job to search his deeds for the cause of his suffering and to repent before God. Job does not deny that he has sinned, only that his sins were small and that the punishment is out of all proportion to his sins (7:21; 13:23,26). Gradually, Job asserts his complete innocence (9:15,20-21; 12:4; 23:10-17; 29:12-17; chapter 31) and couples strong denunciations of his friends' views (12:2-12; 13:2-12; 16:2-5; 19:2-5,21-22; 21:23; 26:2-4) with fierce accusations against God (9:17-24; 10:3; 13:24-28; 16:11-17; 19:6-22; 21:7-18; 24:1-25; 30:19-23). The controversy has slowly been shifting from being a dispute between Job and his friends to a controversy between Job and his God. Job is now the plaintiff and God the defendant, from whom Job demands   an   accounting   (9:14-19,32-35;   13:3,15-28;   24:1;

31:35–37). But even while He is a party to Job's lawsuit, God is also the judge to whom Job is appealing for justice (9:32–35; 10:2; 13:13–19; 16:18–22; 19:23–29; 27:1–6; 31:35–37). In chapters 29–30, Job contrasts his righteous past with his present misery one last time. This final recitation of the facts of his case leads him to take drastic action. Job has already expressed the desire to take God to court a number of times. Only in the highest court (God's court) could God the defendant be confronted; only there would Job receive the vindication of his innocence by God the Judge. This is what Job seeks to accomplish in chapter 31.

Chapter 31 represents Job's closing argument before the Heavenly Judge. Without Elihu's address (chapters 32–37), generally considered to be a later addition,[32] Job's last words are immediately followed by the theophany of chapter 38. In chapter 31, Job swears a series of oaths designed to ascertain his innocence (31:1–4,5–8,9–10,13–17,19–23,24–28,29–34,38–40).[33] In this series of oaths (which are remarkable in that they are full oaths complete with conditional curses),[34] Job ceases to accuse God; he now takes steps to compel God to act (35–37). Yehezkel Kaufmann describes Job's situation this way:

> Job is portrayed as righteous out of love of God alone. He challenges God only because he considers it a moral duty to speak truth before Him. . . . His final word is this great oath. Though his world has collapsed, he clings to the one value that is left him, his righteousness. That has become an intrinsic value, without hope of any reward.[35]

The oath is a direct challenge to God to intervene in the case at hand. If Job has perjured himself, then God is invited to punish him more. If Job is innocent, the oath proves it and he should be restored. If neither results, God must personally intervene—which is what Job wants above all else—to have the opportunity to confront his accuser and judge. And this is what occurs immediately following the oaths.

The answer to the central problem of the book (the issue of God's justice) lies in God's revelation to Job and Job's response (38:1–42:6). But God's revelation, while it ends doubts about God's remoteness and inattentiveness, does not seem to offer a direct answer to Job's charge: "Why do the innocent suffer?"

Instead, God overwhelms Job with questions about the function-
ing of the universe and nature. The theme of the theophany is the
magnitude and scope of divine knowledge contrasted with the
minuteness and presumption of human knowledge.[36] Job only
knows a fraction of the whole. This is the point of God's concluding argument: How dare one presume to contend with the all-
knowing God whose concern extends over everything (40:2,7–14)?
Job's response is a confession of humility. Like Abraham, Job
realizes that he is as naught before God (Genesis 18:27; Job 40:4)
and without true knowledge (Job 42:2–3). Therefore, Job repu-
diates his earlier stand (40:4b–5; 42:3b,6). The direct experience of
"seeing" God and the content of the revelation change Job's outlook. Now Job knows that God indeed does exercise divine providence and that, in the end, God is just (because He has answered
Job).

What then is the specific answer to Job's charge? There is none
explicitly given. God's appearance, the revelation, is Job's vindication.[37] Moreover, God confirms Job's stand and condemns the
views of his friends who had sought to justify God's ways to Job
(42:7–8). God, it would seem, is expressing approval of Job's vociferous insistence of his innocence and of his right for justice at the
hand of God, all of which, let it be remembered, is very close in
outlook to the psalms of national lament and the Book of Lamentations. This is more than coincidence, for like these works, Job is
generally considered to be an exilic or postexilic work. As such, it
is attempting, no doubt, to address the same problem that these
and other works (such as Ezekiel) do, namely, to reconcile the new
reality of the destruction of the Temple and the misery of the Exile
with the inherited covenantal view of God. Job's suffering, like
that of the mysterious individual of Lamentations 3, has suprapersonal significance.[38]

Who is Job? It is significant that Job was "blameless and upright, one who feared God, and turned away from evil" (Job 1:1,8;
2:3). It is also significant that he lives in a foreign land, but even so
is "God's servant" (1:8; 2:3; 42:7,8). Job, like Jeremiah, like the
individual in Lamentations 3 and Isaiah 62, like the individual in
the psalms who links his misery with that of the nation, is the
prophet as paradigm; he is Israel personified as an individual. Job
symbolizes Israel in exile. More specifically, he represents the

generation after the destruction, the generation innocent of whatever sin was supposed to have brought on God's wrath. Job's anguish is paralleled by the anguish found in the national laments in Psalms and Lamentations. Both Job and the nation are bent in suffering; both appeal to God to see His justice.

For this generation, the possibility of a loss of faith or a renunciation of the God of Israel was all too real. The threat was twofold. First, the people might begin by despairing of their God, but they could end by forsaking their God (Lamentations 3:18; Isaiah 40:27; 49:14; 59:13; 63:11–15; Ezekiel 9:9). The lament, left unanswered, could just as easily swing the people from hope to denial. Second, the crisis in faith produced by the exile also made possible the denial of God's omnipotence, His justice, or both. This second threat was given concrete form by the beliefs of the religion under whose influence the Jewish people now fell. The religion was Zoroastrianism, the religion of the rising Persian Empire, and it advocated a dualistic theology with the god of the moral and natural order, Ahura Mazda (Wise Lord) on the one hand, opposed by the forces of evil (Angra Mainyu and Shaitin) on the other. This theological system surely offered the downcast and despairing among the Jewish exiles a sound explanation for what had befallen their nation. This twofold threat was the challenge that Job, Lamentations, Deutero-Isaiah, and Ezekiel attempted, by various means, to meet.

The Book of Job is a drama, but it is also a work of didactic theology, offering a message of hope and instruction in the understanding of God's justice to the exiled people of Israel. Job's understanding of divine justice, hence his teaching on the subject, thrusts as much against the Sinaitic view of divine justice (Exodus 34:7) and the Deuteronomic view of suffering (see Deuteronomy 31:16–21, for example) still current in the faith of Israel, as it does against the nations of the world who pass judgment on Israel, as did Job's friends upon him. This twofold attack is common to many of the exilic and postexilic biblical works. To counter the traditional views of divine justice and suffering, Job couples a devastating critique of a God whose justice allows the wicked to prosper and the righteous to perish (Job 21 and 24) with a protestation of innocence (see also the petitionary psalms and lamentations) and argues instead for a system wherein each is rewarded or punished according to his deeds (Job 21:19–20, and also the references to his own case—compare with Ezekiel 18). To counter the judgment passed on Israel by the nations of the world (Job's friends correspond to the enemies in the laments), Job teaches Israel that although God's presence and God's providence may not be discernible at the moment, even so Israel should not despair. God has no doubt of Israel's (Job's) integrity (faithfulness) as the prologue and epilogue of Job make clear.[39] Eventually God will manifest His justice and restore them. Just as Job's friends changed from being Job's judges to being witnesses to his vindication, for whom he must intercede with God, so too will the nations eventually bear witness to God's true plan and stand in need themselves of Israel's help (compare Job 42:7–8 with Isaiah 53 and Zechariah 8:14–17,20–23).

Job is not the only work to deal with the problems arising out of the Exile. Lamentations, Deutero-Isaiah, and Ezekiel also attempt new alternative theological interpretations. The period between the sixth and third centuries "represented that one period in the history of biblical religion which is not covered, or, at best, very scantily covered, by one or the other form of this idea of divine justice."[40] Yet it was just in this period when the problem of the suffering of the innocent was probably the greatest. Although each work presents a different point of view, some larger themes emerge.

First, against the threat of Persian dualistic theology, we find the assertion that the Lord is the sole author of all, both light and dark, good and evil (Job 2:10; Lamentations 3:38; Isaiah 42:18–25; 44:6–8; 45:5–8,18–23). But beyond this, there exists a division, often within the individual works themselves. Job's vigorous protestation of his innocence, like the protestations found in Jeremiah's confessions, Lamentations, the psalms of petition, and Isaiah 63:11b–19, is given divine sanction. But this approval of the argumentative stand must be balanced by the assertion of God's greatness and by the inability and presumption of man to know God's plan in its entirety (the view of Elihu and God in Job; Lamentations 3:37–9; Ezekiel 18:25,29; Isaiah 40:12–31; 42:18–25; 45:9–13; 55:8–9).

Second, Job (21:19–20) and Ezekiel (18; 33:10–19) propose a system wherein each individual, each generation, is rewarded or punished according to their deeds alone (compare with Deuteronomy 24:16). This is also advocated, by implication, in the national laments of Psalms and Lamentations, and in Deutero-Isaiah (Isaiah 63–64), where God is asked to behold the plight of His people, to see their innocence, and requite the wicked "according to the work of their hands" (Lamentations 3:64). But while Job himself, and the laments, do this via protest (Job; Lamentations 3:41–45,49–50; Isaiah 62:1–7; and in many psalms), others do it via faith. Ezekiel (18:25,29), Malachi (2:17; 3:13–15), Deutero-Isaiah (Isaiah 65:11–12), and Elihu affirm that God is in the right. They side with God and not with those who would argue and complain against God.

Third, all these works hold out to Israel the hope of redemption. Job, like Jeremiah in the confessions, like the individuals of Lamentations 3, Isaiah 62, and Psalms, offers Israel the hope of obtaining a hearing in God's court with the expectation that God will grant them a favorable verdict and vindicate them. These individuals are paradigmatic figures; their revelations teach that God will answer and restore Israel. On the other hand, however, are the views of Ezekiel, Zechariah, Malachi, Deutero-Isaiah, and Elihu. While they too look for a redemption, they state that it was Israel's sins that led God to withdraw, and that it is for the people to repent and for God to pardon. Deutero-Isaiah, in particular, has God answering all the charges that Israel (or Job) raise against Him.[41] As opposed to the protest and argument of Job and company, these works advocate trust in the Lord, an attitude given its fullest expression in Psalm 73.[42]

This brings us to the very threshold of the rabbinic point of view, which *ultimately* resolves the problem of theodicy along the lines developed by the postexilic prophets and Psalm 73, that is, through the belief in the Messianic Redemption, retribution in the World to Come, the resurrection of the dead to eternal life, and the acceptance of suffering as chastisements of divine love. I stress ultimately because such a view was adopted not without opposition. The arguing with God sort of prayer, as developed in Prophets and Writings, marked those occasions when protest and argument were advocated as a response to individual and national suffering. This same response continued to have its advocates throughout the rabbinic period and beyond, for it remained a viable response to the experience of suffering that the Jewish people endured throughout their subjugation at the hands of Rome and Christian Europe.

CONCLUSION

The arguing with God motif and law-court pattern in prayer in Prophets and Writings build upon the foundations laid by the final redactors of the Torah. Both utilize many of the same motifs in their arguments: the appeal to God's justice, to His name's sake, to God's past acts and promises, to the inequity and injustice of the punishment vis-à-vis the sin(s) committed, or with reference to their own innocence. Both appeal to God as judge, but in Torah, God is appealed to solely as judge. In Prophets and Writings, He is both judge and defendant. Both believe in the efficacy of prayers of intercession by the righteous; but in Torah, only God's chosen representatives use the law-court mode of prayer. Prophets and Writings follow this line but add something new as well. Jeremiah and Isaiah are, of course, prophets. Job, while not a prophet, is God's servant and, like the individual of Lamentations 3, does receive a revelation. But Prophets and Writings suggest a wider application of the law-court prayers stretching to the common people perhaps, but at least to the people as represented or personified by some holy and righteous individual. In the Torah, Abraham and Moses generally stand as third parties, lawyers, to disputes between God and the world (Sodom and Gomorrah, Israel). In Prophets and Writings, less emphasis is placed upon this intercessory type of role. Finally, both forms are meant to be experienced and understood on a dramatic-historical and didactic-theological level: both have but one intention—to affirm God's justice. Yehezkel Kaufmann has already noted this important and distinctive point:

> Complaints about the evil in the world, especially about moral evil, are voiced by pagan thinkers as well. . . . Only in Israel, however, does this question touch the very essence of God. . . . On the one hand, there was no evil principle; good and evil came from YHWH. On the other hand, Israelite religion tolerated no fault or blame in God. He was altogether good and just. When

harsh reality challenged the conventional view of divine justice, concern for the honor of God violently disturbed the devout. They could not break out in insults or surrender to despair; they could only complain and question and go on seeking an answer. At bottom, it is not so much the human side of undeserved suffering that agitates the Bible as the threat it poses to faith in God's justice.[43]

2

RABBINIC USE OF BIBLICAL ARGUMENTS

INTRODUCTION

Moses received the Torah at Sinai and handed it to Joshua; Joshua to the elders; the elders to the prophets; the prophets handed it down to the men of the Great Assembly . . . [so-and-so] received [it] from them. . . .[1]

To listen to the recounting, according to *Pirkei Avot*, of the chain of the transmission of the Torah down through the ages is to hear several cardinal principles of the traditional Jewish world view being articulated. First, that there was an actual transmission of the Teaching from earliest times down to the present. Second, that the Teaching consisted of two components: explicitly, the written Torah, the Five Books of Moses, and implicitly, the oral Torah, which consists of the traditional interpretations, likewise handed down from teacher to teacher and further interpreted by the leading scholars in each generation.

But the chain of transmission established by *Pirkei Avot* is equally important for what it downplays and omits. Downplayed is the fact that textual fundamentalism is not—despite the fact that the Torah is considered the direct word of God to Moses—mainstream in Judaism. The chain assumes exactly what tradition affirms—that an oral interpretive Torah accompanied the written Torah. Also *Pirkei Avot* omits notice that the Pharisees (the precursors of the Rabbis who flourished 150 years before the

41

destruction of the Second Temple) and their heirs, the Tannaim, were in actuality but one of several "parties" or "schools" with conflicting theological and political world views. Ultimately, the views of the Pharisees and Rabbis triumphed, but up until the upheavals of the first and second centuries C.E., their views and interpretations were not normative.

The age loosely referred to as the rabbinic or talmudic period (roughly comprising the first six centuries of the common era) was the formative period for Judaism as we know it today. The teachings of these ancient Rabbis provide the classic texts of Jewish law (*halakhah*) and lore (*aggadah*): Mishnah, Talmud, and Midrash. Theirs was a time of religious and political upheaval, a time of internal and external crisis for the Jewish people. Within the span of about a century they had to cope with a loss of sovereignty, military defeats at the hand of Rome, the loss of Jerusalem, the destruction of the Temple, the rise and challenge of Christianity and Gnosticism, and the crisis in Jewish belief and practice that all these catastrophes entailed.[2]

The chapters that follow focus on the Rabbis' use of the arguing with God motif and the law-court pattern of prayer as found primarily in the Midrash. For our purposes, it will be most helpful to define midrash as a process. According to one scholar, Norman J. Cohen, midrash was the means by which the Rabbis filled in "the spaces between the sacred words of Scripture," extending "the text as far as they could, detailing the characters' missing actions, thought, and feelings" in order to answer a multitude of questions and to articulate a message of contemporary and often timeless value. "Midrash is the 'literature of response,' and the midrashic process was the tool by which the Rabbis bolstered the courage and faith of their followers" as well as offering their responses to the exigencies of their life-situations and their polemical replies to the challenges the Jewish community faced.[3]

THE RABBINIC MODEL OF
THE LAW-COURT PATTERN

Throughout the rabbinic period, the arguing motif and the law-court pattern remained in constant use, and in fact, their application was greatly broadened.[4] In the rabbinic period, the form served three primary functions: to expound certain biblical passages, to help explain the problem of the Exile, and to act as the personal mode of prayer when certain sages (or the people on whose behalf they prayed) found themselves in dire straits.

Let us note at the outset that all three functions of the arguing with God motif are tied together by their use of the law-court pattern of prayer. Unlike the biblical use of the pattern, the rabbinic application evinces a much higher degree of uniformity in structure. Whether cast in the mouths of biblical characters or expressed contemporaneously, the law-court prayers remain cast in one mold—they are thoroughly rabbinic in form and content. All partake of certain common theological and methodological concepts which serve as the point of departure for the Rabbis. These concepts include the belief in the existence of an ongoing Covenant between Israel and God, and the belief that the Torah includes both the written and the oral law. They include the belief in a God who, while endowed with omnipresence, omnipotence, and omniscience, remains nonetheless a God of justice and mercy; a God with whom prayer is efficacious; a God who is linked to the world—and especially to Israel—through bonds of love and concern as its Creator and Judge, and, in the case of Israel, as its husband/lover as well. Methodologically, the law-court prayers are grounded in the rabbinic concept of there being no sense of time (chronology) in the Torah (*"ein mukdam v'ein m'uhar batorah"*) as well as in the classic principles of hermeneutic exposition.

The theological outlook of those rabbis who make use of the law-court pattern of prayer is but one of a number of differing rabbinic theological outlooks, all of which co-exist in tension with one another. Julius Guttmann has had the following to say on this matter:

> All the most important ideas in connection with the problem of theodicy can be found in the Talmud; yet it is impossible to construct from them a systematic doctrine . . . What the Talmud has produced is not theology, but scattered theological reflections. This accounts for the sometimes strange coexistence of ideas. . . . The ideas of providence, retribution, and miracles were firmly established as elements of the Jewish faith through their connection with belief in revelation. Their factual truth

was beyond doubt; only in regard to their precise understanding was there freedom for philosophical interpretation. . . . The
whole complex of religious convictions that had grown up in the
Talmudic period served as an incontestable, valid norm of faith
for future Jewish generations and for their philosophies.[5]

THE ROLE OF
THE LAW-COURT *AGGADAH*

With regard to the vast number of aggadic law-court prayers
attributed to biblical characters, it is significant to realize that, in
general, the Rabbis employed the law-court prayers in exactly
those situations where it had been used in the biblical narrative.[6]
This suggests that the Rabbis themselves were conscious of the
existence of the form and that they used it for a similar purpose in
addressing problems current in their own day. The primary purposes of the law-court prayers in the *aggadah* seem to have been
(a) to clarify certain difficult biblical passages that cast doubt
upon fundamental rabbinic beliefs, and (b) to expand upon and
defend their own teachings. One problem that arises as a result of
the ages-long process of compilation is that few of the midrashim
have retained their original form. Many stories are repeated in
variant forms by different sages, but few kept the full law-court
pattern. Many partial examples have, however, been preserved—
primarily the defense argument section.

In some cases, the law-court prayers in the *aggadah* merely
expand existing biblical arguments; in other cases they serve to
complete an argument only hinted at in the Bible. In still other
cases, the Rabbis' use of the form had a much more explicit purpose, serving as a counterattack against the teachings of Gnosticism and Christianity, both major threats to Judaism in the late
tannaitic and early amoraic periods (second–fourth centuries C.E.).[7]
Gnosticism, given its "finest" formulation in the teachings of Marcion, espoused a dualistic theology, opposing "the Demiurgos, the
god of the Jews, the god of this world, the known god, on the one
side, and the highest god, the great unknown god, on the other
side."[8] According to the *Clementine Homilies* (ii. 48 f.), Marcion,
supporting his case with appropriate biblical proof-texts, taught
that the God of the Jews and of the Bible was a God who:

lies, makes experiments as in ignorance, deliberates and changes his purpose, envies, hardens hearts, makes blind and deaf, commits pilfering, mocks, is weak, unjust, makes evil things, does evil, desires the fruitful hill, is false, dwells in a tabernacle, is fond of fat, sacrifices, offerings, etc., is pleased with candles and candlesticks, dwells in shadow, darkness, storms and smoke, comes with trumpets, shoutings, darts and arrows, loves war, is without affection, is not faithful to his promises, loves the wicked and adulterers and murderers, changes his mind, chooses evil men.[9]

As much of a threat as he was for the Christian Church (which declared his teachings heretical), Marcion represented an even greater threat for the Jewish people, whose faith remained intimately linked to its sources in the Bible. It was therefore incumbent upon the Rabbis to meet the Gnostic challenge head-on and to counter Marcion's attacks on their God directly, lest his views negatively influence the beliefs of a Jewish people still attempting to cope with the national disasters of 70 C.E., 115 C.E., and 135–138 C.E. The threat posed by the Gnostics was compounded by the polemics of the emerging Christian Church, which sought to undermine and repudiate rabbinic Judaism even as it advanced its own beliefs and its claim to be the "True Israel" and holders of a "New Covenant."[10] Here too, it was crucial for the Rabbis to launch a defensive and offensive war of words. This they did through the *aggadah.*

The *aggadah* performs this polemical function through its dialogues in which the biblical characters contend with God. These dialogues thus, in part, serve to defend Israel and to uphold certain fundamental beliefs concerning the nature of God and His relationship with Israel and the world. God's true nature and Israel's unique status in the world are affirmed through the arguments and admonishments these figures hurl toward God.

ABRAHAM'S AGGADIC ARGUMENTS WITH GOD

Our first example is drawn from those arguments that the Rabbis created to complement the arguments Abraham uses in the Bible when he intercedes on behalf of Sodom and Gomorrah:

Address: Master of the Universe!
Argument/Petition: You swore that You would not bring a flood upon the world [again], as it is written: "For this is as the waters of Noah to Me; for I have sworn that the waters of Noah shall never again go over the earth" [Isaiah 54:9]. A flood of water You won't bring, but a deluge of fire You would bring!? Would You with subtlety evade Your [the] oath? If so, You shall not have fulfilled the oath. As it is written: "Far be it from You— shall not the Judge of all the earth do justly?" (Genesis 18:25). If You seek [absolute] justice, there can be no world here. If it is a world You seek here, there can be no [absolute] justice. You would grab a rope by both its ends; You would have a world, and You would have absolute justice. If You don't let up a bit, Your world cannot endure.[11]

This argument functions in exactly the same way as did its biblical counterpart, dramatizing the historical moment and simultaneously teaching, explaining, and clarifying the theological significance of the event. Through the Rabbis' words, Abraham's argument becomes more explicit and more daring than in the Torah. Consider other snatches of argument attributed to Abraham on this same occasion: "In this world one has recourse to appeals in a higher court; but You, because no appeals [to a higher court] can be made, 'Will You not do justly?'" "The anger [*ha'af*] which You bring to Your world, would You destroy the righteous with the wicked? It's not enough that You do not suspend the judgment of the wicked for the sake of the righteous, but You would destroy the righteous with the wicked!" "Is Your anger like a she-bear on the rampage—if it can't find another beast to kill, it kills its own young?"[12]

Here Abraham's remarks verge on the blasphemous, yet are very far removed from blasphemy. The Rabbis contrast Abraham's charge (Genesis 18:25) with a similar accusation leveled at God by Job (Job 9:22), and find that Abraham is of a much superior mettle than Job.[13] Job, they say, spoke out in rebuke, whereas Abraham spoke in a tone of love and intercession; Job's accusations were statements of fact, Abraham's accusations were rhetorical. As in the biblical story, each of Abraham's charges is to be answered with a resounding "No!" by its audience.

God's proposed destruction of Sodom and Gomorrah, like His judgment of the Flood and the Tower of Babel, represented a serious challenge to the rabbinic belief in a just and benevolent God. Stories such as these three were seized upon by Marcion and other Gnostics to prove the true nature of the Jewish God. That Abraham's law-court prayer is meant to counter the Gnostic view is made clear by other comments made by the Rabbis in discussion of the episode. Rabbi (Judah HaNasi) said: "A human being is conquered by anger, but The Holy One Blessed Be He conquers His anger—'The Lord is vengeful, but masters anger (Nahum 1:2).'"[14] R. Yudan and R. Aha remark that the judgment which God intends to hand down is a profanation [*hillul*] of His name and foreign to his nature.[15] Elsewhere it is said that God knew there were no righteous men in Sodom, but allowed Abraham to say his piece anyway.[16] More to the point are a series of midrashim wherein God submits His judgment of Sodom and Gomorrah to Abraham's scrutiny. In Genesis *Rabbah* 49:10, God says to Abraham: "They [people] cast aspersions upon Me and say 'He does not judge correctly.' . . . Go and examine My judgment and if I have erred, 'you teach Me' (Job 34:32)." In *Tanhuma* (Buber), God submits not only His judgment of Sodom and Gomorrah, but also His past judgments as well, to Abraham's scrutiny, in order to be cleared of the "charges" made against Him.[17]

Parallel aggadic arguments raised by other biblical characters make the charge against God even more explicit. The prayer/argument offered by Abimelech, who, it is significant to note, is a non-Jew, challenges God as follows: "Will You slay even a righteous nation? [Genesis 20:4]—If this was the way You judged the generations of the Flood and the Tower, they were righteous!"[18] God faces similar accusations in the aggadic accounts of the return of the spies (Numbers 14), but this time it is Moses who accuses Him! Actually Moses employs these accusations as part of his defense of Israel, saying that if God does indeed destroy Israel in the wilderness, He will only be adding fuel to the fire. He will give the nations cause to say that God is weak and cruel and destructive.[19] In the case of Sodom and Gomorrah, as in the case of the spies, God does not want to provide substance to this provocation and so relents. In both episodes, God is, of course, cleared of all charges made against Him.[20]

Two fundamental beliefs are affirmed in these midrashim. In gratitude to Abraham for arguing successfully, God praises Abraham and rewards him by choosing (or rather, by having chosen)

to address him alone from among all preceding generations with
"*leikh l'kha*," "Go forth" (Genesis 12:1, but quite possibly Genesis
22:2 is intended as well). In Moses' case, the Talmud has God say
"*Heheitani bed'vareikha*"—"You have revived me with your
words"—which Rashi interprets as "you have preserved My esteem among the nations."[21] In response to the Gnostic charge
that God is evil, the Midrash affirms the belief in God's justice.
And, in response to the Christian denial of the unique station of
Israel in the world, the Midrash affirms God's choice of Abraham
as His witness and as father of His people.

These same two beliefs also play an important role in the rabbinic understanding of the *akeidah*, the near sacrifice of Isaac. In
the story of the *akeidah*, Abraham again expresses some of the
very questions raised by the Gnostics: "Why must God test Abraham?" "What kind of God would propose such a test?" However,
in the case of the *akeidah*, unlike in the case of Sodom and
Gomorrah, Abraham's charge is not meant rhetorically:

> **Address:** Master of the Universe!
> **Presentation:** It is revealed and known to You that when You
> told me to offer up my son Isaac, there was something I could
> have said to You: Yesterday You said to me "for it is through
> Isaac that offspring shall be called to You [Genesis 21:12] and
> now You say "offer him there as a sacrifice." Heaven forbid, I did
> not do so [offer such a retort], but I conquered my inclination
> and did Your will.
> **Petition:** Thus may it be Your will, O Lord my God, that when
> the children of Isaac, my son, enter into sorrow and there is no
> one to plead their defense, You plead their defense. "The Lord
> will see"—You remember for their sake [for them] the binding of
> Isaac their father and be filled with compassion for them.[22]

What is remarkable about this midrash is the fact that in the
biblical account—and in most midrashim—Abraham is celebrated for his silence in the face of God's inexplicable command.
Abraham's unquestioning faith is held up as a virtue for later
generations to emulate, but obviously R. Yohanan, the source for
this midrash, thought an argument was also an appropriate response for the man who argued with God over the fate of Sodom
and Gomorrah. Thus, in this passage, Abraham launches a fierce
accusation against God—that God all but went back on His own

word.[23] As judge, God has no choice but to acknowledge the justice of Abraham's complaint and grant him his request. God is forced into admitting His error in testing Abraham as He did, and such an admission must be balanced by the compensation He awards Abraham and his descendants.

It would seem that the Rabbis were less concerned with clearing God's good name than about establishing the centrality of the *akeidah* as the redemptive act par excellence. What is meant by Abraham's request that God act as Israel's advocate when they have no one else to plead their case is made clearer in one of the parallel texts to this prayer. In Leviticus *Rabbah* 29:9, Abraham tells God that in remembrance of the *akeidah* He should pardon Israel's sins and convert His Attributes of Justice into the Attribute of Mercy in the seventh month (on Rosh Hashanah).

In his arguments, Abraham is doing nothing less than laying the foundations for (or rather, reinforcing) the centrality of the *akeidah* both for the Exodus from Egypt and still later for the yearly High Holy Day ritual of atonement. And Abraham's argument actually was used in the Rosh Hashanah liturgy of third century C.E. Palestine.[24] In Genesis *Rabbah* 49:11 the fast ritual is described in which the Ark is brought out into the public square and ashes are sprinkled before it in remembrance of the merit of Abraham ("I am but dust and ashes") and Isaac (the *akeidah* burnt-offering ashes). Abraham's argument thus must be understood on one of its levels as an attempt by the Rabbis to emphasize the central redemptive role of the *akeidah* both in Jewish history and in the religious life of their times. On another level it also represents their attempt to polemicize against the redemptive qualities ascribed to the crucifixion of Jesus.[25]

MOSES' ARGUMENTS

The servitude of Israel in Egypt had a deep resonance for the Jewish people under Roman rule. Thus when Moses protests against God's inactivity (or ineffectuality) early in his mission, the Rabbis found a ready hook on which to hang their own generation's complaints.

Moses exchanged words (literally, returned words) with the Holy One, blessed be He:

I have taken the Book of Genesis and
read in it. I observed the deeds of the
Generation of the Flood and how they were
punished. It was done according to justice.
And the Generation of the Separation [Babel]
and of the Sodomites and how they were
punished. It was done according to justice.
But what has this people done that
they are more abjectly enslaved than all
earlier generations?

And if it is because Abraham [doubted Your word
and You decided to punish his descendants]
then Esau [Rome, Christian Empire] and
Ishmael [the Arab world] are also his children
and they too ought to have been enslaved
[as was Israel]. And even [if this were the reason],
then it should have been the generation of Isaac
or the generation of Jacob that was
enslaved, but not this people in my generation![26]

Rabbi Ishmael and R. Akiba debate the meaning of the words: "But indeed You have not delivered Your people" (Exodus 5:23). Rabbi Ishmael insists that the words be interpreted literally, that is, that God in truth had not saved and would not save his people. R. Akiba, however, offers an interpretation of Moses' words that is at once more hopeful and more audacious. According to Akiba, Moses declared: "I know that you will save them in the future, but what do You care about those entombed under the buildings [in the meanwhile]?"[26]

Speaking to his own generation, R. Akiba was saying: "Yes, God will redeem us someday but I, Akiba/Moses, call God to accounts over our suffering here and now."

Opinion was divided over the appropriateness of Moses' impatience and lack of faith. This same midrash continues: At that moment the Attribute of Justice sought to strike Moses down. But when the Holy One, blessed be He, saw that Moses had spoken so only out of love on Israel's behalf, Justice did not punish him. On the other hand, in Sanhedrin 111a, R. Eleazar, son of R. Yossi, taught that upon hearing Moses' words God lamented: "Alas for those who are gone and no more to be found! For how many times did I reveal Myself to Abraham, Isaac, and Jacob . . . and they did not question my Attributes, nor say to Me, 'What is Your name?'" And for this Moses is punished by being denied entrance into Canaan. The appropriate attitude of a Jew to suffering was, apparently, not uniform.

The aggadic accounts of Moses' arguments with God at the time of the Golden Calf likewise occupy a very significant place in the Rabbis' attempts to answer the charges brought against Judaism by Gnosticism and Christianity. According to the Gnostics, the episode of the Golden Calf showed yet another example of the Hebrew God's destructiveness, changeability, jealousy, and anger. According to the Christian Church, the episode of the Golden Calf marked Israel's (first) rejection of God, and consequently, God's ultimate rejection of Israel.[27] Thus, in their aggadic interpretation of the Golden Calf story, the Rabbis had to respond to both these attacks.

In a number of midrashim, God actually wants Moses to intercede with Him on Israel's behalf. In one case, God deliberately says: "*Vayomeir*"—"*Emor li*"—"Tell me what I did to deserve this of them?"—in order to provide Moses with the opportunity to intercede.[28] In another instance, God is compared to a king who is on the verge of beating his son and, anxious over what he might do, says within hearing of his adviser: "Were it not for my adviser here I would kill you!," by which the adviser (Moses) realizes that he must act to defuse the situation.[29] Elsewhere, Moses feigns such anger with Israel that God tells Moses that they both cannot be angry and that therefore Moses had better pray on Israel's behalf.[30] In yet another midrash, Moses, like Abraham before him, tells God that such an act as He contemplates would be a profanation of His name.[31] This sort of exposition effectively clears God of the accusations of wanting to destroy Israel.

Moses then attempts to plead on Israel's behalf. He begins with arguments based on Israel's own merit:

Address: Master of the Universe!
Accusation: Be reminded for their sake, that when You sought to give the Torah to the Children of Esau, they rejected it, but Israel accepted it (Exodus 19:8).
Divine Response: God replied: "They have transgressed against the deed [of taking the Torah]" (Exodus 32:8).

Accusation: Be reminded, for their sake, that when I went on Your mission to Egypt and I said Your name to them, immediately they believed and worshiped You (Exodus 4:31).
Divine Response: God replied: "They have transgressed against [their] worship [of Me]" (Exodus 32:8).
Accusation: Be reminded of their firstborn whom they sent to offer sacrifices before You (Exodus 24:5).
Divine Response: God replied: "They have transgressed against their sacrifice" (Exodus 32:8).
Accusation: Be reminded for their sake, of that which You said at Sinai—"I am the Lord your God" (Exodus 20:2).
Divine Response: God replied: "They have transgressed against that too—'And they said: These are your gods'" (Exodus 32:8).

Israel has no merits of its own with which to protect itself, and Moses calls upon the merit of the ancestors (*zekhut avot*) to bolster Israel's case.

The Rabbis, curiously, were ambivalent in their attitude toward the merit of the ancestors. Generally speaking, they placed great emphasis on the redemptive and atoning powers of the merit concept.[33] With reference to the story of the Golden Calf, we see both tendencies at work. In a number of midrashim, Moses obtains no forgiveness for Israel's sins until he makes mention of the ancestral merit.[34] In one example, Moses uses examples drawn from the trials of the Patriarchs to prevent Israel's destruction at the hands of God. Moses argues:

If they [Israel] warrant burning, remember Abraham who was ready to be burnt in the furnace for the sake of Your name, let his burning stand [go forth] for the burning of his children. And if it is death [by the sword] they warrant, remember Isaac, their father, who stretched his neck upon the altar for Your name; let his slaughter take the place of the slaughter of his children. And if it is banishment that they deserve, remember Jacob, their father, who was exiled from his father's house to Haran; let these stand for theirs . . . [and spare them.][35]

In another midrash, Moses prays: "Master of the Universe! Were the Patriarchs righteous or wicked? Distinguish between the two. If they were wicked then it is fitting what You plan to do to their children. Why? Because their fathers have no deeds [stored up] with You. But if they were righteous, give them [Israel] the deeds of their fathers . . . [and spare them.]"[36]

Moses also uses the three Patriarchs to refute God's expressed wish to make of Moses a second Abraham: "Sovereign of the Universe! If a three-legged stool cannot stand before You when You are angry, how much less a one-legged stool? I would be ashamed to face my ancestors who would say: 'See what a leader He has set over them! He sought greatness for Himself and not mercy for them [Israel].'"[37]

In other instances, however, the merit of the ancestors does not accomplish all that is expected of it. In Ecclesiastes *Rabbati* 4:5, Moses calls upon the Patriarchs to battle the angels of God's anger, but God discredits the merit of each: Abraham because he lacks faith (Genesis 15:8), Isaac because he loved Esau, whom God hated (Genesis 25:28 and Malachi 1:3), and Jacob because he intended to deceive God (Isaiah 40:27). But then Moses adds "to whom You swore by Your own self" and God immediately repents.[38]

In another case, Moses reminds God that He had sworn to the Patriarchs not by transitory objects like heaven and earth, but by His own name, saying: "Master of the Universe! Did you not swear by Yourself to their fathers that You would not destroy their children?" And God must respond: "Just as I live and exist for all eternity, even does My oath stand forever and ever."[39]

God's promise to Israel is the crucial matter, a concern brought home by a dialogue between God and Zion in *Berakhot* 32b. Israel accuses God: "When a man takes a second wife, he remembers the deeds of the first! You have both forsaken and forgotten me" (Isaiah 49:14). God responds: "My daughter, I made the whole universe for your sake. 'Can a woman forget her suckling child?' [Isaiah 49:15]. Can I forget the burnt offerings . . . in the Wilderness?" Israel then asks anxiously: "Since there is no forgetfulness with You, will You not forget the Golden Calf?" God: "I have forgotten it." Israel: "But will You forget Sinai?" And God reassures Israel: "I will not forget you."

In the main then, the Rabbis did place great trust in the powers of the "merit of the ancestors," citing its redemptive power at the time of the Golden Calf and on many other occasions. This was both an attempt to affirm their own faith and to mount a counter-polemic against the Christian Church, which inveighed against the merits of the ancestors even as it asserted the redemptive power—the merit, if you will—of Jesus.[40] And even for those Rabbis who placed less of an emphasis on the ancestral merit, God's promise to the Patriarchs still remained intact, for Israel's Covenant with God was an eternal Covenant, a Covenant never to be repealed and never to be superseded.

The Rabbis by no means discounted the seriousness of Israel's worship of the Golden Calf and of its implications for the Covenant. Israel, in these cases, has no merit upon which to base its defense, and Moses must defend them himself even to the point of risking his life. Moses' breaking of the Tablets, according to several midrashim, was an act of desperation, by which Moses sought to lessen Israel's punishment and prevent its annihilation, similar to the tearing of a *ketubah* to prevent an unchaste woman from being punished as an adulteress. Yet in daring such an act, Moses risks his life. As in Exodus 32:32, Moses links his fate with Israel saying: "They have sinned, and I have sinned for I have broken the Tablets." "If You pardon me, You must also pardon them."[41] The Covenant at Sinai is thus temporarily but purposely suspended in order to prevent a stricter punishment from befalling Israel. In another midrash, Moses does incur God's wrath for breaking the Tablets, yet saves himself by juxtaposing the merit of Abraham's ten trials with the ten broken Words.[42]

In another group of midrashim Moses attempts to save Israel by pointing out that God addressed the Commandments to him alone (that is, in the singular) and hence Israel had not broken its pledge, since it was not party to the agreement.[43] Moses attempts a similar semantic defense by answering God's command: "Go down! Your people have sinned," with, "If you say they are my people [and not Your people], then *my* people have sinned and not *Your* people. So 'Why are you angry against Your people?'" (Exodus 32:11).[44] Moses also urges God to be realistic and patient—had not Israel just left a land steeped in idolatry? How could they not but be influenced by the Egyptians' practices?[45]

Some midrashim also continue the anti-idolatry polemic of the Bible—but with a twist of intention and a touch of humor. Moses proposes: Sovereign of the Universe! They made an assistant for You and You are angry with them?! This Calf which they made will be Your assistant. You make the sun rise, and it—the moon. . . ." God replies in astonishment: "Moses! Are you going astray just like them? Surely there is nothing to it!" And thereupon Moses retorts: "If so, why are You angry with Your children?"[46] In a variation on this theme God admits: "I must be angry to show that I am against idol worship—but there's nothing to it really," and Moses responds as before.[47]

In still other midrashim, Moses uses God's past or future behavior to press for Israel's acquittal: Here is one example:

> **Address:** Master of the Universe!
> **Accusation:** [When You sent me to Pharaoh I asked about the merit of Israel for they were idolators] but You said to me, "You see them now as idolaters, but I see . . . when I shall give them the Torah." . . . But if before You redeemed them, You told me that they would worship the Golden Calf, now that they have made it, why do You seek to kill them?![48]

Israel's ongoing relationship with God, the Covenant, must be affirmed and defended above all. In the Rabbis' eyes, Moses was Israel's greatest defense attorney, marshaling so many arguments that he literally wearies God with their multitude.[49] But in a number of midrashim, Moses exceeds himself and becomes a Prometheus-like figure standing against God in the protection of Israel.

In several midrashim Moses confronts God directly. In Numbers *Rabbah* 16:25, Moses declares: "Master of all worlds! 'You have been seen eye to eye' . . . the scales are balanced. You say 'I will smite them' [Numbers 14:22], but I say 'Pardon I pray' [Numbers 14:19]. Let us see whose words stand [take effect]!"

In another midrash, Moses charges:

> **Address:** Master of the Universe!
> **Accusation:** They broke the beginning of the Commandment, "You shall have no other gods" . . . but You seek to break its end "Showing loving kindness [*hesed*] for thousands of my beloved" [Israel]. . . . And how many generations [have there been] from Abraham until now? Seven. . . . And if You cannot show *hesed* to seven [generations], how are You going to show *hesed* for two thousand [generations]? Thus, they have nullified the first clause of the Commandment, and You seek to nullify its second clause.[50]

But Moses does not rely only on the power of argument. R. Abbahu, while apologizing for the extreme anthropomorphism of this teaching, says that the text (Exodus 32:10) teaches that Moses took hold of God like a man who seizes his fellow by his garment and said: "Sovereign of the Universe! I will not let You go until You forgive and pardon them!"[51]

Raba, in this same midrash, plays on the verb found in Exodus 32:11 and, based upon its recurrence in Numbers 22:19, says that Moses remitted God's vow for Him. A parallel, but perhaps earlier text explains that God had previously vowed that those who sacrificed to other gods would have to die (Exodus 22:19). God regretted it, but He, of all "people," could not possibly break His vow. Thereupon Moses declared:

> **Address:** Master of the Universe!
> **Accusation:** Have You not given me the power to nullify oaths? (Numbers 30:3). A person can absolve himself, but a sage can absolve his oath for him when requested. Any elder who gives instruction, if he wishes that others will receive [accept] his teachings, must himself observe [establish] it first, and You have commanded me regarding the annulment of vows. It follows that You must permit Your vow [to be absolved] as You have commanded me regarding others.

Thereupon Moses wrapped himself in his *tallit* and sat like a sage while God stood before him like one asking about his vow. Said Moses, "Do You regret Your vow?" God replied: "I regret [repent] the evil which I thought to do to My people." And Moses then declared: "You are absolved. There is no vow here, and there is no oath here."[52]

God is pleased that Moses has dissuaded Him. In several midrashim God admits that had He won, He actually would have lost.[53] In other midrashim Moses is confirmed in his role, complimented or thanked.[54] Moses' argument was, in some cases, so valid that the Rabbis say that God actually learned from Moses.[55] Finally, God rewards Moses by giving him the second set of Tablets—the Tablets containing both the written and oral Law.[56]

In the episode of the Golden Calf, as in many other instances, Moses appears as a master lawyer, using every technique he (and the Rabbis) know to defend Israel. But it is not just ancient Israel at a time of crisis whom Moses is defending. His words, not surprisingly since they were set in his mouth by the Rabbis, were also very timely with regard to the problems of the second through the fourth centuries C.E. The same is true for Abraham and his arguments with God. Taken together, Moses and Abraham both defend and polemicize for rabbinic Judaism. In answer to the Gnostics, the aggadic law-court prayers of Moses and Abraham show that God is by nature just and good, and that God desires not the destruction of the sinner but his repentance. In response to the Christian Church, the aggadic prayers of Abraham and Moses defend God's choice of Israel as His people, and affirm the continuity and continued efficacy of God's Covenant with Israel.

ARGUMENTS AGAINST THE HUMAN CONDITION

Through certain biblical stories, the Rabbis protest against God's apparent injustice as it applies to the human condition: childlessness, the evil inclination, and death.

Childlessness

In the Bible, Hannah, Samuel's mother, prays fervently but silently that God give her a child (1 Samuel 1:13). In the words of the Rabbis, her silent biblical prayer becomes a series of audacious arguments with God:

> **Address:** Master of the Universe!
> **Accusation/Petition:** Of all the hosts and hosts that You have created in Your world, is it so hard in Your eyes to give me one son?

And

> **Address:** Master of the Universe!
> **Accusation:** Among all the things You have created in a woman, You have not created one without a purpose: eyes to see, ears to hear, a nose for smell, a mouth to speak, hands to do work, legs to walk with, breasts to give suck. These breasts that

You have put on my heart, are they not to give suck?
Petition: Give me a son, so that I may suckle with them.

And most brazenly, in an effort to force God's hand:

Address: Master of the Universe!
Accusation/Petition: If you will look, it is well, but if you will
not look, I will go and shut myself up with someone else
[another man] in the knowledge of my husband Elkanah [who
will be jealous and suspect me of adultery]. And, as I shall have
been alone [with a man other than my husband] they will make
me drink the water of the suspected adulteress [but I will be
innocent] and You cannot falsify Your Law, which says, "She
shall be cleared and shall conceive seed" (Numbers 5:28).[57]

God, of course, grants Hannah's prayer.

The Evil Inclination

In the Torah, Cain's argument consists of an appeal and a protest:
"My punishment is too great to bear! Since You have banished me
this day from the soil, and I must avoid Your presence and become
a restless wanderer on earth—anyone who meets me may kill me!"
(Genesis 4:14). Yet this was enough of a beginning upon which
the Rabbis could build an elaborate defense argument for Cain.
When confronted by God and asked, "Where is your brother Abel?"
Cain retorted:

You are He who is the guardian of all creatures and You ask of
him from me?! This is like a thief who steals utensils and is not
caught. In the morning the gatekeeper catches him and says:
"Why did you steal the utensils?," to which the thief replies: "I
stole but I did not forsake my craft. Your craft is to stand guard
by the gate, why did you forsake your craft? And yet now you
inquire of me?!" Thus said Cain: "I have killed him. But You
created the evil inclination in me. You are the guardian of
everything, yet You allowed me to kill him. You are the one who
killed him . . . for if You had accepted my sacrifice as You did his,
I would not have grown jealous."

[The rabbis explain:] This resembles the case of two who quar-
reled and one is killed. But a third fellow was there who did

nothing to intervene between them. Upon whom does the blame rest if not the third fellow? Thus it is written: "[His blood] cries out to Me [Ěly]—it cries out against Me [Aly]."

Cain said to Him: "Master of the Universe! I have not known about, or ever seen a slain person in my life. How was I to know that if I smote him with a stone that he would die?" [God curses Cain and Cain asks:] "Master of the Universe! . . . My father and my mother dwell on earth and they did not know that I had killed him. You however are in Heaven, how did You know?" God replies: "I roam the entire earth and I bear everything, as it says: 'I have made, and I will carry; I will bear, and I will save'" [Isaiah 46:44]. Thereupon Cain retorts, "You bear all the world in its entirety, but my sin You cannot bear?! My sin is too great to bear!" And God says: "Since you have repented, you are [only] exiled from this place."[58]

Cain's complaint, set in his mouth by the Rabbis, becomes a strong critique of the nature of things—of the imperfection of human nature, of the lack of divine providence, the interrelationship between human and divine moral responsibility, and the existence of the evil inclination, against which the Rabbis often inveighed.[59]

Cain's accusations against God do present a powerful condemnation of the nature of God's justice regarding the human condition. But Cain, like Esau, was generally considered a wicked person, one who approached God with devious intent by demanding God's forgiveness rather than confessing his sin.[60] In light of this, certain Rabbis took Cain to task. Another midrash states that God asked Cain his brother's whereabouts only to offer Cain the chance to repent as He had with Adam. But Cain was one of several men who answered God wrongly, saying: "Am I my brother's keeper?" rather than acknowledging that God knows and sees all.[61] (In the Midrash *Tanhuma* passage cited above, Cain answers God properly, that is, by acknowledging God's omniscience.) Job too, according to Raba, sought to excuse himself by placing all responsibility for sin in the hands of God (Job 10:7). For this blasphemy, Raba said: "Dust should be stuffed in the mouth of Job."[62]

But even if the charge was blasphemous, it still had to be answered nonetheless. This the Rabbis do in a number of ways. First, as in the Midrash *Tanhuma* passage, God acknowledges

His responsibility.[63] In other midrashim, God regrets having created the evil inclination in man and creating him from earthly parts.[64] But the deed is done, and man is what he is. Does this leave God standing accused of creating an imperfect world or of being malicious? This prompts a second rabbinic response—that *all* creation *is* good. The Rabbis saw a positive value in the evil inclination. It was seen as the source of all productivity.[65] Beyond this, the rabbis assert that all of God's work is perfect, that all His ways are just:

> His work is perfect in regard to all who come into the world, and one must not criticize His ways. . . . He is a God of justice: He judges each one justly and gives him his due. A God of faithfulness: He had faith in the world and so He created it; for He did not create men that they should be wicked, but that they should be righteous.[66]

That God was perfect, just, and faithful was an assertion the Rabbis made both to counter the tenets of Gnostic dualistic theology and in response to their own theological world view. But with regard to the latter, since God had created in us an evil inclination, then we cannot be wholly responsible when we do sin. This is Cain's argument. If God were to judge us as if we were wholly to blame, then He would be a malicious and unjust God. But God is not so, say the Rabbis. God has intended humankind to be righteous, but has also endowed us with the evil inclination. This leaves human beings free to choose. This is the third response— that free will exists. But God does not leave humanity to founder on the rocks of temptation. In His mercy, He has provided an antidote to the influence of the evil inclination: "I have created the evil inclination," says God, "but I have also created the Torah as a remedy against it. As long as you busy yourselves with Torah, sin will not master you."[67] If Cain has sinned, God too has erred, and both atone for their wrongdoing—God by creating the Torah, and Cain by doing *teshuvah* (repentance).

This leads to the fourth response—the important role ascribed to repentance by the Rabbis. Unlike several other midrashim, a midrash in Deuteronomy *Rabbah* sees Cain's repentance as genuine and his confession sincere.[68] By repenting, Cain, the prototype of the sinner, appeals to God's mercy. The repentance of the sinner was seen by the Rabbis as God's chief joy, for it allowed Him to be merciful.[69] Cain repented and his sentence was lightened. Adam, upon hearing this, struck himself, and wondered: "Is the power of repentance as great as this? I did not know it was so."[70] God desires repentance even from the most sinful. Thus, King Manasseh repented after a fashion, and God forgave even him: "You deserve not to be answered, for you have angered Me, but so as not to shut the door upon the repentant, lest they say 'Manasseh sought to repent but he was not received'; therefore I will answer You." God proceeds to pardon Manasseh even though His decision meant going against the wishes and actions of his Angels.[71]

Israel stood in great need of these teachings regarding the nature of God, the value of observing the Torah, and the role of repentance in order to survive the traumas of the national disasters of the Roman era. But Israel also made use of Cain's argument on occasion. Thus Israel says to God:

Address: Master of the Universe!
Accusation: You have said, "Behold, like clay in the hands of the potter, so are you in My hand O House of Israel" [Jeremiah 18:6]. Therefore, even though we sin and anger You, do not withdraw from us. Why? Because we are the clay and You are our potter. [Come and see: If a potter makes a jar and leaves a pebble in it, when it is taken forth from the kiln, if a man puts a draught in it, it will leak from the place of the pebble, and will lose the draught inside of it. Who caused the jar to drip and to lose what was inside of it? The potter who left the pebble in it!] Thus Israel said to God:
Address: Master of the Universe!
Accusation: You created the evil inclination in us from our youth [as it says in Genesis 8:21], and it causes us to sin against You but You do not remove cause of sin from us.
Petition: We beg of You, remove it from us in order that we may do Your will.
Divine Response: God said to them: So shall I do in the future [to come] as it is said: "On that day, says the Lord, I will assemble the lame and gather those who have been driven away and those whom I have wronged [afflicted]" (Micah 4:6).[72]

The Rabbis recognized that even someone like Elijah made use
of this argument, when he said to God on Mount Carmel, "You
have turned their heart backwards" (1 Kings 18:37). While one
rabbi states that such a statement was insolent—a hurling of
words against Heaven (*hatahat devarim k'lapei ma'alah*),
another rabbi states that God acknowledged the truth of Elijah's
words in Micah's prophecy, "those whom I have wronged" (Micah
4:6). R. Hama (in the name of R. Hanina) and R. Papa (elsewhere
R. Yohanan and R. Papa) go on to say that had God not said these
words through His prophets, Israel would have had no excuses, no
basis for pleading for mercy. But since God has acknowledged His
responsibility for our condition, we have a loophole (*pithon peh*)
upon which we can build our defense. God, in His justice, can be
forced to recognize the justice of Israel's complaint.[73] Thus, Israel
can argue as it did above, gaining a promise from God that in the
future He will make their hearts whole by removing the evil inclination from them. In other midrashim, the demand is more immediate. In *Tanna de be Eliyahu*, God compensates for the dam-
age He had done in creating the evil inclination by opening the
gate of mercy to receive the sinners of Israel (when they repent).
And Israel prays: "Master of the Universe! It is revealed and known
to You that the evil inclination incites us. In Your abundant
mercies, receive us in complete repentance" [that is, receive us
who repent with complete forgiveness].[74] And R. Alexandri prays:

> **Address:** Master of the Universe!
> **Accusation:** You know it is our will to do Your will. But the
> leaven in the dough [the evil inclination] and the servitude to
> the kingdoms prevent it.
> **Petition:** May it be Your will to save us from their hand, so that
> we may return to do the statutes of Your will with a perfect
> heart.[75]

R. Alexandri suggests that if God wants Israel to return and
observe His laws, then He will first have to remove the stumbling
blocks from their path. Not only is this an appeal to God's self-
interest,[76] but also implies that Israel cannot completely effect
repentance on its own. God must turn and aid Israel against the
impediments of the Exile and the evil inclination if Israel is to rise
above its present sinful state and return to do God's will.[77]

To summarize: God has created all things for a good purpose. God has created the evil inclination but He has also created the Torah to help Israel learn to overcome the evil inclination. The temptation to sin is strong, but God's mercy is infinitely more so, for the possibility of repentance is always available. The act of repentance (*teshuvah*) represents a turning of the sinner to God and of God to the sinner.[78]

Death

Just as the Rabbis told stories of Israel's attempts to destroy the evil inclination, so too they told of a similar antipathy toward the Angel of Death.[79] An early tradition has Israel receiving the Torah only upon the condition that the Angel of Death will no longer have power over them, although they then lost this unique privilege by worshiping the Golden Calf.[80] Furthermore, various heroes and sages, David and Joshua b. Levi, for example, attempt in vain to triumph over the Angel of Death.[81] But the one who protested the most vociferously was Moses.

In the Torah, there is but one argument near the time of Moses' death—Moses' appeal to enter the Land.[82] But the Rabbis understood Moses' protest on that occasion to include both an argument to enter the Land and an argument against his impending death, since in the Torah Moses' death follows directly upon the heels of his viewing of the Land. Many of Moses' arguments mirror this fact by raising similar points in each case. We shall focus, however, on Moses' protest against death since it represents an issue of great importance to the rabbinic world view.

As with the concept of the evil inclination and the story of Cain's sin, Moses' death raised questions not only about the justice of the event itself, but also questions about the justice (or goodness) of death in general. If these questions were put to the Rabbis by the Gnostics, it was not because rabbis to ask them were lacking. Moses' death, and death in general, were issues over which the Rabbis themselves pondered.

The Rabbis had to develop answers to refute the charge that God was wronging Moses by taking his life just as Israel was about to enter the Land of Canaan. This they did in a number of ways. As with regard to the evil inclination, the Rabbis assert that death, too, is good—it represents punishment for the wicked, who, by dying, cease to anger God, but it is a reward for the righteous, who gain a deserved rest. But death comes to one and all lest the wicked feign repentance in order to continue living.[83] Death, together with suffering, *Gehinnom*, and punishment are good because they are part of God's system of justice by which He rewards the righteous and punishes the wicked.[84] Furthermore, although in the future God intends to abolish death, for the present death is an established decree, a fact of life, something that God Himself refuses to abolish either for Israel or for Moses.[85]

Second, the Rabbis seek to determine specific reasons why Moses should be punished. The Torah gives one reason—Moses' and Aaron's inappropriate action at Meribah—to which the Rabbis also refer, saying that this represented a public exhibition of Moses' lack of faith.[86] But the Rabbis also saw Moses' previous arguments as due cause for his being punished.[87] Moses' death is also conceived as being part of the overall working-out of divine justice. Thus, just as the sin of Adam brought death into the world with a "Behold" (*hen*)—(Genesis 3:22), so too Moses must die with a "Behold" (Deuteronomy 31:14); this in addition to Moses himself first having sinned with a "Behold" (Exodus 4:1).[88] But Moses was God's chosen servant, and though he must die, God will in the future reward him and all Israel by bringing the Messiah with a "Behold."[89] In another midrash, God tells Moses that he must die in the wilderness lest people think that the generation of Israelites who died there had no share in the World to Come. Moses must remain with them until God summons him to bring them in (up?) to the World to Come.[90]

All this proves, in response to the Gnostics, that God is just and His decrees are just. But however much the Rabbis justify Moses' fate and theorize about death's "redeeming" qualities in the Midrash, Moses still argues his case. When all was said that could be said about death, it still remained a source of anxiety—if not for the Rabbis then for the people. Thus Moses' arguments over his impending death are replete with all the human emotions connected with death: fear of the unknown, regret at what is to be left behind and what still remains to be accomplished, and a defiance coupled with a sense of betrayal for having been created, given a mission to fulfill, and then, in the end, to be removed from life's activities while life continues, oblivious to the change.

To annul the decree of death, Moses draws a magic circle around himself and hurls his prayers to the Heavens. God orders the Gates of Heaven shut but Moses' prayers batter against the gate and set all the angels atremble.[91] To no avail. Thereupon Moses prayed:

> **Address:** Master of the Universe!
> **Accusation:** The labours and pains which I have devoted to making Israel believe in Your name are manifest and known to You, to what trouble I have gone with them in connection with the precepts in order to fix for them Torah and precepts. I thought: Just as I have witnessed their woe, so too I would behold their reward. But now that the reward of Israel has come, You say to me, "You shall not go over this Jordan" [Deuteronomy 31:2]. Behold You make a fraud of Your own Torah, as it is written: "You must pay him his wages on the same day, before the sun sets, for he is needy and urgently depends upon it; else he will cry to the Lord against you and you will incur guilt" [Deuteronomy 24:15]. Is this the reward [I get] for the forty years labour that I went through in order that [Israel] should become a holy and faithful people?[92]

Moses and God engage in a duel of words and proof-texts. Moses complains: "In all Your acts [one sees] measure for measure; [will You now repay me with] a bad measure for a good measure, a short measure for a full measure, a grudging measure for an ample measure?"[93] God replies that Moses will be well rewarded in the World to Come. Moses pleads: "Master of the Universe! If You will not bring me into the Land of Israel, leave me in this world so that I may live and not die." God replies that Moses must die in order to reach the World to Come. To deny death to Moses would likewise render God's Torah untrue and thereby make God a liar. God uses the same type of argument here as Moses does. Moses entreats God: "If You will not bring me into the Land of Israel, let me become like the beasts of the field that eat grass and drink water and live and enjoy the world; likewise let my soul be as one of them." God replies: "Let it suffice you." Moses says, "Master of the Universe! Let me become like the bird," and God replies, "You have spoken sufficiently."[94] But Moses clings to life. Defiantly, he takes up writing a Torah scroll and the Angel of Death fears to approach him to take his soul. When ordered to return a second time, the Angel of Death receives a beating from Moses' staff.[95] Finally, God resolves to act, and calms Moses' fears directly. God Himself, not the Angel of Death nor human beings, will attend to Moses' burial. With sweet words God calls forth the soul, and weeping, gives Moses the kiss of death.[96] When Moses died, his body was laid on the wings of the *Shekhinah*, and the ministering angels lamented over him saying: "He executed the justice of the Lord and His judgments with Israel" (Deuteronomy 33:21). And God declared: "Who will rise up for Me against the wicked? Who will stand up for Me against evil-doers?" (Psalm 94:16).[97]

In the *aggadah*, Moses' death becomes an opportunity for the Rabbis to calm people's apprehensions regarding death. Thus God attempts to reassure Moses saying, "Let it suffice you"—"You will have much in the next world ... don't embarrass Me by further pleading."[98] "Let it suffice you, lest people say how severe is the Master and how persistent is the student."[99] Moses must cease protesting lest people question God's nature and begin to doubt in the reality of the World to Come. Moses may have lost the argument, but he was comforted by learning and personally experiencing what every human being longs to know—that death is not the end, that God does care, and that He has provided a future beyond the grave in the World to Come. This is one of the major points of the entire dialogue/argument. On one level, it is meant to quell anxieties over death by having Moses give expression to these feelings and by having God reassure him. On another level, the didactic level, the dialogue serves to instruct about the rabbinic concept of the World to Come and its place and role in the system of divine justice.

CONCLUSION

With regard to both the evil inclination and death, as with the midrashic treatment of biblical events, there are two divergent, but not unrelated, attitudes among the Rabbis. On the one hand, these problematic aspects of human existence were held to be good, necessary parts of the divine plan. God is just, faithful, and perfect in all His work; therefore "one must not at all criticize or ponder."[100] On the other hand, the Rabbis do voice strong criticism about the human condition by placing law-court arguments in the mouths of various biblical characters. These two views are not contradictory; rather they exist in tension with each other as parts within a larger whole. The first view affirms in a positive way the teachings of the Rabbis; the second affirms the rabbinical world view indirectly as it combats the attacks of Gnosticism and Christianity and the doubts of the people themselves. This dual approach exists toward the suffering of the Exile as well.

3

ARGUMENTS AGAINST THE EXILE

INTRODUCTION

"For a brief moment I forsook you, but with great mercy I will gather you," said God through Isaiah to comfort and buoy up the people of the First Exile. "In overflowing wrath I hid my face from you for a moment, but with eternal *hesed* [loving-kindness] I will have mercy upon you."[1] Such also was the consolation that Israel longed to hear after the national disasters of the late first and early second centuries of the common era. However, as the psalmist said, "a thousand years in Your sight are but as yesterday when it is past,"[2] and the longer Israel suffered in Exile the more pronounced their anguish became. The destruction of the Second Temple and the resultant persecutions represented a serious problem that the Rabbis and the people had to confront, namely, the injustice of the suffering of the innocent vis à vis the traditional belief in a just, omnipotent, loving, and long-suffering God.

In its own right, the national disaster probably would have prompted a reinterpretation and a revision of the God–concepts, explanations for suffering, and world views of the pre-Destruction era. But this need was exacerbated by the polemic attacks of the Christians and the Gnostics. To the Gnostics, the catastrophe that befell the Jewish people was proof of the weakness and maliciousness of the Hebrew God. To the Christians, the national calamity testified to the sinfulness of Israel in rejecting Jesus, and it confirmed the divine rejection of the Jewish people and the

election of the "New Israel." The Rabbis, therefore, had manifold
reasons for rejecting the full implications of the concept of divine
retributive justice, at least temporarily, because it implied that the
Jewish people had sinned a great sin. The latter thought ran
against both common sense and the shared experience. It also
would have fed the fires of Christian polemics. If, on the other
hand, the Rabbis asserted that the suffering of the Exile was not a
manifestation of God's will, they would have compromised God's
omnipotence and lent credence to the Gnostic position. Addition-
ally, if the Rabbis affirmed God's omnipotence alone, this would
have implied that God, either willingly or capriciously, had in-
flicted suffering upon Israel. And from this the conclusion could
be drawn that either God was not all-just and all-merciful—a
teaching sure to delight the Gnostics—or that Israel's Covenant
with God had been terminated—one of the "rocks" upon which
the Christian Church was built.

Thus, the Rabbis were in a dilemma. On the one hand, they had
to develop a positive message with which to inspire themselves
and the people, and on the other hand, they had to counter
Christian and Gnostic polemics.[3] The Rabbis met these challenges in several ways. First, under R. Akiba's leadership, they
drew upon biblical sources and developed a new rationale for the
meaning of suffering and an alternative to the concept of quid pro
quo divine justice. National and/or individual suffering were seen
as gifts from a loving God who tries the righteous, to cleanse them
of sin now in order to reward them in full later on. In the case of
Israel, suffering was conceived of as a badge of honor, a sign of
Israel's chosenness, and the means by which Israel attains its
divine rewards.[4] Second, but connected with the first, the Rabbis
transposed the arena for the ultimate execution of divine justice
from this world to the World to Come. Third, they emphasized the
role of study, prayer, and repentance in place of the Temple service
and sacrificial cult. Fourth, they utilized the law-court argument/
prayer to give voice to the complaints of Israel and to counter the
anti-Jewish polemicizing of their time.[5] And fifth, concomitant
with the fourth, the Rabbis built upon the anthropopathetic God-
imagery of the Prophets and Psalms to envision an empathetic
God who could be simultaneously just and merciful, wrathful and
grief-stricken, omnipotent and self-limiting.

The recitation of the tribulations of the Babylonian Exile was, for the Rabbis, an opportunity to recount the sufferings endured during the Second Exile. For them, the Book of Lamentations not only depicted the horrors of the Babylonian conquest of Jerusalem; it also spoke prophetically of the persecutions and suffering endured under Rome. The two events merged together, and in many instances when the Rabbis refer to the events of the First Exile, they are actually addressing the situation of their own time. One motivation for this blending of the two events may well have been as an act of political prudence, designed to avoid incurring the wrath of the government. Another motivation was, no doubt, the Rabbis' own belief in the redemptive aspect of Jewish history which led them to see their future through the redemptive events of the past.

In a number of midrashim, Job becomes a paradigmatic figure for the Jewish people, and his story mirrors Israel's tragic history. Thus, the sack of Jerusalem by the Babylonians (and therefore by implication also by the Romans) is reflected in the story of Job. Both Jerusalem and Job suffer at the hands of the Chaldeans who are but emissaries of God's will. Both Job and Jerusalem sat on the ground, clothed in sackcloth and dust; both receive no comfort in their grief. But just as Job was first afflicted by God and was later given a double reward, so too will Jerusalem eventually be granted a double measure of comfort by God.[6] With the final comparison the Rabbis have turned to speak directly to their contemporaries. But the analogy between Job and Jerusalem (Israel) actually goes much deeper than is discussed in the Midrash. Just as Job suffered and protested, so too Israel, in many midrashim, suffered and was not hesitant in protesting. These protests, cast in the form of law-court prayers and set in the mouths of Knesset Yisrael (the People Israel), Zion or the Ancestors in Heaven, occur primarily in the books of Lamentations *Rabbah*, *Pesikta de Rav Kahana*, and Midrash *Tehillim*. Of our sources, only one, Lamentations *Rabbah*, is early (400–500 c.e.); the others were all compiled in the latter half of the millennium. This suggests, perhaps, that the problem of the Exile continued to plague Israel well beyond the period of the Tannaim and Amoraim, that the solutions to the problem of suffering and exile proposed by the Rabbis were never totally satisfactory, and that the people were neither wholly comforted nor content.

THE ARGUMENTS OF
KNESSET YISRAEL

Building upon the imagery of the prophets, the Rabbis portrayed the events surrounding the covenant-making at Sinai as the betrothal and marriage of Israel to God. But this analogy did not end there. From the first moment in Jewish history when it became apparent that God had ceased to act as He had in the past, Israel was depicted as a widow (Lamentations 1:1) The Rabbis likewise describe Israel's situation in terms of widowhood, compare it to a rejected first wife, or, most apt of all, as an *agunah*, an abandoned wife. Israel is likened to a woman whose husband has left her; no one knows whether he lives or has died, or if he shall ever return. And so Israel waits. She can neither remarry, get a divorce, nor live in peace with her mate, for He has abandoned her and left her without support. In an early midrash, Israel doubts that God will ever take His "wife" back, and she cites Jeremiah 3:1 as proof of this. But God responds: "That is written only with regards to a man. 'I am God and not a man' (Hosea 11:9). If I have divorced you, where's your bill of divorce? Have I not already said: 'Where is your mother's bill of divorce with which I sent her away?'" (Isaiah 50:1).[7]

Rabban Gamaliel must answer precisely this same charge, though it is directed at him by a hostile pagan philosopher: "Is it possible that you still say 'We wait for the Lord to deliver us?'" Rabban Gamaliel responded in the affirmative: "Then you are uttering a lie. God will never return to you, for does not Scripture say 'He has drawn off from them?'" (Hosea 5:6). But Gamaliel answers that, according to the laws of the *halitzah*, the woman, not the man, draws off the shoe, and although God has drawn Israel off, Israel has not drawn off from God (proof-text: Song of Songs 5:6). Therefore, God's action is an invalid *halitzah* and the bond between Israel and God remains. Israel can only cry out against her abandonment.[8] And so Israel protests:

> **Address:** Sovereign of the Universe!
> **Accusation:** When a man takes a second wife he remembers the deeds of the first! "You have both forgotten me and forsaken me!" (Isaiah 49:14).

> **Divine Response:** God replies: "My daughter, I have made . . .
> [the entire universe] . . . for your sake. Yet you say 'You have
> forgotten me and forsaken me.' Can a woman forget her suck-
> ling child? (Isaiah 49:15). Can I forget the burnt offerings . . .
> you offered to Me in the Wilderness? . . ."
> **Address/Accusation/Petition:** Sovereign of the Universe! Will
> You forget my conduct at Sinai?
> **Divine Response:** I will not forget you.[9]

Similarly, when Jeremiah sees what God has wrought against
Jerusalem, he cries out: "Master of the Universe! If You intend to
return [to her], why have You struck us without healing?" (Jeremiah 14:19). God replies: "I will say to you what I have said to
Moses: 'I will not reject or abhor them'" (Leviticus 26:44). But God
does not answer Jeremiah's earlier protest regarding "forsaking
and forgetting" (Lamentations 5:20,22), so Zion herself accuses
God, saying: "The Lord has forsaken me, my Lord has forgotten
me" (Isaiah 49:14).[10] The existential dilemma remains: Israel
suffers in Exile, and God remains silent and aloof.

Israel take it upon herself to remind God:

> **Address:** Master of the Universe!
> **Accusation:** You told us "Remember" (Deuteronomy 25:17),
> but of us forgetfulness is to be expected. You must remember,
> however. There can be no forgetfulness before the Throne of
> Your Glory, "Remember, O Lord, the day of Jerusalem against
> the children of Edom" [Rome] (Psalm 137:7).

And impatient to see God manifest His justice, Israel complains:

> **Address:** Master of the Universe!
> **Accusation:** You had a House from which You had pleasure,
> but enemies rose up and destroyed it. But they still stand while
> it lies waste. There were righteous men from whom You had
> pleasure, but the wicked rose up and slew a great number of
> them and so despised Your name. Yet still the wicked stand!
> (proof-text Psalm 10:3).[12]

But when God reproaches Israel for impudence in addressing
Him in such a manner, Knesset Yisrael replies:

Address: Master of the Universe!
Accusation: It is seemly and right and proper for us to do so, seeing that no other nation except us accepted Your Torah.
Divine Response: God retorts: It was I who disqualified all the other nations for your sake.
Accusation: They said to Him: If that is so, why did You carry Your Torah around for them to reject it?[13]

The Covenant gives Israel the right to argue with God. It also provides Israel with a precedent and a strong basis upon which to dispute with God.[14]

The rehearsal of God's saving acts in the past, brought to mind with each reading from the Torah and each holiday celebration, roused Israel's bitterness at her present lot. Recognizing the timeless quality of the psalms of national lament, the Rabbis said: "[The B'nai Korah] prophesied concerning the present generations who say to the Holy One Blessed be He":

Address: Master of the Universe!
Accusation: You did wonders for our fathers, will You not do them for us? . . . What a work You performed in bringing them forth out of Egypt and dividing the sea for them! But You have not done anything like that for us! . . . You did it for them, but not for us. What does it profit us what You did for our ancestors? When shall the profit be ours? When will You work a good sign for us as it is said: "Work a sign for good in my behalf" (Psalm 86:17). You did great work for the former generations in the days of Abraham. . . . You did a great work for Abraham's children also. You showed favour to them, but You show no favour to us.
Petition: As Scriptures say: "Lord, You have been favourable to Your land. . . .Show us Your mercy, O Lord, and grant us Your salvation" (Psalm 85:2,8). . . . You were favourable to them, but You are not favourable to us.
Divine Response: God replies: Indeed, I shall be favourable to you also. And of this the B'nai Korah were to say: "Lord, You have been favourable to Your land, You have brought back the captivity of Jacob" (Psalm 85:2).

The specific laws of the Covenant are also used in arguments. In a number of midrashim, Israel, supported by the Holy Spirit on occasion, points out that their enemies act both against them and against God's Torah by killing the mother together with the child (see Deuteronomy 22:6; Leviticus 22:28), committing sexual offenses (see Leviticus 18:13), and by abandoned bloodshed (see Leviticus 17:13).[16] While in these cases God is expected to take note of these transgressions for eventual judgment, in other midrashim God Himself is in violation of His law. Israel declares:

> **Address:** Sovereign of the Universe!
> **Accusation:** How long will the Temple remain in ashes? Haven't You written in Your Torah: "He that kindled the fire shall make restitution" (Exodus 22:5)?
> **Petition:** You kindled the fire—You are obliged to rebuild it and to comfort us—You, not an angel.
> **Divine Response:** And God said: I will do it (proof-text Psalm 147:2).[17]

Israel challenges God to realize that His apparent rejection of Israel and of the Covenant also damages the sanctity of His name:

> **Address:** Master of the Universe!
> **Accusation:** Is one a king without a throne? Is one a king without a palace? "How long O Lord? Will You forget me, O Eternal One?" (Psalm 13:2). Do You forget that You said to the prophet Samuel: "The Eternal One of Israel will not lie nor change His mind" (1 Samuel 15:29)? Surely in the covenant made between You and the Patriarchs, You, who are the Eternal One of Israel, did not act the liar. Surely You do not repent [change Your mind regarding] Your gifts that You will not bring them to us. For Scripture says: "God is not a man that he should lie; neither the son of man that he should repent" (Numbers 23:19).[18]

Voicing a similar "concern for God's name," the women of Jerusalem pray: "Master of the Universe! If You have no pity on us, why have You no pity on the sanctity of Your name?"[19] And from another source, Israel chimes in: "If we have good works, redeem us. But if we have no good works, redeem us for Your name's sake."[20]

It is also out of respect for God's attribute of truth, and in the knowledge that God would not want false things said about Him, that Jeremiah and Daniel delete key words from the phrase that Moses had set down in praise of God "great, mighty and awful"

(Deuteronomy 10:17). Jeremiah says: "Aliens are demolishing His sanctuary—where are His awful deeds?" So he refuses to say "awful" (proof-text Jeremiah 32:17). Daniel comes and says: "Aliens are enslaving His children—where are His mighty deeds?" And Daniel refuses to utter "mighty" (proof-text Daniel 9:4).[21] As daring as this midrash is, its impact becomes even greater when one realizes that Moses' words form the opening part of the first blessing in the *Amidah* prayers. Speaking through Jeremiah and Daniel, the anonymous author, at least in his midrash, presumes to repudiate Moses' praise of God. The midrash, therefore, has a strong, contemporaneous note of protest to it.[22]

Israel clings to her God in faith and in hope, even though, as we have seen, these qualities are often expressed as protests and accusations rather than as confessions of trust or acknowledgments of dependence. It is the hope for redemption that comforts Israel—the expectation that God will act for the present generation as He had for earlier generations. "Only when I am delivered," says Israel, "can I open my mouth to speak and answer those who taunt me, even though I cannot answer them now"—"I am dumb, I open not my mouth because You did it" (Psalm 39:10). . . . But it is Your will that I am to answer them, and so "Remove Your stroke from me; I am consumed by the blow of Your hand" (Psalm 39:11).[23] It is this faith that gives Israel the strength to persevere and the courage to answer her foes.

THE ARGUMENTS OF
THE ANCESTORS IN HEAVEN

But Israel does not stand alone. The prophets of Knesset Yisrael on earth are strengthened by the protests of the Patriarchs, Matriarchs, and Prophets in Heaven, all of whom attempt to use their influence, their *zekhut* (merit), in the attempt to intercede with God in behalf of Israel. Often, the Angels, and even the Holy Spirit, join in the tumult. In perhaps the most famous of these midrashim, the twenty-fourth proem of Lamentations *Rabbah*, Jeremiah, at God's behest, rouses the Patriarchs and Moses from their graves to weep and lament over Israel's destruction for (and with) God.

But the occasion for lamenting soon turns into a confrontation between Israel's ancestors and God in which the Patriarchs and Moses accuse God of great injustice. When Abraham comes weeping and mourning before the Lord, the ministering Angels join in his lamentation and cry out:

> **Address:** Sovereign of the Universe!
> **Accusation:** Broken is the covenant which You made with Abraham their father, through which the order of the world was established and through which men recognized You as the most high God, creator of Heaven and earth. You have despised Jerusalem and Zion which previously You had chosen.

Soon after Abraham speaks:

> **Address:** Sovereign of the Universe!
> **Accusation:** Why Have You exiled my children and delivered them over into the hands of the nations who have killed them with unnatural deaths? And why have You laid waste to the Temple, the place where I offered my son Isaac as an offering before You?
> **Divine Response:** Your children have sinned and transgressed against the whole Torah, all the twenty-two letters that are in it.
> **Address/Accusation:** Sovereign of the Universe! Who testifies against Israel that they have transgressed against Your law?

God calls first the Torah and then each letter of the alphabet to testify against Israel. But Abraham, with the finesse of an expert defense attorney, convinces all the witnesses for the prosecution not to testify against Israel. Then he commences Israel's defense:

> **Address:** Sovereign of the Universe!
> **Accusation/Defense:** When I was one hundred years old You gave me a son, and when he had acquired intelligence and was thirty-seven years old, You ordered me "Offer him as a sacrifice before Me." I steeled my heart against him and I had no compassion on him; I myself bound him.
> **Petition:** Will You not remember this and have mercy upon my children?

Then Isaac begins and says:

> **Address:** Sovereign of the Universe!
> **Accusation/Defense:** When my father said to me, "God will provide the lamb for the burnt offering, my son," I raised no objection to the carrying out of Your words, and I willingly let myself be bound upon the altar and I stretched out my neck beneath the knife.
> **Petition:** Will You not remember this on my behalf and have mercy upon my children?

Then Jacob begins and says:

> **Address:** Sovereign of the Universe!
> **Accusation/Defense:** Did I not stay twenty years in Laban's house? And when I left his house, the wicked Esau met me and sought to kill my children, and I delivered myself [to him] to die in their stead. Now they are delivered into the hands of their enemies like sheep to the slaughter, after I had raised them with as much difficulty as a hen has raising her chicks. I have experienced great trouble for their sakes.
> **Petition:** Now will You not remember this for me and have compassion upon my children?

Then Moses begins and says:

> **Address:** Sovereign of the Universe!
> **Accusation/Defense:** Was I not a faithful shepherd for Israel during the forty years? I ran before them in the Wilderness like a horse. And when the time came that they should enter the Land, You decreed that my bones should remain in the Wilderness. Now that they are exiled, You have sent for me to lament and weep over them. [My case is] like the proverb which people use: "Of my Lord's good I do not partake; but of His evil [or misfortune] I do!"

Moses and Jeremiah then journey to Babylon to redeem Israel only to be thwarted in their attempt by the decree of the *Bat Kol* (Heavenly Voice). Moses and Jeremiah return to Heaven and describe all the horrors of the Exile to the Patriarchs. Together they weep and lament. Moses then proceeds with his defense of Israel:

Address: Sovereign of the Universe!
Accusation: You have written in Your Torah: "Whether it be a cow or a ewe, you shall not kill it and its young in one day" (Leviticus 22:28), but now they [the Chaldeans] have slaughtered a great many mothers and children together. And yet You are silent?!

Then Rachel, the Matriarch, leaps up before God and says:

Address: Sovereign of the Universe!
Defense: It is known to You that Jacob, Your servant, loved me with a special love and that he served my father because of me for seven years. But when the seven years were over and the time of my marriage had arrived, my father determined to give my sister to my husband instead of me. And it was hard for me because I knew of the plot. I disclosed it to my husband and I gave him a sign so that he could distinguish between me and my sister. . . . But afterwards I repented and I overcame my desire and I had pity on my sister that she should not be put to shame. . . . And I gave my sister all the signs that I had given to my husband, so that he might think that it was I. Not only that, I crept under the bed in which he lay with my sister and when he spoke with her, she was silent and I spoke for her so that he would not recognize my sister by her voice. I acted lovingly towards her and I was not jealous and I did not put her to shame.
Accusation/Petition: Now if I, who am but flesh and blood, dust and ashes, was not jealous of my rival and did not put her to shame, why should You, O Eternal King, the loving and merciful One, be jealous of idols who have no reality in them, so that You have sent my children into Exile and let them be slain by the sword and suffered their enemies to do what they wished to them?

Then the mercy of God is aroused, and He says:

The Divine Response: For your sake, Rachel, I will restore Israel to their land, as it is said, "Thus says the Lord, A voice is heard in Ramah [on high], lamentation and bitter weeping; Rachel weeping for her children refuses to be comforted, because they are not. Thus says the Lord, Refrain your voice from weeping, and your eyes from tears, for your work shall be rewarded, and they shall come again from the land of the enemy" (Jeremiah 31:15–16).[24]

Note that after God the prosecutor has presented His witnesses, God does not speak again until the very end when He appears as God the judge. Also significant is the fact that the use of *zekhut* (merit) by the Patriarchs and Moses is of no effect, nor is Moses' use of the "they go against Your Law" argument. Only Rachel's argument moves God to compassion—an argument in which she compares her own qualities of patience, understanding, and compassion with those of God. But unlike the other pleaders, she does not ask directly that Israel be forgiven for her sake (her merit). She only points out that it would seem that she, a mere woman, is more compassionate than God and that God is angry over an inconsequential matter. It is the combination of these two factors that causes God to change His mind. Rachel does not make her petition depend directly on her own merit (see *Berakhot* 10b) and her petition pointedly contrasts God's attributes with His apparent behavior—behavior very reminiscent of the Gnostic polemics against Him.

But this cosmic court case has still further dimensions. The generation of Israel that suffers on earth can also appeal to the court on high. In a midrash very similar to the story of Hannah and her seven sons in 2 Maccabees, a mother (Miriam) urges her seven sons to martyrdom at Roman hands rather than have them commit idolatry by worshiping the emperor. And to her last child she says: "Tell Abraham: You bound one son upon the altar; I have bound seven. Yours was but a test; mine is a real deed." Soon after she kills herself, too.[25] Miriam and her seven sons are more faithful than Abraham or Isaac, and Miriam calls upon Abraham to acknowledge the truth of her words. This is one reason why she directs her words not to God, but to Abraham. But there is a second reason as well. As in the twenty-fourth proem, Abraham serves as Israel's defender in Heaven. Miriam's pointed comparison between her deed and his mere test is expected to urge Abraham on to further and more forceful pleading. If, based on the test of the *akeidah*, Abraham could win concessions for his children from God, how much the more so should he be able to win concessions from God based upon the actual sacrifice of seven sons and the martyrdom of a mother.

Many other accounts of martyrdom are recounted in Lamentations *Rabbah* and we might well ask why these horror stories should be repeated four or five hundred years after the fact. Why are stories of the martyrdom of tannaitic sages also recited in the Yom Kippur *Musaf* service? The Patriarchs are Israel's defenders; like Moses in the twenty-fourth proem, they are witnesses to Israel's suffering and act as advocates in Israel's behalf. Each act of martyrdom adds to Israel's *zekhut* (merit) and further bolsters the arguments of the Patriarchs on high. Ultimately, God will turn in compassion toward Israel. He too will witness and testify to Israel's faithfulness in suffering and will reverse His decree against them.[26]

But when God does indeed do so, Israel will not be so quick to forget and to forgive Him the long and painful delay. In a number of midrashim God sends Abraham, Isaac, Jacob, and Moses, and following them, all of the Prophets, to comfort Zion with words of consolation. But Zion refuses each and every one of them.[27] God then realizes that He Himself must lead the procession of comforters since He Himself is personally responsible for her plight. Even with this realization on God's part, it will not be easy to comfort Jerusalem. According to one midrash, Jerusalem will refuse God's comfort until she can utter reproaches (*tokhahot*):

> Let me show You the nations of the world whom You lavish with all kinds of good things, yet they deny You nonetheless.
>
> Why didn't You act like Joseph to us? He forgave the evil done to him and did good to his brothers (Song of Songs 8:1; Genesis 50:21).
>
> No other nation would take Your Torah. Is this how You reward us who took it?

And God accepts Israel's rebukes, saying: I have acted foolishly with you. Jerusalem responds:

> **Address:** Master of the Universe!
> **Accusation:** This has been a private conversation between You and me. Who will let the nations know that we have been doing Your will? They oppress and persecute us saying, "You rebelled against your God and sinned [acted treacherously] against Him."

> **Divine Response:** I will let them know of the deed of your righteousness, as it says: "I will declare your righteousness" (Isaiah 57:12).

Then Israel and Michael acknowledge God's deeds, saying: "The Lord has brought forth our vindication: come let us declare in Zion the work of the Lord our God" (Jeremiah 51:10).[28]

Israel demands nothing less than total vindication by God before all the nations for all the suffering she has endured since the destruction of the Temple. And God, in His justice, acknowledges the justness of Israel's complaint and acts accordingly.

RABBINIC RESPONSES TO THE EXILE

The Rabbis were, above all, teachers with responsibilities to the people. Hence, though in the Midrash they could contend with God, they also had the obligation to respond on behalf of God to the people who attended the synagogues and houses of study. Let us now briefly examine how the Rabbis depicted God's role in, and His reaction to, the national cataclysm of the Exile.

First, the Deuteronomic view of retributive divine justice was never wholly relinquished. It still served as (at least) a partial explanation for what had befallen Israel. Thus the Rabbis sought to determine the specific sins for which Israel was punished by God.[29] This was coupled with a renewed emphasis on the acceptance of the divine decree and by having God answer Israel's charges with counteraccusations. "Is it I who have forgotten you? Is it not you who have forgotten Me?" (Psalm 106:21). "Have I hid My face from you? Is it not you who have hid your faces from Me?" (2 Chronicles 29:6; Jeremiah 2:27).[30] But while this may affirm the justice of God's decrees, it does not represent God's (or the Rabbis') final word on the subject, which was always one of consolation (*nehamta*). This message of comfort occurred primarily at the conclusion of law-court arguments uttered by the Patriarchs, Prophets, a personified Zion, or Knesset Yisrael. God states: "I will not forget you";[31] "I have not rejected nor abhorred";[32] "I will comfort you";[33] "I am not like man who cannot take back a rejected wife. I have not divorced you";[34] "I will act as a compassionate father and mother to you";[35] "I have not lied regarding the

Covenant or the redemption";[36] "Israel shall flourish again";[37] "You will be rewarded for your suffering";[38] "I will do great deeds for you too";[39] "I was silent for the three kingdoms, but for Edom [Rome] I shall cry out."[40]

Words of future consolation, however, cannot wholly soothe the pains of the present, nor do they totally acquit God of the charge of injustice. Several early sources depict God, or His *Shekhinah*, as suffering when Israel suffers, as being enslaved when Israel is enslaved, and as being redeemed when Israel is redeemed.[41] In one case this connection is proposed linking God's activity to Israel's observance of the Torah.[42]

With regard to the destruction of the Temple, the Rabbis further develop the anthropopathetic God–imagery of the Bible, making it even more explicit. In one instance, God wants to punish Israel because He is angry, but He does not want to destroy her totally. Nor can He, as Israel's God, permit Israel's destruction without damaging His good name. Therefore, God, as it were, closes His eyes to what is about to happen.[43] God empathizes with Israel in their suffering. He feels pain when they feel pain,[44] He weeps and mourns for Jerusalem like a king of flesh and blood.[45] Indeed, as one midrash states, it only appears that God is asleep. In fact, He weeps over Jerusalem together with His prophets.[46] Other images include depicting God as being ill,[47] or being led into exile,[48] or as having bound His right hand.[49]

But if God has truly not abandoned Israel, if He is grief stricken for their sake, if He writhes with them in suffering, if the Covenant still exists, and if God really intends to deliver Israel in due time, then what remains as Israel's task until their redemption? One midrash, reminiscent of an early tannaitic teaching in the *Mekhilta*, has God say to Israel:

> My Torah is in your hands and the End is in My hands. We need each other. Just as you need me to bring the End, so too I need you to observe My Torah to bring closer the building of My House, and Jerusalem. As I cannot bring Myself to forget the time of redemption [which is as likely as My forgetting My right hand], so too you are not free to forget My Torah.[50]

But this too needed clarification by the Rabbis, for with the Temple in ruins and with entry often forbidden into Jerusalem, let

alone near the Temple Mount, how could Israel still serve God?
This prompts Israel to ask of God:

> **Address:** Master of the Universe!
> **Accusation/Complaint:** If the princes sin, they bring a sacrifice
> and it atones for them. If the anointed [priest] sins, he brings a
> sacrifice and it atones for him. But we have no sacrifices.
> **Divine Response:** God replies that if they sin they too should
> offer up a sacrifice (Leviticus 4:13).
> **Defense:** Israel repeats itself: We are poor and we have nothing
> to bring for sacrifices.
> **Divine Response:** And God says: I desire words as it is said:
> "Take with you words and return to the Lord" (Hosea 14:3), and
> I will wipe out your transgressions. [By] words [I mean] words of
> Torah as it is written: "These are the words which Moses spoke"
> (Deuteronomy 1:1).
> **Defense:** But Israel said: But we do not know [its words].
> **Divine Response:** So God said to them: Cry and pray to Me and
> I will receive [it]. Didn't I redeem your ancestors from their
> servitude in Egypt because of [their] prayers? (proof-text Exo-
> dus 2:23). Didn't I do miracles in the days of Joshua on account
> of prayer (proof-text Joshua 7:6; 8:18). [And in the days of
> the Judges I hearkened to their cries, and likewise I heard the
> prayers of Israel in the days of Samuel.] And so too with the
> people of Jerusalem. Even though they angered Me; because
> they wept before Me, I had pity upon them (proof-text Jeremiah
> 31:6). Therefore I desire neither offerings nor sacrifices from
> you, only words.[51]

In a law-court petition similar to God's response above, Israel asks
that God accept their fasts of repentance:

> **Address:** Master of the Universe!
> **Accusation:** When the Temple existed, we used to burn the fat
> and portions for atonement. Now behold our own fat, blood, and
> souls.
> **Petition:** May it be Your will that they atone for us.[52]

This multi-faceted adaptation of Pharisaic Judaism by the Rabbis enabled the Jewish people to survive the traumas that befell
the nation in the late first and early second centuries of the
Common Era. Rabbinic Judaism consisted of a series of complex

and intertwined dialectics. To mention but a few: an increasingly "philosophical" God-concept coupled with a heavy reliance on anthropomorphism; the encouragement of an attitude of submission to God's will when confronted by inexplicable suffering opposed by the continued use of the law-court argument to protest against such unwarranted suffering; the desire for divine retribution in this world balanced by the transference of divine retribution to the World to Come; the frequent use of the *zekhut avot* (ancestral merit) and the attempt to limit the role of the ancestral merit; the belief that God alone will bring the redemption and the belief that Israel can affect the redemption by righteous behavior and observance of the Torah. These, and other dialectical opposites remain in Jewish theology to this very day.

These arguments between Israel and God regarding the Exile would appear to mark the climax of the rabbinic usage of the law-court pattern of prayer. No other event, except perhaps Israel's worship of the Golden Calf, sparked so many law-court arguments as did the suffering of the Exile. Encapsulated in these midrashim we have seen virtually all of the themes and motifs found in the biblical and aggadic law-court arguments: that God must be true to His nature, that He must not act contrary to His Torah, that He must be merciful as well as just. We see reference to the inviolability of the Covenant, to the *zekhut avot* (merit of the ancestors), and to God's great deeds in the past in the expectation that He will act in a similar fashion in the near future. We see that Israel alludes to her own meritorious behavior in the past, primarily to the acceptance of the Torah, to her continued faithfulness, and to the fact that she suffers for the sake of God. But in the law-court arguments that protest against the Exile, the Rabbis are directly addressing the problems of their day—the despair and anguish of the Jewish people and the attacks leveled against Judaism by Gnosticism and Christianity. Only in these midrashim do the Rabbis have the freedom to give vent to the full expression of their feelings; only here, when speaking through some other figure, do they have the license to contend vociferously with God, demanding to know why Israel continues to suffer and why God delays the execution of His justice for so long. Some Rabbis and Sages, however, primarily in the tannaitic period, did make personal use of the law-court pattern. Let us now examine some examples of the Rabbis' own law-court prayers.

4

PERSONAL LAW-COURT PRAYERS IN THE RABBINIC PERIOD

FORCING GOD TO SEND RAIN

As we would by now expect, the Rabbis, in the main, resort to the law-court argument prayers in times of personal or communal distress.[1] Thus R. Tsadok uses it when he enters the ruins on the Temple Mount,[2] Levi b. Sisi and R. Eleazar of Modi'in use it to thwart enemy troops,[3] Rabban Gamaliel uses it to save himself and his companions from drowning,[4] and R. Judah HaNasi uses it on his deathbed.[5] But by far the most common situation in which the Rabbis and Sages utilized the law-court pattern of prayer was the time of drought.

In biblical times, so too in the rabbinic period, drought was considered a sign of divine displeasure.[6] Several midrashim even attempt to delineate for what sins rain is withheld, while other midrashim stress the magnanimity of divine love and mercy that the bestowal of rain signifies.[7] God's mercy could also be appealed to to end a drought. In both the biblical and rabbinic periods, the divine decree of drought was never sealed; the decree could be averted by a confession of guilt, acts of repentance, and an appeal for divine mercy on the part of the sinful people. According to the Book of Joel, the standard biblical procedure for averting a decree of drought seems to have been one that included a communal (or national) assembly and fast, coupled with special prayers and laments spoken by the priest accompanied by the blowing of *shofarot*.[8] It was not always the priest who interceded with God. Certain Prophets also appealed to God to bring rain. Elijah successfully and dramatically brought the rain with a law-court argument consisting of an oath and accusations during the contest on Mount Carmel.[9] And Jeremiah, too, attempted to intercede for the people but God forbade him to do so.[10]

All these elements are found in the rabbinic discussions on the subject. First of all, the established procedures to end droughts, as set down in tractate *Ta'anit*, included a fast, an assembly in the market place, the donning of sackcloth (and other signs of mourning and repentance), the blowing of *shofarot*, the recitation of special prayers, and a call to repentance by an elder or a scholar.[11] Underlying both the biblical and rabbinic procedures was the essential concept of *teshuvah* (returning or repentance).[12]

Of curiosity is the fact that while the benedictions that accompany blowing of the *shofar* were recorded, the actual prayer for rain was not.[13] If the commentary of the later Amoraim in *Ta'anit* 16a is any clue to what had been done in the earlier period, or in their own time, then probably these prayers were argumentative, and took the form of the law-court pattern. In many cases only fragments of the complete prayers have been transmitted. Thus, regarding the transporting of the Ark into the market place, R. Hiyya b. Abba said: "We have prayed in private but we have not been answered, [therefore] we will humiliate ourselves in public"; while Resh Lakish said: "We have exiled ourselves [from the synagogue]; may our exile atone for us"; and Joshua b. Levi said: "We had a utensil/vessel which we kept hidden, and now because of our sins it has become despised." Regarding the donning of ashes, Levi b. Hama said: "We are considered before You like ashes," while R. Hanina said: "That God may remember for our sake the ashes of Isaac." (See also Levi b. Hama's and R. Hanina's dispute and prayers concerning the procession to the cemetery.) The repentant people of Nineveh are held up as an example of how a repentant Israel should behave, and here too the Amoraim provide us with law-court prayers set in the mouths of the inhabitants of Nineveh. According to the Amoraim, the people of Nineveh separated the animals from their young and said: "Master of the Universe! If You will not have mercy upon us, we will not show mercy to these," thereby implying that they would be forced to transgress God's Torah (Leviticus 22:28). Moreover, they would cry to God saying: "Master of the Universe! If one is humbled [pitiful] and one is not, if one is righteous and one is wicked, who should yield to whom?"[14]

However, the strongest proof for postulating that the actual prayer for rain in the rabbinic period (as in the biblical period) was a law-court argument/prayer, are the stories about those rabbis and other righteous individuals who interceded on behalf of the people to pray for rain. In doing so, these figures served a function parallel to the intercession of other prominent and righteous individuals in the biblical and aggadic tales.[15]

We begin our study of the Rabbis' and Sages' prayers for rain with perhaps the best-known example of its kind, the stories about Honi HaMe'agel (the Circledrawer).

> It happened that [the people] said to Honi HaMe'agel, "Pray that rain should fall." He said to them: "Go and bring in the ovens [in which you have roasted] the paschal offerings so that they do not dissolve." He prayed, but no rain fell. What did he do? He drew a circle and stood within it and said: "Master of the Universe! Your children have turned to me for I am like a member of Your household [literally: a child of Your house]. I swear by Your great name that I shall not move from here until You show mercy to Your children."[16]

The rain came grudgingly at first, Honi retorted with another prayer; the rain then descended in such torrents that Honi had to respond with yet another prayer said over a bull prepared as a sin-offering:[17]

> "Master of the Universe! Your people Israel, whom You have brought out of Egypt, can stand neither too much goodness nor too much punishment. When You are angry [and withhold the rains] they cannot stand it; when You pour out Your goodness upon them they cannot stand it. May it be Your will that the rains stop and that there be ease [rest] in the world."[18]

Let us note some of the major motifs in these two prayers. Prior to his first law-court prayer, Honi confidently tells the people to take in their ovens—a sign that he had no doubts whatsoever about his abilities to intercede with God. But perhaps because of this lack of modesty, or perhaps because of the people's sin, no rain was forthcoming. Honi then resorts to forcing God's hand by means of a drawn circle and an oath based on his personal merit.[19] But the oath is softened by the preceding sentence in which Honi explains that he is interceding on behalf of the people. He calls himself a "*ben bayit*," a child of God's house (more on this later), and asks God to have mercy upon His children. This allusion to Israel's chosenness and God's mercy is reinforced in the second law-court prayer, in which Honi refers to Israel as God's people, to God's deeds at the time of the Exodus, and to the need for God to be temperate in His dealings with humankind (a request similar to that of Abraham in several midrashim on Sodom and Gomorrah). Also significant is the fact that while in the first prayer Honi relies on his personal merit and obtains less than satisfactory results, in the second prayer Honi refers only to the merits of Israel and the nature of God, and thereby achieves the desired result.

The ability to bring rain runs in Honi's family. Two of his grandsons, Abba Hilkiah and Hanan HaNehba, were also appealed to by the Rabbis to intercede with God on the people's behalf and to pray for rain. On one occasion, the Rabbis sent school children to beseech Hanan HaNehba to pray for rain, which he did saying: "Master of the Universe! Act for the sake of those who cannot distinguish between the Father who gives rain and the father who does not give rain."[20]

Two other righteous individuals who also managed to bring rain with their prayers were Nakdimon b. Gurion and Hanina b. Dosa. Nakdimon b. Gurion, a wealthy and prominent citizen of Jerusalem, borrowed twelve cisterns of water from a heathen nobleman to provide for the needs of the Jewish pilgrims in a time of drought upon the condition that he would repay the loan in kind or in cash by a certain date. But the due date arrived and the drought remained unbroken; thereupon Nakdimon wrapped himself in his cloak and prayed:

> **Address:** Master of the Universe!
> **Defense:** It is revealed and known to You that I acted not for my honor, nor for the glory of my father's house, but for Your honour alone, that the pilgrims for the festival might have water.
> **Divine Response:** (Immediately it began to rain in abundance.)[21]

However, the heathen lord claimed that the time limit had already passed, as the sun had set, and that therefore Nakdimon still owed him the twelve talents of silver. Nakdimon turned once again to God and prayed:

Address: Master of the Universe!
Petition: Make it known that You have beloved ones in Your world.[22] Perform a miracle for me now as You did before.[23]
Divine Response: Immediately the clouds dispersed and the sun broke through [thereby showing that Nakdimon had repaid his loan within the time limit].

Hanina b. Dosa, the last of the "men of deeds," "a man of rank for whose sake favour is shown to the entire generation," also could bring on rain with but a simple prayer.[24] Once, while on a journey, rain began to fall, and Hanina b. Dosa uttered the following, somewhat frivolous but successful, prayer, thereby overriding even the prayers of the High Priest said on behalf of the entire nation:[25]

Address: Master of the Universe!
Petition: The whole world is at ease while Hanina is in distress?!
Divine Response: The rain stopped.

Upon reaching his home, Hanina b. Dosa prayed:

Address: Master of the Universe!
Petition: The whole world is in distress while Hanina is at ease?!
Divine Response: And it began to rain again.[26]

The Rabbis themselves often assumed, or were invited to assume, the role of intercessor. Thus we find that R. Eliezer b. Hyrcanus and R. Akiba led prayers for rain, as did R. Judah HaNasi, R. Hama b. Hanina, and Joshua b. Levi, and also Raba, R. Judah, Levi, Nahman, Huna, and Hisda, among others.[27] Few of these prayers have been transmitted, but those that have are all law-court prayers. For example, following R. Eliezer's ineffectual attempt to produce rain, R. Akiba, in his own mild style, prayed:

"Our Father our King, We have no king but You. Our Father our King, for Your own sake, have mercy upon us." And the rain fell.[28]

Others, however, were more forceful in their approach. After he had proclaimed a fast, which failed to bring rain, Levi prayed: "Master of the Universe! You have ascended and taken Your seat on high and You do not have mercy upon Your children?!"[29]

R. Tanhuma also proclaimed a fast that proved ineffective in ending a drought. He then advised the people to be compassionate to one another in the hope that this would inspire God in turn to be compassionate with them. Soon after, R. Tanhuma received a report that a certain man was seen giving his ex-wife money—clearly a sign that the two were engaged in something illicit. When the man was brought before him and the situation explained, R. Tanhuma turned in prayer to God:

> **Address:** Master of the Universe!
> **Petition:** If this man, upon whom the woman has no claim for sustenance, saw her in distress and was filled with mercy [compassion] for her, how much the more so must You be compassionate upon us, for it is written about You "gracious and merciful" [Psalm 103:8], for we are the children of Your beloved ones, the children of Abraham, Isaac, and Jacob.
> **Divine Response:** Immediately the rain fell.[30]

In this brief prayer, R. Tanhuma utilizes a number of by now well-known motifs: the expectation that God should be more merciful than a mere mortal, that God should act according to His revealed nature, that God should be merciful to His children Israel, and that God should bring to mind the merit of the Patriarchs for the sake of their children.

R. Hiya b. Luliani uses Israel's merit, which it gained in accepting the Torah, to bring the rain clouds from Moab and Ammon to cover the Land of Israel instead: "Master of the Universe! When You were about to give the Torah to Your people Israel, You [first] offered it around among all the nations of the world, but they would not accept it. And now You would give them rain?! Let them [the clouds] empty their waters here." And it rained.[31]

Last, Raba offers a prayer that appears to be both a prayer for rain and a prayer to be saved from the persecution of King Shapur, by whom he had been threatened with punishment unless he could make it rain. Thereupon Raba prayed: "Master of the Universe! 'O God, we have heard with our ears, our fathers have told us, a work You did in their days, in the days of old' (Psalm 44:2)—but as for us, with our own eyes, we have not seen [it]."[32] Rain fell, but Raba's life was saved only by a rebuke and a warning from his Father in Heaven in a dream. What makes this prayer still more audacious is that it also paraphrases Job's words following his controversy with God (Job 42:5), implying perhaps that Raba was demanding a similar accounting from God in addition to expecting to see God manifest His justice against his persecutor.

RESPONSES TO PERSONAL ARGUMENTATIVE PRAYERS

Having examined a number of examples of the Rabbis' and Sages' personal use of the law-court prayer form, we turn to a weightier issue—whether such prayers were considered appropriate by their contemporaries and acceptable to God. With regard to the latter, there is little question that such prayers were generally acceptable to God since so many of them were "answered" immediately. Much, however, depended upon the merit of the individual uttering the prayer.[33] Thus, in the one clear instance of divine displeasure at such a prayer by an inappropriate individual, Levi b. Sisi's disciple attempted to ward off enemy troops with a law-court oath based upon his observance of the Torah as his master had done. The troops left, but his hand withered. This unfortunate disciple's pupil also tried the same technique but his hand did not wither nor did the troops leave. His prayer was simply ignored.[34]

In another case, Levi becomes lame subsequent to his uttering a harsh law-court prayer for rain, and R. Eleazar sees in this a sign of divine displeasure: "A man should never hurl words against Heaven, since a great man did so and became lame."[35] His conclusion is questionable for two reasons: first, because R. Eleazar was offended even by the biblical characters' "hurling of words,"[36] let alone his contemporaries' doing so, and second, because Levi's lameness was also seen as the result of his having done a *kiddah* (a kind of bow) before Rabbi (Judah HaNasi).[37] In a third case,

Raba receives a rebuke from his Father in Heaven for having
troubled Heaven so much with his prayer, and is warned to
change his sleeping place to avoid being murdered. This may be
considered a sign of divine displeasure, but Raba's prayer had
been answered and he was forewarned that his life was endan-
gered.[38] It would seem then that, according to some of the Rabbis,
God is believed not to be opposed to the personal use of law-court
argument prayers, at least by worthy individuals.

Much more evidence is available about the Rabbis' own views of
such prayers.[39] The primary problem to be dealt with here regards
the deprecatory remarks made by certain important rabbinic figures, primarily in response to the law-court prayers of such charismatic characters as Honi and Hanina b. Dosa. At first glance,
these statements would seem to condemn both the usage of law-
court argument prayers and those individuals who used them.
However, this form of prayer already had a long history, and
furthermore it was also widely used by some of the most prominent rabbis. The character of those who used this mode of prayer
is also crucial. Both Honi and Hanina b. Dosa were considered
extremely righteous men in their day and their righteousness
(their merit) gained them the influence they had with God.[40] As
Buechler has stated with regard to both Honi and Nakdimon b.
Gurion:

> The whole account rests on the prevailing conviction that in a
> calamity God accepts the interceding prayer of worthy individu-
> als, and even more readily than that of the whole community or
> the congregation; for their supplication is supported before God
> by their piety.[41]

In light of this, the stories concerning these exceptional "rain-
makers" are introduced into the talmudic discussion precisely
because the extraordinary piety of these individuals, like that of
certain rabbis, exemplifies the necessary qualifications for the type
of person needed to lead the community's desperate prayers.[42]
Honi and men of his ilk are not exceptional for the type of prayer
they uttered; they are exceptional because of their merit. Honi and
Hanina b. Dosa are two individuals of whom it is said: "The
righteous decree and God fulfills," a phrase also said of Jacob,

Amram, Moses, Elijah and Micaiah, Judah HaNasi, and of the righteous in general.[43]

But all this notwithstanding, the prayers of Honi and Hanina b. Dosa were depreciated and deprecated by certain rabbinic figures. Following Honi's successful prayers for rain, Simeon b. Shetah sent Honi this message:

> Were you not Honi, I would have decreed excommunication for you, for if these years were like the years of Elijah, in whose hands were the keys of rain, would not the name of Heaven have been profaned at your hand? But what can I do to you since you ask petulantly of God and He does your will, as a child who importunes his father and he does his [the child's] desires. . . . Of you Scripture says: "Let your father and your mother be glad, and let her that bore you rejoice" (Proverbs 23:25).[44]

The first point of criticism raised by Simeon b. Shetah is that Honi's use of an oath could have led to a public profanation of God's name. But Simeon b. Shetah qualifies his remarks, saying "were you not Honi" and "were these years like the years of Elijah," when Elijah had proclaimed that there would be no rain for years (1 Kings 17:1). Under different circumstances, an oath such as Honi's might have led to a profanation of God's name; but under the circumstances of Honi's time, and with Honi being who he was, there was no such danger—Simeon b. Shetah's objection is purely hypothetical. The talmudic story further relates that God sent a drizzle to annul Honi's oath, further proof of Honi's special merit. And this is supported by the text itself in which Honi's disciples say: "We look to you to save us from death; we believe that this rain descends only to absolve you of your oath."[45] Furthermore, even Simeon b. Shetah acknowledged Honi's righteousness. In the Talmud Yerushalmi, Simeon b. Shetah and Honi engage in the following dialogue:

> You deserve excommunication, for had it been decreed [now] as it was in the days of Elijah, would you not have brought the people to a profanation of the Name? And he who brings the multitude to a profanation of God's name deserves excommunication.

Honi replied, Does not God annul His decree in favor of the
decree of the righteous?

Simeon b. Shetah replied: Yes, God does [so], but God does not
annul the decree of one righteous man in favor of the decree of
another righteous man [who is] his colleague. [But] so what can
I do to you since you importune God like a child who petulantly
asks [things] of his father, and he does his desires.[46]

Honi's reputation was impeccable, even if his conduct was
questionable to some. But if Simeon b. Shetah saw Honi as deserving of punishment for potentially leading the people into sin,
even so he also realized that Honi's special merit with God pro-
tected him from both divine and rabbinic punishment. Not all of
Simeon's contemporaries shared his negative estimation of
Honi's act. Another *baraita* states that the *bet din* (rabbinic court
of justice) supported and even praised Honi for his successful
intercession on behalf of the people.

"You decreed a thing and it was established for you. And upon
your path light will shine . . ." (Job 22:28–30). You have decreed
a thing—you have decreed on earth and God has established
your word from Heaven. . . . You have illumined with your prayer
a generation in darkness. . . . You have raised with your prayer a
generation sunk low. . . . You have saved by your prayer a generation bent in sin. . . . You have delivered by your prayer a generation that is not innocent. . . . You have delivered it through the
work of your clean hands.[47]

As Buechler has noted, Honi's first (and unrecorded) prayer
may have been ignored by God perhaps because of his presump-
tuousness; but Honi's second prayer succeeded because of his
special merit.[48] Furthermore, the difficulties Honi had in procur-
ing the sort of rain he desired were due, not to misbehavior on his
part, but rather, as the above *baraita* suggests, to the sinfulness
of his generation, on account of whom the rain was originally
withheld and on behalf of whom Honi had been asked to intercede.[49]

Simeon b. Shetah also characterizes Honi's behavior as resem-
bling that of a child. Various scholars have viewed this negatively.
This isn't necessarily the case.[50] First of all, not only is Honi called

a child, he calls himself a child, a *"ben bayit"* of God, who is interceding on behalf of God's own children, Israel. The appellation, "child," in this case is hardly pejorative; it parallels Honi's reputation as a *tzaddik* (a righteous person). Just as the *tzaddik* has a special status and influence with God, so too does a child with his own father. The *tzaddik* is a child of God in every sense of the word; he is God's beloved and is listened to and indulged by God.[51]

Similarly, R. Yohanan b. Zakkai said of Hanina b. Dosa, who had just successfully prayed for the recovery of R. Yohanan's son: "He is like a slave before the king, while I am like a noble [high official] before the king."[52] Both Honi, like a "child of the house," and Haninah b. Dosa, like a "slave," are able to intercede with God because their *zekhut* (righteous merit) has gained them the status of God's *familiaris*, which entitles them to come and go in God's presence (in prayer) without having to ask God's permission.[53]

Akiba, too, uses a similar metaphor to describe the success of his own prayer for rain after that of his master has failed. He tells a parable of a king who had two daughters, one of whom was impertinent and the other modest. The king took long delight in beholding the presence of the modest daughter, but the brash one got what she wanted. When the latter petitioned the king, he would say: "Give her what she wants so that she will go away!"[54]

In Song of Songs *Rabbati*, the prophets are compared to women in that they are unafraid to demand the requirements for Israel, like women who ask their husbands for their household needs.[55] If, according to a world view in which Israel herself is compared to a slave (or servant) when it comes to petitioning God,[56] the application of the designation "child of the house" or "slave" to oneself can only be considered a compliment.

It is obvious, however, that Simeon b. Shetah and Yohanan b. Zakkai did not intend their words as compliments. At least a few rabbis saw something unacceptable in the prayers of these righteous individuals. In Honi's case it was the possibility that he might have led the people to a profanation of God's name; in Hanina b. Dosa's case it was the fact that his frivolous and selfish prayers for rain were uttered in opposition to the prayer of the High Priest and contrary to the welfare of the entire nation.[57] But such contemporaneous criticism was more than balanced by their reputations and their deeds.

RABBINIC OPPOSITION TO MIRACLES

Criticism was also voiced after their lifetimes, and it is this criticism that is, perhaps, the more telling. Honi, Nakdimon, and Hanina b. Dosa were all individuals who lived primarily before the destruction of the Second Temple. The destruction of the Temple, the resultant persecutions and uprisings, and the growing inroads made by Christianity and Gnosticism all led to a profound revamping of the rabbinic outlook. One notices this in the teaching of Nahum of Gamzu and R. Akiba regarding the rewards of suffering and the absolute justice of the divine decree. One notices it also in the changing attitude of many of the Rabbis toward contemporary miracles and miracle workers. Thus R. Yohanan b. Zakkai declares that Hanina b. Dosa, the last of the "men of deeds," may be likened to a slave in the king's court, but he, R. Yohanan, is of a higher status—he is like a noble before the king. The slave may have easier recourse to the king, but the noble has the loftier and more important position. This represents an attempt to change (or to channel) the lines of authority in Judaism.

In the post-Temple era, one finds the Rabbis acting as prayer leaders or intercessors in times of calamity. Buechler suggests that either the age of the "men of deeds" had passed, or that the Rabbis no longer countenanced their special brand of piety.[58] Such a claim is supported by the fact that Honi's grandsons, Hanan HaNehba and Abba Hilkiah, were both reluctant to put their skills of intercession to work, and Abba Hilkiah in particular was loath to have others (especially scholars?) dependent upon him. In the mid-third century, Eleazer b. Pedat, expounding the types of individuals who deserve excommunication by the rabbinical court, singles out Honi as one who made himself too familiar toward Heaven—something that is equated with the insulting of a rabbi.[59] All the clues point to a growing disfavor, in rabbinic circles at least, with such heterodox individuals. Eleazer's remarks clearly indicate a defense of the rabbinic authority against any individuals who might arise to challenge this authority.[60] The reason for this change in attitude was primarily a result of the Christian challenge to Judaism that developed after 90 C.E.

As Christianity developed, the Rabbis grew increasingly opposed to the use of miracles (including the *Bat Kol* or Heavenly Voice) by their contemporaries, particularly when invoked to determine Jewish ritual observance. This new attitude is best illustrated by the famous controversy between R. Eliezer b. Hyrcanus and the Sages.[61] These second generation Tannaim disputed over the ritual cleanliness of the oven of Aknai, with R. Eliezer declaring it pure while the Sages, led by R. Joshua, insisted it was impure:

> It has been taught: "On that day R. Eliezer brought forward every imaginable argument but they did not accept them. He said to them: "If the *halakhah* agrees with me, let this carob tree prove it!" Thereupon the carob tree was torn a hundred cubits out of its place—others say four hundred cubits. "No proof can be brought from a carob tree," they replied.
>
> Again he said to them: "If the *halakhah* agrees with me, let the stream of water prove it!" Whereupon the stream of water flew backwards. "No proof can be brought from the stream of water," they replied.
>
> Again he said to them: "If the *halakhah* agrees with me, let the walls of the schoolhouse prove it!" Whereupon the walls inclined toward falling. But R. Joshua rebuked them saying: "When scholars are engaged in a halakhic dispute, what right have you to interfere?" Hence they did not fall, in honor of R. Joshua, nor did they resume the upright, in honor of R. Eliezer, and they are still standing thus inclined.
>
> Again he said to them: "If *halakhah* agrees with me, let it be proved from Heaven!" Whereupon a *Bat Kol* sounded and said: "Why do you dispute with R. Eliezer, whereas the *halakhah* agrees with him in every instance?"
>
> Then R. Joshua arose and exclaimed: "It is not in Heaven!" (Deuteronomy 30:12).
>
> What did he mean by this? Said R. Jeremiah: "Since the Torah had already been given at Mount Sinai, we pay no attention to a *Bat Kol*, because You have long since written in the Torah at Mount Sinai, 'After the majority must one incline'" (Exodus 23:2).

What is so extraordinary about this story is that in so miracle-minded an age, the Rabbis could reject all proofs based on miracles, which is to say they rejected divine input—even revelation by means of the *Bat Kol*—in their halakhic decisions. While Eliezer has all the gifts one associates with Honi or Hanina b. Dosa, and he uses them to full measure, his views are rejected explicitly by the Sages. It is as R. Jeremiah interprets: once God gave the Torah to Israel, it is Israel's to use. God is bound by Torah's laws as much as is Israel, and Israel has the freedom to challenge God's will based on the laws themselves. That is why, as the text continues, Elijah is supposed to have related God's delighted reaction to this momentous decision: "The Holy One, blessed be He . . . laughed and said: 'My children have defeated Me, My children have defeated Me!'"

For Eliezer, the results were not so pleasant, even if God was pleased. Despite his great learning and his great standing as a leader and teacher, his ritual decisions were nullified and he himself was excommunicated by his former colleagues and disciples. R. Akiba delivered the bad news to his master. The ban remained in place until moments before his death.

Guttmann makes the case that the Sages' opposition to the invocation of miracles and revelations is their direct response to the rise of Christianity and its own reliance on miracles and new revelations. The fact that Eliezer was once arrested, but later cleared, by the Roman authorities on suspicion of Christian heresy, that his dispute with the other Rabbis focused on ritual purity matters (an issue of dispute with Christian sectaries), and that the decline of miracles as an influence on halakhic decision-making began only after this controversy, all lend credence to his theory.[62] As a result of this growing conflict with Christianity, the Rabbis emphasized only the biblical miracles, made them into public events, and provided them with prayers, while at the same time they downgraded the value of contemporary miracles, all but outlawed the reliance on the *Bat Kol*, and declared: "One does not mention miracles" in halakhic disputes.[63]

CONCLUSION

Law-court argumentative prayers remained in constant use throughout the rabbinic period not only in the *aggadah*, but also in prayers uttered in times of distress. With regard to the rituals for ending a drought, forceful law-court prayers may well have had an actual liturgical function. This, however, was a last resort, to be used only in times of grave crisis, after regular prayers and acts of repentance had failed, and only by righteous individuals, who by their special merit or rabbinic status, were worthy to act as intercessors with God on behalf of the community. While many rabbis, well into the amoraic period, continued to act in the role of intercessor in times of calamity and continued to utilize law-court argument prayers, nonrabbinic characters certainly came to be discouraged from doing so. The Rabbis also were most wary about fostering belief in post-biblical miracles and trust in miracle-working individuals, even other Rabbis, since both threatened the developing legal and interpretive foundations of rabbinical authority and Judaism as a whole.

5

EXCURSUS ON A BIRD'S NEST (or Out on a Limb)

INTRODUCTION

In *Berakhot* 33b and *Megillah* 25a, we read: "If one [in praying the *Amidah*] says: 'Your mercies extend to a bird's nest'; 'Your name will be mentioned for the good'; or 'We give thanks, we give thanks'; he is silenced." The *Gemara* clearly understands the reason for prohibiting the two latter phrases. Both expressed heretical concepts popular in the rabbinic period, that is, the belief that there were two powers in Heaven and that man must bless God only for the good, in either case thereby denying that both good and evil come from a single divine source. However, "Your mercies extend to a bird's nest" is not so readily understood, and various Amoraim offer differing rationales for its inclusion.[1] This confusion in the amoraic period is further suggested by the contradictory reactions of Rabbah and Abaye to the prayer of one who prayed, "You have shown mercy upon the bird's nest, [so too] show compassion and mercy to us," (or, as is added in *Megillah* 25a, "You have shown pity to an animal and its young, [so too] have compassion and mercy upon us"). Rabbah declares: "How well this student [this rabbi] knows how to placate (*tzuvrah*) his Master," to which Abaye retorts: "But we have learnt 'he is silenced!'"[2]

The singling out of this prayer for condemnation is indeed mysterious. The mystery is heightened by the fact that the Mishnah condemns a pattern of prayer and a prayer motif found elsewhere in a number of places. Thus Jacob prayed:

103

Address: Sovereign of the Universe!
Accusation: You have written in Your Torah: "Do not kill a cow or ewe and its young on the same day" (Leviticus 22:28). If this wicked one [Esau] comes and destroys all at once, what will happen to Your Torah which in the future You will give on Mount Sinai? Who will read it?
Petition: I entreat You: Deliver me from his hand, that he will not come and kill both mother and children [together].[3]

A similar argument fragment found in Genesis *Rabbah* 76:6 refers to the complementary commandment of Deuteronomy 22:6 prohibiting the complete emptying of a bird's nest. Knesset Yisrael uses the identical motif in complaining that her enemies, by their slaughter, are going against God and His Torah.[4] Another midrash sees Leviticus 22:28 interpreted in the light of Proverbs 12:10, "The *tzaddik* regards the life of his beast," as referring to God, while "the mercies of the wicked are cruel" refers to Sennacherib and Haman who killed (or sought to kill) mothers and their children together.[5] And we have noted that other Amoraim put a very similar law-court prayer into the mouths of the repentant inhabitants of Nineveh.[6] Clearly the Mishnah had a reason for forbidding the use of "Your mercies extend to the bird's nest" prayer, but whatever it was was lost to later generations who actually did make use of it. Let us try to determine what possibly motivated this mishnaic prohibition.

THE APOSTASY OF AHER

Two parallel accounts in the Babylonian and Jerusalem Talmuds relate the story of four rabbis who entered *Pardes*—ben Azzai died in the process, ben Zoma looked and was stricken, Aher (Elisha b. Abuyah) became an apostate, and only Akiba emerged unscathed.[7] The term *Pardes* itself is a code word for the study of esoteric philosophy,[8] although the exact subject matter remains in question to this day. Thus, the experience of the four who entered *Pardes* has been given various interpretations. Rashi and Tosafot, respectively, have described it as the Rabbis' ascent, or seeming ascent, to Heaven. Gershom Scholem believes that the account in *Hagigah* shows the dangers inherent in delving into the mysteries (the experience of the ascent) of *Merkabah* (Throne of God) mysticism.[9] Samson R. Levey has suggested that *Pardes* refers to the teachings and doctrines of the early church and that the *Hagigah* accounts describe "the probing study of Christian origins and beliefs" by the four.[10] Other scholars have linked ben Zoma and Aher with Gnosticism and various other kinds of heresy.[11]

The *Hagigah* account relates that Aher saw Metatron acting in such a way as to suggest that Metatron and God were both gods. This experience led Aher to embrace some form of Gnosticism, and to act in a manner destructive to rabbinic Judaism.[12] In other sources, however, the cause of Aher's apostasy is made more explicit. According to one story, Aher was once studying when he saw a man climb a palm tree on Shabbat, take both the dam and its young from the nest and descend unharmed, thereby transgressing both the Shabbat laws and Deuteronomy 22:6 with impunity. After the Shabbat, he saw a second man ascend a tree and take only the young from the nest while allowing the dam to remain, in accordance with the laws. But when this man descended, a snake bit him and he died. Thereupon Aher exclaimed: "It is written: 'Let the mother go, and take only the young, in order that you may fare well and have a long life' [Deuteronomy 22:7]—where is the goodness and length of days for this man?"

Another story relates that when Aher saw the tongue of R. Judah HaNahtom in the mouth of a dog, he declared: "If this is the reward of a tongue which toiled all its days in the Torah, how much the more so a tongue which did not! Since this is so, there is no reward for the righteous nor any resurrection for the dead."[13] In a variant on this latter story, Aher's apostasy was due to his seeing the tongue of Hutzpit HaMeturgaman cast upon a dungheap.[14] In all these stories, Aher's belief-shattering experience was his encounter with the problem of unwarranted human suffering, which led him to doubt the reality of divine providence, and according to the story in *Hagigah*, to doubt the unity of God.

Nor was his experience unique. The problem of suffering in general, and the tribulations of Israel in particular, were problems that plagued the Rabbis throughout that epoch.[15] Considering the cataclysmic times in which Aher lived, it is probable that he was one, but not the only one, of many who lost their faith.

Whatever the exact nature of Aher's experience, his was but an early example of what became a serious threat to the continued survival of rabbinic Judaism.

THE CHALLENGE OF GNOSTICISM

It is our contention that the story of the four who entered *Pardes* represents the Rabbis' attempts to grapple with the problem of theodicy and to comprehend (and make comprehensible) the nature of God's justice. Like Aher, Moses, in a number of aggadic sources, seeks to understand this fundamental problem of existence. In Exodus 33:13 and 18, Moses asks to be granted knowledge of God's ways and to behold God's presence. This request God grants only in part, saying: "You cannot see My face, for man may not see Me and live. . . . I will take My hand away and you will see My back; but My face must not be seen" (Exodus 33:18–23). The midrashim develop this ambivalent divine response, and opinion remains divided as to whether Moses gained a full understanding of God's ways, whether he was granted a partial understanding, or whether he was refused any understanding at all.[16] In *Menahot*, Moses, like Aher, also questions the nature of divine providence, for, when he is shown Akiba's grisly fate, he cries out: "Lord of the Universe! Such Torah and such a reward!" This earns him a sharp rebuke from God.[17] It may be, therefore, that the ascent to *Pardes* represents not so much the delving into mysticism, but rather the delving into the more concrete problems of theodicy, in much the same manner as Moses' request had included both elements together.

This hypothesis, however, is purely conjectural, since it relies upon analogy rather than upon actual texts. But in support of our contention, we have seen that a great deal of energy was expended by the Rabbis to counter the attacks launched against rabbinic Judaism by Gnosticism and Christianity. It is not unreasonable, therefore, to suggest that certain sages, like the four in the *Hagigah* account, did attempt to fathom the mystery of divine justice, particularly in light of severe suffering that occurred in their lifetimes. It is also plausible to suggest that certain sages, like Aher and ben Zoma, were unable to arrive at an answer capable of reconciling the traditional God–concept of rabbinic

Judaism with the suffering of Israel to which they bore witness. Their inability to comprehend the mystery of divine justice then led them to embrace one or another kind of heretical position as part of their attempt to explain the events of their day.

Against this hypothesis, it must be noted, stands other research that has shown that Aher's actual sin was not theological at all, but rather was political in nature. These activities, and not heresy, were what led Aher into direct conflict with Akiba and his disciples.[18] It was this conflict that led later generations of rabbis to attribute to Aher the controversies of their own day, specifically, the heresy of Gnosticism. Thus, in a number of amoraic accounts, Aher founders on the rock of the incomprehensibility of divine justice and becomes an antinomian heretic, while in the *Hagigah* legend, Aher is described as having fallen under the Gnostic delusion of divine dualism.

It is indeed unlikely that Aher actually did become a Gnostic heretic. The amoraic ascription of Gnosticism to Aher testifies more to the issues of the day than to Aher's times. The mishnaic prohibition mentions the "bird's nest" in context with two other prayers clearly recognized as dualistic in amoraic times. However, only the rationale for prohibiting the bird's nest prayer was in doubt. The existence of a legend which attributes Aher's apostasy to his having seen the commandment regarding the bird's nest (Deuteronomy 22:6–7) broken with impunity, may have helped the Amoraim to clarify what they considered the mishnaic rationale for prohibiting a law-court prayer based on this same commandment. Given the existence of a tradition that alluded to Aher's apostasy in a most vague manner, the Amoraim, evincing the concerns of their own day, readily attributed to Aher the sin of Gnostic heresy.

The mishnaic prohibition may have understood the bird's nest prayer to be dualistic in some way, without providing any explanation on the subject. But both in structure and in content, the bird's nest prayer was no different from other law-court prayers; the Amoraim might well have been puzzled by its inclusion in the mishnaic prohibition. The legend of Aher and the observance of the commandment regarding the bird's nest might then have been created to help explain why a law-court prayer based upon Deuteronomy 22:6 had dualistic overtones, the answer being that one prominent tannaitic sage was led to Gnosticism as a result of his doubting divine justice in this matter. The mishnaic prohibition against the bird's nest prayer thereby acquired a historical rationale for its existence. This conclusion is also most tentative and is suggested here only as hypothesis.

AKIBA'S UNDERSTANDING OF DIVINE JUSTICE

There is a broader and more obvious objection to the use of the bird's nest prayer which adequately explains the mishnaic prohibition against it. It should be noted that the Mishnah itself offers no explanation as to why the three prayers should be prohibited. It is possible that they were originally prohibited for reasons other than those perceived by the later Amoraim (that is, dualism). The mishnaic prohibition may simply reflect the growing acceptance of Akiba's views regarding the exercise of divine justice and their incorporation into the halakhic system.

It is related that Akiba alone entered *Pardes* in peace and that he alone left in peace. What peace? Peace of mind. Only Akiba arrived at an understanding of divine providence capable of withstanding the tribulations of his day. Armed with the teaching of "precious are sufferings" and an indefatigable faith in God's justice in all matters, Akiba was able to transcend the many national and personal tragedies of his age.[19] The lot of succeeding generations was hardly better than that of Akiba's day; therefore, his teaching on the subjects of theodicy, divine justice, and providence remained extremely relevant to those later generations. Moreover, his teachings were much more applicable to the real-life problems facing these generations in a way in which the law-court type of response could not be. Protest and argument are fine in the *aggadah* or in times of emergency, but because of the basically immediate nature of the law-court prayer (that is, the demand that God intervene or respond directly to the complaint brought before Him), the law-court pattern was incapable of sustaining hope or fostering a positive expression of faith and observance on a day-to-day basis. Akiba's teachings, on the other hand, based on submission to, and acceptance of, the divine decree, promoted continued adherence to rabbinic Judaism without sacrificing the hope of beholding the ultimate triumph of God's justice. Thus Akiba's understanding of the problem of divine justice became the more normative Jewish view on the subject, blending smoothly with the general tone of the statutory liturgy as it developed.

Perhaps, given its source, Akiba's understanding of divine justice was mystically inspired; *Pardes*, after all, did refer to esoteric, mystical knowledge. Curiously enough, mysticism also may account for the prohibition against uttering a bird's nest law-court prayer, although this only can be argued a posteriori.

The *Zohar* (2:8a–9a) uses the phrase "bird's nest" to refer to the hidden abode of the Messiah, a secret place in the Garden of Eden to which, every day, the Messiah goes, to add his laments and tears to those of the Ancestors in Heaven in protest against Israel's suffering in the Exile. This ritual of daily protest will continue until God acts on the promise with which He placates the Messiah every day; until God, in fact, redeems Israel. Although it is generally accepted that the *Zohar* was written in the late thirteenth century, one cannot know the origins of the oral sources that served as its foundation. One may postulate, therefore, that the *Zohar's* use of the term bird's nest may have had ancient roots, and so its usage may have some bearing on the mishnaic prohibition against uttering a bird's nest prayer.

Seen from this perspective, the mishnaic law prohibits precisely those prayers that would "hasten the End" by imploring God to "extend His mercies to a bird's nest," that is, by ending the Messiah's daily protest and commencing the Redemption. This view is supported by the fact that although the Rabbis did use the bird's nest prayer in the *aggadah*, they did not use it during the *Amidah*, where its use was prohibited. (Only Rabbah, and then only conjecturally, considered it a fitting prayer in the *Amidah*.) It may be, then, that such a prayer was considered out of keeping with the submissive tone of the *Amidah*.[20] Almost certainly it was viewed as a complaint against God. In the Jerusalem Talmud, *Berakhot* equates one who utters a bird's nest prayer with one who complains (*karah tigar*) about God's ways and attributes.[21] That this sort of prayer could be considered as rebellion against God should be expected—we have seen the general opposition of Akiba and his followers to those who would argue against or complain about God's justice.[22] Such a prayer may have been acceptable in the *aggadah* and in personal, nonstatutory prayers offered in times of emergency, but certainly not in the *Amidah*.[23] Alternatively, the prohibition possibly may be explained by the esoteric nature of Jewish mysticism and the unwillingness of its practitioners to impart its teachings except when appropriate, or to see its teachings misapplied. In either case, what the Rabbis sought to limit were unhealthy theological speculations or despair among the people.

CONCLUSION

Law-court prayers remained an effective polemical and didactic device, utilized in rabbinic sermons and the *aggadah*, to refute the attacks of Gnosticism and Christianity while responding to the ultimate questions and doubts of the Jewish people. But the law-court prayer never acquired the stamp of legitimacy, nor gained the currency in normative Jewish practice, that Akiba's teachings did, nor could it, for it was unsuited to the task of sustaining the people over an indefinite length of time such as the Exile represented. When cast as actual petitionary prayer, the law-court prayer created a forced confrontation between God and the people that could only either result in a revelatory action (in deed or word) on the part of God or produce despair on the part of the people if the prayer were not directly answered by God. The longer the Exile became, the more anxious the Rabbis grew to avoid any situation that could potentially lead the people to despair of God's justice and to turn elsewhere for consolation. The law-court prayer pattern, although suited to controlled usage in the *aggadah*, or even by a bona fide *tzaddik* (although its usage by the latter was, as we have seen, also discouraged by the Rabbis), was inadmissible in the realm of public, statutory prayer since, as Simeon b. Shetah is reputed to have observed, it could lead the people to a profanation of the name of God.

This perhaps is the reason underlying the mishnaic prohibition against the use of the prayer "Your mercies extend to the bird's nest." And in light of this, the Amoraim stated that had Aher known (that is, accepted) Akiba's exposition of Deuteronomy 22:7, which shifted the reward of the righteous and observant to the World to Come, Aher might not have been led to despair.[24] Had

Aher accepted Akiba's understanding of the nature and exercise of divine justice, he would not have become an apostate. In other words, addressing the people of their own day, the Amoraim were advancing Akiba's teachings as an efficacious means of countering the attacks of Gnosticism and Christianity, which represented a very real threat to the day-to-day survival of Judaism and the Jewish people.

PART II

6

ARGUMENT MOTIFS IN THE STATUTORY LITURGY

CONFLICTING ATTITUDES TO SUFFERING AND THE TRIUMPH OF AKIBA'S VIEW

In the Bible, God frequently is supposed to use punishment (suffering) as an instrument to effect Israel's repentance and her return to the observance of the Covenant. God tries the righteous and punishes the wicked; suffering, therefore, has a purpose—a divinely ordained purpose. Espousing an attitude of trust in God and accepting one's lot was the means to affirm and acknowledge directly the reality of the exercise of divine justice in the world.[1] This submissive attitude found its rabbinic champions in Nahum of Gamzu, R. Akiba, and many others. Their attitude toward Job's arguments was a case in point. According to Akiba, Job was wrong to question and rebel against his suffering. Job stood on the lowest level of those whom God smote.[2] Elsewhere, Akiba praises the attitude of Job as expressed at the beginning and conclusion of the Book of Job.[3] A later source relates that had Job not questioned or rebelled against his sufferings, today we would begin the *Amidah* by addressing "the God of Abraham, Isaac, Jacob, and Job."[4] Job's rebellion is deemed the way of *goyim* and their prophets.[5] The proper Jewish attitude, they held, is one of patience and submission in affliction.[6]

115

On the other hand, the vast numbers of rabbinic law-court argument prayers testify to the fact that this passive stance was never wholly accepted. Furthermore, what was meaningful to one generation did not necessarily satisfy the next. Marmorstein has noted that although the teachers of the second century had decided that suffering should be borne in love and patience, the scholars of the third century returned to address the heart of the issue themselves.[7] The problem posed by Israel's suffering was too great an issue to be answered once and for all time.

The conflict between these two views carried over into the midrashim themselves. We have seen that Abraham and Moses, for example, were praised and rewarded by God for engaging Him in law-court arguments.[8] But we have also seen instances when Moses, Jeremiah, David, and others were criticized or punished for arguing with God and questioning His judgment.[9] In some cases God (or a Rabbi) criticizes certain figures for not arguing; while in other cases, those individuals who do question God end up repenting their words and acknowledging God's justice.[10]

Opposition to the use of forceful law-court prayers existed for good reason. Although rabbis could use them in midrashim, or as personal prayers in times of emergency, their usage nonetheless was confined exclusively to righteous individuals (biblical or rabbinic), and then primarily on behalf of their community. In the proper hands, law-court prayers served many valuable functions, but in the wrong hands, their use could lead the people to despair. Thus the Rabbis encouraged popular acceptance of Akiba's teachings on suffering while at the same time reserving for themselves the right and the responsibility of arguing with God when the need arose.

Nowhere was the triumph of Akiba's submissive attitude toward suffering more pronounced than in the statutory liturgy.[11] In this realm, the law-court pattern of forceful prayer was definitely out of place. This aggressive form of prayer, which "hurled accusations at Heaven" and asserted the rights of the petitioner, stood in sharp contrast with the statutory liturgy whose prayers stressed humility and sinfulness, longings for forgiveness and mercy, and a general dependence upon God. The Sages of the Talmud decreed that the law-court pattern of forceful prayer be strictly reserved for emergencies only, when all other means of petition have failed, and only then by pious men interceding on behalf of the community.[12]

The law-court pattern never achieved a position of any significance in the statutory liturgy. Its influence can be observed in the structure—though not the tone or content—of prayers of thanksgiving and confession.[13] Its motifs and modes of argument, all in mild form, also appear here and there in the statutory liturgy itself. The paucity of examples testifies to the completeness of the victory of the Akiban school in the realm of public prayer.

The law-court motifs most often in evidence in the liturgy are "quoting God's words back to Him"; "past arguments," that is, using arguments that had been successful in the past; "merit of the ancestors"; and "past precedents." The four motifs are closely intertwined. In many cases the words quoted back to God were those very words spoken by God in response to a successful argument uttered in the past by a great Jewish leader, an Abraham or a Moses who, in his lifetime, was held in high regard by God and whose memory—if not actual presence in Paradise—could be invoked by later generations for their benefit. The use of previously successful arguments had a twofold thrust: to ensure the success of a contemporary petition by using—perhaps with magical overtones—the exact words of an Ancient that were proved efficacious in the past; and to remind God that, at least in order to be consistent, He should be as heedful of the contemporary petition as He was to the original. Thus the employment of an argument based on quoting God's words back to Him or past arguments also relies on past precedents to make its case.

THE QUOTING GOD'S WORDS
BACK TO HIM MOTIF

The most common prayer that utilizes this motif is the concluding benediction to *"Mi Khamokha"* (Who is like You?) for the morning service. It reads: "Rock of Israel, arise to the help of Israel and redeem, *according to Your word*, Judah and Israel."[14] Standing alone, this line presents only the vaguest of arguments—

"redeem according to Your word"—without even citing an example of God's promise. However, coming as it does on the heels of the *geulah* prayer (the prayer for redemption that follows the *Shema*), in which God's saving act at the Sea of Reeds is recounted and His praise as a redeemer is uttered, it represents the climax of the entire section. This brief reminder of God's promise is the pivotal point in the prayer, by means of which the recollection of God's saving acts in the past is turned into a petition for the present.

The *Kedushah* (sanctification) of the *Shabbat Amidah* (standing prayers) and of the *Musaf* (additional service) also offer examples of this motif. The *Kedushot* constitute, perhaps, the most intimate and awesome moment of prayer. Here Israel's praise of God is linked with that of the divine chorus on high. At this special moment in time Israel petitions God to appear and redeem them from the Exile. In honor of the Day of Rest, the tone is urgent but polite.

> From Your place, Our King, appear and rule over us, for we wait for You. When will You rule in Zion? May it be soon, even in our days, that You dwell [there]. May You be exalted and sanctified within Your city Jerusalem for all generations, now and forever.

> Then our eyes will see Your Kingdom [established] *according to the word spoken in the songs of Your might by David, Your righteous anointed*: "The Lord will reign forever; Your God, O Zion, through all generations. Hallelu-yah!"[15]

The *Musaf Kedushah*, known as the "great" or "high" *Kedushah*, operates on an even higher mystical plane. The *Shabbat* morning *Kedushah* has the worshipers repeat the words of the heavenly hosts, thereby sharing in their words. But the *Musaf* version has the people render its own homage together with the divine beings. And Israel's plea to God is, here, even a little more direct:

> From His place, may He turn in mercy and be gracious to the people [nation], who, evening and morning, proclaim the Unity of His Name, by repeating twice every day, constantly and with love, saying "Sh'ma—Hear, O Israel. . . ."

> ... In His mercy, *He will proclaim to us a second time* in the presence of all the living [His promise]" ... to be to you a God."

> "I am the Lord, your God."[16]

Though the argument motif used is as mild as can be, it is clear. God's promise "to be a God" to Israel, through revelation and redemption, is first mentioned and then actually enacted. Thus, on the most holy day of the week, at the most special moments of that day, Israel dares—and rightly so—to allow reality to intrude and to remind God of her most pressing needs.

Another place in which this argument motif of "quoting" is used is the prayer that concludes the priestly blessing (given by the *kohanim* [priestly descendants] to the congregation during the *Musaf* holiday service). After blessing the people, the *kohanim* turn to God and say:

> Lord of the Universe! We have done what You have decreed for us, so too should You do *as You have promised*: "Look down from Your holy dwelling, from heaven, and bless Your people Israel and the land which You gave us—as You swore to our fathers—a land flowing with milk and honey" (Deuteronomy 26:15).[17]

A recurring prayer in the *slihot* (penitential) service, "*Zekhor lanu brit rishonim*" (Remember in our favor the Covenant of the Fathers, for You have said),[18] is based entirely on this argument motif. In this prayer, God's words are quoted back to Him to remind Him of His promises. The entire process of the Redemption is documented here, beginning with God's promise to remember the Covenant, His pledge never to wholly abandon or destroy Israel, and His word to gather in the dispersed once again. In the second half of the prayer, God is asked, through the use of His own words, to sweep away Israel's sins, to have mercy and not to destroy them, to open their hearts to the love of God, to be with Israel when they seek Him, and to bring them back to His Holy Mountain, there to offer sacrifices and prayers. But as much as God is bound by His promises and is reminded of them in this prayer, so too is the recollection of His promises meant to comfort and inspire the congregation that hears them.[19]

The *slihot* services and the *tahnunim* (supplications) for Monday and Thursday offer a number of prayers based on the motifs of quoting, past arguments, and past precedents.[20] These prayers all quote the Thirteen Attributes (of Mercy) by which God revealed Himself to Moses on Mount Sinai (Exodus 34:6–7). The argument in all of these, such as it is, consists solely of quoting God's own expression of His attributes back to Him so that Israel can confess and obtain forgiveness. This is derived first from Moses' precedent (in Numbers 14:17–19) during which he successfully invokes God's benevolent attributes (Exodus 34:6–7) in his plea for God to forgive Israel. The Rabbis saw this invocation as a sure means of obtaining forgiveness. R. Yohanan taught: "This is to teach us that the Lord taught this prayer to Moses, saying 'Whenever Israel will sin, let them recite these [words] according to this order and I shall forgive them.'"[21] By quoting the Thirteen Attributes back to God, Israel is thus guaranteed, as it were, a way of obtaining perpetual forgiveness.[22] As R. Judah says (in the same passage as R. Yohanan), "A covenant has been made with the Thirteen Attributes that they [Israel] will not be turned away empty-handed."

PAST ARGUMENTS,
PAST PRECEDENTS,
AND THE MERIT OF
THE ANCESTORS MOTIFS

Both the past arguments and past precedents motifs are closely linked with that of the merit of the Ancestors motif. The arguments of the ancestors and the deeds God wrought for them provide the content for prayers based on these motifs. Similarly, a successful past argument becomes a past precedent for the present generation to employ.

The most prominent argument in the category of past argument is Abraham's midrashic prayer following the *akeidah*.[23] It appears in two forms and in two places: first in the preliminary daily morning service following the reading of the *akeidah*,[24] and second in the *zikhronot* (remembrance) benedictions of the *shofar* service, found in the *Musaf Amidah* for Rosh Hashanah.[25] Since the version used in the morning service is more direct and more closely related to Abraham's prayer, we will quote it as our example:

> Master of the Universe! May it be Your will, O Lord our God and God of our fathers, to remember in our favor the covenant of our fathers. Just as Abraham our father conquered his mercy for his only son and desired to slaughter him in order to do Your will, so too may Your mercies conquer Your anger from [falling] on us. May Your mercies prevail over Your [other] attributes and gather us in from [the attribute of] strict justice. Rather, conduct Yourself, O Lord our God, according to the attributes of loving-kindness and mercy, and in Your great goodness, turn Your fierce anger from us and from Your city and Your land and Your heritage. And fulfill for us, O Lord our God, the promise which You made to us through Moses Your servant as it says: "I will remember My covenant with Jacob, also My covenant with Isaac, and also My covenant with Abraham will I remember; and I will remember the land" (Leviticus 26:42).

As in the original midrashic version, this prayer urges God to emulate Abraham's behavior and also to remember the merit of Abraham's deeds (and the *akeidah* in particular) for the benefit of His children. In both this and the Rosh Hashanah version, an additional petition is made using a quoting God's words back to Him motif to plead for an end to Exile (the ultimate instance of God's mercy conquering His anger). (The Rosh Hashanah version quotes Leviticus 26:45.) Both prayers obviously draw upon the merit of the ancestors (*zekhut avot*)—the Rosh Hashanah version more dramatically as it also utilizes a ram's horn (*shofar*) to remind God of the *akeidah*—and both evince the intercessory nature and redemptive power originally attributed to them.

The arguments of Moses are also utilized in the liturgy. In a recurring prayer of the *slihot* services, "*El erekh apayim Atah*" (You are a God slow to anger),[26] reference is made to Moses' argument with God on Mount Sinai. There Moses pleads, "Turn from Your fierce anger" (Exodus 32:12), following which God reveals Himself to Moses by His Thirteen Attributes. Thus this prayer uses the quoting back to God of His Thirteen Attributes in the context and remembrance of a previously successful argument in which Moses argued with God to forgive and God did indeed forgive.

In another common *slihah* prayer, "*Kerahem av al banim*,"[27] God is urged, by analogy to human behavior, to be merciful "as a father has mercy on his children." This petition is followed by a quotation from Moses' argument with God at the time of the spies, "O forgive the iniquity of this people, I pray You, according to the greatness of Your kindness, as You have forgiven this people from Egypt until now" (Numbers 14:19). It is expected that by repeating Moses' exact words, God will respond to the present generation as He had in the past with "I have forgiven according to Your word" (Numbers 14:20), as in fact He does in this prayer.[28] The prayer continues with a portion of Daniel's mild law-court prayer for redemption (Daniel 9:18–19):

> **Address:** O my God!
> **Argument:** Incline Your ear and hear. Open Your eyes and behold our desolations and the city which is called by Your name. Not because of our righteousness do we utter our supplication to You, but because of Your abundant mercies.
> **Petition** (with concluding point of argument): O Lord, hear. O Lord, forgive. O Lord, hearken and act, do not delay. For Your own sake, my God, because Your city and Your people are called by Your name.

Like the *slihot* services, the *tahnunim* (supplications) section of the daily liturgy combines submission with protest, praise with argument, confessions of guilt and pleas for forgiveness with assertions of innocence and faith, and the acceptance of the divine decree with the demand for redemption. The *slihot* focus on obtaining forgiveness; the *tahnunim* are exilic prayers for redemption.

The elegies at the heart of the *tahnunim* service display a host of argument motifs all meant to convince God to act—pleas for forgiveness, confessions of sinfulness, pleas for God to act, descriptions of the intolerable present, assertions of faithfulness, and calls for God to remember the Patriarchs, the Covenant, His past deeds, His honor, and so forth.[29] The language is direct and forceful. Psalm-like imperatives abound: "do not forsake us," "look upon our troubles," "hear the voice of our prayer," "remember," "show us a sign," "answer us," "have mercy," and "be not silent." Of special note is the inclusion of portions of successful biblical law-court prayers: that of Daniel (Daniel 9:15–19) in the first and second elegies, and that of Moses (Exodus 32:12) in the sixth. Reference is also made several times to the mockery of Israel by her enemies, who say: "Where is their God?" and "Their hope is lost!" In the light of these sentiments and Israel's history, David's plea, which is uttered immediately following the seventh elegy, is most poignant: "Let us fall, I pray, into the hand of the Lord, for many are His mercies, but let me not fall into the hand of man" (2 Samuel 24:14). If Israel deserves continued punishment, let God be the one to announce and execute it, not Israel's enemies.

After a personal confession and the recitation of the psalm, the service once again turns from personal to national concerns. The following eleventh-century *piyyut* (liturgical poem) is a major component in this renewed protest against Israel's suffering in exile and is recited on Monday and Thursday mornings. It utilizes a portion of Moses' argument on Mount Sinai (Exodus 32:12) as a petitionary refrain throughout:

> **Address and Introductory Petition/Refrain:** O Lord, God of Israel, "turn from Your fierce wrath, and repent the evil against Your people" (Exodus 32:12).
>
> **First Argument:** Look from Heaven and see how we have become a scorn and a derision among the nations. We are counted as sheep brought for the slaughter, to be slain and destroyed and smitten and reproached. Yet, despite all this, we have not forgotten Your name. We beseech You—do not forget us.
>
> **Refrain:** O Lord, God of Israel, "turn from Your fierce wrath."
>
> **Second Argument:** Strangers say: "There is no hope or expectancy for you." Be gracious to a people that hopes in Your name. O Pure One, bring our salvation near. We are weary and there is no rest for us. May You conquer Your anger from [descending] on us. We beseech You—turn from Your fierce wrath and have mercy upon the treasured people whom You have chosen.
>
> **Refrain:**
>
> **Third Argument:** O Lord, spare us in Your mercies, and do not give us into the hands of the cruel. Why should the nations say:

"Where now is their God?" For Your own sake, deal kindly with
us and do not delay. We beseech You—turn from your fierce
wrath and have mercy upon the treasured people whom You
have chosen.
Refrain:
Fourth Argument: Hear our voice and be gracious. Do not forsake us in the hand of our enemy to blot out our name. Remember what You swore to our Fathers—"I will multiply your
seed as the star of the heavens"—but now we are left a few out of
many.
Yet despite all this, we have not forgotten Your name. We beseech You—do not forget us.
Refrain:
Concluding Petition: Help us, O God of our salvation, for the
sake of the glory of Your name and deliver us, and pardon our
sins for Your Name's sake.
Refrain: [30]

In all *slihot* services, past precedent plays an important role.
The prayer "*mashiah tzed'kikha*" (Your righteous anointed),
found near the conclusion of each *slihot* service but in its fullest
form in the service for Rosh Hashanah eve,[31] quotes the successful prayers for forgiveness uttered by David, Micah, Daniel, and
Ezra. Other argument motifs, specifically quoting God's works
back to Him and the "merit of the ancestors," are also employed in
this prayer. As the service moves toward a final crescendo in its
pleas for forgiveness and redemption, two standard litanies are
utilized, one urging God "to act" (*assei*), the other urging Him to
"answer us" (*aneinu*) for a host of reasons: His Attributes, the
Patriarchs, Zion, the Temple, the martyrs, the innocent. A final
standard litany, "*mi she'anah*" (He who answered), concludes
this portion of the service by rehearsing many of the crucial
instances in the past when God had answered His people. The
litany begins "He who answered Abraham our father on Mount
Moriah—He shall answer us" and continues, citing a host of
biblical examples, ending with "He who answered all the righteous, pious, pure and upright—He shall answer us."[32] The thrust
of the implied argument cannot be ignored. Just as God had
answered and helped Israel's ancestors in times past, so too must
He respond to the present generation's petitions in their time of
need.

PETITIONS WITH A
CONDITIONAL ELEMENT

Certain prayers contain an implied argument, which, like Jacob's vow in Genesis 28:20–22, suggests that if God will do what is requested of Him, then in return Israel will (again be able to) do what God has required of them. The clearest example of this sort of argument, oddly enough, is the prayer "*u'mipnei hata'einu*" (But on account of our sins), which is read during the festival *Musaf Amidah*. I say oddly enough because the first sentence of the prayer typifies the normative Jewish response to adversity, namely self-castigation, while the rest of the prayer presents a mild argument that denies the intent of the opening line.

> But on account of our sins we were exiled from our country and driven far from our land. We cannot make pilgrimage up to appear in Your Chosen House, to bow before You and to perform our obligations in the great and holy House which was called by Your name because of the hand [The Hand?] which was stretched out against Your Sanctuary.
>
> May it be Your will, O Lord our God and God of our fathers, O merciful King, that in Your abundant mercies, You will return and have mercy upon us and upon Your sanctuary. Rebuild it speedily and magnify its glory. Our Father our King, reveal the glory of Your kingdom speedily to us. Shine forth and be exalted over us in the eyes of all the living. Gather our dispersed from among the nations and our scattered from the ends of the earth. And bring us to Zion, Your City, with song, and to Jerusalem, the home of the Sanctuary, with everlasting joy. And there we will offer our obligatory sacrifices, the daily offering and the additional offerings according to their rules.[33]

It is implied here that if Israel is to be able once again to perform her sacrificial obligations as God has commanded and as she wants to do, then God will have to act first. Before Israel can do God's will, God must withdraw "the hand which is stretched out against" the Sanctuary, rebuild the Temple, cause His kingdom to come, gather Israel from the four corners of the earth, and lead them to the Sanctuary in Jerusalem. Then Israel will once again perform all her obligatory sacrifices in love, faithfulness, and devotion, as she has yearned to do all the years of the Exile. Thus a prayer that opens on a note of confession of guilt ends with an assertion of continued faithfulness and impatient expectation. Rather than focusing on repentance, which would be the expected corollary to a confession of guilt, the prayer dwells on what God must do to enable Israel to serve Him as fully as He has commanded.[34]

If God truly wants Israel's service, then He will have to act first. Before Israel can once again serve God in all the ways He has ordained, God must first clear the way. The omnipotent God of an impotent people must demonstrate His potency by rescuing Israel and restoring her to her rightful place. Only then will Israel be able to demonstrate that indeed her love of God and her faithfulness to His commandments have remained undiminished and constant despite the many centuries of suffering.

CONCLUSION

The statutory liturgy represents the triumph of Akiba's attitude toward suffering. The prayers are meant to reassure and to inspire, to raise confidence and heighten faith. The forceful prayers of the law-court pattern also intend the same objectives, but they do so "*ki l'aher yad*"—in a backhanded manner and carry in themselves the risks of public blasphemy and an unanswered confrontation with God. Thus the Sages first limited the use of the statutory liturgy to emergencies and by only the most pious; later they raised doubts as to the use of the mode altogether.

Yet the law-court pattern and its motifs were neither lost nor forgotten. They remained preserved in the Bible, Talmud, and Midrash, and transmitted through study to future generations. But the primary focuses of the Sages were the more concrete issues of formulating the *halakhah* and developing the liturgy in consonance with the teachings and views of Akiba and his disciples. Eventually, forceful argument did find its way into the liturgy. When historical events gave the Jewish people renewed reason to protest to God, they did so using the law-court pattern of prayer in the form of poetic insertions to the statutory public prayers. These poems of prayer and protest, called *piyyutim*, are the subject of our next chapter.

7

POETRY AS PRAYER
AND PROTEST

THE ORIGINS AND DEVELOPMENT
OF *PIYYUTIM*

In his short but excellent introduction to medieval Jewish liturgical poetry entitled *Theology and Poetry*, Jakob Petuchowski
traces the growth of the statutory liturgy and the origins of the
liturgical poem. He writes:

> The traditional Jewish liturgy, as it has come down to us, con-
> sists not only of the standard prayers ordained in the Talmud
> and the ritual codes, but also contains poetic embellishments of
> all kinds. Such poetic embellishments take the form of hymns
> to be sung prior to, or after, the standard prayers, and of poetic
> inserts in the standard prayers themselves. . . .
>   Technically, such poetic embellishments and inserts are
> known as *piyyutim* [singular: *piyyut*].[1]

As a fully developed form, the *piyyutim* contain a wealth of quotes
and allusions from biblical and rabbinic literature, and were
meant to enhance the meaning of the particular holiday or prayer
for which they were written.[2]

Petuchowski delineates the conflicting scholarly opinions as to
when the *piyyutic* tradition commenced. Although scholars still
debate the date of its origins (now considered to be somewhere
between the second and sixth centuries C.E.), it is now accepted
that its place of origin was Palestine. Attempting to clarify the
origins of the *piyyut*, Petuchowski suggests that its beginnings
are to be found in the developmental process of the liturgy itself.

127

... until the ninth century there was no such thing as a Jewish
prayerbook. The content of certain prayers was fixed, and so
was the sequence of the prayers as well as the concluding eulo-
gies of the major benedictions. But when it came to the actual
wording of the prayers, a great deal of leeway was given—and
more so in Palestine than in Babylonia. Not only did the precise
wording of the prayers differ from congregation to congregation—so that, even in later centuries, no two manuscripts of the
Palestinian rite are exactly alike—but also the same prayer
leader in the same congregation may have chosen different
words on different occasions for one and the same prayer.[3]

The *piyyut*, according to Petuchowski, has its origins in this loose
format and in the freedom given the prayer leader (*shaliah tzibur*)
to embellish, at will, the more standardized prayers (in particular
the *Amidah*) with prayers and poetry of his own creation. Petuchowski continues:

All of this suggests, therefore, that, at a time when prayer texts
were not yet fixed, several versions of the same prayer vied for
popular acceptance—some more simple, others more elaborate
or more "poetic." As prayer texts then became more fixed and
more "traditional," particularly in the Babylonian rite, the earlier freedom to create liturgically presented itself, and was often
fought, as an *alternative* to fixed prayer, until a compromise
solution was arrived at.[4]

That compromise, first set down in the ninth century C.E., but
disputed by other rabbinic figures until well into the twelfth
century,[5] decreed that it was permissible for a congregation to
recite *piyyutim* "as long as the *piyyut*, at its conclusion, provides
a 'bridge' to the theme of the concluding eulogy of the traditional
benediction."[6] With this modest endorsement, the piyyutic tradition began to flower, and it flourished mightily until the early
nineteenth century.[7]

In tracing the development of the statutory liturgy and the
piyyutim, Petuchowski alludes to the role the *piyyutim* played in
the "rebellion against the *idea* of standardized fixed prayers."[8]
Elsewhere, Petuchowski describes the development of the
piyyutim as being a manifestation of "the old conflict between
qebha' (*keva*—fixed times and a fixed liturgy) and *kawwanah*

(*kavanah*—inwardness and spontaneity in worship), between the fixed and the spontaneous elements of the worship service" in which the *piyyutim* "served the purpose of revitalizing the synagogue service."[9] Petuchowski describes the dialectic tug of war between *keva* and *kavanah* in the liturgy, noting that the synthesis of *keva* and *kavanah* gave birth to a dialectic of its own in which "one generation's expression of *kawwanah* becomes the next generation's heritage of *qebha'.*"[10]

PIYYUTIM OF PROTEST, *KEVA* AND *KAVANAH*

At the conclusion of Part I of this work, we observed a dialectical process in the rabbinic attitudes toward suffering. We saw that the two streams of rabbinic thought on the subject—that of protest (or argument) and that of submission (to God's will)—existed side by side, balancing each other, complementing each other, yet at the same time contradicting each other, working against each other. For a time both views had a more or less equal legitimacy; both served a specific function. When Akiba's teaching of submission became more dominant and was developed as the primary attitudinal base of statutory public worship, the stance of protest and argument went into eclipse. Yet just as in the case of the dialectic pull between *keva* and *kavanah,* so too did the pendulum eventually swing back in the dialectical pull between protest and submission, and the law-court pattern of forceful prayer found its way into the prayerbook as poetic additions to the statutory liturgy. If the standard fixed prayers (*keva*) may be said to represent, as suggested earlier, the triumph of Akiba's submissive theology, then the *piyyutim,* in particular those based on the law-court pattern, may likewise be said to represent the spontaneous expression (*kavanah*) of a later generation that also saw reason to address God with prayers of protest. The emergence of the *piyyutim*—and of the *piyyutim* of protest in the specific— represents a move against both fixed prayers and a submissive attitude in favor of a move for contemporaneous, spontaneous prayer and an argumentative stance vis-à-vis the deity. With the acceptance and incorporation of this sort of *piyyut* into the prayer book, the original bipolar faith of the ancient Rabbis was effectively reinstated in a new synthesis.

This new synthesis was both a synthesis of *keva* and *kavanah*, and of the two major rabbinic attitudes toward suffering. It also resulted in a dialectic dialogue between the statutory liturgy (*keva*) and the *piyyutim* of protest (*kavanah*) on the subject of suffering. Like the liturgy itself, this dialectic dialogue transcends time and space as the sages and poets of different ages and places speak in counterpoint to one another. For the knowledgeable and discerning worshiper, this dialectic dialogue could only have been therapeutic. On the one hand, the *piyyutim* of protest voice the doubts and anger born of the experience of suffering that all too often typified the life of Israel in Exile. Thus the worshiper was enabled to voice *all* his innermost thoughts and feelings in prayer to God. Prayer was whole; it hid nothing; it mirrored experience. It affirmed the reality of Jewish existence by attributing to God— and simultaneously holding God accountable for—both the experience of perceived good and the experience of perceived evil (suffering and injustice).

There are many types of *piyyutim* and thousands of poems extant. The majority of these poems complement the tone of the traditional liturgy, but *piyyutim* of protest are found in almost every type or category of *piyyut*. The greatest number of *piyyutim* of protest are found in the various penitential services for the High Holy Days and Fast Days. These *piyyutim* are known as *slihot* (penitential poems) and *kinot* (laments or elegies).[11] *Slihot* are recited on the days preceding and during the Ten Days of Repentance (the ten days from Rosh Hashanah through Yom Kippur inclusive), and on the Fast Days of 17 Tammuz, 3 Tishrei (Fast of Gedaliah), 10 Tevet, 13 Adar (Fast of Esther), and 20 Sivan (in the Polish rite). *Kinot* are recited on the evening and day of the Ninth of Av, which commemorates the destruction of both the First and Second Temples. It should be stressed that argument and protest are not found in every *slihah* or *kinah*. But a great number of *slihot* and *kinot* do protest against the harshness of the divine decree and raise arguments in Israel's favor that were expected to induce God the Judge to execute justice for His people. Such *piyyutim* in particular both continue the law-court pattern of prayer and utilize the argument motifs developed by earlier generations.

A HISTORY OF SUFFERING

Living in the shadow of the Holocaust dims our perception of Jewish suffering in the past. But other generations too have known immeasurable sorrow. As in our day, each generation saw their suffering as the nadir of the Exile, as something uniquely horrible, surpassing and dwarfing all misery before it. Perhaps a brief reminder is in order: During the First Crusade alone, an estimated 5,000 Jews were killed, and thousands more were murdered in subsequent Crusades; the anti-Jewish attacks that followed in the wake of the Black Death decimated a full 50 percent of the German Jewish population; in Reconquista Spain the total number of Jews slaughtered is estimated at over 70,000, with thousands killed in Seville in one day, June 6, 1391. The Chmielnitski rebellion in the Ukraine and Poland between 1648 and 1658 totally destroyed Polish Jewry. A chronicler of the anti-Jewish pogroms that accompanied the rebellion called the period the Third Destruction, equating it with the destructions of the First and Second Temples. Jewish sources of the time put the number of dead at 100,000, 6,000 in the city of Nemirov alone. More pogroms occurred in 1768. There are *piyyutim* of protest lamenting all of these events.

The *piyyutim* of protest continued to be used, with some differences—language being a major one—down to our own century. There are *piyyutim* in Hebrew and Yiddish lamenting the pogroms in Russia in the 1880s, and again from 1903 to 1906, including the infamous Kishinev pogrom. There are others protesting the massacres in the Ukraine during World War I and the Civil War that followed. There, Ukrainian nationalist forces under Petlyura slaughtered tens of thousands of Jews—2,300 in one day—for four years from 1917 to 1921. Beginning in 1919, the counterrevolutionary army under General Denikin—whose motto was "Strike at the Jews and save Russia"—massacred some 60,000 Jews, annihilating some 530 communities. Between these bloodlettings and the famine and disease, an estimated 250,000 Jews lost their lives. This later period will be covered in the chapter on arguing with God in the Eastern European Jewish tradition. Suffice it to say here that until the modern era, the law-court pattern of prayer and its various argument motifs set the form and tone for all *piyyutim* of protest down through the generations.[12]

HOW A *PIYYUT* OF PROTEST WORKS

To understand how a *piyyut* of protest works in its interaction with the liturgy, we will examine how a dialectic dialogue is set up between two *piyyutim* and their liturgical contexts. In the first example, dialectic dialogue is created because the *piyyut* simultaneously complements and contrasts with the liturgy, while in the second example, it arises solely through the sharp juxtaposition of the *piyyut* and the liturgy.

The first *piyyut* is of the *geulah* type (a "redemption" type of *piyyut*—inserted into the *geulah* benediction following the *Shema*). Entitled "*Birah Dodi*" (Hasten My Beloved), it was composed by the tenth century German poet Simeon bar Isaac bar Abun. It is recited in the *Shabbat* morning service during the week of *Pesah* (Passover).

Immediately preceding this poem is the "*Mi Khamokha*" (Who is like You?) prayer, which celebrates God's quintessential act of redemption, the parting of the Sea of Reeds during Israel's exodus from Egypt. This prayer concludes: "Rock of Israel, arise to the help of Israel. Redeem Judah and Israel according to Your word. Our redeemer, the Lord of Hosts is His name, the Holy One of Israel. Praised are You, O Lord, who has redeemed Israel."[13] Then Simeon bar Isaac bar Abun's poem is recited. Here are three stanzas from Petuchowski's translation of the poem:

Hasten, my Beloved, to the tranquil site.
If we have wearied You by making our way perverse,
Then see, we have been smitten by every painful hurt.
But You, O Lord, are our refuge and our hope.
In You we hope the whole day long
That You will redeem us and make us like a watered garden.

Hasten, my Beloved, to our sanctuary's place.
If sins have risen far above our head,
Then see, our life by iron chains beset.
But You, O Lord, are our Holy One and Redeemer.
To You we pour forth our whispered plea
That you will redeem us from Your holy habitation and
    set us free.

Hasten, my Beloved, to our Righteous City.
If we have not hearkened to the voices bidding us do right,
Then see, those who would crush us have consumed us with
    an open mouth.
But You, O Lord, are our Judge and Legislator.
Upon You we cast the burden of our fate.
That You will redeem us and, with calm and trust,
    will make us strong.[14]

The liturgy then resumes with the *Amidah* (the Eighteen Benedictions) which begins:

> Praised are You, O Lord, our God and God of our fathers, God of
> Abraham, God of Isaac, God of Jacob. The great, mighty, and
> awesome God, God on High, who bestows lovingkindness and
> possesses all, who remembers the righteousness [pious deeds]
> of the Fathers, and in love brings a redeemer to their children's
> children for His name's sake. O King, Helper, Saviour, and
> Shield—praised are You, O Lord, Shield of Abraham.[15]

The first item to note is that each stanza of the poem follows the
law-court pattern in the fashion of the psalms of lament. Taking
the first stanza as our model, we see:

Address and introductory petition	"Hasten, my Beloved" (God) (and use of second person address throughout)
Argument	"If we have wearied You by making our way perverse" (limited and conditional confession of guilt)
	"Then see, we have been smitten by every painful hurt" (description of present situation, that is, complaint/lament)
Expression of trust and faithfulness	"But You, O Lord, are our refuge and hope. In You we hope the whole day long"
Petition/ supplication	"That You will redeem us and make us like a watered garden"

Simeon bar Isaac bar Abun argues that, while it may be conceded that Israel has sinned, nonetheless her punishment far exceeds the proper measure. Therefore, since Israel still trusts only in God, she expects that God will hear her prayers, take note of her situation, and redeem her.

One notices that the introduction of the poem into the liturgy results in a dramatic shift in tone away from one of thanksgiving, praise, and petition toward one of confrontation, complaint, and petition. As we turn now to examine the poem in its liturgical context, we will see that it can be said to operate in both a complementary and contradictory fashion. In both cases, however, we are dealing with the same elements. The "*Mi Khamokha*" ends with a petition calling upon God to redeem the remnants of Israel as He has promised. The poet then presents his case in lawcourt fashion. The *Avot* benediction of the *Amidah* then adds a third element to the poet's argument: God is praised as the God of the Patriarchs who remembers their merits for the sake of their descendants in order to redeem them. (The prayers and the poem work as one unit to form a potent argument against the Exile.)

The poem may be said to work with the liturgy in a complementary manner. This may be summarized as follows:

Mi Khamokha (Who is like You?)	praising and reminding God of His past redemptive acts and of His promise to redeem
Birah Dodi (Hasten, my Beloved)	describing the desperate straits in which Israel now lives (with a confession of some guilt)
Avot (First benediction of *Amidah*)	referring to the saving influence of the Patriarchs (*zekhut Avot*) and praising God as one who remembers, protects, and redeems

According to this schema, the three elements work together to form one continuous appeal, citing God's past deeds, His promise to redeem, a description of current troubles, a partial confession of guilt, and the merit of the Patriarchs in an attempt to move God to intercede.

But the poem may also be said to operate in juxtaposition to the liturgy. This may be summarized as follows:

Mi Khamokha	celebration of God's past redemptive acts
Birah Dodi	description of intolerable conditions of present with a demand that God act justly and save
Avot	God is praised as the God of the Patriarchs who, in the future, will act to redeem Israel

According to this schema, the poem's description of the unredeemed present is placed in sharp contrast with the past and future in which God has manifested, or will make manifest, His saving power.

Thus, this particular poem derives its power in two ways: by combining with the liturgy to form a more effective argument, and by placing itself in sharp contrast with the tone and content of the prayers around it.

Our second poem, "*Ein Kamokha Ba'ilmim*" (There is none like You among the dumb), by Isaac bar Shalom, commemorates the massacres of the Second Crusade in Germany. The *piyyut* is recited on the first *Shabbat* morning after *Pesah*. Unlike our first example, this example derives its power solely through the juxtaposition of the intolerable present with the praise of God as Israel's redeemer. The prayer before Isaac bar Shalom's poem declares:

> True it is that You are the Lord our God and God of our fathers, our King and King of our fathers, our Redeemer and the Redeemer of our fathers, our Maker and Rock of our salvation, our Deliverer and Rescuer. Your name is from eternity; there is no God besides You.[16]

Immediately following the poem, the liturgy continues: "You have been the help of our fathers from of old, a Shield and Saviour to their children after them in every generation."[17] Sandwiched between these two pious assertions lies Isaac bar Shalom's bitter protest. "There is no God besides You," says the liturgy—"There is none like You among the dumb," cries out Isaac bar Shalom. Here are some stanzas of his poem, excerpted from Petuchowski's translation:

> There is none like You among the dumb,
> Keeping silence and being still in the
>   face of those who aggrieve us,

Our foes are many; they rise up against us,
As they take counsel together to revile us,
'Where is your King?' they taunt us.
But we have not forgotten You nor deceived You.
Do not keep silence! . . .

In answer [to the Crusaders' demand that they convert]
   cried the smitten ones:
"From our God we turn not, nor shall we worship yours! . . .
Alive and enduring is our Redeemer,
Him we shall serve, and Him we praise.
In time of trouble, He is our salvation."
Do not keep silence! . . .

They made ready to slay their children,
Intending the blessing of sacrifice,
"Hear O Israel, the Lord is our God,
The Lord is One." Let us proclaim His Unity!
For His Name's holiness are we slain,
Our wives and children are falling by the sword.
Do not keep silence! . . .

A charred and overflowing pile,
Like an oven both uncovered and unswept;
All Israel weeps for the burning.
But those falling in God's fire
Are destined for His initiates' abode,
Like Hananiah, Mishael and Azariah.
Do not keep silence!

As refuse they treated Moses' Law,
The Talmud of Rabhina and Rabh Ashi.
Can You, at this, restrain Yourself and keep Your peace?
Pages and parchment, destroyed by flailing sword,
Yet holy letters flying on high—
God's writing on the tablets is engraved.
Do not keep silence!

The foe was strutting with his sword,
Destroyed my precious ones, made them to nought.
And he slew all who did my eye delight.
The year: four thousand nine hundred and seven,

When trouble closely followed trouble,
And, for my feet, they set a snare.
Do not keep silence! . . .

Almighty God, be zealous for Your law.
Put on Your vengeance and Your zeal.
Arouse Your mighty power—
As You once rebuked the swinish beast
With destruction and havoc and breaking.
Him and his people You smote with the plague.
Do not keep silence! . . .

Make our remnants Your own once again.
Among the crowds show us Your wonders.
Establish peace upon us!
Pity, O our Holy One, those whom You have dispersed;
Let a willing spirit uphold us.
Arise for our help, and redeem us!
Do not keep silence![18]

First let us focus on the structure of the poem, which is, not surprisingly, in the law-court pattern. The first stanza will serve as our model:

Address/ accusation	"There is none like You among the dumb"
Argument/ complaint	"Keeping silence and being still in the face of those who aggrieve us. Our foes are many; they rise up against us, As they counsel together to revile us, 'Where is your King?' they taunt us." (accusation, complaint, description of situation, blasphemy of the enemy)
Expression of trust and faithfulness	"But we have not forgotten You nor deceived You."
Petition	"Do not keep silence!"

The poem as a whole also follows the law-court pattern with stanza one serving as the overall address and introductory petition, stanzas two through ten as the argument (description of the situation, faithfulness of the martyrs, acts of barbarity committed), and stanzas eleven through thirteen serving as the concluding petitions (calls for vengeance, justice, and redemption).

It is obvious that the tone of Isaac bar Shalom's poem is wholly out of keeping with that of its adjacent prayers. His poem derives its power not only from the strength of the verses themselves, but also from the juxtaposition of a liturgy of faith with a *piyyut* of protest. As his poem testifies, Isaac bar Shalom, for all his anger, still has faith in God. He demands that God not keep silent, that God act in justice to avenge the wrong done His innocent people. The contrast between the liturgy and the poem only heightens his protest-petition.

The total argument therefore would go something like this:

Ein El Zulatkha (affirmation)	"True it is . . . that there is no God besides you"
Ein Kamokha Ba'ilmim (negation and petition)	"There is none like You among the dumb, Who keeps silence" in the face of our suffering. "Do not keep silence!"
Ezrat Avoteinu Atah (reaffirmation)	"You have been the help of our fathers from of old, a Shield and Saviour to their children after them in every generation"

The inferred question that results from this juxtaposition is: "But are You in fact our Helper, Redeemer, and Savior?" This reinforces the poem's lament and petition. In effect, the poem argues, "You have not acted as You should, so act now!" We say, "You have been the help of our fathers in every generation"—but have You in fact acted as our Shield and Savior? Act now on our behalf as You should have acted then. Punish our enemies and redeem us now!"

The juxtaposition of the *piyyut* of protest with the liturgy of faith, in this case, draws attention to the redemptive element inherent in the statutory liturgy by giving it an added sense of urgency. The obligatory praise of God as the Redeemer thus becomes an occasion for protest; it provides an opening for the reality of Jewish existence to challenge the ideals and visions of

Jewish tradition. And, as the liturgy continues, it makes the messianic argument of the poem most explicit.[19]

The dialectical way in which these two *piyyutim* of protest interact with the statutory liturgy can be observed with other single poems as well. Time and again, a prayer of faith and promise is given a new depth of meaning and, by a twist of phrase, is interpreted to refer to the predicament of the Exile.[20] In this way, the faith of the generations is artfully melded with the existential protest of the present generation. In the prayer book, protest came to coexist with faith; the celebration of the redemptive past became coeval with the lamentation of the unredeemed present. The dialectic dialogue that resulted was whole, a complete expression of the people's state of being and of their total religious sentiment.

The resolution of this dialectic dialogue resides in the future, in the shared expectation, common to both the form of faith and the form of protest, that God would soon redeem and save Israel as He had done in the past. And it was precisely this hope and trust in the future manifestation of God's justice that sustained the generations who languished in the present, who continued to suffer in Exile. For them, protest, no less than faith, was a means of affirming God's justice.

LONG-SUFFERING IN HER LOVE

From Jeremiah and Hosea to the rabbis who interpreted the Song of Songs as an allegory for the love between Israel and God to the poets and mystics of the medieval world, a favorite metaphor to describe the relationship between God and Israel has been marriage. The marital state is an especially apt analogy. It offers numerous possibilities for depicting the relationship between God and Israel: first, love and courtship, marriage, consummation of the marriage, quarrels, infidelity, divorce. The metaphor provides continuity while allowing for alienation, discord, anger, and, unfortunately, violence. But more significantly, there always exists as well the possibility of a reconciliation and of a renewal and ever-deepening love. Therein lies the power of the metaphor—hope remains no matter what happens in the interim.

Many *piyyutim* utilize various stages of the marital relationship either for the purpose of confession (admitting Israel's infidelity to her Husband) or for the purpose of protest (Israel as an abandoned and abused wife). In Isaac b. Judah ibn Ghiyyat's *slihah*, "I will go and return," the covenant of Sinai, the establishment of the Temple, and the Exile all are expressed in terms of the love relationship. His poem is a fine example of the fusion of biblical elements (drawn from the Song of Songs, Hosea, and Lamentations) and rabbinic interpretations. In this poem a personified Zion speaks as a repentant wife, lamenting the state to which she has been reduced:

> I will go and return to my first Husband,
>> who once kept me as the apple of His eye . . .
> With His arm He redeemed me from among the harlots [a licentious people],
>> He beautified me and adorned me with new garments.
> He spoke with me through holy ones,
>> He bound me to His side with a marriage contract and a marriage ceremony [giving of the Torah at Sinai].
> He gave me a rich bride-price and possessions, [the Land of Israel]
>> He increased my joy in every way . . .
> My Bridegroom, the King, brought me to His chambers [the Sanctuary in Jerusalem].
> I bathed and put on my most precious ornaments,
>> My perfume gave forth the scent of love.
> He came to my bed and rested between my breasts,
>> His right hand embraced me—the caress of hands.
>
> But a moment passed and then it happened.
>> He withdrew His glory and broke the engraven law [Destruction].
> I wandered with the wind inarticulate,
>> I was mocked and harried, but my Beloved turned away and was gone [Exile].
> My whole being yearned for my Beloved, my Husband,
>> "Why has my lover annulled His contract?" [That which was stipulated for me in the marriage contract.]
> He has gone from me and not comforted me.
>> I said, "I sought Him but did not find Him."
> I called to Him but He did not answer me,
>> "Return, O my Lord, return," I begged Him repeatedly.
> He turned away and did not heed me.
>> I hoped in vain.

My heart sounded like a [mournful] harp,
   My eye wept and did not cease.
He changed my glory into lowest poverty, my purity into impurity,
   My cleanliness was altered into the onset of [menstrual] im-
      purity.
He tossed me like a ball in my oppression,
   I am bound and troubled as one living in widowhood.
I yearn intensely, O Lord, for the Day of Comfort,
   The abandoned are buried in anger and wrath.
Flames of fire surrounded her like a wall,
   Have mercy upon her who has not been pitied.[21]

ISRAEL'S LIFE IN EXILE: "BEHOLD OUR PLIGHT"

Insufferable is the word that best describes the life of Israel in Exile portrayed by many of the *piyyutim* of protest. Whether the poet lived and wrote during the so-called Golden Age of Spain—like ibn Ghiyyat—or during the Dark Age of the Crusades, the sense of Israel's suffering in Exile was keenly felt by all. The description of Israel's torment was sometimes realistic and sometimes metaphoric. It may have corresponded to a specific event, a Crusader massacre for example, or it may have derived from life in general. But wherever the poet's home and whatever the era in which the poet lived, one of the more prevalent features in a great many of these poems was a description of Israel's life in Exile. This description both provoked the lament/complaint/protest to God and it served as the major point of argument in Israel's favor.

Ephraim of Bonn creates a litany of specifics in his lament for the massacre at Blois where, in 1171, the charge of blood libel led to the burning of the entire Jewish community at the stake.

I am stoned, I am struck down and crucified. I am burned, my neck is snapped in shame. I am beheaded and trampled on for my guilt. I am strangled and choked by my enemy. I am beaten, my body is scourged. I am killed, I am at the mercy of a lion. I am

crushed [as if] in an oil press, my blood is squeezed out. I am
hung, despised, exiled in pain. I am stamped on, ruined, made to
pine away. My blood is shed, my skin turned inside out, my
home overturned. I am pursued, thrust back by my opponent. I
am raped, I am damned by my enemy, I am driven into hiding
and led into captivity.[22]

One of the most graphic poems in its detailing of various horrors
is Kalonymous b. Judah's elegy for the communities of Speyer,
Worms, and Mayence (Mainz), all martyred during the First Crusade in 1096. It is recited on the morning of *Tishah B'Av.*

O that my head were water, and my eyes a fountain of trickling
tears, that I might weep all the days and nights [of my life] for
my slain children and babes, and the old men of my congregation, and indeed cry aloud: "Woe! Ah! Alas! And weep greatly,
even more copiously."

(Refrain) Alas, for the house of Israel and the people of the Lord,
for they are fallen by the sword.

My eye shall weep bitterly, and I will go to the weeper's field, and
I will make those who are distraught [with grief] and bitter of
heart weep with me for the fair maidens and tender children
who were enwrapped in their school books, and were dragged to
the slaughter . . . they were trampled and cast down like the dirt
of the streets . . .

The Torah, the Scriptures, the Mishnah and the Aggadah . . . I
have seen them torn, bereft and solitary. Bear witness and sing
dirges to set forth the tale—where is the Torah, [where are] the
disciples who studied it? Is not her place desolate with none to
dwell therein? . . .

So for these do I weep, and my heart groans exceedingly, and I
call to the hired mourning women and to the skilled keeners, all
moan, mourn and wail. Is there any anguish that can be compared to my anguish? . . . My wounded, and those who are
riddled with sword thrusts, lie naked. Sucklings, young men
and maidens [together] with hoary old men, their corpses are
like carrion for the wild beasts of the land . . .

> My oppressors mock and increase their reproach: "Where is their God," they say. "The Rock in whom they trusted until death? Let Him come and save [them], and restore their souls [to life] . . ."[23]

Another poet-rabbi of the same era bids God take note of specific horrors: "Let this sight come before You: young women, who put their trust in You, slaughtered naked in broad daylight, the fairest of women—their wombs slashed open and the afterbirth forced out from between their legs."[24]

Accounts of martyrdom like these constitute a major portion of the "behold our plight" argument motif. The more accurate and specific the account, the more moving the depiction, the better the case that the poet-rabbi-lawyer could present before God.

These accounts also often serve as the focus of a poem of general complaint. This is entirely understandable. To describe suffering in general is one thing, to describe the death of martyrs is to deal with the reality of the loss of actual human lives, in some instances the annihilation of entire communities. This suffering was very real and immediate for the poets and their congregations—the fate of the martyrs could easily have been theirs as well—so the horrors they recounted had a concreteness beyond that of a general description of Israel's suffering in Exile. The accounts of martyrs, therefore, represent the pinnacle of the behold our plight argument motif.

It is difficult to comprehend the intensity of religious conviction that seized the medieval world. But during the Crusades, for example, the Jews were as fanatical as were the Crusaders and Muslims—all were willing to die for "God's sake." The Crusaders killed in God's name and Jews allowed themselves to be killed or, as was sometimes the case, killed themselves in God's name.[25]

This twofold form of martyrdom—at the hand of another or at one's own hand—echoed in the *piyyutim*. Each martyr was regarded either as a sacrificial offering to God or as a participant in the reenactment of the *akeidah* [the binding of Isaac] in which the descendants of Abraham and Isaac actually complete the deed without divine intervention. In either case, each martyr added to the merit of Israel on high, testifying to the fact of Israel's faithfulness below.

Kalonymous b. Judah wrote a number of powerful elegies in response to the horrors of the First Crusade. In "*Amarti*" ("I said, look away from me") he graphically portrays the act of martyrdom, punctuating it with cries of lamentation and outrage:

> Behold: the nations have gathered together at the appointed time. O Living God, they make a pact against You according to their desires . . . They said: "Come, let us destroy them from being a nation that the name of Israel may no longer be mentioned" (Psalms 83:4–5). But the children whom He had called proclaimed: "Though [if] God kill us, yet we will trust in Him, we will still adore His awesomeness." The Lord has prepared a sacrifice; He has sanctified those whom He has called.

> Then my adversaries and enemies chastised me sore, they multiplied my slain, and murdered my noble ones . . . They have destroyed all my righteous ones instantly—all the best of my people [lit. every good piece, the thigh and the shoulder, i.e., the sacrificial motif] [because] I refused to take part in idol worship. Daughters of most excellent beauty, babies newly weaned, just taken from the breast, were led to the slaughter like lambs and kids. The father subdued his compassion, brought his children to the sacrifice like lambs to the slaughter; indeed he prepared the slaughter house for his own children. When the women set aside the children of their tender care for the slaughter, and dragged them to the slaughter house, they said to their mothers: "Behold we are being slaughtered and massacred!" . . .

> Who can hear [of this] and not shed tears? The son is being slaughtered and the father recites the *Shema*. Who has seen or heard [things] such as this? A fair virgin of the house, a daughter of Judah, did whet and sharpen the knife and stretched out her neck [to ease the sacrificial act]. The Eye saw it and will bear witness.

> The mother was afflicted and breathed forth her soul. She prepared herself for the slaughter [sacrifice] as a mother, rejoicing in her children, prepares a meal. Betrothed maidens and wedded daughters did exult as they danced joyfully to meet the scourging sword, that their blood [be shed] upon the bare rock, never to be covered. The father turned away weeping and wailing, plunging himself down to be pierced through by his sword, wallowing in his own blood upon the highways . . .

Who will shake [his head in sympathy for] my mishaps, devasta-
tion interwoven with destruction as the delight of my eyes were
delivered [over to the sword] for destruction and annihilation?
Was such murder ever before wrought?[26]

The following lines, also from the Crusades, draw upon the
akeidah motif, contrasting God's saving intervention then with
His inactivity in the present day:

Before that patriarch [Abraham] could in his haste sacrifice
   his only one,
It was heard from heaven: "Do not put forth your hand to destroy!"
But now how many sons and daughters of Judah are slain—
While yet He makes no haste to save those butchered nor those
   cast on the flames.[27]

If, as in these lines, it was apparent that God was not acting as He
should and thus deserved Israel's reproach, in other *piyyutim* the
poets were not so quick to condemn. Instead they struggled to
accept God's apparent judgment.

THE STRUGGLE TO COMPREHEND
AND TO SPEAK

The poet-rabbis faced an unenviable task—how to tread the fine
line between public blasphemy and voice the questions and anger
of the people, their flock? Some assumed the role forthrightly on
behalf of their congregation; some urged the congregation to join
their lament; some hesitated, not knowing what to do at first, then
yielding to their feelings of outrage and horror. The following
verses, all from the Crusades, typify each form of response:

I shall speak out in the grief of my spirit before my small
congregation. I shall wail and lament, for the Almighty has dealt
bitterly with me. Be silent, hear my words and my prayer. If only
He would hear me.[28]

I said: "Look away from me, while I will weep bitterly" [Isaiah
22:4]. I will relieve the bitterness of my soul and spirit with

> those ready to raise their cry of woe . . . O how did this evil come
> about? O surviving remnant, give [yourself] no rest, raise your
> voice and cry bitterly for disaster follows disaster.[29]

> Woe is me if I speak and cast doubt on my Maker; woe is me if I
> do not speak, venting my sorrow. Woe is me, my day of goodness
> has declined. My Comforter and Relative is far away from me.[30]

In spite of the fact that the martyrs, at the very least by virtue of
their act of martyrdom, were innocent victims and wholly faithful
Jews, the attempt was still made to uphold the on account of our
sins (are we punished) doctrine in which both the guilt of Israel
and the justice of God's judgment were affirmed. But the facts of
Israel's suffering were overwhelming, and thus even when the on
account of our sins doctrine was repeated, it was often done
within the context of argument with God.

> Who should murmur and argue at Your methods?
> Who should arm himself to dispute with You?
> We have turned away and have been scattered and
>   the oppressor's sword was drawn.
> But with You is justice, and the upper hand is Yours.
> Let not the tyrant say "I have overcome," nor let
>   Judah's enemies exult over my fall.
> Proclaim the year of release for those who are sold for naught,
>   and let the wicked man who spoils be turned back and cut
>   down . . .
> The produce which You have sanctified is swallowed up, both
>   ears and straw.
> Let judgment for their wickedness fall upon them and convict
>   them.
> Bring upon them devastation according to their misdeeds.[31]

Here the acceptance of God's decree is combined with a call for
justice and revenge. Implied are arguments stating that even if
Israel has sinned, she has suffered more than enough in recompense, and that the sinful deeds of the wicked far outweigh Israel's deserved punishment. Justice from God will vindicate the
martyrs.

A supplicatory prayer by Saadya Gaon also evinces this unusual
commingling of submission and protest:

Submission: Behold, we have been plunged into subjection to foreign domination . . . It was not from want of power that You have not saved us, nor from hardness of hearing that You have not heard our prayer, for our iniquities have made a barrier between ourselves and Your salvation, and You are righteous in all that has come upon us, for You have acted truthfully, but we have acted wickedly.

To You, O Lord, belongs righteousness, but to us shame of face. To the Lord, our God, belong mercy and forgiveness although we have rebelled against Him. And to you, O Lord, belongs kindness, for You will render to each according to his deeds.

Protest: But You, O Lord our God, are the Redeemer of Israel and his Holy One—will You be angry with us forever? Will You prolong Your anger to all generations? Far be it from You! Will You cast [us] off and never again be favorable [to us]? Far be it from You! For Your kindness has not ceased forever, and Your mercies have not ended, for they are new every morning, they are at hand at all times and at every moment . . .

Petitions: For the sake of Your name, O Lord, deal with us [do it for us] for that is Your praise, for we are called by Your name— Lord God of Israel. And for the sake of the covenant of our fathers, Abraham, Isaac and Jacob, which You established with them . . . and for the sake of Your people and Your inheritance . . . and for the sake of Jerusalem . . .

O Lord, God of Hosts, how long will You have no mercy on the cities of Judah, and Jerusalem, against which You have had indignation these many years? Behold now, Your people Israel is greatly persecuted. We turn to the right and there is none to help—to the left, and there is none to uphold.

And behold the time and season have come for You to save us. Our God, we are ashamed of our deeds . . . and we have no mouth to reply, nor boldness to lift up our heads. We have no one to rest on but on You, our Father who is in heaven.[32]

What is remarkable about this supplicatory prayer is the way in which the poet makes the transition from a confession of guilt and an acceptance of God's decree to a protest against the length of the Exile and a petition for redemption. One must understand this prayer in the context of the law-court. One might say that the defense attorney is throwing himself and his client on the mercy of the Court by (a) acknowledging his guilt; (b) affirming the justice of God's previous judgments; (c) praising God for His mercifulness and forgiveness, then complaining about the severity of the present sentence; and finally, (d) asking God to reverse the verdict in light of his client's change of heart and for a host of extraneous reasons (His name's sake, the Covenant, His choice of Israel as His people, their faith in Him, and for Jerusalem).

For other poet-rabbis, the shock of events was totally overwhelming; the words their hearts brought forth leapt from protest to submission and back again. In the elegy, "I said, 'Look away from me,'" Kalonymous b. Judah begins by advancing the classical rabbinic concept of *havivin yisurin*—that the righteous suffer now to merit the rewards of the World to Come.

> I have set my mind searching for the reason of such happenings, yet I know that His judgments are just and right. It will be well with those who fear God, who stand in awe before Him. God puts no trust in His holy ones, He is strict [with] their sins to a hair's-breadth. It is a good sign for a man that he is not mourned and given due burial [that is, the fate of the martyrs]. He will not fear on the Day of Anger [that is, he suffers now but because of this he will not suffer in the End of Days].

But even as he makes this pious affirmation, the poet cannot accept what he has seen befall his people, and he continues:

> At this my heart trembles, [it] starts up in anguish.
> My mighty ones are overthrown and humbled to the lowest
>   depths, fallen as one falls before bandits.
> O how long will You be like a warrior who is powerless to save?
> Make known in our sight the avenging of the blood of Your
>   servants.
> The Lord is a God of vengeance. O God of venegeance, shine forth!
> Wreak my vengeance upon them that afflicted me, it is a time of
>   vengeance to judge my cause, O zealous and avenging God.
>   O Lord, go forth like a hero [and] repay Your debt . . . break the
>   arm of the wicked and of the evil.[33]

An anonymous poet of the First Crusade likewise cannot reconcile his feelings about what he has experienced with his beliefs.

Lamenting the martyrs of Mainz, the poet reaches a pinnacle of protest, a near public blasphemy. But then, perhaps shocked by his own words, he jumps back in the next stanza to the comfort of the on account of our sins position.

> Almighty Lord, dwelling on high, in days of old the angels cried out to You to put a halt to one sacrifice. And now, so many are bound and slaughtered—why do they not clamor over my infants?

> But we must not question the fate of the dead, for they have been destined for eternal life. We must question ourselves, for we have been found very guilty; we have transgressed the precepts of right.[34]

The matter does not end here though. For this poet, as for many others, the words of submission and protest ultimately merge in the singular petition for justice at God's hand.

THE MERIT OF THE MARTYRS

Although the suffering leading to martyrdom was often understood as divine punishment for sins committed, the act of martyrdom itself was viewed as an assertion of Israel's continued faithfulness in the face of adversity. As the following excerpt shows, the act of martyrdom proved God mistaken in His anger against Israel and His punishment of them.

> The judgment of their Creator they accepted. They did not break off His yoke. They justified the righteousness of the Rock, whose work is perfect. . . . All say . . . "Let us fall into the hand of the Lord, but not into the hand of man" . . .

> They remembered their Creator and they did not break the covenant. May their blood be more acceptable to You than that of a lamb or bullock. O earth, do not cover their blood with dust, but only with the blood of him who shed it, let it not be atoned for [forgiven] until it is covered . . .

> The voice of the cry of my people [is heard] in a distant land, but worthless men have slain the righteous. Whether for life or for

death they cleaved to the Lord, they did not transgress the Laws,
nor did they change the precepts . . .

They sought You in distress when Your chastening was upon
them. Each one gave up his soul and poured forth his blood.
May this be pleasing to the great King . . .[35]

The point of these numerous depictions of martyrdom was to
induce God to cease being angry, to reverse His decree, to punish
the wicked, and to redeem Israel speedily. Israel may have sinned,
she may continue to sin, but she remains loyal to God as her many
martyrs make clear at the cost of their very lives. Thus, this
ultimate act of piety became a source of merit—a major point of
argument in Israel's favor.

The martyrs' deaths provide the basis of an appeal to God in two
ways. First, as we have seen, their sacrifice can be used as proof of
Israel's devotion and hence as the basis for a petition for redemption, forgiveness, and so forth. Second, their sacrifice has a redemptive, intercessory nature all its own, adding to the accumu-
lated merit of Israel in Heaven.

Lamenting the victims of Speyer during the first Crusade in his
poem "O God do not silence my blood," David b. Meshullam also
celebrates their joyful willingness to be martyred. He concludes
his poem with a petition that links the current martyrs to the
archetypal act of self martyrdom—the (near) sacrifice of Isaac by
Abraham.

Once, long ago, we could rely upon the merit of Abraham's
sacrifice at Mount Moriah, that it would safeguard us and bring
salvation age after age.
But now one sacrifice follows another; they can no longer be
counted.
O Living God, may the merit of their righteousness protect us
and call a halt to our miseries![36]

Similarly, Ephraim of Bonn, witness to the Second and Third
Crusades, also joins the martyrs of his day with Isaac of old by
linking their fate to that of Isaac in an elaborate midrashic treatment of the *akeidah* in which Isaac is actually slaughtered and
resurrected.

> O Righteous One; deal kindly with us,
> You promised our fathers steadfast love;
> Your love for Abraham. Let their merit [righteousness]
> answer for us and make us prosper . . .
>
> Remember, in our favor, how many have been
> slaughtered—pious men and women murdered for
> Your sake. Oh reward the martyrs of Judah . . .[37]

Like the Patriarchs, Matriarchs, and various individuals from Seleucid and Roman times, the countless martyrs, named and unnamed, had a unique standing in God's eyes. Their acts of martyrdom, acts demonstrating unswerving loyalty, and the merit that accrues from such acts, could be utilized by Israel in her appeal to convince God to forgive and redeem.

The merit of the martyrs is thus closely tied to the *zekhut avot*—the merit of the ancestors, itself a powerful argument motif. It was used by Moses in the Bible and by the Rabbis in their midrashim. It is most prominent in the famous midrash in Lamentations *Rabbah* (Proem 24) in which the Patriarchs and Moses gather in Heaven to argue and plead with God to reverse His decree against Israel at the time of the destruction of the First Temple. It is also widely used in a great many *piyyutim* of protest.[38]

THE BEGINNING OF PROTEST

The concept of the merit of the martyrs makes the most of a horrible truth—that innocent people have been killed while God stands by. It is an attempt to impose sense on something that potentially could shake a person's belief to the core. It made a virtue of the otherwise inexplicable, and transformed the unavoidable from the negative into the positive. Yet although martyrdom was an act held in highest esteem by the Jewish people and, as it was believed, by God, still the darker side of the issue kept emerging.

Martyrdom was only a last resort, the only honorable route of escape when no choice, save conversion, was offered. But the majority of Jews was not compelled to choose martyrdom. For them (as for the martyrs) life was highly desirable, a tangible sign of God's goodness. But life in Exile meant suffering—suffering by the will of God. When events reached the threshold of the intolerable, a complaint was lodged on high. In a number of *piyyutim*, this complaint echoed a motif found in the psalms of lament. Thus, during the Crusades, Moses b. Samuel b. Absalom (c. 1160) asks, as part of his prayer for forgiveness:

> What profit is there in my blood, in my being destroyed?
> Who, like me, acknowledges Your unity in love and awe?
> O awesome and fearful One, my soul calls out to You.
> Accept the freewill offering of my mouth as a burnt offering.[39]

Similarly, in an earlier time, Saadya Gaon pleads:

> Do not be exceedingly angry with us, do not remember iniquity forever. For what profit is there in our blood if You will destroy us and what benefit [is there] if You cast us down into the pit of destruction on account of our sins? And what advantage is there if You punish us according to our ways? Not in these is Your glory, not in these is Your praise. Rather, that which serves as Your name and glory is acting towards Your children according to Your attribute of mercy, extending over them the attribute of lovingkindness.[40]

The questioning of God did not end with this mild rebuke. To buttress their descriptions of Israel's suffering and martyrdom, the poet–lawyers hurled harsh questions and accusations toward Heaven. "Why does the Lord impose it?" wondered one poet.[41] "How can food and drink be sweet to me when I must look on while dogs drag Your [Mother Zion's] young lions? Or how can the light of day be pleasing for my eyes when I must see corpses of your eagles in the mouth of ravens?" laments Judah Halevi in his famous poem *Tzion ha'lo t'shali* "O Zion, shall You not ask. . . ."[42] The greatest poets, renowned for their pious verse, were at the same time champions of their people's protest. Thus Solomon ibn Gabirol laments:

> Everything has an end, but my misery has none!
> Generation follows generation, but my wound still is
>   not healed . . .
> How long, O God, will our enslavement last?
> How long will strangers rule over us?
> Ishmael [the Arab kingdom] is like a lion;
>   Esau [The Christian kingdom] like a bird of prey.
> The remnant that the one leaves of us, the other devours.[43]

Another poet of the Golden Age of Spain, Abraham ibn Ezra, sets his complaint in the mouth of the people:

> I have studied the books of the Prophets,
> And the words of Isaiah in his writing
> Were read in my presence, saying:
> "For My salvation is near to come."
> Yet generations pass away and are born.
> While God's people remains in pain.
> For a millennium, quite appallingly,
> It has sunk; and, in the bitterness of its heart,
> It says: "If you will redeem, then redeem! But
> If You will not redeem, then tell me."[44]

Even more despairing was Moses ibn Ezra:

> Over their pitch-black night the morning star does not appear.
> The day of their exile knows of no tomorrow,
> The star of their redemption is hidden under the earth
>   and does not appear. It has hidden itself in nethermost Sheol.
> False are all his hopes; his reckonings have been wrong.
> Their days—passed away; all their lights—snuffed out; the
>   secret of his dreams—buried (hidden).
> There is none to break their sighs (console them).
> Without a redeemer are the exiles, without a protector to
>   bring back the despoiled.[45]

QUESTIONS FOR GOD

In a number of poems the recitation of Israel's suffering or the expression of despair results in a bitter outcry to God. Ephraim of

Bonn, for example, utters this poignant question to God and couples it with a bitter complaint:

> To whom can You liken me, who is my equal in suffering?
> Is there a nation, of all those around me, that has been broken
> for its sins as I have been? Your wrath has swept over me and
> made me writhe in pain.[46]

Another poet, writing in the thirteenth century, builds upon the previous question, asking:

> O heaven, in what way are we worse than other people?
> Is our strength a strength of stones, is our body of copper,
> that we should be able to endure our tribulation? . . .
> It is already 1230 years since the enemy has devastated
> everything, and his hand still stifles us . . . Our
> adults, young children, women and children, old and
> young men, bridegrooms and brides—all are being burned
> alive and murdered . . . Ask all the inhabitants of the
> earth: Has this happened to any other people?[47]

Most frequently, the outcry is phrased as a rhetorical question, drawing upon the psalms of lament and Book of Lamentations both for their precise questions and for an archetypal description of their plight. One *slihah*, by Solomon b. Menachem (fourteenth century), has a refrain made up entirely of such questions. To the reader's statements, the congregation responds with a refrain consisting entirely of psalmic lament questions. The following is an excerpt:

Reader   If their guilt be so great as to reach the heavens and stars, I beseech You, whose every attribute befits You, I plead for mercy for them, to avert from them what is written: "I thought I would make an end of them" (Deuteronomy 32:26).

Congregation   Why should the nations say, "Where is their God?" (Psalm 115:2).

Reader	If their iniquities be grievous and innumerable, I beseech You, whose every attribute befits You, to cast [iniquities] away, and conceal them, and with forceful words do I supplicate You to avert from them what is written: "I will hide My face" (Deuteronomy 32:20).
Congregation	"Why do You stand afar off, O Lord? Why do You hide Yourself in times of trouble?" (Psalm 10:1).
Reader	If presumptuous sins have misled the foolish and proud hearts, I beseech You, O Lord, whose every attribute befits You, to deliver them from blows that wound; hasten to come, and lift up the voice of redemption.
Congregation	"Why do we [lit. I] go mourning under oppression?" (Psalm 42:10).
Reader	If they have framed falsehood in their thoughts and deeds against You, I beseech You, whose every attribute befits You, remember the love of those who extol You, and may Your tender mercy be moved toward the remnant of Your people.
Congregation	"Why, O Lord, shall Your anger be kindled against Your people?" (Exodus 32:11).

And so on. Other questions include: "O God, why do You cast us off forever?" (Psalm 74:1); "Why have You broken down her walls, so that all who pass along the way pluck her fruit?" (Psalm 80:15); "Why do You forget us forever, [why do You] forsake us for evermore?" (Lamentations 5:20): "Why do You hold back Your hand, Your right hand? [Draw it out] from the midst of Your bosom to destroy" (Psalm 74:11); "Why should You be like a man confused, like a mighty man who cannot save?" (Jeremiah 114:9).[48]

Note that the reader does not assert that Israel has sinned. He only suggests that if indeed they have, then God should forgive them—for His own sake—because of and according to His Thirteen Attributes by which He revealed Himself to Moses. The congregational response complements the reader's portions by voicing the petition that is meant to conclude each stanza. The result is a powerful and timeless lament against the Exile and God's inexplicable inactivity on His people's behalf.

WHERE ARE YOUR
MIRACLES NOW?

Questions such as the above examples simultaneously demand action on God's part and call Him to account. Often God is challenged to account for His present inactivity in the face of His past deeds. Asks Gershom b. Judah (960–1028), "O Lord of Hosts, where are all Your great and awesome wonders of which our fathers told us?"[49]

In another poem, the poet Benjamin b. Zerach (1050) has a personified Israel lament:

> Where now is my Hope? Who is there to see my Hope? . . .
> Where is the word of the Lord? Let it come now! . . .
> Where is Your zeal and Your might? . . . You have forsaken
> Your people, the house of Israel, in the land of their
> captivity. They are tossed about on earth like a vessel in
> the heart of the sea. Babes ask their fathers, "Where
> are the wonders of that Shepherd? Where is He who
> brought them up from the sea?" . . . We said: "We are cut
> off, our hope is lost." "Where are all Your miracles of
> which our fathers told us?"[50]

Finally, in an outcry against Chmielnitski's pogroms in seventeenth-century Poland, the poet asks with impatience:

> When will the [day of the] final miracles come?
> Your sons and Your daughters are given [into the
>   hands of] an alien nation and Your eyes see.
> Show us Your miracles as during our exodus from Egypt![51]

WHY ARE YOU SILENT?

The tension between past and present provoked strong questions; God's silence was equally heartbreaking. The accusatory questions are repeated as often as Jewish tears flowed. "There is none like You among the dumb," cries Isaac b. Shalom in response to the outrages of the Crusaders, "keeping silence and being still in the face of those who aggrieve us." And, after reciting the horrors he has witnessed, the poet shouts: "Can You at this restrain Yourself and keep Your peace?"[52] So too does Kalonymous b. Judah lament the Jewish martyrs of the Crusades:

> O mighty Lord, who is like You keeping silence
> Will You restrain Yourself and keep Your peace and not gird
> Yourself in wrath at those who mock me saying: "If He is God,
> let Him contend [for you]"?[53]

In no less vehement a tone is this excerpt from a poem by Menachem b. Jacob:

> Who is like You among the dumb, my God? You kept silence.
> You were silent when they destroyed Your Temple.
> You remained silent when the wicked trod Your children
>   underfoot, and You sold Your people without gain or profit.
> We came through fire, water and flame,
> They mastered us, stoned us, and hung us on scaffolds.
> They rode on our heads, but we declared our love for You.
> We descended into Sheol [Hell] while living and we were
>   swallowed.
> There we died, we are all lost . . .
> You are the zealous One and Avenger—where, then is
> Your vengeance?[54]

ACCUSATIONS AND HOSTILITY TO GOD

On somewhat rare occasions, a poet may come close to crossing the line of piety and propriety. In his poem "I longed for You and hoped in You," Elijah b. Shemayah (1160) approaches this limit in one stanza:

> You have despised, forsaken, and cast off those who cleave to You. You have cancelled Your covenant with the three beloved ones [the Patriarchs]. You have made us an offscouring; we are stricken and scourged, torn by the locust and devoured by canker worms [references to the Crusaders].[55]

Baruch of Magenza (Mainz) lived at the time of the Third Crusade. In this poem for the martyrs of Blois in 1171, God is presented as a devouring fire:

> [Dressed in] His purple cloak, gleaming red, He—a fire that devours fire—gathered to Himself His loyal servants, their flesh and blood. . .

> Remember this and abandon hope: they were given away and devoured, though they sang Your praises daily in their multitudes. Did You, their Helper and their Shield, think this just? "You took for Your own the most holy sacrifices, the offerings by fire, all they had to offer. . ."

> You forbade the uncircumcised to offer You even rams. Then why did You hide Your face when they ravaged the holy people, the feeble Jews, who put their trust in You? "Smoke rose from His nostrils, devouring fire came out of His mouth, and glowing coals."

> We offer You thick clouds of incense [as if] on a golden altar. Our skin is always ready for the sacrifice, so great is our faith in You. You made us Your own with words of fire, how are we [now] set aflame? "The house of Jacob is fire; the house of Joseph flame."[56]

This powerful elegy reaffirms the ancient relationship between God and Israel—but the relationship is scarcely one of love. Baruch comes close to casting God as the adversary in this particular poem. Perhaps it was only his deep learning—Baruch was a noted scholar—that provided a cushion against the blows experience struck against belief. But the key here is that Baruch still prays to God, accuses God, demands justice of God. All this reaffirms God.

The questions—the accusations of inactivity, silence, and outright hostility—and the cry for vengeance are no less than a call for divine justice. The two go hand in hand. Zinberg notes: "This twofold motif—how the God of justice can look calmly on such horrible deeds, and the bitter, anguished cry for vengeance and justice—echo powerfully in many supplications and laments of that bloody era."[57] God was expected to act because His honor was at stake, because His people were mocked and degraded, because they remained faithful in spite of everything, because of His consideration of the merit of Israel's ancestors, His past promises and His acts of old.

Each of these reasons were major argument motifs in the *piyyutim* of protest; all are closely intertwined and build upon one another. Each warrants an example or two.

THE MERIT OF THE
ANCESTORS MOTIF

The Patriarchs and other figures—biblical characters and martyrs—in Heaven were conceived as actually being able to intercede with God on behalf of Israel. Thus, for example, in Eleazar Kallir's "Then when Jeremiah went," the famous midrash of Lamentations *Rabbah* is paraphrased. Each ancestor in turn argues with God stating, "I did thus and so, where is the promise You made to me, and I quote . . ."[58] In some poems, the Patriarchs are joined by angels (or planets), while in other poems by a personified Zion, in their intercession and lamentations.[59] In still other poems, the angels, planets, Zion, and the Torah—either separately or in combination—are asked to intercede on Israel's behalf.[60] In her attempt to gain God's ear and hasten the Day of Redemption, Israel sought help from every friendly quarter. Because merit functions on several levels (its saving power, God's past promises to the Patriarchs, and as past precedents), the *zekhut avot* (merit of the ancestors) is often applied in conjunction with other argument motifs, or as the last word in a petition.

A *kinah* for *Tishah B'Av* recalls the analogy of the marriage between God and Israel in the context of "merit." Meir b. Eleazar exhorts Zion to intercede with God on her own behalf and for her children:

> O Zion . . . cry out on high for your lost ones . . .
>   to entreat and supplicate God to set you and your chosen
>   children in peace.
> The Husband of your choice, whose love was for you, has
>   turned as a stranger against you and also against your
>   hosts . . .
> Cause your Beloved to return to your bed, to rest in your shade,
>   and to walk in your enclosed garden and roses.
> [Purchased] with a bride-price, [joined] by marriage rites and
>   with a wedding contract, they are your help. They are your
>   choicest of gifts.
> Have you not born offspring and well-proportioned children for
>   your Husband? How are you now bereft [childless] of
>   righteous ones?
> He turned and passed by and was gone from you, but you were
>   not sent away. No bill of divorce ever came into your hand.
> He accuses with a complaint of refusing Him in rebellion, and so
>   you have been scorned and the people of your Beloved have
>   been brought low . . .
> O Zion, how long will you keep silent? . . .[61]

THE PAST ARGUMENTS MOTIF

Just as the meritorious deeds of the ancestors and God's promises to them could be used to bolster a petition, so too could the successful arguments of biblical ancestors be utilized on behalf of the present generation. Like the merit of the ancestors, past arguments function on several levels. Because the biblical arguments were efficacious in the past, quoting their exact wording presumably guaranteed success in the present as well. Second, the fact that God heeded arguments in the past provided the present with a precedent upon which to base its current petition.

Frequently, the arguments of an Abraham or a Moses are melded as one. Thus in the k'rovot for the Musaf service for the first day of Rosh Hashanah, Abraham's midrashic *akeidah* argument is blended with his biblical argument on behalf of Sodom and Gomorrah:

> Incline from Heaven's heights to the *shofar* blast and change Your seat of judgment into that of mercy. For the sake of the only son who was judged in the binding, may his offspring be spared from being judged. "Far be it from You" (Genesis 18:25) O God of Justice. Remember [the words]: "He shall not act justly" (Genesis 18:25).[62]

The pivotal quote in this argument is "He shall not act justly," which has the sense of "He shall not act by justice alone." Based on a midrashic interpretation, the poem transforms the biblical line, "Shall not He [the Judge of all the earth] act justly?," into an indicative sentence, "He [the Judge of all the earth] shall not act justly," by switching the interrogative article for the definite article. Abraham's biblical and midrashic arguments for Sodom and Gomorrah thus blend smoothly into his midrashic argument following the *akeidah* in which he tells God that He should permit His mercies to conquer His sense of justice when judging Israel in the future. In this poem, both arguments are joined to culminate in one potent petition.

Similarly, in the poem "When Israel sinned in the wilderness," Rav Amram Gaon begins by quoting the argument of Moses during the episode of the spies: "'My King and God! Pardon, I pray, the iniquity of this people, according to the greatness of Your kindness, as You have forgiven this people from Egypt until now'" (Numbers 14:19). To this the poet adds a petition to protect Israel, a reminder of the Covenant made with Abraham, and an appeal to God's reputation. Both of the latter, however, are derived from Moses' argument with God on Mount Sinai (Exodus 32:12–13). The poet continues by paraphrasing Moses' concluding argument with God on Mount Sinai: "If You will forgive their sin [well and good], but if not then blot me out of Your book" (Exodus 32:32). The poem then concludes with God's pardoning words at the time of the spies: "I have forgiven according to your [Moses'] word" (Numbers 14:20).[63] It is as though all of Moses' arguments were one!

THE PAST PRECEDENTS MOTIF

Closely related to the invocation of past arguments with God and the merit of the ancestors is the argument motif based on past precedents. In this motif, the appeal is made by contrasting the needs of the present (directly or indirectly) with God's deeds for the needy in the past. This argument motif is used most prevalently in the litanies for *Sukkot, Hoshana Rabba*, and in the *slihot* services. In the litany, example is piled upon example in a most repetitive style, building a powerful case for God to act in the present as He has in the past. In a sense, it demands that God be consistent. The distinctive style of the litany has a twofold function. First and foremost, it reminds God in simple and direct terms of His past assistance (with the implication that God should remain consistent in His activity now as then). Second, the repetitive style has magical overtones—especially when combined with circular processions and other unusual actions.[64]

In the *slihot* liturgy, the most prevalent litany is the *Mi She'anah* "He who answered," found near the conclusion of each service. It is an ancient prayer, and is first recorded in *Mishnah Ta'an* 2:4.

He who answered Abraham our father on Mount Moriah—
   He shall answer us.
He who answered Isaac his son when he was bound on the altar—
   He shall answer us.
He who answered Jacob at Bethel—
   He shall answer us.
He who answered Joseph in prison—
   He shall answer us.
He who answered our fathers at the Sea of Reeds—
   He shall answer us.
He who answered Moses at Horeb—
   He shall answer us.
He who answered Joshua at Gilgal—
   He shall answer us.
He who answered Samuel at Mizpah—
   He shall answer us.
He who answered Elijah on Mount Carmel—
   He shall answer us.
He who answered Daniel in the lion's den—
   He shall answer us.

He who answered Mordecai and Esther in Shushan the capital—
  He shall answer us.
He who answered Ezra in the Captivity—
  He shall answer us.
He who answered all the righteous and pious and perfect and
    upright—
  He shall answer us.[65]

Although not technically an argument, nonetheless the litany has a point to argue, namely that God's past actions have set a precedent (in expectation at least) for a speedy response in the present.[66] It should be noted that the invocation of past precedent also has an element of merit in it since the very individuals to whom these litanies refer are those whom God has especially loved and honored.[67]

But other forms of *piyyutim* also utilized this motif. A *kinah*, or lament, for *Tishah B'Av* by Eleazar Kallir is entitled "How in Your wrath You hastened." Each stanza begins with *eikhah* (how), the first word in the Book of Lamentations, and asks how God could forget the specific merits of Israel when He destroyed the Temple and exiled His people. Each stanza concludes with a congregational refrain: "Recall O Lord, what we had [in our favor]" (Lamentations 5:1). In this lament, God's angry punishment of Israel (called God's faithful ones, His redeemed, His lambs, His witnesses) is contrasted with His promises, His previous saving acts, Israel's past faithfulness, and the glory of the now ruined Temple.[68] The explicit criticism and argument states: "How could You do this to Your people and not recall these past precedents—these examples of our favor? Therefore we cry out, 'Recall what we had!'" The implicit criticism is that God has acted rashly, without due regard for Israel's merits or His own word, when He destroyed the Temple. This reference to God's past promises brings us to yet another argument motif.

THE QUOTING GOD'S WORDS BACK TO HIM MOTIF

A third variation on the use of the past as an argument motif is quoting God's words back to Him.

In a *kinah* for *Tishah B'Av*, ("Where is the saying of 'thus'?),"
Kallir plays upon the word *eikhah* (how?), rendering it as *ei koh*,
"Where is the 'thus'?." Each stanza asks God: "Where is the 'thus'
with which You promised our ancestors and us good tidings?"
These promises are contrasted with the suffering of Israel in exile
and with the destruction of the Temple and Jerusalem. To reinforce this contrast, Kallir concludes each stanza with phrases and
questions drawn from the first ten verses of Psalm 74, a national
lament. The following verse provides a taste of the poem:

> Where is the saying of "thus" [koh], spoken in joy to the
> father (Abraham) at the covenant between the pieces—
> "Thus [numerous shall your descendants be] forever"?
> (Genesis 15:5).
> But behold! Now my bones are broken through murder. "Why,
> O God, have You forsaken [us] forever?" (Psalm 74:1).[69]

By bringing to God's attention the promises He has made, and
contrasting these with her present state, Israel hopes to awaken
God's memory, stir His mercies, and speed the fulfillment of His
word. In this regard, let us examine a poem that portrays the
martyrdom of the Ten Rabbis (including Akiba) at the hands of
the Romans. This famous poem, the *Eileh azkarah* "These things
will I remember," is recited during the *Musaf* (additional) service
for Yom Kippur afternoon. The line in parentheses does not appear; it must be read into the poem as part of the words being
quoted back to God.

> You have said: "The house of Jacob shall be a fire and the house
> of Joseph a flame" ["and the house of Esau stubble. And they
> shall kindle in them, and devour them; and there shall not be
> any remaining of the house of Esau"] (Obadiah 1:18). But now
> the stubble has quenched their fire! O Living One! Hear my cry
> and bring near the burning of the Coming Day for they agreed
> to slaughter Ten Righteous Men.[70]

This example's power is not readily apparentexcept to God and
the knowledgeable reader. Perhaps this was intended, given the
close scrutiny Jewish texts received from time to time by Chris-

tian leaders intent on persecution. Certainly, once the meaning is made explicit, one's doubts as to the reason for the subterfuge are removed. First, as mentioned earlier, the second half of the verse— the part being quoted back to God—must be read into the poem. Second, one must know that from midrashic times Esau symbolized first Rome and then the later Christian kingdoms. Put the two together and you get a protest that says, in effect: "You promised that we [Israel] would emerge victorious over our Christian oppressors but now look what has happened! They have all but destroyed us! You had better heed Your own promise and do what You swore You would!"

One vein of argument within this particular argument motif is worthy of special mention, namely those poems that hold God accountable for violating His own laws. God is considered the author of both the natural laws and the laws of the Torah. Two Spanish poets built their cases on the laws regarding the manumission of (Hebrew) slaves (Exodus 21:2) and the redemption of Hebrew slaves from heathen owners (Leviticus 25:48–49). Isaac b. Judah ibn Ghiyyat sets his argument down as follows:

> "God is not a man that He should lie and change His word"
>   (Numbers 23:19).
> But You have decreed "After six years the slaves shall be
>   released."
> But how many times six years have passed me by and I have
>   not loved my masters [i.e., expressed a desire to remain a
> slave].
> And if I am sold to a heathen and I am not
>   redeemed by the number of years, the law of [ransom
>   from the] heathen falls upon kinsman [relatives], and
>   You are my relative and my redeemer.
> O Lord, hear my voice in the morning.[71]

More artfully, Solomon ibn Gabirol pleads:

> Six years were decreed for a slave desirous of redemption
>   to wait.
> But the years of my enslavement have neither termination
>   nor end.

Why should I, my King, be slave to the son of a handmaid
    [i.e., Ishmael, the Arab kingdom],
And by the hand of a slave find distress and trouble?
From day to day I hope but I do not hear a thing.
What will You answer me, my King, and what will You say
    [lit. open]?[72]

ISRAEL, THE FAITHFUL WIFE

All these arguments make one point: that as much as Israel has
suffered, she has still not given up her claim to a special relationship with God. That is why the metaphor of marriage is so perfect.
God may have left Zion as an *agunah* (an abandoned wife), but He
has never divorced her. Though she may now sit in despair, she still
has cause to hope that one day He will return. What will win her
Husband back? In one poem, soft in tone but vehement in urgency,
Judah Halevi suggests love itself will suffice, and so Zion pleads:

My love, have You forgotten Your resting place between
    my breasts?
Why then have You sold me forever to those who enslave
    me?
Did I not, long ago, follow You through an unsown land?
Seir, Mount Paran, Sinai and Sin are my witnesses!
And my love was Yours, and Your favour was in me.

Then how can You now bestow my glory [on all] but me?
Thrust towards Edom, pushed towards Kedar, [the Christian
    and Muslim nations]
Tested in the hearth of Greece, afflicted with the yoke
    of Persia.
Is there a redeemer, other than You—and one bound by
    hope, other than me?
Give me Your strength, for to You I shall give my love.[73]

For another poet, the longevity of Israel's exile—symbolized as a
pregnancy awaiting delivery—is seen as an anomaly in the divinely ordained natural order. The poet therefore asks Zion:

O Zion, how long shall you put your hand to [your]
    mouth [i.e., keep silent]?

> How the time of your giving birth [i.e., redemption] is
> long delayed! How long will you be bound up, ached
> with the pangs of pain that pierce you?
> The time of every pregnant woman is nine months, yet
> how many years is it since you have conceived children?
> Cry [to God] who watches [to aid] the hinds in labour,
> and [He] will ease your labour pains on the birth stool.[74]

In our next example, the poet advances the fact of Israel's continued faithfulness as both proof of her love and as an argument for her redemption:

> The beloved wife of Your youth, whom You betrothed with
> great bride-price and large bounty—How now does she sit
> disgraced, slighted, despised and forsaken? . . .
> How now is she considered as one violated, contempted,
> disgraced, and cursed? . . .
> How now does she bruise her feet on the mountains
> following her babes?
> O You who sits about the cherubim, see that despite all
> this she has not turned towards the insolent nor to the
> horsemen and chariots; but to Your abundant mercies.[75]

Faithfulness is also the theme of our final example, a forceful poem by Judah Halevi, which is bold in its argument and brazen in its analogy. In the poem, a *geulah* for the seventh day of Passover, Judah Halevi likens Israel's relationship with God to the relationship between Judah and Tamar (see Genesis 38). Quoting Genesis 38:25 in Israel's defense, Halevi casts Israel as the wronged but innocent Tamar, while casting God in the role of the twice-wronging Judah. (Judah not only refused to give Tamar the husband due her by law, but also unwittingly slept with her. When she became pregnant, he accused her of gross misbehavior deserving of death. She then presented evidence of his own misconduct and turned the tables, wringing from him an acknowledgment of the justice of her cause.) Applying this story to his poem, Judah Halevi in effect argues: "We have been faithful to Your Covenant all these years—recognize these visible tokens of our faith and admit the justice of our grievance. Are we not worthy of redemption?"

After being confronted by this evidence, in this case the sign of circumcision and the wearing of *tzitzit* (fringes), God can only admit, as did Judah: "She is more righteous than I." But this admission is unstated—perhaps because Halevi wanted to avoid the outright blasphemy of putting these words in God's mouth, perhaps because he was playful and expected his reader to fill in the blanks. But the admission of guilt by God is clearly implied because in the next stanza, Halevi bases his petition upon God's acknowledgment of the justice of Israel's complaint. Thus, after presenting his pivotal argument—the twenty-fifth verse of Genesis 38—Halevi pleads:

> Then return, marry her [Israel] a second time.
> Do not continue to divorce her [drive her away].
> Cause the light of her sun to rise, that the
> shadows shall flee away.[76]

With this poetic argument, Judah Halevi gives added strength and emphasis to the prayerbook's otherwise quite weak argument for Israel's redemption. In contrast to the liturgy, the poem is audacious in its demand and daring in its depiction of the relationship between God and Israel.

PETITIONS FOR JUSTICE
AND REVENGE

In many poems the faithfulness of Israel in adversity is juxtaposed with the blasphemy and prosperity of the nations. Numerous poems describe the mockery and misguided exultation of the wicked as they torment both Israel and her God. Why is it that the wicked prosper while Israel languishes in Exile? How, the pious ask, can God refrain from acting in the face of such behavior?[77] These questions demand justice of God. What comprises justice? Justice means the vindication and redemption of Israel; justice means the execution of vengeance and the punishment of the wicked. Their twofold demand is the petition that underlies all other petitions whether for forgiveness, for the rebuilding of Jerusalem, or for the end of the Exile. None of this can come about without God's mercy and then God's justice.

Kalonymous b. Judah contrasts the perfect faith of the martyrs with the mockery of the Crusaders. In their mockery is the implied petition that God answer their taunts with action:

> My oppressors mock and increase their reproach: "Where is his [Israel's] God," they said, "the Rock in whom they trusted till death? Let Him come and save [them] and restore their souls [to life]!"
> O mighty Lord, who is like You keeping silent? Will you keep Your peace and restrain Yourself and not gird Yourself in anger when my scoffers say: "If He is God, let Him fight [contend] [for you]!"?[78]

The call for vengeance is the response of a powerless people, for whom no redress of wrongs is possible save through God's activity. The longer He delays, the more His reputation—and that of His people—is tarnished. Thus the call for vengeance could link the insult done to Israel, the Torah, and God:

> You Almighty God, will You not have compassion on the blood of Your children that has been shed? Behold Your sacred Torah is trodden in the dust underfoot and they mock and laugh: "Where is He, their royal helper and redeemer?" King of all worlds, mighty and fearful, You omnipotent Lord, repay them speedily, speedily send them ruin, overthrow them like Sodom and Gomorrah![79]

Given Israel's faithfulness (her acknowledgment of guilt notwithstanding, which is, at any rate, a further sign of her faithfulness and observance) and the unrestricted violence of the nations against God, His Torah, and His people, could the call for vengeance have been less vociferous? Could the manifold horror wrought upon Israel have inspired anything other than the demand for divine accountability and the manifestation of divine justice?

Thus Ephraim b. Isaac of Regensburg both laments and demands:

> How wide have my enemies opened their mouths against me;
>   all my possessions and fortune have they swallowed.
> They have vanquished me and greedily drink my blood.
> From all sides hostile people surround me, oppress and
>   persecute my brethren.

Esau's children cry out, "Destroy them, annihilate them."
"Come," they call, "let us root them out, wipe out their
memory!" . . .
O God, You God of vengeance, repay them for their deeds,
frustrate their hopes, break their support.
Let their ruin be immense! . . .[80]

Kalonymous b. Judah cries out:

O requite them according to their deeds. Speedily throw
down my enemies and destroy them, for the Lord is a God
of retribution. He shall surely demand recompense.
Cut off those who hate You, make them drink the cup of
poison [as punishment] [for it is written:] "If one
dies by his hand, he shall surely be punished" (Exodus
21:20). Will You not take vengeance on such [deeds as
they have done to us]? [If You will not take revenge
for this, then for what?]
Are You not called "A man of war," Your enemies to destroy
and upon them to take vengeance? The Lord is an avenger
and is full of wrath.
Be zealous for Your name, for Your sake, O God, and for
the shed blood of Your servants, and for the ruins of the
Temple. Avenge the children of Israel!
The drops of my blood are counted one by one. Show Yourself
in Your purple [robes], their lifeblood stained upon Your
garments. Execute judgment among the nations. Fill [their
place] with corpses.
I am weary of bearing all this hardship. Hasten my redemption
and quicken the vision, for the day of vengeance is in my
heart and the year of my redemption has come.[81]

This demand for justice and revenge also was meant as a form of
affirmation and consolation for the survivors. The elegy, *Av h'arah-
amim* "The Merciful Father," first written in response to the First
Crusade and later incorporated into the liturgy, displays this con-
soling call for vengeance:

The merciful Father, dwelling on high, will revenge, in His boundless abundant mercies, the pious, upright and pure; the holy
communities who gave their lives for the sanctification of the
[divine] Name . . . Remember them, O our God, for good with the

other righteous of the world. He will avenge the spilt blood of His servants as it is written in the Torah: "The nations shall give His people cause to rejoice, for He will avenge the blood of His servants" (Deuteronomy 32:43). . . . and [in the Prophets] it is written: "I will avenge their blood which I have not yet avenged" (Joel 4:21). . . . and [in the Writings] it says: "Why should the nations say, 'Where is their God?' Let the avenging of the spilt blood of Your servants be made known among the nations in our sight" (Psalm 79:10).[82]

Consolation is derived not simply by affirming that God will avenge, but by reminding God (and Israel) of His promises to take revenge. God *will* remember to exercise justice against those who have wronged His people. Of this they were certain.

Thus despite all the complaints and accusations hurled against God, the medieval poet nonetheless maintained a steadfast relationship with God. That relationship, both personal and national, was expressed not only through a faithful observance of the Torah, but also through trust in the ultimate triumph of God's justice. In the liturgy proper, this trust was affirmed through praise and petition. In the *piyyutim* of protest, it was expressed through argument and a petitionary demand. The petitions were the same—only the structure and tone differed.

CONDITIONAL PETITIONS

One way in which a number of *piyyutim* express this difference in tone is by offering a conditional petition. A conditional petition, like Jacob's vow in Genesis 28, states: "If God does such and so, then I shall do the following." In the context of oppression and persecution, a conditional petition expressed the tentativeness of Israel's love relationship with God.

In his elegy for the martyrs of York and Beaufort in 1190, Menachem b. Jacob links his petition for twofold justice—redemption and revenge—with his conditional praise of God:

Exalted One, thus pay his [England's] descendants:
A sevenfold retribution. Pull them out to the slaughter.

Grant [lit. show] the requests and desires of those
   who wait for You.
"The righteous shall rejoice when he sees vengeance"
(Psalm 58:11).

Bring the miracle of salvation to Your people . . .
For the love of her martyrs [her killed ones], forgive
   [her] transgression . . .
Cause rejoicing and delight to the portion of Your lot,
"[Israel] shall wash his feet in the blood of the wicked"
(Psalm 58:11).

Then shall I rejoice in You, my Creator,
I will sing to You, my Rock and my Redeemer . . .
O God who grants revenge to me.[83]

In his lament for the martyrs of Blois in 1171, Ephraim of Bonn challenges God to make His words come true and offers God a bonus of additional praise and sacrifices.

. . . Is the Lord's arm so short that it
cannot change my lot? Let Your words come
true and we will pay homage to You in my city,
Jerusalem.

There I shall offer young bulls daily on
Your altar. Oh, let it be Your pleasure to
adorn Your city Jerusalem with all its glory
and to preserve the daily offering forever . . .[84]

These conditional petitions reflect a certain reality. Israel alone is God's people on earth; because her very existence is in jeopardy, God's reputation on earth is threatened. Israel is the test case of God's power and of God's attributes. God's rule—at least on earth—is dependent upon His redemption of Israel. As Elijah b. Shemayah puts it: "How shall it be made known that You are their Redeemer, if the enemy has stiffened [his] persecution [of Israel] and made heavy their yoke?"[85] God helps Himself by helping Israel. Thus Israel's redemption is linked with the praise of the righteous and with the universal acknowledgment of God's sovereignty:

You, whose might is in the heavens and whose dominion is on the earth, have the power to raise up the downtrodden.

The righteous shall indeed praise Your name when You raise aloft those who have been purified seven times [i.e., through suffering]. Then shall all those who are near and far say: "The Strong and Mighty One, has fulfilled His promise to [Israel] . . ."[86]

And similarly:

Have mercy and gather us from these corners [of the Exile]. Then they shall say among the nations: "The Lord has done a great [thing] for them" (Psalm 126:2).[87]

Just as, in some poems, God must act to save Himself and Israel,[88] so too it is implied in these examples that God's sovereignty will never be acknowledged by all unless He keeps His promise to Israel. The choice is His as to when He will commence the process of salvation. But in the meantime Israel sits, an abandoned wife, neither at peace with her Husband in her arms nor free to marry another. All she can do is to lament and hope, argue and pray that one day her Lover will return, as we overhear in this anonymous dialogue of complaint and comfort between Israel and God:

Lord, how much longer will this separation make me a homeless fugitive? The fires of wandering are ablaze, and I am ready for the stake . . .

. . . My enemies say that I have been abandoned, left widowed by my God. He is far from me and that, they say, is proof enough . . .

. . . The parting makes me moan and the fires make me cry and gasp. Lord, will You forever be incensed against this destitute people? Oh, extend Your compassion to me, have done with wrath.

And I, though darkness cover me, shall make You my refuge; though Your parting grieve me, You are all I have. Only Your mercy can shield me from my violent enemies. Even if You beat me down or plague me with persistent sickness, You will send Your deliverance and restore me, for a father has mercy on his child.

But one day God shall return and say:

> My love for you, O My beautiful daughter, is broader than the
> sea. I shall take you back to Me, and the people, who were
> overcome, will forget their misery. I shall endow those who love
> Me with laws and wisdom. I shall assemble their captives. I shall
> say to the North: "Give them up, give up all those who sleep in
> the ghostly underworld!" For instead of sackcloth they will yet
> dress themselves in fine linen, in purple and scarlet.

And Zion shall be able to exult:

> All of you who mocked me yesterday in the hour of my peril, in
> the day of my distress—my Beloved has truly taken me back and
> my illness has disappeared. I shall stamp on my enemies and
> fling my shoes at my adversaries. And to the idol-worshippers,
> who had said that He hates me, I shall proudly declare: "My
> Husband loves me now, and for all time."[89]

AFTERTHOUGHT

Although one school of rabbinic thought sought to provide Israel
with a prayer book capable of inspiring the people to emulate
Akiba's example of faith, later generations could not accept these
prayers alone. History time and again forced them to ponder the
problem of Israel's suffering and the nature of divine providence—
issues that Akiba and those after him may have thought had been
dealt with satisfactorily. While the doubts, questions, and answers
of earlier generations of rabbis manifested themselves in the Midrash, the later generations found self-expression—and solace—in
the writing of *piyyutim* of protest. When these poems were incorporated into the worship service, a dialectic dialogue was created
in which the faith and love of one generation were displayed
alongside the doubts and anger of a later generation. But whether
the worshiper identified with one attitude or the other or both
was important only to that individual. Both stances had legitimacy as a Jewish response to suffering. And more significantly,
both sought to affirm the same beliefs and values: love of God,

faithfulness to the Torah, trust in God's power, which would manifest itself through the judgment and punishment of the wicked, the vindication of Israel in the eyes of the nations, the redemption of Israel from Exile, and their return to the land of Israel. As we have seen, the *kinot, slihot,* and other *piyyutim* of protest utilized many of the motifs found in the biblical and rabbinic law-court prayers. These poems were part of a tradition all their own, a tradition of arguing with God which co-existed with the more normative concepts of piety, suffering, and prayer.

At first, these *piyyutim* of protest represented the *kavanah*— the rebellious, spontaneous aspect of prayer. However, after these medieval *piyyutim* were incorporated into the liturgy, they became the *keva,* or fixed aspect, of still later generations. Thus, as Petuchowski notes, in the nineteenth century Reform Judaism led a rebellion against the continued inclusion of the *piyyutim* in the liturgy.[90] To this day—and in spite of a movement to return to tradition—most of the medieval *piyyutim* remain excluded from Reform prayer books, their place occupied by often less daring prayers of modern origin. Although more *piyyutim* are included in their liturgies, the Conservative prayer books offer much the same fare. Today it would not be unfair to state that for the majority of Jews the piyyutic tradition represents a little understood and nearly forgotten form of religious expression. And if this is the case for *piyyutim* in general, how much the more so for the *piyyutim* of protest in particular! Not only has the piyyutic tradition been lost, but also—and more significantly—the alternative theological positions the *piyyutim* of protest represent. It is a loss not only of material and ideas, but also of concept and principle: the concept of theological pluralism and the principle of contemporaneous religious self-expression. By contrast, the traditional *siddur* (prayer book) encourages and gives voice to a variety of theological views and attitudes. Petuchowski notes that the traditional prayer book

> which is the product of centuries and millennia, rather than the work of a single man or a . . . committee, must of necessity reflect the manifold changes in religious mood and theological consensus which the vagaries of a long and eventful history have wrought among the Jewish faith-community. Thus it

could happen that poems expressing unconventional theological positions became imbedded within a framework of standard liturgical formulae speaking in quite different accounts.[91]

Simply put, the traditional *siddur* has a wider range of theological expression—and is more tolerant of unconventional theological ideas—than many a modern prayer book.

Many modern Jews pray with half a heart. Torn between a desire for faith on the one hand and the existence of unsuppressible doubts on the other, modern Jews are at a loss when it comes to building a relationship with God through prayer. Prayer as praise, thanksgiving, and petition represents only half their thoughts and feelings. The other half is overflowing with anger, doubts, and questions arising from the experience of the Holocaust. Is it possible today to pray without the incursion of troubling thoughts? Yet this is exactly what our *piyyut*-less prayer books ask us to do. Cut off from the tradition of protest and argument that is the heritage of earlier times, ignorant of the concept of prayer as protest, and deprived of the rich vocabulary of liturgical protest, modern Jews have no outlet to express their darker thoughts to God—certainly not through conventional worship services in a contemporary synagogue or temple! If the reformers of the nineteenth and early twentieth centuries saw fit to curtail the use of the *piyyutim*, perhaps we can soon look forward to the emergence of a new generation of reformers who will reintegrate the medieval *piyyutim* of protest—and add new *piyyutim* of protest as well—into the worship service once again. The Holocaust martyrs deserve it, the contemporary generation needs it, and future generations will hold us accountable if we fail to add our post-Holocaust laments and protests to those of our ancestors.

8

ARGUMENT WITH GOD IN THE EASTERN EUROPEAN TRADITION

INTRODUCTION

From the Babylonian Exile to the Roman domination, from the Crusader massacres to the Chmielnitski pogroms, the law-court pattern of prayer was used to register a protest with God and against God concerning the unending suffering of His people Israel. First as psalm and prophecy, later as midrash and still later as *piyyut*, the law-court pattern of prayer was an accepted, albeit unorthodox, form of communicating with God.

It would be difficult, if not impossible, to determine how these fierce prayers were actually received in their day. How did these public "blasphemies"—even though a part of a longstanding tradition and justified by the events of the day—sit with the more normatively pious of any given generation? Since the debate between Job and his erstwhile friends, whose points were multiplied a thousandfold in the teachings of the Rabbis, the dual traditions of passivity and protest inherited from Abraham did not always co-exist peacefully. Passivity in the face of suffering and the acceptance of one's fate has long held the upper hand as the normative and preferred form of piety. But the arguing with God tradition

177

persisted and indeed flourished in every age. The fact that many
of the authors of these prayers of protest were among the rabbinic
leadership of their day does confer more than a token legitimacy
to this mode of prayer.

The emergence of Hasidism (itself a reaction to the violence of
the Chmielnitski era) saw a revival of both the argument motif
and the law-court pattern. With its emphasis on the role of the
tzaddik (a completely holy individual—the *rebbe*), Hasidism
evinced a return to the charismatic style of religious leadership
characteristic of a Moses or a Honi. The latter is an especially apt
precedent since he, like the hasidic masters, was opposed by the
rabbinic sages of the day. And perhaps some of the rabbinic
opposition to Hasidism stemmed from their fears of where a
charismatic individual could lead his followers and of what could
result from an injudicious—and unanswered—use of the law-
court pattern of prayer.

As champions of their people and as intimates of their Father in
Heaven, the hasidic masters frequently argued with God, calling
Him to account for His lapses in obligation. God is addressed from
a strong sense of intimacy; He is praised or bullied or hoodwinked,
depending on Israel's needs. Many stories have come down to us
concerning the lawsuits and arguments brought against God by
various *rebbes*.

These stories are significant in several ways. The first regards
language. The midrashim and *piyyutim* were written in Hebrew;
the hasidic tales were told and later transcribed in Yiddish. This
change of language, from that of the scholar to that of the people,
also marked a shift in the intended audience for the prayers of
protest. Midrash and *piyyut* were, by and large, written in an
esoteric language and formalized manner by a rabbinic elite for
other learned people; the hasidic tales were written in Yiddish for
the masses. The third item to note is that the hasidic stories
represent a shift in the usage of the protestant mode. The
piyyutim were direct prayers intended for use in the worship
service; the hasidic prayers are recounted in story form, similar in
many ways to the stories of the medieval *ma'aseh* books and
other folk tales. Other hasidic prayers became folksongs. As part
of a folk tradition, these hasidic tales mark a transition from the
solely rabbinic and liturgical use of the protestant mode to the
wholly popular—and often secular—use of the form in Yiddish

folksong and twentieth-century Yiddish poetry. (Only a handful of modern Hebrew poets—and of these almost all have East European backgrounds—continued, or returned to, the tradition of penning protest in the language of the Bible.)

Although the hasidic tales are intrinsically problematic, both in the unreliability of the sources for the tales and in the discontinuity between the actual writings of, for example, Rabbi Levi Yitzhak of Berditchev and the tales about him, they do nonetheless exist, and they have continued to exert a strong influence down to our own day. The issues that prompted an outburst on the part of an hasidic master are ancient, even by Jewish standards: the hardships of life and the sufferings of the Exile.

These themes are echoed in Yiddish folksong and in modern Yiddish poetry, which adopted the protestant mode for their audience and their day. Of greater importance is the fact that even as rabbinic Judaism increasingly defined passivity as the norm for piety, the motif of arguing with God (*krign zich mit Got*) and the concept of protestant piety were incorporated and preserved in the Eastern European Yiddish folk culture, and thence to the present generation.

HASIDIC TALES OF PROTEST

The power of the *tzaddik* is based on the principle "What the Lord decrees, the *tzaddik* may annul; but what the *tzaddik* decrees, the Lord will confirm." As Rabbi Levi Yitzhak of Berditchev put it: "In our generation, the Holy One, blessed be He, says to the *tzaddik*, who now stands in the place of Moses: 'I, the Lord, am your God! You may' [Exodus 20:2]—dare one utter the words?— 'do with Me as you wish!'"[1] And the hasidic masters—the *tzaddikim*—did just that. Levi Yitzhak is the best known of all the hasidic masters who took God to task because of the sufferings of the Children of Israel. Since so many tales are concerned with his incessant challenging of the Holy One, Blessed be He, Levi Yitzhak is the focus of our study, but the tales of other *tzaddikim* also make their appearances from time to time.

Prayer was the preferred means of confrontation, the natural occasion for such endeavors, when petition could be reinforced with protest. On many an occasion, while leading his congregation in prayers, Levi Yitzhak would interrupt his chanting of the Hebrew and, breaking into the Yiddish tongue, set forth before God the case against Him. These private prayers of protest must have left an indelible mark upon those who eavesdropped.

The power of his private prayers derive from his ability to heighten or dramatize the tension that exists between the ideal (or written word) of the liturgy and the real—the hard world of the Exile. By articulating what the people experienced and, as it were, drawing God's attention to this reality, Levi Yitzhak was confirmed in his role as the champion prosecuting attorney of the Hasidim.

Rabbi Levi Yitzhak's use of private prayer and his conception of the role of the *tzaddik* are clearly evident in the following story:

> Once, in the *Musaf* service of Rosh Hashanah, when he reached the words "And Your throne will be established in mercy and You shall sit upon it in truth," Levi Yitzhak stopped praying to explain the meaning of these words to the Almighty.
> **Address:** O Lord,
> **Argument:** If You want the throne of Your glory to be established so that You may sit upon it in that glory which alone is fitting for the King of kings, then deal mercifully with Your children and issue decrees for their salvation and consolation. But if You deal with us harshly and issue harsh decrees, Heaven forbid, then Your throne will not be established and You will not sit upon it in truth. For the *tzaddikim* of the generation will not permit You to sit upon Your throne. You may decree, but they will annul.
> **Petition** (implied): Therefore I entreat You, O Eternal King: If "Your throne be established in mercy," then "You will sit upon it in truth."[2]

Perhaps the most famous of his private prayers of protest is his "*Din-Torah mit Got*" ("Lawsuit with God"), also known as "*Kaddish*" since it was interjected into this particular prayer. His poem-prayer became a folksong famous in its own right, so beloved was it by the people.

> **Address:** Good morning to You, Master of the Universe.
> I, Levi Yitzhak, son of Sarah of Berditchev,

I come to You with a Din Torah [lawsuit] from Your people
   Israel.
Argument: What do You want of Your people Israel?
For everywhere I look it says, "Say to the Children of
   Israel,"
And every other verse says, "Speak to the Children of
Israel,"
And over and over, "Command the Children of Israel,"
Father, sweet Father in Heaven,
How many nations are there in the world?
   Persians, Babylonians, Edomites.

The Russians, what do they say?
   That their Czar is the only ruler.
The Prussians, what do they say?
   That their Kaiser is supreme.
And the English, what do they say?
   That their King is the sovereign.
But I, Levi Yitzhak, son of Sarah of Berditchev, say,
"*Yisgadal v'yiskadash shmei raboh—*
Magnified and sanctified is Thy Name."

Petition: And I, Levi Yitzhak, son of Sarah of Berditchev, say,
"From my stand I will not waver,
And from my place I shall not move
Until there be an end to this Exile.
Yisgadal v'yiskadash shmei raboh—
Magnified and sanctified is only Thy Name."[3]

Like the rabbinic law-court arguments, Levi Yitzhak's prayer
stresses the themes of Israel's faithfulness and devotion to God,
her present suffering and the request (demand) that her misery
end. Note also the motifs of "the attitudes of the nations," "the
attitude of Israel" and the urging of God to act "for His name's
sake" and vindicate Israel's trust in Him. Note as well Levi Yitzhak's role as intercessor—one that combines his authority as a
rabbi with his charisma as a Honi-like *tzaddik*.

That Israel alone acknowledges God as her King and that Israel
alone is subject to and willing observer of all God's commandments are the implicit reasons that God should render judgment
in favor of Israel and put an end to the Exile. But lest these points
be insufficient, Levi Yitzhak uses his status as a *tzaddik* and

attempts, like Habakkuk and Honi, to force God's hand by refusing to budge until he sees results. Typical of the stories about Levi Yitzhak is the fact that, his reputation notwithstanding, he was never successful in winning results with his lawsuits on high. The stories about other rabbis' arguments do, on occasion, end with a miraculous reversal of the divine judgment, but even in those stories, as in Levi Yitzhak's, victories were won only in small claims court, never in the one major case whose judgment all hoped to see reversed.

At times, Levi Yitzhak could be more demanding and less loving with God. Once he argued that just as Israel observed all that God commands, God should, at times, do no less than treat Israel in the same manner He has commanded them. By analogy, since a Jew is required to lift up, dust off, and kiss a pair of fallen *tefillin* (prayer phylacteries), God should do likewise with His people Israel.

> Your people, Israel, are the *Tefillin* of Your head, for the *Tefillin* glorify their wearer, and it is through Israel that You are glorified. For what verse is enclosed in Your *Tefillin*? It is a verse of David's, of Your anointed: "Who is like Your people, Israel, a unique nation on earth!"
>
> Lord, Your *Tefillin* have fallen to the ground and have lain in the dust of exile and suffering lo! these two thousand years. Why do You not raise them up once again?

Then he added:

> If You will forsake Your way and adopt our way and forgive our sins and redeem us, all will be well. If not, I shall be compelled to reveal publicly that Your *Tefillin* are false.[4]

Similarly, one Rosh Hashanah, Levi Yitzhak urged God to sound the Great *Shofar* of Redemption, based on Israel's observance of God's commandment to sound the *shofar.*

> **Address:** Lord of the Universe,
> **Argument:** You have commanded us, "A day of sounding the *shofar* shall there be for you." And because of this commandment in Your Torah, we, Your children, sound a hundred *shofar*

blasts each Rosh Hoshanah, and thousands upon thousands of
Jews have sounded these hundred blasts for many centuries.
Now these thousands upon thousands of Jews, Your loyal chil-
dren, cry out and pray and beseech You, and have beseeched
You for these many centuries, to sound but *one* blast for our
freedom on the Great *Shofar*.
Petition: Still You have not blown it![5]

Even though Rabbi Levi Yitzhak argued in earnest with God, he
was not always serious. A little holy humor or divine play often
entered into his petitions, as the following episode relates:

It was during one Yom Kippur service, when the people had
confessed their sins and were asking for forgiveness, that suddenly everyone grew silent as they noticed their rabbi turn from
the prayer book before him and say:
Address: "Eternal Lord,
Argument and petitions: There was a time when You went
around with that Torah of Yours and were willing to sell it at a
bargain, like apples that have gone bad. Yet no one would buy it
from You; no one would even look at You! And then we took it!
Because of this I want to offer You a proposition. We have many
sins and misdeeds, and You an abundance of forgiveness and
atonement. Let us exchange! But perhaps You will say: 'Oh, like
for like!' My answer is, 'Had we no sins, what would You do with
Your forgiveness?' So You must balance the proposition by
giving us life, and children, and food besides!"[6]

Sometimes the line between earnestness and humor, between
boldness and blasphemy, is indistinct. At times it becomes difficult to tell whether Levi Yitzhak was joking with his Father
or provoking Him with an insolent slap. On one Yom Kippur
when, according to tradition, God inscribes the fate of humanity
in the Book of Life, Levi Yitzhak interrupted his prayers to
pray:

Address: Lord of the Universe!
Argument and petition (implied in threat): It is only allowed
according to Your Holy Commandments, that a doctor should
write on the Day of Atonement, when, by so doing, he may be the
means of saving a soul; therefore O God, if You intend to save,
then affix Your signature bearing forgiveness to a prosperous

year. But if You mean to condemn, then I, Levi Yitzhak, Rabbi of
Berditchev, forbid You to write on the Day of Atonement.[7]

The Talmud (*Sanhedrin* 105a) states: "Boldness is effective—
even against Heaven."[8] This was a principle Levi Yitzhak and
other *tzaddikim* practiced, and one he also encouraged others to
practice, as the story of a simple tailor's Yom Kippur prayer illustrates:

> The Berditchever called over a tailor and asked him to relate his
> argument with God on the day before. The tailor said: "I de-
> clared to God: You wish me to repent of my sins, but I have
> committed only minor offenses: I may have kept leftover cloth, or
> I may have eaten in a non-Jewish home, where I worked, with-
> out washing my hands.
>
> "But You, O Lord, have committed grievous sins: You have
> taken away babies from their mothers, and mothers from their
> babies. Let us be quits: may You forgive me, and I will forgive
> You."
>
> Said the Berditchever: "Why did you let God off so easily? You
> might have forced Him to redeem all of Israel!"[9]

This well-known story is but one example of the common person's
use of the argument motif and of this typically Yiddish ability to
use humor to lighten life's loads.[10] (Over a century later, the writer
Sholom Aleichem raised the form of holy humor in argument with
God to a fine art in the prayer monologues of Tevye the milk-
man.[11])

Humor had its role, but so did teaching. On occasion Levi
Yitzhak would endeavor to teach God the true meaning of His own
scriptures:

> **Address:** Master of the World,
> **Argument:** David Your servant said, "They stand this day for
> Your judgments, for all things are Your servants" (Psalm
> 119:91), and I, Levi Yitzhak, will explain these words:
>
> "They stand this day for Your judgment," that is, the Children of
> Israel, the people You have chosen, the people who fulfill Your
> law, they stand this day—if one may utter it—to judge You!

"For all things are Your servants," that is, they judge You for everything we bear—wicked and cruel decrees, pogroms and persecutions, poverty and sorrow—all these things are come upon us only because "we are Your servants." Just as King David said elsewhere: "For Your sake we are slain all the day long, and are we taken as sheep for the slaughter" (Psalm 44:23).

Petition: O Master of the World, since it is "for Your sake" that we die before our time, the judgment is that You must redeem us, and without delay.[12]

Similarly, when the Sassover Rebbe, Moshe Leib, explicated a prayer for God's benefit, he also took advantage of the opportunity to point out how much God needs Israel's sins!

Address: O Lord,

Argument: Consider that You perforce must need that Israel should sin for the fulfilment of Your thirteen attributes which are like thirteen gems in "Your Crown." Otherwise You would lack some of Your most precious gems: "Long-suffering and Forgiving Iniquity" (Exodus 34:7), and Your Crown would lose much of its glory.

Petition (implied): Thus, even by their sins the children of Israel contribute to Your glory, and they deserve to be treated with clemency.[13]

The concept of Israel sitting in judgment of God is evidence of the persistence of the law court imagery that is part of so many hasidic arguments. In his "*Kaddish*," Levi Yitzhak comes with a lawsuit against God. On other occasions, Levi Yitzhak would cite chapter and verse of the Bible or Talmud in his efforts to "hasten the End."[14] This motif of "quoting God's words back to Him" is as ancient as Moses, yet the hasidic masters used it often, many times in an actual courtroom setting, to win a reversal of an evil decree. As Olsvanger noted: "From the moment when He revealed the Torah to man, He lost the autocratic powers of an absolute monarch. For the Torah is the constitution which God gave to humanity, and He must observe its statutes as mindfully as His people."[15]

The following stories are but two examples of the hasidic masters' use of the quoting God's words back to Him motif, in which God is called upon to appear as a defendant in a rabbinical court.

A terrible famine once occurred in the Ukraine and the poor could buy no bread. Ten rabbis assembled at the home of the "Spoler Grandfather" for a session of the Rabbinical Court. The Spoler said to them:

"I have a case in judgment against the Lord. According to rabbinical law, a master who buys a Jewish serf for a designated time [six years or up to the Jubilee year] must support not only him but also his family. Now the Lord bought us in Egypt as His serfs, since He says: 'For to Me are the sons of Israel serfs,' and the prophet Ezekiel declared that even in Exile, Israel is the slave of God. Therefore, O Lord, I ask that You abide by the Law and support Your serfs with their families."

The ten judges rendered judgment in favor of the Spoler Rabbi. In a few days a large shipment of grain arrived from Siberia, and bread could be bought by the poor.[16]

The Emperor of Austria promulgated a new law that a tax of 400 guldens be levied on every Jewish marriage. A poor man came to the Lizensker and complained: "I have a case in judgment against God. He commanded that men multiply, and yet He permitted a decree which makes marriage impossible for most Jews. My daughter is betrothed, but neither I nor the bridegroom can pay so enormous a tax."

The Lizensker pondered a moment, and then exclaimed: "Let the Dayyanim [rabbinical Court] sit in judgment." In his argument he said: "It is the law that if a man is half-serf and half-free, his master must give him his freedom in order that he may be able to marry, since a Jew may not wed a female serf, and a Jewess may not be given in marriage to a male serf [*Gittin* 41b]. We are partly serfs of God, and partly freemen because of our free-will. It is because we are serfs that the decree has been directed against us Jews only. Let God, Our Master, either free us from this decree, or else give us freedom from our service to Him, so that we may marry as other nations may."

Soon after a messenger arrived with the joyful tidings that the harsh decree had been abolished.[17]

Day-to-day life in Exile was fraught with hardship—as Levi Yitzhak pointed out to God once when he argued on behalf of Israel:

Address: Master of the World,
Argument (with implied petition): What claim do You have against Your people? By my life, had I not seen with my own eyes

the way in which the Children of Israel hasten to perform
mitzvot—giving charity, keeping the Sabbath, and studying the
Torah—I would not have believed it was in the power of flesh
and blood to do such things while confined to this bitter exile![18]

Even a non-hasidic rabbi would still, on occasion, avail himself
of the law-court pattern for private prayer. The revered Rabbi
Israel Meir Hacohen of Rudin, the Hafetz Hayyim, used this personal prayer of intercession for Israel, asking for an end to the
Exile solely because of all that Israel had accomplished regarding
the Torah despite the Exile:

> **Address:** Behold, O, You Master of the Universe,
> **Argument:** The honor which Your people Israel bestows upon
> Thee. Just look down from Heaven and see the crowns with
> which they have crowned Your Torah. You have given to Your
> people a Torah small in size, yet see how many mighty towers
> they have built upon it. They studied every word, every letter,
> every dot. All of these they have adorned and illumined with
> ornaments as white as pearls and bright as sapphires. Just
> consider the two Talmuds—the Babylonian and the Jerusalem
> Talmuds; and then further chaplets of grace without number:
> the Midrash, the Zohar, the Sifra, the Sifri, the Mekhilta, the
> Tosefta, Alfas, Rambam, the early Sages, and the Later Sages!
> Consider also the circumstances under which these expansions
> of the Torah were created: In the long and bitter Exile, between
> the fire and the sword, under conditions beyond human endur-
> ance and yet, they studied, and learned, and wrote. So, dear
> Master of the Universe, why are You wrathful with Your people
> Israel? Do You have any other nation to compare with it?
> **Petition:** Therefore, how long, how long, dear Father in Heaven
> will You allow Your faithful people Israel to endure its sorrows
> and sufferings?![19]

If the sufferings of the Exile preoccupied the hasidic masters of
the early modern period, the nature of life itself—which is to say
the question of what transpires after death—also was of much
concern to them as well. Specifically, they wondered how it was
that the generations of *tzaddikim* who had passed through
death's portal had, as it were, neglected their duty in urging God
to send the Messiah when they appeared before Him on high.

Many a hasidic rabbi vowed prior to his death to confront God, but to his disciples who survived him, it was obvious that none ever succeeded.

Before his own death, Levi Yitzhak, it is said, vowed neither to rest nor to be silent once in Heaven, until God permitted the Messiah to come. But to no avail. His disciples waited in vain. According to Rabbi Abraham Joshua Heschel of Apt, Levi Yitzhak was overwhelmed by the marvels of Heaven and forgot his previous vow. But he, the Apter Rebbe, vowed he would not forget, and he uttered this prayer:

> **Address:** Master of the World,
> **Argument:** I know that I am not worthy to be allowed to enter heaven with the other righteous men. Perhaps You will permit me to enter Gehenna with the wicked. But You, O Master of the World, You know how much I hate those who transgress Your will. You know I cannot bear to be with them. How should I then make my dwelling among them?
> **Petition:** Therefore, I beg of You that You will remove all the wicked of Israel from Gehenna in order that You might be able to bring me there.[20]

A *tzaddik*, like the Apter or Moshe Yehudah Leib, might be able to redeem lost souls from *Gehenna*, but none was able to force God to redeem Israel by sending the Messiah.

Believing in a life after death and in the inevitability, however long delayed, of the World to Come, the legends concerning the hasidic masters show them as champions of Israel, waging legal battle after legal battle with their beloved Father in Heaven, both in life and after death. As the quality of Jewish life in Eastern Europe deteriorated, stories such as these sought to bolster the people's faith and their will to live. These stories, like those found in the Bible and Talmud, are based not on "the questioning of faith, but the rebellion that arises out of the profoundest confirmation of that faith."[21]

But one hasidic master, perhaps the most complex and enigmatic, Rabbi Menachem Mendel of Kotzk, argued from a different vantage point, on that narrow ridge between faith and despair that is so typical of the post-Holocaust modern Jew. Torn between love of God and rebellion against Him in his life (he remained in seclusion for the last twenty years of his life), the Kotzker Rebbe is said to have once uttered this totally desperate and defiant prayer:

> **Address:** Master of the Universe!
> **Petition:** Send us our Messiah, for we have no more strength to suffer. Show me a sign, O God. Otherwise I rebel against You. If You do not keep Your Covenant, then neither will I keep the promise, and it is all over: we are through with being Your Chosen People, Your unique treasure.[22]

His words, as we shall see, are echoed in Yiddish poetry written in response to the Holocaust.

YIDDISH FOLKSONGS AND POETRY OF PROTEST

Folksongs and Early Poetry

The Yiddish folk tradition manifested in the hasidic tales is also expressed in song. The protestant spirit that permeated the hasidic tales just looked at also infused the realm of the Yiddish folksong. In some cases, for example, Levi Yitzhak's "*Kaddish*," a prayer became a popular and beloved folksong.

Some of the earliest folksongs dealt with tragedy. These dirges strongly resemble the Hebrew *piyyutim* in expression and style, except that they were written in Yiddish. The Chmielnitski pogroms of the mid-seventeenth century laid waste many a Jewish community in the Ukraine. The following is an excerpt of a lament that both chronicles the destruction and calls God to account:

> Dear people, let us weep and wail
> Over the dread events occurring in our days,
> In the year of the coming of the Messiah, the
>   Cossacks pursued us
> With a dreadful cruelty, impossible to
>   describe! . . .
>
> They chased and killed everyone alike,
> Many were drowned in the deep river;

Those who swam out were slain without mercy;
No one was spared, young or old, poor or
    rich.

Holy scrolls were mutilated and made into
    slippers,
Holy Torah, how can it not anger you?
Oh, woe, how they defiled your sweet words,
That is why my eyes flow in a river of tears.

Unburied the dead lie under the sun,
One holy martyr covers another, the one
    underneath is the better off.
Oh, this unexpected terrible horror,
Five hundred children drowned in wells.

Women and maidens defiled and raped,
Many forced to turn from their faith in the
    one God,
Many synagogues destroyed down to the four
    walls.
Dear Lord, why do You withhold Your mercy?
    Witness our helplessness!

Lord, how can You restrain Your mercy,
Witnessing the bellies of pregnant women
    split open?
And if the old ones have sinned
Why should the little children be the
    terrible victims?[23]

The pogroms that marked the unsettled times of the late nineteenth and early twentieth centuries inspired—if one can use the word in this context—renewed Zionist fervor (itself a form of protest and rebellion against the divinely imposed Exile), political radicalism, and a burst of creativity in the field of literature, both Hebrew and Yiddish.

Shmuel Frug (1860–1916) lamented the sufferings of his people during the pogroms of the 1880s and 1890s. Several of his poems were set to anonymous melodies and became popular throughout the Yiddish-speaking world. In one such poem–song, "Sand and Stars," Frug reminds God of His promise to Abraham (Genesis

13:16, 15:5) and demands to know why but half the divine vow
has been fufilled!

> Yes, dear God, it is true that like sand and
>   like stones,
> We've been scattered, dispersed, mocked and
>   shamed. . . .
> But where are the stars, those bright
>   brilliant lights—
> The stars, the stars oh, where are they,
>   God?[24]

In a less literate mode is this excerpt from a folksong heard in
Russia in the 1880s:

> Where do they all come from?
> Today we suffer through them
> As in all ages past.
> Shout Jews, shout loud and clear;
> Shout higher for up there to hear.
> You can wake the Old Man up.
> As if He were asleep for real.
> Why's He trying to pretend?
> What are we—a fly?
> Is there nothing in our favor?
> Enough! It's got to end!
>
> Everyone's beaten and bruised.
> Everything is thrown asunder.
> Brides taken from their grooms.
> Children from their mothers.
> Shout, children, shout loud and clear;
> Shout higher for up there to hear.
> You can wake your Father up,
> As if He were asleep for real.
> Listen, and You'll hear the cries
> Of children in their cribs.
> They plead with You that You might say:
> Enough! It's got to end![25]

Subsequent verses urge the feathers from torn pillows and bedding and the parchment fragments of desecrated Torah scrolls also to ascend on High to awaken first God, then Moses that the Jewish people below might hear, "Enough! It's got to end!"

The Kishinev pogrom of 1907 led the great Hebrew poet Hayyim Nahman Bialik to pen two poems, "On the Slaughter" and the longer "In the City of Slaughter." Perhaps owing to his East European Yiddish environment, Bialik was one of the few modern Hebrew poets who argued with God in his poetry. (Originally Bialik wrote in Yiddish, then switched to Hebrew.) The task of arguing with God fell, by and large, to the Yiddish poet who wrote for the masses. But in both of Bialik's poems memorializing the Kishinev pogroms, his protest is as strong as any written in response to the Holocaust. In "On the Slaughter," Bialik cries out:

> Crave pity for me, sky,
> If you hold a God, and ways to Him
> That I have not found.
> Say prayers for me.
> My heart is dead: no prayer comes to my
>   lips.
> My hand is useless: there is no more hope.
> For how long . . . till when . . . when? . . .
>
> If there's any justice let it shine now.
> But if it shines in the sky after I'm killed
> Let its throne be smashed. . . .[26]

Similar, though more pointed, sentiments mark "In the City of Slaughter." In this poem Bialik cries out against both the horrors perpetrated during the pogrom and against the attitude of the victims themselves. It is to the latter that Bialik has God say:

> And see them beating on their hearts confessing
>   their iniquity
> By saying: "We have sinned, betrayed!" Their heart
>   believes not what they say.

A shattered vessel, can it sin? Can potsherds
  have iniquity?
Why, then, their praying unto Me?—Speak unto
  them, and let them storm!
Let them lift up their fist at Me, resent the
  insult done to them,
Insult of ages, first and last:
And let them smash the sky and My own throne with
  their raised fist.[27]

In commenting on these lines, Petuchowski has identified one of the modern innovations in the argument motif. Bialik attacks the age-old "refrain about being exiled on account of our sins" and with it, the "passive submission to the recurring catastrophes of Jewish fate." Bialik's poem is "a call to rebellion against the Exile mentality, against God Himself . . . one of the distinctive undertones of the modern Jewish national revival." Petuchowski continues:

> We see, then, that, during the nineteenth and twentieth centuries, and for a variety of reasons, a doctrine which has held sway during the previous eighteen centuries was both challenged and, in some quarters, rejected. Perhaps this was not the least of the transformations which Judaism has undergone in the modern period. The fact, however, that we are able to associate the challenges so closely with the last two centuries only underlines the seemingly undisputed acceptance of that doctrine in earlier periods.[28]

Although Bialik stood in that time-honored Jewish tradition that found it possible both to argue with God and to call Him to account, his attitude—the rejection of the for our sins are we punished mentality—was uncommon, except perhaps among those Jews who, like Bialik, embraced Zionism's call to "hasten the End."

More in keeping with traditional Jewish values and the traditional modes of protest is the lament *"Eli, Eli"* ("My God, my God"). It was sung by millions of Jews in Russia, Poland, and America. In the original, only the opening and closing lines, both biblical quotations, are sung in Hebrew, the rest is in Yiddish.

Address: "My God, my God, why have You forsaken me?"
Complaint—descriptions of plight, protestation of innocence,
continued devotion and piety, merit of the ancestors:

> With fire and flame they have burnt us,
> Everywhere they have shamed and derided us,
> Yet none among us has dared depart
> From our Holy Scriptures, from our Law.

> "My God, my God, why have You forsaken me?"
> By day and by night I only yearn and pray,
> Anxiously keeping our Holy Scriptures
> And praying: Save us, save us, once again!
> For the sake of our Fathers and our Fathers' Fathers!

Appeal—affirmation of trust in God, recitation of Sh'ma in
unity with martyrs and as witnesses to God:

> Listen to my prayer and to my lamenting,
> For only You can help, You, God, alone,
> For it is said: "Hear, O Israel, the Lord is our God,
>   the Lord is One!"

In another folksong, a song of the Chelm Ghetto written during
World War II, biblical verses (from the psalms of lament and sung
in Hebrew) are interspersed with Yiddish verses. (The Hebrew
verses are in italics.)

Address and introductory complaint:
> *O look from heaven and behold,*
> Look down from the skies and see!
> *For we have become a derision,*
> *A derision among the nations.*
> We are surely a laughingstock to them.
> *We are accounted as sheep to the slaughter.*
> O Creator, how can You look upon this?
> Indeed, we never were at ease,
> We were always to the slaughter.

Complaint—protestation of faithfulness with petition:
> (Refrain)
> Therefore we plead with You ever:
> Help us now, Guardian of Israel,
> Take notice now of our tears,
> For still do we proclaim "Hear O Israel!"

O, take notice, Guardian of this nation.
Show all the peoples that You are our God,
We have indeed none other, just You alone,
Whose Name is One.
(description of plight)
   Strangers say there is no salvation.
   The nations say that for us
   There is no hope.
   We may be driven,
   We may be tormented.
   We have no one to whom
   We can complain.
   But we surely know
   That You are in heaven!
   Of You the Bible says:
(quoting God's words back to Him)
   He doth neither slumber nor sleep.
   You must surely protect
   Your children.
   Therefore we know
   That You are in heaven—
   With miracles and wonders.
          (Refrain)
Petition:
   Spare us O Lord,
   Surrender us not to their hand.
   Have pity, do not yield us
   Into their hands,
(mockery of nations)
   Wherefore should the nations say:
   "Where is their God?"
   That is always their cry.
   O my Jews, my Jews, what are you doing here?
   Gather your packs and take ye to Zion!
   We would have fled
   But the way is not open.
   Why do You let them treat us thus?
          (Refrain)[29]

What is expected of God is straightforwardly expressed: "You
must surely protect Your children. Therefore we know that You
are in heaven."

The song departs from the traditional protest–lament form in one distinctive way. The last stanza has God cry out in loving despair, "O my Jews, my Jews, what are you doing here? Gather your packs and take ye to Zion!" But speaking for the people, the poet answers, "We would have fled but the way is not open." And once again the poet takes up the direct demand for help from God: "Why do You let them treat us thus? Therefore we plead with You ever: Help us now, Guardian of Israel." This injection of contemporary politics—voiced by God, no less—into a classical lament of protest is unusual and indicative, perhaps, of a certain sense of guilt for not having heeded the warnings of the Zionists prior to the war. But as the poet asserts, even this failure cannot let God off the hook. As long as even one Jew remained in trouble, God was duty bound by the laws of justice to come to his or her aid.

POETRY OF THE HOLOCAUST
AND AFTER

The problem of theodicy raised in our own day by the Holocaust, coupled with the changes wrought in our worldview by modern science and philosophy, has demanded that changes be made in traditional Jewish theology, and in the traditional normative response to suffering in particular. Not surprisingly, the arguing with God tradition has found a renewed relevancy in our era and has witnessed a resurgence in application, primarily in the works of modern Jewish authors and poets.

The rejection of the for our sins are we punished doctrine in the modern era has already been noted in the work of Bialik. It is one of the signposts of the post-Holocaust era in particular that only a very few still presume to apply this doctrine to Jewish history anymore.

A second innovation of the modern era, at least with regard to the arguing with God tradition, is that the role of voice of the people has been assumed by poets and authors, whereas in the medieval period the rabbis did not hesitate to call God to account and demand justice of Him.

Speaking perhaps for many modern Jews, the Yiddish poets of the last half-century have returned to argue with God over what has befallen His people. Here we notice a third innovation, also peculiar to the modern era, as Irving Howe and Eliezer Greenberg point out:

> [The heart of the Yiddish poet] was pledged neither to the world nor to God, but to the people who believed in God or had only yesterday believed, or for whom the vision of God was inseparable from the vision of peoplehood. This is one reason that a recurrent theme in Yiddish poetry is the quarrel with God (*krign zich mit Got*), a quarrel undertaken with intimacy, affection, and harshness. If God had lapsed in His obligation toward the Jews, the Yiddish writers would not lapse in their role as spokesmen for the Jews addressing God: and this role, it should be stressed, was assumed by believers and skeptics. . . .
>
> God might be denied by many writers, yet He continued to inhabit their work, equally real to believers and disbelievers.[30]

God is addressed—prayed to, if you will—by poets speaking from a variety of viewpoints. In prayer–poetry, God's justice is questioned; in prayer–poetry, God is rejected; and in prayer-poetry, God is reaccepted. Often the works of a single poet—Jacob Glatstein comes most readily to mind—will embrace a multitude of attitudes from questioning to rejection to reacceptance.

One last innovation to note before turning to the poems: the absence of the law-court pattern. In the modern poetry what remains is the theme or motif of arguing with God, but the law-court pattern itself is rarely to be found, perhaps due to the changing nature of Jewish education (and the knowledge of classical Jewish prayer formats), perhaps due to the full transformation of the theme from liturgy to folk culture.

The Issue

A famous midrash in the Passover *haggadah* relates how a group of sages in Bene Berak stayed up all night discussing the implications of the Exodus from Egypt in their day. Writing in German, the poet Paul Celan recorded a discussion about God and the Holocaust he had had with Nobel Prize winner Nelly Sachs. The poem contains the kernel of a modern midrash:

The talk was of too much, too
little. Of thou
and thou again, of
the dimming through light, of
Jewishness, of
your God. . . .

The talk was of your God, I spoke
against Him, I
let the heart that I had,
hope:
for His highest, His deathrattled, His
angry word—

Your eye looked at me, looked away,
your mouth
spoke to your eye, I heard:

We
simply do not know, you know,
we
simply do not know
what
counts.[31]

So overwhelming was the experience or knowledge of the Holocaust that, time and again, the issue of theodicy surfaces in the
works of Jewish poets writing in many languages. Only in modern
Hebrew poetry does there seem to be a general reluctance to deal
with this issue. Not surprisingly, it is those modern Hebrew poets
of East European origin—Uri Zvi Greenberg and David Shimoni,
to name but two—who are primarily responsible for continuing,
in Hebrew, the tradition of arguing with God.[32]

The topic of argument is ancient; only the context is new. Writing in German, Friedrich Torberg juxtaposes the Passover seders
of old, of the innocents, with the seder of 1944:

Lord, I am not one of the just.
Don't ask me, Lord, for I could not answer.
I do not know, you see, why for your servants
    here
this night is so different
from all the others. Why?

The youngest child was happy once
to learn the answer at the table feast:
Because we were slaves in Egypt,
in bondage to wicked Pharaoh
thousands of years ago. . . .

And so we give thee thanks, O Lord,
for saving us from harm,
as we gather believing
today, and here, and in every land,
and "next year in Jerusalem."

The youngest child who heard all this
has long since lost his faith.
The answer of old no longer holds,
for "next year" never came, O Lord,
and the night weighs down heavy and dark.

We still have not wandered across the sands,
we still have not seen the Promised Land,
we still have not eaten the bread of the
     free,
we still have not done with the bitter herbs.

For time and again in our weary wanderings
Pharaoh has set upon our trail,
behind us he comes with his bloody henchmen—
the carts, O Lord, do you hear their clatter—
O Lord, where have you led us to!

You sent us on without a star,
we stand at the shore and stare on high,
O Lord, the flood has not returned,
O Lord, the night is not yet past,
"Why is this night so different from . . ."[33]

The unstated question of the youngest child stands as an eternal, silent accusation against God.

For the Yiddish poet Jacob Glatstein, the Holocaust is cause for an ever-increasingly necessary quarrel with God, because when the Jewish people is threatened with destruction, so too is their God. This concept of an immanent, suffering God, articulated first in the Bible, later in the Midrash, and revived in kabbalistic and hasidic thought, proves daringly bold in the modern, post-Holo-

caust era. Glatstein is more concerned—and rightly so—with Israel than with God. But in the following post-Holocaust prayer-
poem, Glatstein warns God of His impending demise in order to
save Israel.

> If we leave this world
> The light will go out in your tent . . .
>
> Now the lifeless skulls
> Add up to millions . . .
> The memory of you is dimming,
> Your kingdom will soon be over.
> Jewish seed and flower
> Are embers.
> The dew cries in the dead grass! . . .
>
> Who will dream you?
> Who will remember you?
> Who deny you?
> Who yearn for you?
> Who, on a lonely bridge,
> Will leave you—in order to return?
>
> The night is endless when a race is dead.
> Earth and heaven are wiped bare.
> The light is fading in your shabby tent.
> The Jewish hour is guttering.
> Jewish God!
> You are almost gone.[34]

A part of what empowers a poem such as this is the way in which
traditional Jewish theological concepts are adapted—in some
cases turned on their head—and integrated with contemporary
experience. This synthesis, unique among the Yiddish poets and
poets of other languages who came from the East European Jewish milieu, offers a compelling language of protest and a host of
unusual, new theological ideas to those in search of a way of
response to the Holocaust.

Simcha Bunen Shayevitch, murdered in Auschwitz 1944, also
utilized classical Jewish theological motifs in his poetry. In his
poem, "Slaughter Town," Shayevitch utters a warning similar to
Glatstein's: "When a man is slaughtered,/His God is slaughtered

also." Shayevitch's poem, based on the famous poem of a similar name by Bialik, calls upon the dead poet to play the role of Elijah and to awaken Mother Rachel and Rabbi Levi Yitzhak of Berditchev from their eternal sleep. The scene is but an updated version of the famous midrash in Lamentations *Rabbah* in which the Patriarchs and Rachel are awakened to protest the Destruction of the Temple and the Exile of Israel. Bialik, Rachel, and Levi Yitzhak are to go, all three, to God's side, to argue Israel's case one more time before Him with the black threat that if He does not redeem living Jews, God will have but dead bones to redeem.[35] As in Glatstein's poem, God's imminent demise is a threat, an argument, meant to rouse Him from His torpor and back into action.

For another poet, H. Leivick, it matters little whether God exists or not—He is still accountable for what has befallen His people.

> The accounting is still Yours, Creator,
> Even if it be true that You're not there.
> And however much people may have denied You—
> You are still there for the reckoning,
> To ask and to demand of You
> In our days which are dimmed over with death.
> —The final reckoning is still Yours, O
>   Creator! . . .
>
> Even more than it is with him—Your own
>   creation . . .
>
> The accounting is still Yours, Creator,
> Even though no one is demanding payment—
> A pile of ashes, however, is clear evidence . . .
> That from Mount Moriah to Maidanek
> It is no more than a leap of Isaac.
> Judgment is still Yours, O Creator.[36]

Responses

While all the Yiddish poets recoiled in horror at what was happening—or what had happened—to Israel in Europe, only a few could retain the "passive" response to suffering that the normative tradition proposed. Uri Zvi Greenberg attempts to retain the for our sins response in a poem in which he accuses Israel of bringing punishment upon itself by aping the ways of the Gentiles.[37] Aaron Zeitlin reaffirms his belief in the one God, Source of all good and evil in his poem "I Believe," balancing hell-on-earth with a paradise-in-Heaven, a punishing God with a rewarding God, and a suffering people with a suffering yet omnipotent Father.[38] And the poet Isaac Katzenelson paints a magnificent portrait of traditional Jewish martyrdom—the chosen fate of so many Jews—in his epic "Shlomo Jelichovski."[39] All three are powerful poems which present the traditional response to suffering in a challenging and dynamic manner.

The arguing with God tradition offered another route of response, allowing poets to voice the anger and anguish of their people. Some, like Uri Zvi Greenberg and Isaac Katzenelson, assumed the role of protesting poet of the people only reluctantly. Greenberg hesitatingly adds "a rung to the ladder of Hebrew prayer" "as a man replaces his comrade in battle" to chastise, in prophetic fashion, Israel, the nations and God.[40] Katzenelson at first refuses to heed an anonymous command to lament, then acquiesces after summoning the multitude of murdered souls to appear, screaming, before him.[41] Some spoke, feeling the weight of generations upon them,[42] others, Kadia Molodowsky, for example, assumed the role freely, on their own, without hesitation. And still others chose to protest by relating a specific incident of the Holocaust and voicing their outrage through the story's characters.

Questioning God's Justice and Indifference

But for one and all the question hurled heavenward remains the same. "Did my dear ones know that Jews have no Father in Heaven to defend them . . . that vain was the good longing, vain the warm tear and the lofty prayer? . . . ," demands Greenberg.[43] Katzenelson accuses God indirectly by protesting against Heaven's silence in his awesome ode to the martyred millions, "Song of the Murdered Jewish People."

> This is how it began, from the start . . . O heavens,
>   tell me why,
> Why must we be so shamed on this great earth?

The deaf-mute earth's eyes seem shut. But you,
    heavens, you saw,
You watched from above and yet did not collapse! . . .

Away! I will not look at you, see you, know you!
O you deceitful, tricky, lowly heavens on high. . . .

Away! Away! You deceived us, my people, my ancient
    race!
You have always deceived us, my ancestors and my
prophets!
To you, kindled by your flames, they lifted their eyes.
For you they had longed with all their hearts . . .

Don't you know us, recognize us? Have we changed so?
Are we so different? We are the same Jews we were,
Even better . . .

O blue heavens, why are you so blue and beautiful while
    we are being murdered? . . .

Millions of dying children lifted their hands to you,
    yet you were not moved!
Millions of noble mothers and fathers—yet your blue
    skin did not quiver. . . .

You watched . . . There is no God in you, false, empty
    heavens![44]

And later in the poem:

. . . Listen:
All the better that there is no God . . . To be sure,
    it's bad without Him, very bad.
But if He existed it would be even worse! Both God
    and Mila Street . . . What a combination!
O take out your children hidden in bags. Fling them,
    dash them, against the wall!
Set huge fires. Wring your hands, tear your hair, and
    leap into the flames.
There is a God! Yet such injustice, such mockery and
    such terrible shame![45]

Jacob Friedman, a survivor who made his way to Israel, poses the question for the believer in a tragic poem of a rabbi whose martyred son is held in his arms in place of the Torah scroll for the *Kol Nidrei* prayer on the night of Yom Kippur.

> Look, Father in Heaven, how I say Kol Nidrei
> This Yom Kippur Night!
> Lord God, Creator of the worlds
> A little Jew is calling to You.
> He cannot understand your ways.
> Where is Your mercy, Your justice, where?
> Or do Your worlds revolve in darkness?
> Do You not care![46]

Jacob Glatstein echoes Friedman's doubts and questions, leaving it for future generations to seek an answer while averring that no answer will ever do justice to or make sense for the lost generation of Isaac's children.

> Perplexed I shall leave
> This world of chaos,
> Where the seed of my people has been cut off,
> Without a Voice from heaven, on a blood-drenched way.
>
> Let my children's children
> Unravel this tangle,
> And I will lie among my own,
> An unrecognised one.
>
> No matter how much the scales justify,
> They will never exonerate for us the heavens.
>
> And no matter how many weeping generations will
>   howl over us,
> They will still hear our dead lips mutter.
> For we shall be always demanding,
> "Dear, beloved, Holy Name,
> It was always beyond our understanding."[47]

Grief

Questioning God's justice or attempting to penetrate the mystery of why God would allow such evil to be perpetrated against His people was perhaps the elementary or basic response to the Holocaust. Grief was another. Poem after poem is at least tinged with lament and reproach. But on occasion, as with Katzenelson, the lament serves as the terrible culmination of a horrific tragedy. In his epic lament, "Song of the Murdered Jewish People," Katzenelson voices this tragic concluding dirge:

> The end. At night, the sky is aflame. By day the smoke coils and at night it blazes out again. Awe!
> Like our beginning in the desert: A pillar of cloud by day, a pillar of fire by night.
> Then my people marched with joy and faith to a new life, and now—the end, all finished . . .
> All of us on earth have been killed, young and old. We have all been exterminated. . . .
>
> Never will the voice of Torah be heard from *yeshivoth*, synagogues, and pale students,
> Purified by study and engrossed in the Talmud . . . No, no, it was not pallor but a glow,
> Already extinguished . . . Rabbis, heads of *yeshivoth*, scholars, thin, weak prodigies,
> Masters of Talmud and Codes, small Jews with great heads, high foreheads, bright eyes—all gone.
> Never will a Jewish mother cradle a baby. Jews will not die or be born.
> Never will plaintive songs of Jewish poets be sung. All's gone, gone.
> No Jewish theater where men will laugh or silently shed a tear.
> No Jewish musicians and painters, Barcinskis, to create and innovate in joy and sorrow. . . .
> Woe is unto me, nobody is left . . . There was a people and it is no more. There was a people and it is . . . Gone . . .
> What a tale. It began in the Bible and lasted till now . . . A very sad tale.
> A tale that began with *Amalek* and concluded with the far crueller Germans . . .
> O distant sky, wide earth, vast seas, do not crush and don't destroy the wicked. Let them destroy themselves![48]

Anger and Rejection

But grief could easily turn to anger and hatred against God—even a rejection of God and of the uniquely Jewish relationship with God. The poet Itzik Manger relates a story of a *Din Torah* (lawsuit) against God in the death camp of Belshitz. Three rabbis gather to try God. The reason? "God above has not guarded His vineyard. Here is proof of it, the heaps of ash on the ground." The verdict of the rabbinic court—"Creator of the worlds, You are mighty and terrible beyond all doubt. But from the circle of true lovers of Israel, we Galicians, forever shut You out!"[49] And God is excommunicated. Such trials actually occurred in various camps during the Holocaust.[50]

I. J. Segal in his poem "Yiskor" accuses God of indifference, negligence, even outright malice toward His people, and vows, as the title suggests, remembrance.

> We shall remember, Lord God, that in these years,
> You settled with Your eternal people every old
>   score,
> You plunged us down into the deep black pit,
> And the last thread from our ancient body tore. . . .
> And with Your strong right foot kicked us,
> Where on the cold ground we lay. . . .
>
> You stood great and high in Your Almight,
> And watched with eyes that were cold grey steel,
> How they lashed to death Your people,
> And trod us under their heel.
> Our old people groveled before You on their
>   knees.
> But You were dumb.
> You would not lift Your arms to help us.
> You let the Churban Destruction come.
>
> And when the slayers had slain,
> You went coldly away.
> Your copper red beard gleamed in the sun,
> And we saw the ends of Your departing robe move
>   through the sky.
> The streets were smoke and fire, the roofs were
>   flame.
> Back in a pillar of fire and a pillar of smoke you
>   came.
>
> They thrust into our hands Your Decalogue,
> And our blood drenched it right through.
> They stifled our voice when we wanted to call,

To cry out in our agony to You.
That is what they did to Your people,
And You stood and watched them, Lord!
How they practise holiness with the axe, and love
    with the sword.

Our Ghetto town went up in flames and smoke,
And You could stand still, high and great, and
    look!
On Your Day of Reckoning with us,
You stood high and great,
And with a quiet hand locked behind us the Ghetto
    gate,
Till the morning comes.
We wait.[51]

For Segal, it is not just that God was passive in the face of injustice and oppression—God actively supported the perpetrators! When all is said and done, God stands convicted and rejected. Thus Jacob Glatstein thunders the refrain, "We received the Torah on Sinai and in Lublin we gave it back. Dead men don't praise God, the Torah was given to the living,"[52] while Uri Zvi Greenberg tells God to His face, "You know their end: that death, that terror beyond all thought . . . making clear: the time has come to disperse all parchment words, all letter combinations so that they stand in uncombinable isolation as before the giving from Mount Sinai of the Law."[53] God has rejected Israel; Israel will reject God and Torah. The world—the Jewish world in particular—is no longer the same. The Tree of Life (the Torah) has brought death for all those who held fast to it; it can no longer be cherished, it has lost its validity, its Author is a fraud: so say these poets at the nadir of their bitterness.

But even at this point, the poet still would fling prayers to God. Thus Kadia Molodowsky defiantly cries out:

O God of Mercy
For the time being
Choose another people.
We are tired of death, tired of corpses,
We have no more prayers.
For the time being
Choose another people.

We have run out of blood
For victims.
Our houses have been turned into desert,
The earth lacks space for tombstones,
There are no more lamentations
Nor songs of woe
In the ancient texts.

God of Mercy
Sanctify another land
Another Sinai
We have covered every field and stone
With ashes and holiness.
With our crones
With our young
With our infants
We have paid for each letter in your
    Commandments.

God of Mercy
Lift up your fiery brow,
Look on the peoples of the world,
Let them have the prophecies and Holy Days
Who mumble your words in every tongue.
Teach them the Deeds
And the ways of temptation.

God of Mercy
To us give rough clothing
Of shepherds who tend sheep
Of blacksmiths at the hammer
Of washerwomen, cattle slaughterers
And lower still.
And O God of Mercy
Grant us one more blessing—
Take back the gift of our separateness.[54]

"We have no more prayers"—and yet, despite its hostile tone,
Molodowsky's poem is, in fact, one more prayer.

Reconciliation

Sooner or later, a healing between Israel and God begins. Perhaps
we are in the midst of it even now, for only in recent years, long

after the fact, have Jewish thinkers broken their silence and begun to grapple in their writings with the issue of God and the Holocaust. Uri Zvi Greenberg knew that such a time would come, when God "will count the few forsaken ones, those who have survived. . . . And they who light the smallest candle of hope in their darkness will be heartened"—and he was disgusted. He saw the entire cycle of Jewish forgetting and assimilation beginning once again.[55] But for others, this healing was seen as a joy and felt as a comfort. For Jacob Glatstein, life begins anew with God and the poet as two DP refugees:

> I love my sad God,
> my brother refugee.
> I love to sit down on a stone with him
> and tell him everything wordlessly
> because when we sit like this, both
>   perplexed,
> our thoughts flow together
> in silence. . . .
>
> My poor God,
> how many prayers I've profaned,
> how many nights I've
> blasphemed him
> and warmed my frightened bones
> at the furnace of the intellect.
> And here he sits, my friend, his arm around
>   me,
> sharing his last crumb.
>
> The God of my unbelief is magnificent,
> how I love my unhappy God,
> now that he's human and unjust.
> How exalted is this proud pauper
> now that the merest child rebels
> against his word.

To this tired God, the poet asks, "How much destruction can a people suffer and still believe in rebuilding?" and while God falls asleep in his arms, the poet is left to ponder God's enigmatic answer.[56]

Glatstein expands upon this refugee image and, in another poem, directs this softer, more loving prayer-poem to God:

Shall we perhaps begin anew, small and toddling,
with a small folk?
We two, homeless wandering among the nations. . . .
Shall we perhaps go home now, you and I,
to begin again, small from the beginning?
Begin once more! Be the small God of a small
   people!
Go back, beloved God, go back to a small people! . . .

You will become closer to us,
and together we shall spin new laws,
more suitable for you and for us.

Shall we perhaps begin anew,
small and toddling,
to grow with the growing borders
of a blessed land? . . .
Shall we perhaps go home, you and I?
Shall we perhaps, unconquering, go home? . . .

Save yourself! Together with the pilgrims,
   return,
return to a small land.
Become once more the small God
of a small people.[57]

Glatstein has undertaken a remarkable odyssey, from doubt to despair, from anguish to anger, and on to reconciliation of a sort and rebirth. His intensely anthropomorphic God is far from the gods of modern philosophy and theology, but very true to classical Jewish religious thought. Perhaps his vision of a broken, anthropopathetic God, a God who is being rejuvenated as the Jewish people is rejuvenated, a God with whom one can argue, will speak to the many Jews still struggling for some sort of relationship with God after the Holocaust.

The Ultimate Prayer in Our Day

But Glatstein in these latter poems is already a believer of sorts. For many Jews, belief in God remains unattainable until a con-

frontation occurs. Only then, once a personal relationship has
been cemented by direct experience, can a Jew begin to speak of
faith and belief again. God must bring His people to a second
Sinai or risk losing them in their wanderings through the desert.
And so it is that Itzik Manger, who once yearned only to spit in
God's face,[58] asks the ultimate question of God and, with both
threats and pleas, demands the ultimate consolation:

> Like a murderer, with knife in hand
> Ambushing his victim late at night,
> I listen for your steps, O Lord, I wait;
> I, from whom you hide your smiling light;
> I, the grandson of Iscariot.
>
> I'm ready to do penance with my blood—
> Your prophets' blood still burns my fingertips . . .
> Although a shepherd, in the midst of spring,
> Is fluting silver magic with his lips
> And no one calls me to account for anything.
>
> To see you! Just to see you once.
> To know with certainty there is a You;
> To know you really crown a saint with light;
> To know with certainty your sky is blue . . .
> And then, to hide forever from your sight.
>
> I'll fling the thirty silver coins
> to be confounded with a careless wind;
> And, barefoot, Lord, I'll make my way to you
> To weep before you, like a child returned
> Whose head is heavy with the crown of sin.
>
> Like a murderer, with knife in hand
> Ambushing his victim late at night,
> I listen for your steps, O Lord, I wait;
> I, from whom you hide your smiling light;
> I, the grandson of Iscariot.[59]

The ultimate prayer in our day—no longer a plea for an end to
the Exile—is a plea to meet God face to face, to confront Him as
the Bible relates that Job was able to do.

This dream of confrontation provides the climax to a long Hebrew poem by David Shimoni. Shimoni tells the tale of a father

and son aboard a deportation train. The father tricks the son into
saving himself by jumping off the train into the forest, promising
that he will jump immediately after his son. During the son's
ordeal in the forest, he seeks God, and answers from God, without
success.

> I do not know
> if anyone heard my cries
> in that night in the dark ghetto—
> perhaps because thousands were crying and
>   wailing,
> or because the silence was so great,
> and my cry too was silent.
>
> I do not know
> if anyone heard my cry;
> but He heard, God heard,
> and never answered me. . . .
>
> at night in the wood,
> how I cried to Him, how I cried out to Him,
> to God. . . .
>
> I whispered to Him of the moving fields,
> and of the cars of death,
> the furnaces,
> of everything, of everything. . . .
>
> He did not answer me.

The son somehow survives the hardships of the forest in which he
has landed and, brought to a house, is nursed back to health by
an elderly doctor. During his feverish recovery, the boy dreams of
finally confronting God—or was it just the doctor?

> But this morning, lying half-asleep it seems,
> I was shaken broad-awake.
> A hand stroking my forehead wakened me.
> I opened eyes and saw
> a tall old man was bending over me,
> his white beard on my face
> as white and soft as wool,

his hand in mine.
Knew him at once:
"God!
At last You have answered me. You have come
  to me at last!"
And I wept.
From the day of my coming here
I had not shed one tear,
And now I wept like a stream.
I wept and I asked
about the moving fields,
the furnaces—
about everything, everything.
And asked Him why my father had deceived me,
my dear father, that holy man . . .
And asked Him why
HE   HE   HE
had done all that.
I spoke in a whisper,
for so the stars had taught me
to speak to Him.
I may have cried out suddenly,
for He, stroking my head and forehead,
said to me:
"Dear child, I am the doctor only, the doctor
  only. . . ."

Ha, ha. He the doctor only.
I am not fooled. . . .
And suddenly His face grew red,
and from His eyes the tears began to fall
upon my face.
He wept so much, He wept so much
until I pitied Him,
until my heart grew heavy with my pity,
and I stopped questioning Him.
And then He went away.

But He will come again, will come again,
He said explicitly that He would come.
And when He does, I will not let Him go,
I will not let Him go . . .

And I shall speak right out and to the
  point:
God!
Didn't I once feel pity for You?
Why don't you pity us?[60]

THE PROSE ARGUMENTS
OF ELIE WIESEL

Perhaps it is the intensely personal nature of poetry that permits
the poet to address God directly; perhaps it is the narrative and
often third-person form of the novel that prevents most novelists
from doing the same, but arguing with God appears to be far more
prevalent in the poetic tradition than in the prose. To be sure,
Sholom Aleichem's Tevye argues with God; so do some of Isaac
Bashevis Singer's characters; so does the hero in Zvi Kolitz's short
fictional work *Yossel Rakover's Appeal to God*, but these are
exceptions to the rule. However, one author, Elie Wiesel, returns to
the motif of arguing with God again and again in his works. For
many people, Elie Wiesel represents the voice of the Holocaust
generation; he stands as the most recent figure in the long line of
Jewish protesters who dared to call God to accounts. For Wiesel,
argument with God serves as the basic operative and redemptive
element in his ongoing search for a meaningful and functional
post-Holocaust interpretation of Judaism. In his plays, essays,
and novels, Wiesel has utilized argument with God in his attempt
to forge a path leading from the despair born of the Holocaust
experience to a defiant activism on behalf of oneself, humanity,
and even, perhaps, of God.

    Prior to his experience in the Holocaust, Wiesel dwelt in a world
in which God and the Jewish people were bound closely together.
The devout set their souls toward God, and God, in His own way,
sought to respond. Their world view was not simplistic or primi-
tive. The God—or God–concept—of Wiesel's childhood world was a
complex one, the product of centuries of refinement and interpretation, a heterogeneous mixing of biblical, rabbinic, kabbalistic,
and hasidic thought. But as a young inmate in the death camps,

Wiesel endured firsthand exerience of overwhelming injustice and suffering.

In his premier work, the autobiographical *Night*, Wiesel documents his loss of faith in the flames and smoke of the crematoria:

> For the first time, I felt revolt rise up in me. Why should I bless His name? The eternal, Lord of the Universe, the All-Powerful and Terrible, was silent. What had I to thank Him for?[61]

> Never shall I forget that night. . . . Never shall I forget that smoke. Never shall I forget the little faces of the children, whose bodies I saw turned into wreathes of smoke beneath a silent blue sky.

> Never shall I forget those flames which consumed my faith forever. . . .

> Never shall I forget those moments which murdered my God and my soul and turned my dreams to dust. . . . Never.[62]

> How I sympathized with Job! I did not deny God's existence, but I doubted His absolute justice.[63]

Wiesel's experience of theodicy during the Holocaust is exactly the problem that perplexes so many post-Holocaust Jews still: Where was God—or at least, where was the manifestation of God's justice and compassion—during the Holocaust? God's apathetic absence haunts Wiesel and the heroes of his works. God observed the Holocaust but did nothing. Time and again Wiesel asserts that the Holocaust was the trial and, in a sense, the death, of God. God should be judged for His silence.[64] Faith in God and, in a certain way, God Himself, die with the boy on the gallows in *Night*, with the death of all the victims.[65]

The question must be asked: How can Wiesel speak of God both as One dead and as One still alive? The contradiction is itself the answer, for Wiesel's approach to God is rooted in paradox. The use of paradox is, for Wiesel, the most apt way of expressing the post-Holocaust Jewish experience, one in which the relationship between God and Israel remains unchanged and yet radically different. The paradox is symbolic. It depicts both the deep gulf that separates God from Israel and the ties that continue to bind the two together. It is the expression of what Jews have experienced and of what Jews most desire. The experience of the Holocaust demands a confrontation with God.

For Wiesel, the centuries of suffering, culminating in the Holocaust, present an overwhelming obstacle to faith in the traditional Jewish sense. For Wiesel, the smoke of Auschwitz has obscured the view of Sinai. Sinai remains, but so too does the cloud that envelops it. Wiesel can disregard neither one nor the other. Both experiences must be accounted for, and paradox is perhaps the only conjunction capable of doing justice to both. Wiesel himself refuses to resolve his paradoxical statements about God. He lives with this paradox and, in his works, urges us to learn to accept it as well.

Wiesel's use of paradox also leads him to arguing with God. Wiesel's paradox, based as it is on two seemingly contradictory experiences, serves as a description of the situation that God has allowed to occur, and His indictment for having allowed it to occur. Wiesel has long been familiar with this tradition of arguing with God. He grew up with it. It was an undifferentiated part of his schooling and life. Years later, after the Holocaust, Wiesel returned to study the concept.[66] His cantata *Ani Maamin* links this God-concept directly to the experience of the Holocaust.

In *Ani Maamin*, past and present, legend and reality, are brought together by Wiesel to create a powerful modern midrash to help account for God's absence and lack of activity during the Holocaust. In this reworking of the midrashic legend found in Lamentations *Rabbah*, Wiesel sets a heavenly confrontation between the Patriarchs and God during the time of the Holocaust. The Patriarchs come to earth to visit the Holocaust Kingdom to collect voices of suffering and bring them before the Throne of God, to attempt to persuade God to intercede.[67] Using classic midrashic-style arguments, each Patriarch argues in turn.[68] The plaintiffs argue, but without effect, and all the while, the chorus—the Jewish people past, present, and future—lend their voices to the Patriarchs' suit with the laments and questions of the ages. But God remains silent.[69]

To God's defense comes an angelic voice urging submission, patience, and acquiescence.[70] The Patriarchs continue to dispute, but they realize they have been vanquished. Knowing the truth of the matter—that God knows what is happening to Israel but chooses to do nothing—they resolve to tell the victims to cease praying and hoping, because God refuses to act.[71] On the brink of despair, the Patriarchs rebel against God's will and prepare to abandon Heaven to join the victims in their fate.

The Patriarchs have attempted to intercede on behalf of the present generation: now it is the steadfastness of the present generation that inspires the Patriarchs, forces tears to collect in God's eyes, and finally causes God to break into unrestrained weeping. The Holocaust draws to a close.[72] Their mission successful, Abraham, Isaac, and Jacob leave Heaven buoyed by the hope given them by their children. They leave alone, yet not alone. God accompanies them "weeping, smiling, whispering: *Nitzhuni banai,* my children have defeated me, they deserve my gratitude."[73] *Ani Maamin* concludes not with God's silent apathy, but with His compassion and His empathy for human suffering. Wiesel's God is not a remote, omnipotent God but an anthropopathetic God in need of human redemption.

Of this old/new God, hints have been given in Wiesel's novels. God in imprisoned with the prisoners;[74] He is executed with the victims;[75] He is with the dead in their graves;[76] He accompanies the children;[77] He awaits redemption through His creatures.[78] God is affected—and afflicted—by what happens to, and what is done by, humanity.

Wiesel's God remains a caring God. Yet Wiesel's vision—his recreation and revival of the anthropopathetic God—is tempered by the reality of the Holocaust. God has spoken and His word continues to be heard, but "So does the silence of his dead children."[79] Wiesel's love of God and his presentation of God's response to the Holocaust are never allowed to obscure the fact of God's apathetic inactivity, nor can they ever absolve God of His guilt. The modern Jew, like Abraham, Isaac, and Jacob, must turn to God in love *and* in anger, with faith *and* with questions. Yet when all is said and done, no answer to the questions will be forthcoming. "Perhaps some day someone will explain how, on the level of man, Auschwitz was possible; but on the level of God, it will forever remain the most disturbing of mysteries."[80] Wiesel is, above all, a realist.

In *Ani Maamin,* the arguments of the Patriarchs are quashed by an angelic voice urging submission to God's inscrutable will.[81] The voice is like that which confronted and confounded Job; it is the voice of Nahum of Gamzu and of Akiba; it is the voice of the prayer book; it is also the voice of Sam/Satan in Wiesel's play *The Trial of God.*

In *The Trial of God*, a wandering troupe of *Purimshpielers* (Purim actors), whose ill-timed visit lands them in Shamgorod between two pogroms, joins the local survivors to convene—in jest and yet in earnest—a *bet din* (a Jewish law court) with a suit against God. The players serve as presiding rabbis (judges); Berish, the innkeeper and a survivor, acts as God's prosecutor; and a stranger, Sam/Satan, mysteriously appears to play the role of God's defense attorney.

The play's title is actually a misnomer. It is not so much a trial of God as it is a trial of the two major traditions of the proper Jewish attitude toward suffering. Shamgorod represents the Holocaust in microcosm. The source of inspiration for the play is an actual trial of God that Wiesel witnessed in the death camps.[82] In Shamgorod, as in the Holocaust, God's presence is conspicuously absent even though His people are being annihilated. But in Shamgorod, God's emissary is present in the character of Sam/Satan.

As the trial progresses, Sam/Satan demands to know of Berish:

What do you know of God that enables you to denounce Him? You turn your back on Him—then you describe Him! Why? Because you witnessed a pogrom? Think of our ancestors, who, throughout centuries, mourned over the massacre of their beloved ones and the ruin of their homes—and yet they repeated again and again that God's ways are just. Are we worthier than they were? Wiser? Purer? Are we more pious than the rabbis of York, the students of Magenza? More privileged than the dreamers of Saloniki, the Just of Prague and Drohobitz? Do we possess more rights than they did over heaven or truth? After the destruction of the Temple of Jerusalem, our forefathers wept and proclaimed *umipnei khataenou*—it's all because of our sins. Their descendants said the same thing during the Crusades. And the Holy Wars. The same thing during the pogroms. And now you want to say something else? Does the massacre of Shamgorod weigh more than the burning of the Sanctuary? Is the ruin of your homes a more heinous crime than the ransacking of God's city? Does the death of your community imply a greater meaning than the disappearance of the communities of

Zhitomir, Nemirov, Tlusk and Berditchev? Who are you to make comparisons or draw conclusions? Born in dust, you are nothing but dust.[83]

But Berish is not intimidated by this invocation of faithful ancestors. He responds by pressing his charge that God has been derelict—now as in the past—in His exercise of justice:

And they kept quiet? Too bad—then I'll speak for them too. For them, too, I'll demand justice. For the widows of Jerusalem and the orphans of Betar. For the slaves of Rome and Capadoccia. And for the destitute of Oman and the victims of Koretz. I'll shout for them, against Him I'll shout. To you, judges, I'll shout, for them, against Him I'll shout. To you, judges, I'll shout, "Tell Him what He should not have done; tell Him to stop the bloodshed now. Discharge your duties without fear!"[84]

Begun under the shadow of one pogrom, the trial draws to its inconclusive conclusion under the clouds of another impending pogrom. This time all are threatened with death. In this setting Berish makes his final statement: "I lived as a Jew, and it is as a Jew that I die—and it is as a Jew that, with my last breath, I shall shout my protest to God! And because the end is near, I shall shout louder! Because the end is near, I'll tell Him that He's more guilty than ever!"[85]

Sam/Satan disagrees but remains unperturbed. "God is just," he says, "and His ways are just."[86] When pressed by the "chief justice," he adds:

He [God] created the world and me without asking for my opinion; He may do with both whatever He wishes. Our task is to glorify Him, to praise Him, to love Him—in spite of ourselves. . . .

Faith in God must be as boundless as God Himself. If it exists at the expense of man, too bad. God is eternal, man is not.[87]

As the pogromchiks storm the inn, the judges (but not Berish) beseech Sam/Satan as one of the Hidden Thirty-six *Tzaddikim* (Righteous Saints) to intercede with God to save them. But then

Sam reveals himself as Satan (in Hebrew, the Adversary), and all are lost.

The startling revelation of Sam's true identity masks Wiesel's even more startling interpretation of what he considers to be the proper Jewish response to injustice. For Wiesel, suffering should be met by argument with and defiance against God. Submission to God's will in the belief that whatever happens is ultimately for the best and the acceptance of suffering as atonement for sins committed represent the mainstream teaching of rabbinic Judaism on the subject. The fact that Sam/Satan advocates such a position renders it false, null, and void. Satan is not so much God's emissary as he is man's adversary. This much is clear in that he uses the mainstream rabbinic response to suffering to deceive his victims and deflect them from their legitimate pursuit of justice. Wiesel apparently is saying that submission to suffering is wrong, that it has robbed us of integrity time and again, that we have been deceiving ourselves by castigating ourselves instead of God for our sufferings.

For Wiesel, the violence-prone existence of the Jewish people, typified by Shamgorod and climaxing with the Holocaust, must lead to rebellion against the doctrine of u'mipnei hata'einu—for our sins are we punished. While earlier outbreaks of anti-Jewish violence may have allowed the on account of our sins doctrine to survive, they did not allow it to go unchallenged. But now, for many Jews, the fact of the Holocaust has rendered the on account of our sins doctrine all but obsolete. It is an obscenity and an affront to both God and the victims to suggest that the six million died as punishment for sins committed. Other modern Jewish thinkers concur with Wiesel in renouncing this doctrine.[88]

Wiesel, in *The Trial of God*, acts as a popularizer of this modern rebellion against the on account of our sins doctrine and the cult of submissive martyrdom. With his dramatic and startling juxtaposition of the two basic attitudes toward suffering in the Jewish tradition, he attempts to force his audience (the people) to choose sides. There is no doubt as to where he believes our allegiance should lie. It should be, as always, with the victims—in this case with Berish and the judges who would rule in his favor. But the trial does not, cannot, reach its conclusion. Death dissolves the session. However, as Mendel, the presiding judge at the trial of God, observes just prior to the pogrom:

Who will continue the thread of our tale? The last page will not be written. But the one before? It is up to us to prepare testimony for future generations. . . .[89]

. . . The verdict will be announced by someone else, at a later stage. For the trial will continue—without us.[90]

Wiesel's Holocaust survivor characters constitute the most recent link in the chain of victims as witnesses/prosecutors/judges. In *The Gates of the Forest*, the survivor-protagonist Gregor/Gavriel returns to confront traditional Judaism in the person of the hasidic *rebbe*, to force him to acknowledge the now-completed verdict against God.[91] Gregor tells the *rebbe* a story from his past:

In a concentration camp, one evening after work, a rabbi called together three of his colleagues and convoked a special court. Standing with his head held high before them, he spoke as follows: "I intend to convict God of murder, for He is destroying His people and the Law He gave them from Mount Sinai. I have irrefutable proof in my hands. Judge without fear or sorrow or prejudice . . . ." The trial proceeded in due legal form, with witnesses for both sides with pleas and deliberations. The unanimous verdict: "Guilty."

. . . After all, *He* had the last word. On the day after the trial, He turned the sentence against His judges and accusers. They, too, were taken off to the slaughter.[92]

But after having established that God is guilty and that rebellion is justified, Wiesel tries to provide an alternative, a new way of response. "God is guilty," admits the *rebbe*, "He has become the ally of evil, of death, of murder, but the problem is still not solved. I ask you a question and dare you to answer: 'What is there left for us to do? . . . In what direction are we to go? Where is salvation, or at least hope, to be found?' "[93]

The answer, as Wiesel perceives it, is expressed through faithful defiance. The *rebbe* tells Gregor:

"Who says that power comes from a shout, an outcry rather than from a prayer? From anger rather than compassion? Where do you find certainties when you claim to have denied them? The man who goes singing to death is the brother of the

man who goes to death fighting. A song on the lips is worth a
dagger in the hand. I take this song and make it mine. Do you
know what the song hides? A dagger, an outcry. . . . There is joy
as well as fúry in the hasid's dancing. It's his way of proclaim-
ing: 'You don't want me to dance; too bad, I'll dance anyhow.
You've taken away every reason for singing, but I shall sing. . . .
You didn't expect my joy, but here it is; yes, my joy will rise up; it
will submerge you.'"[94]

This defiance is an expression of rebellion and argument, but
also one of faith. It is, above all, an expression of hope, the hope
needed to combat despair—despair of God and of humanity—
which Wiesel perceives as being the fundamental threat to continued Jewish existence after Auschwitz. Over and over again,
Wiesel advocates faithful defiance as the post-Holocaust expression of a Jew's relationship with God. In *Ani Maamin*, the Patriarchs, on the brink of despair, rebel against God and defiantly
leave Heaven to join their children on earth. In *The Trial of God*,
Berish dies protesting his faith in God and his rebellion against
God's will with words reminiscent of a tale told of a Jewish victim
who sought to escape the Spanish Inquisition.[95] In *Zalmen, or the
Madness of God*, the Rabbi is challenged to rebel against the
oppression of his people in the Soviet Union by speaking out in
defiance of the authorities and the apparent will of God.[96] In *The
Gates of the Forest*, laughter and the refusal to bow down to God's
will, the *hasid's* song and dance, are all signs of defiance.[97] Greg-
or's *kaddish* marks not his return to faith, but his acceptance of
faith as part of his defiance.

Faithful defiance is present in singing and in not singing,[98] in
prayer and ritual observance, and in the refusal to pray or to
observe the traditions.[99] It exists in the last prayer of the believer
and in the death as a believing Jew of a nonbeliever.[100] These
paradoxical expressions are essential to the continued function-
ing of the covenantal relationship in which God must remain
capable of being addressed and of being held accountable for the
people's experience of suffering and perceived divine injustice.
Elie Wiesel *is* a religious Jew. Argument and defiance are his ways
of expressing faith and hope after Auschwitz.

Just as Wiesel turns to faithful defiance to express his sense of
outrage and injustice against God for the Holocaust, so too he

utilizes defiant activism to express his rebellion against God's apparent will (that is, the submission to fate) when such submission would mean that human beings would suffer. This activism is both the defiance of a silent, inactive God and of an apathetic humanity. It is also an expression of hope and faith in God and in humanity. Wiesel writes:

> To be a Jew means to serve God by espousing man's cause, to plead for man while recognizing his need of God. And to opt for the Creator *and* His creation, refusing to pit one against the other. Of course man must interrogate God, as did Abraham; articulate his anger, as did Moses; and shout his sorrow, as did Job. But only the Jew opts for Abraham—who questions—*and* for God—who is questioned . . . Only the Jew knows that he may oppose God as long as he does so in defense of His creation.[101]

Even to those Jews who have become doubters or even unbelievers as a result of the Holocaust, Wiesel offers an alternative to despair and desertion, namely the path of a Jewishly-based defiant activism on both the personal and political levels.[102] "Maybe God is dead, but man is alive," one of Wiesel's characters states. "Suffering is given to the living . . . it is man's duty to make it cease."[103]

Wiesel's activism plays the central, redemptive role in *Ani Maamin*. In *Ani Maamin*, the Patriarchs serve not only as models for their arguments with God, but also as exemplars of Wiesel's defiant activism. Only as a result of the Patriarchs' defiant decision to forsake Heaven and to join their fate with that of their children—which in turn combines with the victims' own faith and hope born of the example of the Patriarchs—is an argument of sufficient weight produced. This argument, more potent than either the Patriarchs or Israel could muster individually, is alone capable of moving God to tears. In the original midrash of Lamentations *Rabbah*, Rachel moves God to tears by identifying with the plight of Leah her sister and their shared desire to wed Jacob. In *Ani Maamin*, the place of Rachel's singularly efficacious argument is taken by the Patriarchs' identification of their fate with that of their children—and Israel's identification of their hope and faith in the example of the Patriarchs.

The world in which Wiesel urges activism remains unchanged in many ways from the Holocaust world. As in the Holocaust, God is silent and inactive; nonexistent as it were—if activity is a mark of Being. Humankind, now as then, is by and large apathetic toward and uninvolved with the suffering of others.

This unredeemed world is the setting of Wiesel's play *Zalmen, or the Madness of God.* The drama focuses on an ailing Jewish community in a city of the Soviet Union sometime after the death of Stalin. Warned by the authorities that their synagogue will be host to a visiting troupe of actors from the West and told not to allow any incidents to occur, the community reaches the nadir of despair. Hope for aid is tantalizingly close with the presence of the Westerners, but the years of submission, surrender, and fear cause the Jewish community to despair of hope. The communal leaders decide to comply with the demands of the authorities, all, that is, except for Zalmen the beadle. Zalmen is "the Teacher," whose function is to enlarge, stir up, and awaken the heart of the hero to the perception of wider horizons and responsibilities, to champion the cause of the sufferers and to act in their behalf. [104] In this case, Zalmen rekindles in the aged Rabbi a prophetic fire; "madness" compels him to action, to speak out against the oppression of his people by informing the Western guests of the plight of the Jewish people in the Soviet Union.[105] Zalmen's "madness" works; despair and submission to fate are transformed, through action, into defiance and hope.

This defiant activism, based on an empathetic identification with the victims of suffering, recurs in many of Wiesel's novels and essays. It is the cardinal message of "the Teacher," who, in one guise or another, appears in so many of Wiesel's works.[106]

In *The Oath*, the hero, Azriel, comes to realize that he must abandon his community's quest to "force the Messiah's arrival" because the means would have nullified the end. On the eve of a pogrom, Moshe "the Teacher" exhorts the Jews of Kolvillag to break the cycle of Jewish history by swearing a terrible oath *not* to bear witness to the world concerning the pogrom that is about to occur.[107] Azriel, the sole survivor of the pogrom, is condemned by this oath to eternal silence, though this is mitigated by a *rebbe* who sets down conditional terms for the release from the oath.

Instead of maintaining his silence to the grave, Azriel must spend his days like some Jewish Ancient Mariner, looking for the right person to whom to tell his tale, through whom he can obtain release from the oath of silence. That point arrives, many decades later, when Azriel meets a young man, a child of Holocaust survivors, who stands on the suicidal brink of despair. Azriel realizes that to save this single life he must break the oath imposed upon him by Moshe his Teacher, for only then will he be able to fulfill the teachings of Moshe. For Moshe had taught:

> What is the Messiah if not man transcending his solitude in order to make his fellow-man less solitary? To turn a single human being back toward life is to prevent the destruction of the world.[108]

> Any messiah in whose name men are tortured can only be a false messiah. It is by diminishing evil . . . that one builds the city of the sun. It is by helping the person who looks at you with tears in his eyes, needing help, needing you or at least your presence, that you may attain perfection.[109]

Thus, although mad Moshe's dream of "hastening the end" by means of the oath of silence might have been successful had Azriel kept his peace, Azriel nonetheless decides to take the risk of ruining that venture for the sake of saving the young man's life. If breaking the vow to save a life means that the Messiah will be delayed, then it is worth the price. Were the price other than this, the Messiah would be a false messiah. The roadway of the Messiah cannot be built on suffering nor by indifference to suffering; it can only be built by rebellion against suffering and the active concern for the alleviation of the suffering of others. For Wiesel, the means are as important—even more important—than the end itself.[110] Everything, even the redemption of God, depends upon how we act in relationship with other human beings.

What, then, is Wiesel's post-Holocaust vision? First, everything centers on how one relates to one's fellow human beings. This, for Wiesel, is primary. Second, by freeing oneself from the prison of one's own suffering and opening up to the suffering of others, one exercises all potential as a human being. By acting to help others, one is "freeing the sparks"; that is, one teaches an example by living an example. Third, such work may lead to the "breaking the chains of the Messiah in exile"—God Himself may be affected, redeemed as it were, by our actions. But underlying this final concept is a significant demurrer, of great importance for nonreligious Jews and for Wiesel as teacher. God's will, His presence or nonpresence during the Holocaust, is forever a mystery, a question with no answer.[111] Thus, while Wiesel, as a religious Jew, connects human activism with the divine redemption, it is equally important for him that those Jews alienated from God also continue to live and act as Jews.[112] The final, ultimate destination of Wiesel's quest remains an unanswerable mystery; hence, at least for the time being, the means become the end. By acting as Wiesel advocates, we bring about our own redemption, even if it occurs piecemeal, a little at a time, with lapses and with leaps. Whether God can be redeemed or not is ultimately beyond our knowing. What matters today, in this post-Holocaust world, is that we do not close ourselves off in indifference and despair, but rather that we live with hope in spite of God and in spite of humankind's long history of inhumanity.[113]

Wiesel's post-Holocaust Judaism builds upon this universal humanistic base. Echoing Pascal and the ancient Rabbis, Wiesel has described Jewish history as a love affair with God, one in which "there are quarrels and reconciliations, more quarrels and more reconciliations . . . yet neither God nor the Jews ever gave up on the other.[114] Many events in Jewish history would have been cause enough to warrant a total rejection of God, yet this has not happened. Instead, Wiesel urges a turn to defiance: arguing with or questioning God while adhering to the Covenant in spite of Him. A Jew today must argue with God,[115] but that argument is, and must be, a two-way interrogation in which the questions put to God rebound to the asker.[116] "To be a Jew therefore is to ask a question—a thousand questions, yet always the same—of society, of others, of oneself, of death and of God."[117] As a result of this "endless engagement with God, we proved to Him that we are more patient than He, more compassionate too. In other words, we did not give up on Him either. For this is the essence of being Jewish: never to give up—never to yield to despair."[118]

The Jew is both an eternal skeptic and a perpetual rebel, living and hoping in defiance of God and humankind. To be a Jew in this post-Holocaust world is to face the human condition realistically but without despair. Wiesel sees the Jewish mission as a number of concentric rings, beginning with oneself and proceeding through one's identification with the Jewish people to embrace the whole world.[119] Argument with God, rooted in the tradition of the Bible and the Rabbis, and defiance of God and humanity expressed by the way in which we live our lives—these are the signposts that mark the way of Wiesel's continuing search for a meaningful response to the Holocaust.

CONCLUSION

Such is the tenor of our contemporary *payyetanim*, a mere taste since we have but grazed the surface of their many works. These post-Holocaust expressions may well set the tone for contemporary Jewish piety. Beaten down but defiant, loving yet bruised, believing still a little but growing increasingly skeptical, modern Jews may find argument to be the only type of prayer possible to express. And even the skeptics may pray thusly! Paradoxically, the prayer of the doubter or disbeliever becomes the more powerful, more intensely demanding argument.

These poetic old-new, post-Holocaust theodicies, the most recent link in a chain of the Jewish tradition of arguing with God, speak directly to the modern Jewish heart and mind. No other response—save that of the normative tradition (for those who can still accept it)—comes close to reconciling the conflict between the Jewish reality (the suffering of the Exile) and the Jewish ideal (history will prove God just when He redeems Israel). Through argument one stands firmly rooted in the real, and grabs the ideal by the scruff of its neck and gives a good, hard shake. This is the modern prayer of protest—a cry of anger, anguish, doubt, and despair that urges renewed fervency on the ancient yearnings and impatience for redemption and vindication. As in the past, these prayers must be incorporated into the liturgy so that prayers portraying the Jewish ideal again are balanced by prayers protesting against the suffering of the innocent. It is important for God to hear these dark prayers; it is even more important for human beings to enunciate them.

Rabbis and scholars once voiced these prayers of protest on behalf of the people. Today, in one of those ironies of history, our spokespersons are once again primarily charismatics—poets and authors—to whom the modern rabbi has taken a subordinate position, being encumbered with the tasks of defending and justifying the God-concept of the traditional liturgy and theology. That which the prophets were able to provide after the First Destruction and the Rabbis and their disciples after the Second, we lack after the Third. Perhaps the experience is still too fresh. But until such time as these healer-thinkers come to be, these poets and authors shall serve as beacons in our search for justice, God and relationship. As David Roskies notes:

> Like the rabbis in Talmudic times who called on Jeremiah, Moses and Rachel to help them weep over the destruction of the Second Temple, contemporary Jewry, overwhelmed by its losses, has erased all previous distinctions [of orthodox and secularist] to reclaim the modernists for its own liturgy of remembrance.[120]

Thus Bialik turns up in the new Conservative High Holy Day prayer book, while Glatstein occupies a place in the litany of laments of the new Reform prayer book for Rosh Hashanah and Yom Kippur.[121] And few *Yom HaShoah* services do not include selections from the works of our modern elegists. Roskies attributes this to "the need for continuity in the aftermath of the last Great Destruction," and certainly this is true; but even more, these poets represent a continuity of their own—as the transmitters of the tradition of arguing with God from a world of traditional values to a world based on secularism and science. Still demanding everything of God but, based on His past performance record, expecting little, praying to a silent God who just might be listening, and yearning only for some tangible sign, our modern *payyetanim* may come to frame the religious discussion and religious mentality for many Jews, all survivors in a post-Holocaust world. Echoing their voices, we may yet find ourselves "turning back to the old Jewish God, not so much the God of orthodoxy or even the God our fathers worshiped, but a God inseparable from Jewish fate, a God with whom one pleads and quarrels."[122]

Rabbi Levi Yitzhak of Berditchev once prayed: "Master of the Universe! I do not ask that You reveal to me the mysteries of Your ways—I could not comprehend them. I do not want to know why I suffer; my only desire is to know that I suffer for Your sake." In our day this is no longer enough. A more contemporary scholar, Rabbi Judah L. Magnes, amended Rabbi Levi Yitzhak's prayer thus: "I do not want to know why I suffer . . . but only if You know that I suffer."[123]

We ask both more and less of God today. More because we need a direct encounter with God; less because we no longer expect sustenance, protection, or other miracles from His hand. But whether questioning the justice of the apparent judgments of the Judge, questioning the existence of the Judge Himself by demanding a hearing in His Presence, or asserting that there is neither Judge nor judgment, modern Jewry continues to wrestle with its distinctly Jewish God in a world in which, for many, the lack of God's presence is felt all too keenly.

PERSONAL AFTERWORD: WHAT ARGUING WITH GOD MEANS FOR ME

INTRODUCTION

Why a Personal Afterword?

"Of making many books there is no end," wrote Kohelet (Ecclesiastes 12:12), and surely what was true in his day is even more so in ours. I pity the forests their trees when I consider the number of books printed each year. Obviously, there must be a need for all these books, and undoubtedly each book is as precious to its author as this one is to me, but nonetheless, as Kohelet wrote, there is no limit to their number, and I wanted to do something more than simply pen yet one more scholarly study. Because I am a rabbi and wish to teach by personal example, because I believe that all study ultimately should be applied study and especially that theology (if that is what I am doing) should be lived, I felt it important to conclude my book with a statement of what my ten-year study of the concept of arguing with God means to me personally. This final chapter, then, is something on a different order from the rest of the book. It is my personal spiritual statement; my personal exploration of the concept and how I apply it in

231

my life as a Jew in the world today. It was important for me to write this afterword; I hope it will be of some value to you as well.

Let me begin with several qualifying reservations. My thoughts only constitute a working toward a solution, not a solution per se. If solutions do exist—and I am not sure they do—they are for each individual and each generation to discover. It is also important to realize that there is no single authoritative response, nor am I offering my ideas as such. Furthermore, what satisfies me today, at this time in my life, may not suffice tomorrow.

Let me also state that, as a liberal Jew, I accept the following:

- There are only interpretations of Torah but no one Torah truth. The oral Torah represents the living thought of the Jewish people through the ages.

- Both the written and oral Torahs are the possessions of all Jews. Their interpretations are myriad and not confined to nor controlled by any one group.

- I cannot believe all that Jews once believed, nor can I believe as Jews once believed.

- All of tradition has a claim on me and I try to be receptive to its totality. My choices are best made when done on the basis of knowledge.

- *I* am *my* measure for what is meaningful *to me*. I have the right to disbelieve and to dissent from tradition, but I also respect the traditions and try to honor the principle of the unity of the Jewish people, *k'lal Yisrael.*

- My confrontation with the inherited teachings and traditions is the way by which I create my own form of Jewish life and spirituality.

THE PROBLEM AND THE NEED

If I had to define my current relationship with God, I would label it "agnostic mysticism." In Jewish terms, the agnostic mystic is one who still covers his eyes with his hand while reciting the Sh'ma, but who keeps his eyes open nonetheless and peers between the cracks of his fingers hoping to sneak a peek at the Divine Presence. The agnostic mystic yearns to "taste and see" God's presence but will not be placated by an I–Thou experience or assuaged by a still small voice. The agnostic mystic has too much skepticism to be swayed from his mystic quest by anything other than an event on the order of a second Sinai. The agnostic mystic's quest is thoroughly empirical. It can end only with a public face to face encounter with God—with the Redemption. And in the meantime, the agnostic mystic lives with the pain of the knowledge of his separation from the Divine Presence and of the hiatus between the accounts of a miraculous past and the miracleless present.

For me, the concept of Galut—Exile—speaks most powerfully and meaningfully. Galut is more than the exile of the people Israel from its land; it also more significantly represents the separation of Israel from the God or, perhaps better stated, the withdrawal of God's presence from the midst of His world and His people. This sense of Galut has nothing to do with the return of the Jewish people to the land and the rebirth of the Jewish state. Even with the existence of the State of Israel, the Jewish people remains in a state of spiritual Galut, as does the whole world.

According to Jewish tradition, as long as the Temple stood and Israel dwelt in her Land, a unique physical and spiritual bond existed linking the world, through the Land of Israel, through Jerusalem, through the Temple, to God, and through the peoples of the world, through the people Israel, through its service, to God. The Temple represented the *axis mundi*, the connecting link between Heaven and earth. Once that physical tie was shattered, the spiritual dimension perforce underwent a major transformation. To be sure, the people were still bound in love to God through the Covenant—and the Rabbis taught that prayer was now to be regarded as even more efficacious than sacrifices—but nonetheless the state of Galut meant the loss of the sense of intense physical intimacy with God. To pursue the love motif: Israel was still beloved of God, but God had withdrawn His presence, had gone away, for an unspecified time. Thus, to pray for a restoration of the Temple and its cult, as traditional Jews still do, was to pray for a restoration of a full, intimate, and immediate relationship with God; it was to pray for an end to physical *and* spiritual exile.

An agnostic mystic like myself deeply desires to feel wholehearted in prayer and through prayer to be united with God's presence. But too many questions and doubts stand in my mind's (or heart's) way. That is why the tradition of arguing with God speaks to my deepest needs and concerns. This tradition asks the right questions of God; its prayers demand all the right things of God. Most of the time, for example, I cannot recite the prayer "Mi Khamokha" ("Who is Like You?"), which celebrates God's redemptive act at the Sea of Reeds, without asking what God has been doing since that miraculous day. But, through study, I know that previous generations have asked the same questions. They ask it for me as well, and this comforts me. On most occasions, I cannot recite the petitionary prayers of the *Amidah*. (Perhaps it is first recited silently to allow for conscientious objectors?) How can I ask God for "small items" like understanding, sustenance, health, forgiveness, and peace when for centuries the petitions for the "big item," for redemption, have gone unheeded? Although I often can still thank God for the gifts of Creation, the gifts of life, and the gift of the Covenant, most of the time I cannot think to ask anything of God other than to add my voice to the ages-old petition for justice. The tradition of arguing with God focuses my intention (*kavanah*) on this fundamental issue. It is hoped that it focuses God's attention on it as well. But regardless, it helps ease my spiritual pain. Knowing that previous generations have felt similarly both confirms the intensity of my yearnings for God's appearance, which constitute my mystic aspect, and also soothes the uniqueness of my equally intense doubts, which constitute my agnostic side. It is good to know that I belong to a chain of tradition, that my feelings are not an aberration of the Jewish religious spirit.

I have always been puzzled and somewhat dismayed at how we Jews remember our history. To me it is clear that Jewish memory is quite distinct from Jewish history. But the Jewish people has survived, at least in part, by transforming the events of Jewish history into an easily remembered myth. The mythic history then replaces true history as the Jewish memory. This "myth-making" is perhaps most clearly articulated in a passage in the Pesah Haggadah dealing with the Exodus from Egypt. In this one passage,[1] all of the myth's basic components are presented: (a) "Blessed be He who keeps His promise to Israel . . . for the Holy One . . . calculated the end [of the time of Israel's bondage], to do that which He swore to Abraham. . . ." From the earliest times, God controls history according to His plan, and when the time is right, He will intervene to save His people. (b) "For it was not one individual alone who arose to destroy us. In every generation they arise against us to destroy us." With some exaggeration but also with justifiable realism, history is portrayed only as a series of persecutions. (c) "But the Holy One . . . saves us from their hand." Just as Jews are commanded to regard themselves as if personally redeemed from Egypt, so too for all subsequent persecutions. In each generation God alone, not Moses nor any later leader, redeems His people. God's role in history is magnified even as the human role is denigrated.

The key point of the myth is the way in which history is presented in order to be remembered. In the Pesah Hagaddah, God appears in complete control; He is the sole agent of Israel's redemption. Israel in Egypt is wholly faithful and true to its heritage; Egypt is archetypically evil, wholly deserving of God's punishment. Excised from the Jewish memory are the subtleties of the Book of Exodus and the Midrash, which discuss Israel's adoption of Egyptian mores, and which relate the ambivalence of Moses and Israel to God and God's plans.

Hanukkah suffers a similar fate in Jewish mythmaking. Unlike the Book of Maccabees, the prayer for Hanukkah, which is inserted both in the *Amidah* and in the Grace after Meals, gives God all the credit for that which Mattityahu and his sons accomplished. Furthermore, in the myth, Hanukkah is remembered not as a civil war that pitted a traditionalist coalition of Jews against radical Hellenistic Jews, but rather as a conflict between the faithful Jewish people and the godless, evil empire of Greece (not Syria). The holiday of Purim is similarly transformed. In the Book of Esther, the Jews are saved solely by the actions of Mordechai and Esther, but in its *Amidah* and Grace after Meals prayers, God is the redeemer and savior.

The way in which the history of these holidays is remembered evinces the triumph of the Deuteronomic and Akiban schools in normative Judaism. History, according to this stream of thought, is God's to shape. All that happens is ultimately for good. Suffering, when perceived to be warranted, comes in the wake of sins committed, as loving chastisements; when perceived to be unwarranted, it is but a test of love. But there is no injustice in what happens to Israel because God *is* perfect. Protest, doubt, and arguing with God therefore can only be seen as rebellion against God's will.

Despite the normative position of the Deuteronomic and Akiban views of history and suffering in Jewish tradition, they are not authoritative. Argument with God has persisted as an alternate but recognizable stream of Jewish thought from biblical sources down through the ages to the modern era. Argument with God takes a very different view of Jewish suffering and Jewish history, even though its premises are the same as those of the normative tradition. History belongs to God. God is just, but all of Israel's suffering is not warranted nor should it be meekly accepted. Suffering cannot be wholly accounted for as either divine tests or loving discipline. It is simply unjust, in whole or in part. And so a protest can be lodged with God the Just Judge against God the Ruler of History. Ultimately it was believed that the Redemption would vindicate Israel. But that was also what the normative tradition sought, only by different means. There it was expressed through total trust (*emunah sheleimah*) in God's plan and by submission to His will. In the arguing with God tradition it was expressed through protest, defiance, and impatience. In fact, the two attitudes were but different sides of the same coin.

Only in our day has the nature of the Jewish argument with God changed. In the past, the argument was raised in the context of a world in which God's existence and power, not to mention His justice, were indisputable. But in the post Holocaust world, the dilemma of theodicy has been compounded by the secular bent of the modern world which fuels the fires of doubt with scientific and humanistic challenges to traditional religious beliefs.

In the past, suffering elicited a cry to see God's justice manifest itself; in the post-Holocaust world, many people yearn to know first and foremost that God exists, and secondarily to know that God is just. In this sense the modern Jewish argument with God has moved one step beyond where it stood for ages. For many of us today, the argument is no longer rooted in faith; it is rooted in doubt. Where previous generations affirmed their belief in God's justice by expecting and demanding it, today's generation asserts its doubts about God's existence by questioning the lack of justice in Jewish history and the lack of meaning in Jewish suffering.

Historical memory, like an individual's memory, has a way of healing life's wounds. Just as an individual may, over time, learn to accept the tragic death of a loved one, so too a people can begin to accept, and make meaning of, the death of millions. It is here that the traditional Jewish historical myth begins to reassert itself. This myth seeks to reimpose, in spite of our knowing better, the ancient way of interpreting tragedy. Since ancient times, Judaism has been rooted in the belief that God is active in the course of history. Jews today, by and large, still cling to this view by refusing to disconnect God from the Holocaust. Those solutions that have suggested otherwise, those that deny either God or the connection, have been rejected by most of us as offering an unsatisfactory solution to the problem. Atheism is far too certain a belief for most of us. At the same time however, a few of us are willing to espouse the traditional on account of our sins doctrine or the precious are sufferings concept as ways of endowing the suffering of the Holocaust with meaning. But the folk memory, the myth of Jewish history, overrides contemporary sensibilities as it reasserts itself.

Suffering must be given meaning and, unless and until creative responses are developed and found satisfying, the ancient myth will reassert itself to fill the void. How does the myth find contemporary expression? The myth is perhaps unwittingly but best articulated in the popular linkage between the Holocaust and the creation of the State of Israel. Now most of us normally would reject the contention that the Holocaust was necessary in order for the Jewish state to be reborn because of the obvious questions it raises about the nature of a God who operates in such a manner. But as time passes, ideas such as this, which the ancient myth fosters, take hold. We know such theories represent affronts both to God and the martyrs, but what our innermost needs dictate is quite another matter. Suffering must be given meaning (that is one point made as early as the Book of Job), and unless and until new creative responses to suffering are proposed and found satisfying, the ancient myth will reassert itself almost as nature's way of forming scar tissue over a bad wound.

But natural healing is not always the best. One may heal naturally and be left severely scarred. The tradition of arguing with God may help prevent or retard this spiritual scarring. As long as grievances against God are kept current—and rehearsing the arguments from ages past and present does this—the wound is kept open and soft. The ancient myth is thus prevented from growing over the wound and administering an imperfect healing. Meanwhile, new responses, representing a more perfect and healthier healing can be formulated, tested, and finally applied. But Elie Wiesel's warning against espousing answers to the inexplicable is well worth heeding. Genuine healing will take much time. The healing process is everything.

Yosef Hayim Yerushalmi has suggested that the popular understanding of the Holocaust is being shaped not by the historian but by the novelist.[2] I would add that the modern rabbi is similarly excluded from the healing process. Today it is the poet and the novelist who lead the people, raising the questions that otherwise might remain unasked by the rabbi. But just as we have doctors to control the healing process of physical wounds and psychotherapists to address the healing process of emotional wounds, so too do we need spiritual doctors to shape the healing of our spiritual wounds. The rabbi must again serve as a physician of the Jewish soul.

In my mind's eye, rightly or wrongly, I see Jewish practice in the past as having fully integrated arguing with God within the normative tradition. The people prayed both the statutory liturgy and the *piyyutim*. They praised God and petitioned God, but protested as well. And the rabbis led them in the latter just as they did in the former, offering up midrashim and *piyyutim* of protest when the situation warranted it. Jews in the past seemed to feel secure enough in their identity and in their faith not only to observe the liturgy and rituals inherited from previous generations, but also to write new prayers (the *piyyutim*) and memorial books commemorating contemporaneous catastrophes, to institute "second purims" marking sudden deliverances and new fast days mourning recent massacres, to formulate new philosophies and theologies in attempts to make their sufferings meaningful.

Knowledge of this idealized past allows me to see myself as a contemporary link in the chain of tradition of arguing with God, as heir to a teaching that, although not a tenet of Judaism, is found in biblical, talmudic, kabbalistic, hasidic, and modern sources. But what I lack is a community and a context in which to study, exercise and transmit this tradition. What I seek is a forum and a format in which I can join others in expressing doubt and anger as well as praise and thanksgiving. Unfortunately for me, the contemporary synagogue ignores the former while embracing the latter. For me, this means that only a portion, at present the lesser portion, of my relationship with God is accounted for. As a result I feel alienated, cut off, an exile among a people in exile. The very place in which I should feel at home, the very home in which I should feel at one with other Jews, and with God, only serves to reawaken my sense of personal alienation and exile. In the contemporary congregation, one must doff one's doubts and anger when one dons a *tallit* and *kippah*. For this I blame the modern rabbinate.

Where once the rabbi served, at least in part, as the people's advocate, the public prosecutor, today he or she serves primarily as God's defense attorney. If today, after the Holocaust, God could be brought to court and sued for "breach of contract," the modern rabbi would be seen as God's accomplice, or at least God's mouthpiece. Plagued by a curious timidity, the modern rabbi has ceased to serve as a genuine *shaliah tzibur*, a spiritual emissary of the congregation, and instead appears content to serve as the upholder of a belief system and a God whose relevance and efficacy many Jews today doubt or even reject.

I believe that the Holocaust, but not the Holocaust alone, has left a deep psychospiritual wound, a real trauma, in the Jewish soul. The longer it is left untreated, the more it is repressed, the more it will express itself in other ways. That is what I think we can observe happening today. Because the issue of God's inactivity and Jewish suffering is not being adequately addressed in the very forum where we would expect spiritual grappling to occur—in the synagogue—Jewish life suffers. Worship services are sparsely and infrequently attended, ritual observance is declining, education is ineffective, a sense of identity is difficult, and increasing numbers of Jews are lost to assimilation: all because the fundamental questions are ignored. The modern rabbi is caught in an unenviable position, wedged between the Scylla of an inactive God on the one hand and the Charybdis of a restive, skeptical, and impatient people on the other. Our questions, doubts, and anger should be the rabbi's prime concern. People expect rabbis, because of their grounding in the tradition, not to have a cure for their spiritual hurt—because that is for each individual to discover independently—but at least to acknowledge their pain and to diagnose its cause. But this most rabbis fail to do. Perhaps I am being too harsh in my judgment, perhaps I speak for none but myself, perhaps I am too impatient with my colleagues. After all, they first must understand the issues for themselves before they can guide others in any direction. But to return to my point of departure, I yearn for a forum in which to offer prayers of praise, petition, *and* protest; prayers ancient and present and (if necessary) future.

Yosif Hayim Yerushalmi also has suggested that "even where Jews do not reject history out of hand, they are not prepared to confront it directly, but seem to await a new, metahistorical myth."[3] I would add that just as much as we need a new metahistorical myth, even more desperately do we need a new metaphysical myth. The arguing with God tradition may well point the way to the development of such a new metaphysical myth for others as it has for me.

First, knowledge of the tradition—if not actual use of it—can help link the present generation to previous generations who also agonized over God's apparent absence. To know that a Kalonymous b. Judah considered the massacres of the first Crusade to be comparable to the destruction of the Temple or that the Chmielnitski pogroms were called the Third Destruction, equating them with the two destructions of Jerusalem and the Temples is to view our generation's tribulations from a different perspective. Perhaps, with this knowledge, our current dilemma, and more important, our feelings of grief and anger become less unique. Perhaps there is comfort in knowing that others before us have felt as intensely as we do.

Second, the arguments of previous generations can provide a rich theological and liturgical vocabulary which can be applied to the struggle to understand the Holocaust. To include *piyyutim* of protest in the liturgy once again is to restore a sense of reality to the contemporary realm of prayer. We cannot pray as if nothing has happened. By making the *piyyutim* of protest accessible to modern worshipers is one way of addressing this need. At the same time, however, the *piyyutim* of our own day, which express for many of our generation what the medieval *piyyutim* did for theirs, must also be included. When these poems, and others even more contemporaneous, make their way into the liturgy, then Jewish worship will again be complete for many more than is currently the case.

Third, unlike the more submissive and dependent posture advocated by the traditional statutory liturgy, the arguing with God approach implies a relationship of interdependence and relative equality with God. According to this view, God and humankind must work together because each is incomplete and unperfected without the other. But together we can act as partners in the ongoing work of creation. In fact, God needs us as much or perhaps even more than we are supposed to need Him. Abraham Kaplan has noted that, in a way, it is humanity who creates God, not because God's existence depends on us, but because "His being the God of worship does depend on there being worshipers." God is a relational term. "God Himself is everlasting, but His Kingship . . . comes to an end when man refuses to acknowledge Him. . . . God cannot be the God of Israel before there is a people of Israel."[4] In this sense, God's existence on earth is dependent on how we think and act.

TOWARD AN UNDERSTANDING OF THE TASK

What was the divine revelation our ancestors experienced at Sinai? It was, perhaps, a violent proof of the existence of a reality, a power and an authority, beyond their world. In its Jewish expression, this revelation produced a set of instructions, the written and oral Torahs, which form the basis of the *Brit* or Covenant between God and Israel. The Covenant defines the way Jews relate to God, to one another, to our fellow human beings, and to all living things. The Covenant orders all action to the fulfillment of a task: to do as God has instructed us. But what exactly did God reveal to us? What specifically is incumbent upon us to do?

Tradition speaks of two revelations at Sinai, the revelation of God's presence and the revelation of the giving of Torah (Instruction, the Commandments). Some sources suggest that when bestowing the Ten Words (Commandments), God spoke the first two directly to the people and the rest through Moses.[5] Thus the first two, corresponding to the revelation of God's presence, were words each Israelite is supposed to have experienced firsthand. Why would tradition attribute only the first two commandments to God and not the others? Perhaps to impress the reality of His presence into the living soul of each Israelite—past, present, and future. The first two commandments serve as the foundation for all the rest. "*If* YHVH, who took you out of the land of Egypt is your God and you take none else as your god, *then* you shall do the following. . . ." First we are called upon to acknowledge the central-ity of God's position and then to respond by doing.

The recognition and acceptance of the centrality of the first two commandments is crucial for the Jew. The irreplaceability of YHVH as God is the singular principle that underlies the Cove-nant. The first two commandments still speak to all Jews—be-liever, skeptic, and nonbeliever alike. Even to those who have trouble accepting the reality of God these commandments say, "If you cannot accept that I am, then at least leave My place of ultimateness one of pristine emptiness. Make no 'idol' your ulti-mate concern; let no man-made god usurp My position." A Jew is one who is committed to maintaining the Covenant, however the individual interprets it. The Covenant is not only our tie with God, it is equally our bond with one another and with the generations of the past and those of the future as well. Therefore, it remains incumbent upon all of us, whatever the condition of our belief, to attempt to observe it in our lives.

Long ago our sages recognized and acknowledged the point at which many in our generation stand. In the Jerusalem Talmud, God is said to say, "Would that they [the Jews] abandon Me, but still follow My commandments."[6] Many of us today have found it all too easy (but with some justification) to observe the first part of this commandment. The difficult part to accomplish is the second half. But this, today as before, remains the primary Jewish task. What we believe is secondary to how we act. And we can begin by keeping faith with the first two commandments, by holding up all our mores, ideas, and ideologies to the scrutiny of the principle of rejecting idolatry. As the Talmud says: "Whoever denies idolatry is as if he has fulfilled the whole Torah."[7] To be a Jew is to live with perpetual questions and doubts about the ways of the world in which we live. It is a way of perpetual creative discontent.

If my point of departure is the principle of the irreplaceability of God/no God in Jewish life, how then does this principle inform my life? According to tradition, one first accepts the "Yoke of Heaven" and then accepts the "Yoke of the Commandments."[8] The commandments are the specifics of the Covenant. Collectively they are called the *halakhah*, literally the "way in which one walks." The *halakhah* seeks to sanctify every action by imbuing it with right intention (*kavanah*). However, as a liberal Jew, I cannot simply conform to the *halakhah* as interpreted by traditional Judaism. For me, each *mitzvah* (commandment) is meant to raise my consciousness from the mundane to a better appreciation and understanding of the pervasive magnitude of the first two commandments. The importance of a *mitzvah*, for me, rests in the Jewish values that underlie it, and which are mine to discover and apply. Ideally, each *mitzvah* should serve as an act of *teshuvah*, something to help return me to the Way, to infuse my daily activities with higher purpose and greater meaning. In this way, eating, doing business, maintaining relationships, all come to be bound together in a totality that is meant to be beneficial and redemptive both for myself and for my world. This is how I strive to implement the first two commandments in my life.

However, even as I construct a rationale for my personal and partial practice of the *halakhah*, I find myself envying traditional Judaism's sense of wholeness, which stretches directly from God, through the Torah and the *halakhah*, to every aspect of human endeavor. As a liberal Jew, I can find no substitute for this sense of surety and connectedness. But at the same time, I yearn for that same sense of inclusivity, that same motivation and commitment, and the knowledge that what I do is what God really wants of me. The freedoms that I, as a liberal Jew, cherish, the freedoms of conscience and choice and action, are at one and the same time also a source of my sense of alienation from tradition.

But following the principle of rejecting idolatry (that is, observing the first two commandments) also leads me to question and doubt the structure I am making. All my concepts are potential "idols" if I make of them anything other than mere theory. And this thought applies to how I view God as well. I may rebel against the traditional, normative concept of God and even posit a different concept of God based on the arguing with God motif, but ultimately, all ideas about God limit God. Ultimately, I cannot say with any assurance what God is, what God's desire is, or what God does. But perhaps that may be how God wishes to be known by us. As God chooses to be so shall God be.

In Jewish tradition, God has a proper name: YHVH. This name, secret and mysterious, unpronounceable since the destruction of the Temple, is commonly replaced with Adonai, or Lord. All names have meaning and God's name is no exception. What does God's name signify? The name is probably a combination of the third person present and future tenses of the verb "*hayah*," "to be." In the Torah, God introduces Himself to Moses as Ehyeh Asher Ehyeh (or Ehyeh for short), also meaning something on the order of "I will be what I will be" or "I am what I am." However one interprets the name—and we are as puzzled by it today as Moses was when he first heard it—the point God wishes to make clear to us (if I can presume to speak in this manner) is that He is a process of being and becoming; God is pure potentiality. God's name signifies incompleteness; if nothing else, God is grammatically imperfect.

The point is that God, even by His own defining name, truly is nameless, formless, imageless, and unknowable except on those occasions when we experience or perceive His presence. When Jacob made his vow with God it was YHVH he invoked. YHVH was present with Jacob in his flight to Haran, and Jacob hoped to ensure that YHVH would continue to be with him until he returned home. When Moses asked for God's name at the beginning of his mission, God replied "I am" or "I will be" (variations on YHVH) perhaps indicating that He would be present with Moses and the Israelites in their struggle for freedom. Perhaps, although it was perceived otherwise, being there was all God really could do, and the act of liberation was up to the Israelites themselves. Moses and the people had to act before God could assist them. In the Jewish mystical tradition is a concept called *tikkun olam* (the repair of the world). According to this theory, the human task is to restore the primordial perfection of creation through the ingathering of the scattered divine sparks, to reunite God with His feminine in-dwelling presence, the *Shekhinah*, to make God one. Through our actions we can either repair the oneness of the world and God or aid the process of fragmentation and dissolution. Thus, it seems to me, when we are commanded to emulate God ("Be holy, for I, YHVH, your God, am holy"), we are asked to create good, to foster unity and the fulfillment of life's potential. God is "built up" when we create more bonds of love and unity in the world; when we choose life, affirm good, do justly, combat evil, practice mercy, and manifest love.[9] It means accepting failures, allowing for change (*teshuvah*, returning to the Way), but never giving in to despair. For us Jews it means trying to live according to the laws and ideals spelled out in the Torah, in the Talmud, in the Codes and ethical writings and rituals, however we interpret them.

The Torah is very clear on the nature of our role. In Deuteronomy it says: "The secret [or concealed] things belong to YHVH our God; but the things that are revealed belong to us and to our children forever, that we may do all the words of this Instruction [Torah]."[10] God remains forever a mystery. Even Moses, the greatest of prophets, found this so. After the first Revelation, Moses prayed, "Oh, let me behold Your Presence [Glory]." But God simply responded: "You cannot see My face . . . [but] I will make all My goodness pass before you, and I will proclaim before you the name YHVH, and I grant the grace that I will grant and show the compassion [mercy] that I will show."[11] God will be what God will be and God will do what God will do. So, odd as it may seem, God is not and should not be our concern. This life and this world are our concern. This is the arena in which, tradition says, God wants us to struggle. Though I continue to yearn to see God, to confront God, to know with certainty that God exists, I nonetheless choose to put God out of my mind. God may or may not appear. This is His choice. In the meantime, though He may tarry, I know that everything depends upon how I act.

We can never know much about God. Our thoughts, our theologies, our structures are only a wall against a perplexing reality upon which we are attempting to impose our sense of order. Because we all too readily make idols of our concepts, we must continually tear down, reexamine, and rebuild our concepts. We must strive to go beyond all our structures, to embrace the whole mystery of God *and* history, of good *and* evil, of life *and* death. The Jewish reality is functional, its way is one of creative discontent. We are called Yisra-el, one who struggles with God. It is our task to struggle continually with God just as we struggle against many idols of our own making.

According to the Jewish mystical tradition and according to some modern thinkers,[12] God is perceived to be self-limiting. God contracts to give His creation space. God limits His power in establishing the Covenant. God should not be described as omnipotent or omniscient but only relatively so, because we human beings also have some power and some knowledge. This view of God appeals to me, it empowers me, it makes me more responsible for my fate and for my world.

Ultimately I have no answers to explain the difference between how God was perceived to act in the Bible and how God is perceived today. I will never know how or why God acts as He has or even if He acts at all. But though I will never put aside these questions, I cannot let my doubts lead to paralysis. The Covenant dictates what my response must be. I must accept that which is unknowable and mysterious and focus instead on what I do know: what I must do as my part of the Covenant.

Although I will never understand God's relationship to the Holocaust or to any other human tragedy, and although this causes me much pain, I will neither forgive nor forget. My chance to call God to account will have to wait for some future day of reckoning. But concerning my relationship to the Holocaust, I can only endorse what Martin Buber has written: "This, in one way or another, is history's challenge to me: this is its claim on me; and so this is its meaning as far as I am concerned. . . . It is only with my personal life that I am able to catch the meaning of history."[13] History's challenge, its meaning, exists only in our present and in what we choose for the future by how we live our lives. It is not enough that we cultivate virtues; we must also struggle against the corresponding evils. Abraham Joshua Heschel wrote that our failure to fight aggressively *against* the forces of the Holocaust led *to* the Holocaust and that in response to our failure, we must redouble our fight against wrong, against injustice, against evil. "God," he wrote, "is everywhere or nowhere, the Father of all men or no man, concerned about everything or nothing. . . . Either we are ministers of the sacred or slaves of evil. . . . God is waiting for us to redeem the world."[14]

This life and this world, this humanity, the here and now, the future, these are my concerns. Because these are all I really can know. These are my domains. As Deuteronomy has God say:

> Surely this commandment which I command you this day is not too baffling for you, nor is it beyond reach. It is not in the heavens . . . neither is it beyond the sea. . . . No, the thing [or word] is very close to you, in your mouth and in your heart, that you may do it. See, I have set before you this day life and good, death and evil. . . . Choose life, that you and your offspring may live.[15]

The choice is always ours to make, each of us individually and in every generation.

A STORY ON THE TASK AT HAND

Once a master built a garden and brought in some workers to till it. One day he said to them: "Tomorrow I am going on a journey. My journey may be of long duration; it may be short. I do not know when I shall return. But here are some instructions to follow in my absence. Care for my garden, improve it if you can. Its fruits are yours to enjoy. When I return, and if you have done well, I shall reward you all greatly."

The next day he left.

Weeks passed into months, and the months turned into years. The workers in the garden began to disagree on the exact meaning of some of the master's instructions. But the work continued nonetheless.

Then after many years, a group of workers cried out in despair: "The master is gone, never to return! Perhaps he is dead. What reward will we have then? What's the use of continuing to follow his instructions?"

But others retorted in anger: "You are wrong! You are faithless! The master will return as he has promised. We will be rewarded. Perhaps he is only testing us so as to increase our meriting a reward upon his return. Perhaps he will return tomorrow. And even if he tarries, even so we will continue to believe in his return and we will continue to work according to his instructions."

The argument raged on persistently, neither side convincing the other, neither gaining over the other. Eventually the argument became so heated that it consumed everyone's attention. And the work in the garden came to a halt.

Finally a third group arose and spoke to the contending sides: "Brothers, sisters! Does it matter whether the master returns or not? Has he not given the garden into our care and granted us its produce as well for our consumption? While you argue this way and that, the garden is going to ruin. If the master returns and sees that we have worked well, we shall be rewarded as he has promised. In this case we should continue working. And if the master never returns, then we shall have this garden and all its fruits as a reward in itself. In this case too it is to our advantage to continue working.

Who knows what the future will hold? But let us cease this arguing to and fro. Let us use the master's instructions and return to our work at once. From either standpoint, our reward is in our continuing the work on the garden."

> My God exists in my dissatisfaction with the present;
> His Torah in my creative discontent.
> I do not wish to know God; I only wish to find Him.
> I shall not find except in seeking,
> I cannot seek except by doing.
> There is no beginning except through asking.

This is what the arguing with God tradition means for me as of today, erev Shabbat Behar, 14 Iyar 5749, Friday, May 19, 1989.

NOTES

NOTES TO THE INTRODUCTION

1. Genesis *Rabbah* 70:3.
2. *Sanhedrin* 10:5.
3. Erich Fromm, *You Shall Be Gods* (Greenwich, CT: Fawcett, 1966), p. 23.
4. *Sifré Devarim*, Va'ethanan 3, piska 26, ed. L. Finkelstein, pp. 39–40, actually provides twelve alternate expressions for *tefillah* (prayer).
5. Edward Ullendorf, "Thought Categories in the Hebrew Bible," *Studies in Rationalism, Judaism and Universalism*, ed. R. Loewe (London: Routledge & Kegan Paul, 1966), p. 279.
6. Sheldon H. Blank, "The Confessions of Jeremiah and the Meaning of Prayer," *HUCA* 21 (1948):337–338. See also his work *Jeremiah, Man and Prophet* (Cincinnati: Hebrew Union College Press, 1961), pp. 95, 236–239.
7. Berend Gemser, "The Rib—or Controversy—Pattern in Hebrew Mentality," *Vetus Testamentum* 3, supp. (1955):124.
8. Ibid., p. 128. Blank, "Confessions," p. 331.
9. Joseph Heinemann, *Prayer in the Talmud: Forms and Patterns* (Berlin and New York: Walter de Gruyter, 1977), p. 193.
10. For a fuller treatment of God's controversies with Israel, see Gemser, "Rib Pattern," pp. 128–133; and Hubert H. Huffmon, "The Covenant Lawsuit in the Prophets," *Journal of Biblical Literature* 78 (December 1959): 285–295.
11. Heinemann, *Prayer in the Talmud*, p. 193.
12. This structure is based on those proposed by Blank in "The Prophet as Paradigm," *Prophetic Thought* (Cincinnati: Hebrew Union College Press, 1977), pp. 24–25; and Heinemann, *Prayer in the Talmud*, pp. 193–194.
13. Gemser, "Rib Pattern," p. 126; Ullendorf, "Thought Categories," p. 279; Heinemann, *Prayer in the Talmud*, p. 207; Blank, "The Prophet as Paradigm," p. 25.

14. Gemser, "Rîb Pattern," pp. 136–137; Heinemann, *Prayer in the Talmud*, p. 208. See also Joseph Heinemann with Jakob J. Petuchowski, eds., *Literature of the Synagogue* (New York: Behrman House, 1975), pp. 1–2, for a more general comparison between ancient Hebrew and ancient Babylonian and Egyptian worship.

15. See, for example, Sheldon H. Blank, "Men against God: The Promethean Element in Biblical Prayer," reprinted as a separate entity from the *Journal of Biblical Literature* 72 (March 1953), and the sources mentioned therein. Although the designation of biblical figures is wrong, which colors the whole development of the article, Blank's work remains a valuable collection of primary sources, which pioneered the way for later studies.

16. Herbert Chanan Brichto, "Images of Man in the Bible," *CCAR Journal* 17 (October 1970):7. For a development of his opinion that "there are no Promethean utterances in the Bible," see pp. 2–9 of the same article. His assertion is supported by Gemser, "Rîb Pattern," p. 136; and Heinemann, *Prayer in the Talmud*, p. 208. Although Blank advocates the existence of a Promethean element in Jewish prayer, he nonetheless also confirms the fundamental importance of God's justice, at least with regard to Jeremiah's confessions. See his "Confessions," pp. 331–354; and "Men Against God," pp. 8–9.

17. *Ta'anit* 24b.

NOTES TO CHAPTER 1

1. Other examples of the law-court pattern of prayer in Genesis include Cain's appeal of his sentence (Genesis 4:13–15); Abimelech's prayer (Genesis 20:4–6); and Jacob's prayer (Genesis 32:9–12). See also the examples cited in note 10.

2. Blank, "Men against God," p. 8; Erich Fromm, *You Shall Be As Gods* (New York: Fawcett, 1966), pp. 24–25.

3. Brichto, "*Images of Man*," p. 7; Nahum M. Sarna, *Understanding Genesis* (New York: Schocken Books, 1970), pp. 146–148.

4. See Sarna, *Understanding Genesis*, pp. 144–145, for the meanings of *za'akah* and *tza'akah* and their relation to justice and the existence of the moral order.

5. Harold M. Schulweis, "Suffering and Evil" in *Great Jewish Ideas*, ed. Abraham E. Millgram (B'nai B'rith Department of Adult Jewish Education, 1964), p. 202. For an explication of the tradition of arguing with God and its relation to the Covenant see pp. 197–202.

6. For a full treatment of the development of the concept of the doctrine of merit and *zekhut avot* in particular, consult Arthur Marmorstein,

The Doctrine of Merits in Old Rabbinical Literature (London: Jew's College Publications, 1920); Solomon Schechter, *Some Aspects of Rabbinic Theology* (New York: Macmillan, 1909), pp. 170–198; and Sarna, *Understanding Genesis*, pp. 149–151.

7. For more on this alternate view of the Exodus, see my article "Remnants of a Dissenting Tradition in the Haggadah" in *Conservative Judaism* 34 (Spring 1981):41–48.

8. Compare Moses' encounter with that of Gideon (Judges 6:13–18,36–40). For a hilarious sendup of Moses' first encounter with God, see Joseph Heller, *God Knows* (New York: Dell, 1985), pp. 32–35. (Who knows, it may be more accurate than the Torah version.)

The following are other instances of Moses' arguments with God, beyond those cited in the text:

1. Following the story of the Golden Calf, when God decides to withdraw His presence from the midst of the people (Exodus 33:12–16); verses 12a—implicit address, 12b—argument, 13—petition, 13b—argument, 15—ultimatum, 16—argument, 17–23—divine response. Also Exodus 34:9: "O Lord"—address; "If now . . . " and "stiffnecked"—argument based on personal merit and confession on behalf of people; "go in our midst," "pardon our sin," "take us for Your inheritance"—a threefold petition.

2. When Israel craved for meat: Numbers 11:11–15; 11a—implicit address, 11b—complaint and petition to God, 12—argument, 13—petition for meat, 14—complaint, 15—ultimatum, 16–20—divine response).

3. Korah's rebellion forces Moses to take an oath before God (Numbers 16:15–17), but God judges Korah and Israel in advance, so Moses must intercede (Numbers 16:21–23). At the time of the actual contest, Moses takes another oath and asks God for a sign (Numbers 16:28–30, and God's answer—31–35).

4. Moses' plea to enter the Land of Israel just prior to his death: (Deuteronomy 3:23–28; 24—address, 24b—praise and argument, 25—petition, 26–28—divine response).

9. The parallel argument in Deuteronomy 9:26–29 has the following structure: 26—address, 27–29—argument, stressing God's deeds during the Exodus, His international prestige, confession of sins, and *zekhut avot*, 26—petition. On the whole, it is more conciliatory and confessional in tone, and emphasizes the concepts of the chosen people and God's saving acts in the past, presumably later concepts. No mention is made of personal merit.

10. Oaths, vows, and signs all function along similar lines; all are related to the motif of the law court. Eleazar asks God to show (him) His steadfast love for Abraham by doing what he asks of Him; he asks God for a sign (Genesis 24:12–14). Moses (Exodus 3–4) and Gideon (Judges 6:13–18,36–40) also ask God for signs before venturing to undertake their missions. While these requests are not usually cast in the law-court pattern, there is an element of argument and hutz-pah in asking God to prove His reliability. Jacob (Genesis 28:20–22), Jephthah (Judges 11:30–31), and Hannah (1 Samuel 1:11) all take vows to obtain what they desire at the hand of God. Unlike the oath, the vow is an exchange. One asks God for something and promises Him something in return—a legal, i.e., punishable, proposition. Moses takes two oaths, one at the time of the Golden Calf (Exodus 32:32), the second when confronted by Korah (Numbers 16:15–30). In the latter case, Moses combines his oath (15) with another oath and a request for a sign (29–30). Elijah likewise combines oaths with re-quests for signs (1 Kings 18:20–40, verses 36–37 in particular; 2 Kings 1:10,12). Job rests his case on an oath (Job 31). For more on Job see pp. 32–33. With regard to all of these, it is fitting to raise the question of whether such oaths, vows, and requests for signs were proper. In Exodus 17:7, the Israelites are castigated by Moses for "testing the Lord," though what they demand is much the same as these other figures demand themselves. It would seem that in the earlier stories, only God's chosen representatives are allowed to exer-cise this privilege. In Prophets and Writings, however, this privilege will be taken over by the people, at least insofar as the people are given voice by their spokepersons in Job, Lamentations, Psalms, and Deutero-Isaiah.

11. The whole section noticeably resembles the Deuteronomic process for the purging of evil from the midst of the people. See, for example, Deuteronomy 21:7–9.

12. Compare Moses' words here with his words to the people on the same occasion (Deuteronomy 1:29–33). He uses the same arguments with both God and Israel—a clear indication of his intermediary role.

13. See Joshua's use of this same motif in his law-court prayer (Joshua 7:7–9).

14. For other examples of the law-court pattern in Prophets, see Elijah (1 Kings 17:20–21), Hezekiah (2 Kings 19:15–19; 20:3–6), Habakkuk (Habakkuk 1:2–4,12–17; 2:1–4), Deutero-Isaiah (Isaiah 62:1–7; 63:11b–chap. 64), and Jonah (Jonah 3:10–4:4). God is not always appreciative of their arguments, or those of the people (Ezekiel 18:25–29; Malachi 2:17; 3:13–15; and compare with Exodus 17:7).

15. See articles by Blank, "Prophet as Paradigm" and "Confessions";

Gemser, "Rib Pattern," pp. 128–133; and William L. Holladay, "Jeremiah's Lawsuit with God," *Interpretation* 17 (July 1963):280–287.

16. Blank, "*Prophet as Paradigm,*" p. 31; Martin Buber, *The Prophetic Faith* (New York: Harper and Row, 1960), p. 180.

17. Blank, "Prophet as Paradigm," p. 31. For the development of Blank's argument see pp. 23, 29–33.

18. Buber, *The Prophetic Faith,* p. 183.

19. Blank, "Prophet as Paradigm," p. 29.

20. This theory is supported by another example of Jeremiah's use of the law-court pattern, which followed his purchasing some ancestral land just before Jerusalem fell. Jeremiah questions God's purpose in commanding him to purchase the lands, and he is given an important divine message in return—a message of hope for an eventual restoration of Israel to its land (Jeremiah 32:17–25, and God's response—verses 42–44 in particular). Here Jeremiah's anxiety clearly serves as a paradigm for the anxiety of the people, and God's response addresses both Jeremiah as an individual, and through him, the people as a whole. The structure of this prayer is as follows: 17—address; 17–25—argument (17–23a—recitation of praise and past deeds of God); 23b–24—confession of sins/justification of God's judgments); 25—complaint with implied petition, "Please explain why You asked me to purchase those lands"; 26–44 (42–44 in particular)—divine response to Jeremiah's question.

21. Blank, "Prophet as Paradigm," pp. 25–26.

22. In this essay we have relied primarily on the works of Claus Westermann. See his article "The Role of the Lament in the Theology of the Old Testament," *Interpretation* 28 (January 1974): 20–21; and his book, *The Praise of God in the Psalms*, trans. Keith R. Crim (Richmond, VA: John Knox Press, 1965), pp. 52–81, in which he proposes a fivefold division to the lament consisting of (a) address and introductory petition, (b) lament and complaint, (c) expression of trust, (d) petition or supplication, (e) vow of praise (in individual laments). Hermann Gunkel, *The Psalms: A Form-Critical Introduction*, trans. Thomas H. Horner (Philadelphia: Fortress Press, 1967), pp. 13–15, 19–22, 32–36, advocates a threefold division: (a) lament, (b) prayer and argument, (c) certainty of a hearing. Artur Weiser, *The Psalms: A Commentary* (Philadelphia: Westminster Press, 1976), suggests a fivefold division in his introduction consisting of (a) invocation, (b) lament, (c) supplication, (d) motivation, (e) vow.

23. Other examples of the national lament include: Psalms 60, 74, 79, 83, 85, 89, 90, 106; Lamentations 2:20–22; 3:40–51; chap. 5; Jeremiah 14:7–9; Isaiah 63:7–64:12; Habakkuk 1:2–2:4. Psalms 4, 10, 51, 82, 94, 102, 115, 123, 130, 131, 137; Lamentations 1:20–22, chap. 3 as a

whole, all combine the lament of the individual with that of the nation.

24. Other examples of the individual lament include: Psalms 3, 5, 6, 7, 12, 13, 17, 25, 26, 27, 28, 31, 35, 38, 39, 42–43, 55, 57, 59, 64, 69, 70, 71, 77, 86, 88, 109, 140, 141, 142, 143; Lamentations 3:1–39,52–66.

25. Westermann, "Role of the Lament," p. 21.

26. On the lament of the individual and the vow of praise, see Wester- mann, *The Praise of God in the Psalms*, pp. 75–78; and Gunkel, *The Psalms: A Form-Critical Introduction*, pp. 13–15, 19–22, 32–36.

27. Westermann, *The Praise of God in the Psalms*, p. 75.

28. Blank, "Men Against God," pp. 95–99, examines this and other motifs of the psalms of petition in detail. I direct the reader to the references made there and to the copious examples found in his notes.

29. The following is the law-court pattern applied to the Book of Lamen- tations as a whole: address—1:20–22; argument—1:1–19, 2:1–19 (complaint), 2:20–22 (accusations); expression of trust—chap. 3; ar- gument—4:1–10 (complaint and accusations), 4:12–20 (confession of wrongdoing); petition and complaint—5:1–18 (complaint), 5:19–22 (petition); certainty of having been heard (instead of a vow of praise)—4:21–22. Note, however, that many of these units can stand structurally on their own as full laments.

30. Gemser, "Rib Pattern," p. 135; Westermann, "Role of the Lament," p. 32.

31. Matitiahu Tsevat, "The Meaning of the Book of Job," *HUCA* 37 (1966): 73–106. In our study of the Book of Job, we have relied heavily on Tsevat's excellent analysis of (but not his solution to) Job. Tsevat sees the central issue as that of justice, and surveys other secondary sources for their understanding of the central issue as well. See pp. 92–96 for a review of these other scholarly views.

32. On the meaning of Elihu's speeches, see Robert Goldsmith, "The Healing Scourge," *Interpretation* 17 (July 1963): 271–279. He links Elihu's speeches with the content of Job's theophany and also with the views of Job's friends (and Deuteronomy). Buber, *The Prophetic Faith*, p. 196, sees Elihu's words paralleling those of the friends, while Yehezkel Kaufmann, *The Religion of Israel*, trans. and ab. Moshe Greenberg (New York: Schocken Books, 1972), pp. 336–337, sees Elihu's address corresponding to the content of Job's theoph- any. It would seem that Elihu's words do link up with the content of both the friends' speeches and God's speeches. Even so, the former's outlook alone is insufficient (and indeed provokes divine displea- sure); the former's outlook must be brought in as part of the latter. In other words, Job's friends are right to a certain degree, but at a certain point their understanding becomes dogmatic. Only when integrated into the context of the theophany do they regain their

proper function (as generally operable principles of divine justice). Elihu's words attempt to combine both the friends' and God's outlooks. The best analysis of Elihu's address (and hence of the theophany) is, in our opinion, Nahum N. Glatzer, "Knowest Thou . . . ? Notes on the Book of Job," *Essays in Jewish Thought* (University, AL: University of Alabama Press, 1978), pp. 82–92. Glatzer points out the underlying theme of true knowledge that unites Elihu's and God's addresses. This theme of true knowledge is a second only to the theme of divine justice in Job, for it is only Job's glimpse of true knowledge that makes him aware of the nature of divine justice.

33. Sheldon H. Blank, "An Effective Literary Device in Job 31," *Prophetic Thought* (Cincinnati: Hebrew Union College Press, 1977), pp. 65–67, analyzes Job's oath in detail. He draws a parallel between Job's oath and the oaths taken by the suspected adulteress (Numbers 5) and the suspected thief (Exodus 22:9–10).

34. Only rarely does the Bible set down full oaths, i.e., with their conditional curses intact. Two other occasions are Psalms 7 and 137. Both Moses and Elijah make use of negative oaths (ultimatums) when confronted by Korah and the contest on Mount Carmel, respectively: "Unless such and such happens, the Lord has not sent me." Moses also uses a partial oath in the episode of the Golden Calf (Exodus 32:32). See note 8, example "3," and note 10, on oaths, vows, and signs.

35. Kaufmann, *The Religion of Israel*, p. 335.

36. This is the theme developed by Glatzer, "Knowest Thou . . . ?," pp. 82–92.

37. The question seems to be: Does God's revelation constitute a show of divine justice, and if so, what is its meaning? Buber, *The Prophetic Faith*, pp. 194–196, and Kaufmann, *The Religion of Israel*, p. 337, say the revelation is a manifestation of divine justice in which God links Himself with the sufferer. Tsevat, "The Meaning of the Book of Job," pp. 97–106, proposes that God and justice must be separated. He believes that Job advocates an end to the principle of exact (quid pro quo) retributive justice. But there seems little in Job to support such an interpretation. As Tsevat notes, the revelation, in that it avoids the issue of justice (i.e., Job's case), does lead one to questions about its intended meaning. Ultimately, the question becomes: Does the revelation contain some "hidden" or "veiled" teaching, or is it itself the teaching, i.e., that God, beyond all His other great concerns, upholds the innocent and champions the right? Tsevat believes the former; we advocate the latter. Tsevat's thesis is weakened because he dismisses the revelation-as-the-message theory without giving it due consideration. "Irrational" is a value judgment on his part. For the Israelites, the belief in, and hope for, revelations was very real. Tse-

vat's answer seems too extreme, too disconnected from anything else written before, during, or after the time of the Exile. True, Job does advocate a change in the people's attitude toward suffering and divine justice, but it is not what Tsevat proposes. If Job were truly meant as a "secret" teaching, then there should be some evidence that someone before Dr. Tsevat also knew of its existence.

38. Buber, *The Prophetic Faith*, pp. 188–189.
39. See Tsevat, "The Meaning of the Book of Job," pp. 74–75, 100, for a full treatment of this view of the prologue and epilogue.
40. Tsevat, "The Meaning of the Book of Job," p. 101.
41. God addresses Israel's despair: Isaiah, 40:28–31; 41; 42:14–17; 43; 44:21–28; 46:3–13; 49:15–50:3; 51–52; 54; 57; 65:8–25. God justifies what He has done to Israel: Isaiah 43:22–28; 48; 57:16–21; 65:1–7. Israel confesses after a prophetic accusation and God responds by acting: Isaiah 59–61. Israel is told not to doubt God's plans but to trust in the Lord: Isaiah 42:18–25; 45:9–13; 55:8–9; 40:12–31.
42. Buber, *The Prophetic Faith*, pp. 196–217, 229–230, links Job to a line of "faithful rebels," leading to Deutero-Isaiah's "servant of YHVH." He attempts to reconcile the diverse views represented in each work, and among the various works, by fitting each work into a conceptual chain. His rationale is that we have received the Bible as a single work so that is how we should attempt to explain it. While I accept his premise, I see no reason why everything must be reconciled. I would suggest that the dialectics set forth above (pp. 36–37) can remain unresolved in the Bible, just as they remain in tension throughout the rabbinic period.
43. Kaufmann, *The Religion of Israel*, pp. 332–333.

NOTES TO CHAPTER 2

1. *Pirkei Avot* 1:1. For an accessible translation with commentary, see Judah Goldin, *The Living Talmud: The Wisdom of the Fathers* (New York: New American Library, 1957).
2. For an excellent introduction to the Judaism of the classical rabbinic period, see George Foot Moore, *Judaism in the First Centuries of the Christian Era: The Age of the Tannaim*, 2 vols. (New York: Schocken Books, 1971).
3. Norman J. Cohen, "The Leap of Nachshon ben Amminadab: A Rabbinic Redemptive Model," *Journal of Reform Judaism* (Fall 1983): 30–31.
4. In contrast with the work presented here and by Heinemann, *Prayer in the Talmud*, pp. 193–217, Solomon Zeitlin, "The Temple and Wor-

ship," *Jewish Quarterly Review* 51 (January 1961):231–236, states that although the argument form and vow form of prayer were known and used in ancient Israel, they were abandoned in postexilic times and ceased completely in the time of the early Second Temple. In the light of so many examples of the law-court pattern in the Midrash and Talmud, one wonders how Zeitlin could ever have uttered such a statement. Perhaps he is privy to some sources unavailable to everyone else! However, his expositions of the *tefillah* and *neder* forms of prayer in the above mentioned article and in "An Historical Study of the First Canonization of the Hebrew Liturgy," *Jewish Quarterly Review* (N.S.) 36 (January 1946):211–229, are quite solid pieces of work.

One wonders whether the Rabbis' use of the law-court pattern is actually a continuation of the form or a revival of the form. The problem arises as a result of that grey area of Jewish history between the return of the first exile and the start of the rabbinic period. Barton G. Lee, *The Private Prayers of the Rabbis: Aspects of Their Form and Content* (Cincinnati: unpublished rabbinic thesis, 1970), pp. 163–168, basing his work on Heinemann's study of the law-court pattern, has noted a strong connection between the prayers of the apocryphal books and the "servant before his master" pattern of prayer. Was this form more prevalent in the Hellenistic period? Was the law-court pattern only revived at a later date (during the period of Roman persecution)? Or did both patterns co-exist in tension as they did in the rabbinic period?

5. Julius Guttmann, *Philosophies of Judaism*, trans. D. W. Silverman (New York: Schocken Books, 1973), p. 44, pp. 48–49.

6. The following are examples of midrashic law-court prayers that parallel biblical law-court prayers:

Hagar—Genesis 21:15–18, and Genesis *Rabbah* 53:13, *Tanhuma Vayeitzei*:5, ed, Lewin-Epstein, p. 39a.

Abimelech—Genesis 20:4–6 and Genesis *Rabbah* 52:6.

Jacob—Genesis 32:9–12 and Genesis *Rabbah* 75:13.

Moses—Exodus 3–4 and Exodus *Rabbah* 3:9,12,13,16; 15:14; *Zevahim* 102a.

Exodus 5:22–23 and Exodus *Rabbah* 5:22, 23; 6:1, 4; *Tanhuma Va'eira*:1, p. 71b; *Sanhedrin* 111a; Ecclesiastes *Rabbah* 7:17, ed. Lewin-Epstein, p. 125a.

Exodus 32—see pp. 51–57.

Numbers 12:13 and *Avot de Rabbi Natan* A:9, p. 41; *Sifré* Numbers, *Beha'alotekha*, piska 105, ed. Horovitz, pp. 103–104.

Numbers 14:13–19 and Numbers *Rabbah* 16:22,25,28.

Numbers 18:11–12, 20 and Numbers *Rabbah* 18:11, 12, 20; *Sanhedrin* 110a.

Deuteronomy 3:23–28 see pp. 264–265.

Phinehas—Psalm 106:3, Numbers 25:9 and *Sanhedrin* 44a, 82b; *Tanhuma Balak* 21, pp. 89a–b.

Joshua—Joshua 7:21–23 and Numbers *Rabbah* 23:6; *Sanhedrin* 44a.

Hannah—1 Samuel 1:11 and *Berakhot* 31b; *Pesikta Rabbati* 43, pp. 179–180.

Elijah—1 Kings 18:20–40 and Numbers *Rabbah* 18:12; *Berakhot* 9b, 31b–32a.

Hezekiah—2 Kings 19:15–19, 20:3–6 and *Berakhot* 10b; Ecclesiastes *Rabbah* 5:4, ed. Lewin-Epstein, p. 120b.

Jeremiah—Jeremiah 14:19 and Exodus *Rabbah* 31:10; Pesikta *Rabbati* 31, pp. 143b–144a. Jeremiah 20:7 and *Pesikta Rabbati* 26, pp. 131a–b.

Job—Job's speeches and *Baba Batra* 16a–b.

Manasseh—2 Chronicles 33:10–13, Apocryphal Prayer of Manasseh and *Sanhedrin* 103a–b; Ruth *Rabbah* 5:6, p. 71b.

Esther—Esther 4:16, Apocryphal addition to Esther 14:3–19 and *Berakhot* 32a; *Midrash Tehillim* 22:6, 16, 18, 19, 27.

Mordecai—Esther 4:1–16, Apocryphal addition to Esther 13:9–17 and Esther *Rabbah* 8:7, p. 17b.

Psalms of Lament—*Pesikta Rabbati* 31, p. 143b.

The following references are to midrashim with no biblical parallels. In each case, however, God is called upon to judge or to intervene. This might explain why the midrashim were created, i.e., to provide God with a reason for intervening.

Sarah—Genesis 20:2–3 and Genesis *Rabbah* 41:2, 52:13.

Midwives—Exodus 1:17–21 and Exodus *Rabbah* 1:15.

7. Arthur Marmorstein, "The Background of the Haggadah," *Studies in Jewish Theology* (London: Oxford University Press, 1950), pp. 1–71. Adolf Buechler, *Studies in Sin and Atonement* (London: Oxford University Press, 1928), p. 130, also briefly mentions the Gnostic threat to Judaism. For the conflict between Christianity and Judaism, see

Rosemary R. Reuther, *Faith and Fratricide* (New York: Seabury Press, 1974).

8. Marmorstein, "Background of the Haggadah," p. 5.
9. Cited in Marmorstein, "Background of the Haggadah," p. 6.
10. Consult Arthur Marmorstein, *The Doctrine of Merits in Old Rabbinical Literature* (London: Jew's College Publications, 1920), pp. 27, 97. For an analysis of the *adversos Judaeos* literature of the Christian Church with regard to their polemicizing against Judaism, consult Reuther, *Faith and Fratricide*.
11. Leviticus *Rabbah* 10:1 (also Genesis *Rabbah* 39:6, 49:9).
12. Genesis *Rabbah* 49:8, 9.
13. Genesis *Rabbah* 49:9. This view was by no means acceptable to everyone. In *Baba Batra* 15b, Job is said to have been greater than Abraham, while in *Sotah* 31a, the two are said to be equals. There is a strong ambivalence toward Job in the Midrash, with some rabbis praising him, other rabbis condemning him, but generally all attempting to tone down the rebelliousness of his speeches. For a good analysis of these various attitudes toward Job, see Adolf Buechler, *Studies in Sin and Atonement*, pp. 119–189; Nahum N. Glatzer, "The God of Job and the God of Abraham: Some Talmudic-Midrashic Interpretations of the Book of Job," *Essays in Jewish Thought* (University AL: University of Alabama Press, 1978), pp. 93–108; and Edward D. Kiner, *Views of Job in the Midrash* (Cincinnati: unpublished rabbinic thesis, 1965).

A similar comparison is made between Noah and Abraham (Genesis *Rabbah* 39:10), and between Noah and Moses and Samuel (with the latter two proving superior) (Genesis *Rabbah* 39:9). Moses takes Abraham, Isaac, Jacob, and Noah to task in order to show the superiority of his merit to theirs (Deuteronomy *Rabbah* 11:3).
14. Genesis *Rabbah* 49:8.
15. Genesis *Rabbah* 49:9 and *Avodah Zarah* 4a. See also those cases where God is not permitted to kill many people for the sins of a few (or single) individuals; Phinehas and Joshua—*Sanhedrin* 44a; Phinehas—*Sanhedrin* 44a, 82b, Numbers *Rabbah* 18:11; Moses and Aaron—Numbers *Rabbah* 18:11.
16. *Avot de Rabbi Natan* A:37 (given as part of addition 1 to version 1, ed. Schechter, p. 149).
17. *Tanhuma Buber*, Va'eira, vol. I, p. 9. God's justice in these and other cases is affirmed in *Sifré* Deuteronomy *Ha'azinu*, piska 307, ed. Finkelstein, pp. 344–345.
18. Genesis *Rabbah* 52:6.
19. Numbers *Rabbah* 16:25, and also Numbers *Rabbah* 16:22 and *Berakhot* 32a, where God's judgments of Sodom and Gomorrah, the

Flood, and the Tower are questioned regarding their cruelty. Also relevant is the following: "Woe to the wicked who make the Attribute of Justice appear as if it were merciless!" (Numbers *Rabbah* 17:3). God is frequently urged to permit His attribute of Mercy to prevail over His attribute of Justice (Leviticus *Rabbah* 29:9; *Berakhot* 7a; *Sifré* Numbers Pinhas, 134, p. 180, Numbers *Rabbah* 16:22, 16:28 [by implication]; *Avodah Zarah* 4b).

20. *Sifré* Deuteronomy *Ha'azinu*, piska 311, ed. Finkelstein, pp. 351–352, expresses a view that would have been unthinkable in the later period, namely, that previous to Abraham's argument with God, God, as it were, *did* judge the world with cruelty!

21. Genesis *Rabbah* 49:9, also *Berakhot* 32a.

22. *Ta'anit* 2, 65d, also Leviticus *Rabbah* 29:9, and Genesis *Rabbah* 56:10. The presence of this law-court prayer in a place with no biblical parallel may be explained by two addresses by God's angel with no intervening response by Abraham (Genesis 22:11–12, 15–18).

23. Genesis *Rabbah* 56:8.

24. See *Rosh Hashanah* 16a; *Mekhilta*, Pisha, ed. Lauterbach, p. I:57, 88, and Beshallah, I:221–223. See also Marmorstein, *Merits*, pp. 76, 148–149.

25. Consult Shalom Spiegel, *The Last Trial*, trans. J. Goldin (New York: Schocken Books, 1967) for a study of the role of the *akeidah* in the midrashim and *piyyutim*. Also Jakob J. Petuchowski, *Heirs of the Pharisees* (New York: Basic Books, 1970), pp. 68–75.

26. Exodus *Rabbah* 5:22.

27. See Marmorstein, *Merits*, pp. 27–28, 151–152.

28. Exodus *Rabbah* 42:2.

29. *Berakhot* 32a; Exodus *Rabbah* 42:9.

30. Deuteronomy *Rabbah* 3:15, Exodus *Rabbah* 45:2. Also *Berakhot* 63b regarding God's ultimatum to Moses regarding the Tent.

31. *Berakhot* 32a.

32. Exodus *Rabbah* 42:12.

33. For a discussion of this ambivalent attitude regarding the *zekhut avot* on the part of the Rabbis, consult Marmorstein, *Merits*, pp. 71, 89, 92, 100–104, 107, 149–154, 164–167, and the references made therein.

34. Exodus *Rabbah* 44:1, 2; and Deuteronomy *Rabbah* 3:15.

35. Exodus *Rabbah* 44:5.

36. Exodus *Rabbah* 44:9.

37. *Berakhot* 32a. In Exodus *Rabbah* 44:9, Moses uses a *kal vahome'ir* argument to make the same point: "If You can't keep a promise made to three, how much the less a promise made to one [me]!"

38. Ecclesiastes *Rabbah* 4:5, p. 118b; also Exodus *Rabbah* 41:7; 44:3,4,8; Deuteronomy *Rabbah* 3:11,15 for full accounts of the battles between the angels of God's anger and Moses, God, and the Patriarchs. Moses, in another case, seizes the Throne of God to prevent the angels from attacking him (Exodus *Rabbah* 41:7; 42:4). There is an interesting dynamic involved here. In certain instances, as above, and at the giving of the Torah, God sides with Moses to protect him from His overzealous angels. See Exodus *Rabbah* 28:1; *Shabbat* 88b–89a; *Pesikta Rabbati* 20, pp. 96b–98b, for stories concerning Moses' struggle to receive the Torah in Heaven. God's angels are divided in their attitude toward humankind and Israel. There are many stories about the angels' opposition to God's favorable judgments to human beings, usually from the Attribute of Justice and like-minded angels. These angels opposed man's creation (Genesis *Rabbah* 8:4,5; *Sanhedrin* 38b), they opposed God's providing Ishmael with water (Genesis *Rabbah* 53:14), they opposed the Exodus (Leviticus *Rabbah* 23:2) and delay the coming of the Messiah (*Sanhedrin* 94a, 97b). Satan (perhaps the testing angel in the Attribute of Justice department) obstructs Abraham during the *akeidah*—(*Sanhedrin* 89b), and the Attribute of Justice seeks to kill Moses when he insults God's honor (Exodus *Rabbah* 5:22,23; 6:1, Ecclesiastes *Rabbah* 7:17, p. 125a), and to condemn Israel at the Judgment (*Megillah* 15b). Almost all these cases represent the attempt on the part of the angels to preserve the integrity of God's justice, hence their opposition to any sin of lese-majesté on the part of mankind and any sign of mercy (i.e., deviation from justice) on the part of God. But just as God has an Attribute of Mercy, so too there are angels of mercy who support and defend Israel and the world. These angels favor man's creation (see references above), they cry out against the *akeidah* (Genesis *Rabbah* 56:5,8), they support Moses and Aaron against Korah (Numbers *Rabbah* 18:20; *Sanhedrin* 110a), and protest against God's destruction of the Temple (*Pesikta Rabbati* 27–28, pp. 134a–135b). One angel in particular has the function of arguing with God, and is called Piskonit or Piskon (Arguer) also known as Gabriel (*Sanhedrin* 44b).

    With regard to the law-court pattern, it is significant to note that, just as in the divine-court proceedings in the Bible, so too in the heavenly proceedings of the Midrash many of the addresses use the law-court pattern.

39. Exodus *Rabbah* 44:10. See also Exodus *Rabbah* 44:6; Leviticus *Rabbah* 23:2; Deuteronomy *Rabbah* 3:5; *Berakhot* 32a.

40. See Marmorstein, *Merits*, pp. 168–171, for Christian views on the *zekhut avot.*

41. Exodus *Rabbah* 46:1. The order in the text seems wrong. It makes more sense if Moses says: "If You forgive me, then You must forgive them."

42. Exodus *Rabbah* 44:4. According to Deuteronomy *Rabbah* 7:10, Moses is punished for arguing with God at the time of the Golden Calf by being refused entry into the Land of Israel.

43. Exodus *Rabbah* 43:5, 47:9, Deuteronomy *Rabbah* 3:11.

44. Exodus *Rabbah* 43:7. In Exodus *Rabbah* 41:7 Moses forces God to acknowledge that Israel is still His people. See also *Pesikta de Rav Kahana* ed. Buber, 128b. Jacob uses the same argument in *Shabbat* 89b. See, however, Exodus *Rabbah* 42:6 where God has an answer to this argument of Moses.

45. Exodus *Rabbah* 43:7,8,9; Leviticus *Rabbah* 23:2.

46. Exodus *Rabbah* 43:6,7; Deuteronomy *Rabbah* 1:2. A similar humorous story depicts God as a king, Israel as the queen who is caught kissing a eunuch (the Calf), and Moses as the adviser who cleverly defends the queen by pointing out the impotence of the eunuch to really do anything that the king could be concerned about regarding the queen (Numbers *Rabbah* 2:15; *Pesikta Rabbati* 11, pp. 55b–56a).

47. Exodus *Rabbah* 43:7.

48. Exodus *Rabbah* 43:8. Moses also uses God's words which had been addressed to him at Marah to urge God "to make Israel's bitterness sweet" (Exodus *Rabbah* 43:3). But in *Sanhedrin* 111a–b, God and Moses argue over God's forgiveness, with Moses wanting God to be strict with the wicked. God warns Moses that he will regret his words, which Moses does (one chapter earlier) at the time of the Golden Calf. Yet even here, God may be proved right regarding Moses' words, but Moses wins the argument!

49. *Berakhot* 32a.

50. Exodus *Rabbah* 44:9.

51. *Berakhot* 32a. In Exodus *Rabbah* 43:1, Moses shoves Satan aside, snatches the Tablets, and breaks them, all in order to save Israel. In *Ta'anit* 4, 68c, Moses and God engage in a tug of war over the Tablets, which Moses wins.

52. Exodus *Rabbah* 43:4. See also the complex exegesis made here to prove that Moses did not really sit before God. He was really standing and God was sitting, all in such a way that it appeared as just the reverse. This section on the annulment of God's vow follows the procedures of *Nedarim* 21b, 77b. For other almost-Promethean stories see above, note 38.

53. *Pesikta Rabbati* 40, p. 168b; *Midrash Tehillim* 103:12.

54. Exodus *Rabbah* 44:9; *Berakhot* 32a.

55. Numbers *Rabbah* 19:33.

56. Exodus *Rabbah* 46:1, 47:9; Deuteronomy *Rabbah* 3:11.

57. *Berakhot* 31b. See also *Pesikta Rabbati* 43, ed. Friedmann, pp. 179a–180a. In each case Hannah is criticized for "hurling words against Heaven." See R. Eleazar's words, *Berakhot* 31b, and also *Pesikta Rabbati* 46, p. 186b.

58. *Tanhuma Bereishit* 9.

59. See in addition to the examples cited in text *Sanhedrin* 64a, *Yoma* 69a, and *Shabbat* 55a, where Israel seizes the evil inclination, imprisons it, and tries to put it to death.

60. *Sanhedrin* 101b.

61. Genesis *Rabbah* 19:11; Numbers *Rabbah* 20:6,9.

62. *Baba Batra* 16a. According to Raba, Job said: "Master of the Universe! You have created the ox with cloven hoofs, and You have created the ass with whole hoofs; You have created Paradise, and You have created Gehinnom; You have created righteous men, and You have [also] created wicked men, and who can prevent You?" (Job 10:7).

63. See also Genesis *Rabbah* 22:9.

64. Genesis *Rabbah* 27:4; *Tanhuma Noah*, ed. Buber, p. 15b.

65. Genesis *Rabbah* 9:7, see also references in note 59, above.

66. *Sifré* Deuteronomy *Ha'azinu*, piska 307, ed. Finkelstein, p. 344.

67. *Sifré* Deuteronomy *Eikev*, piska 45, p. 103–104; *Kiddushin* 30b, *Baba Batra* 16a.

68. Deuteronomy *Rabbah* 8:1. Cain said: "Master of the Universe! You bear with the whole world, yet You will not bear my sin? But you have written: 'Who is a God like You, pardoning iniquity and passing over transgression?' [Micah 7:18]. Pardon my iniquity for it is great."

69. See note 19, above, for references pertaining to God's justice and His mercy, and note 38 regarding God's struggle with His attribute of Justice.

70. Leviticus *Rabbah* 10:5.

71. Deuteronomy *Rabbah* 2:20, *Sanhedrin* 103a, also note 38, above, regarding God's conflict with His attribute of Justice. See also *Tanhuma* Va'eira 8, 10, p. 27a–b, 28a; and *Tanna de be Eliyahu* 14, ed. Friedmann, p. 62.

72. Exodus *Rabbah* 46:4, *Sanhedrin* 96b.

73. *Berakhot* 31b–32a; *Sukkah* 52b.

74. *Tanna de be Eliyahu* 14, ed. Friedmann, p. 62.

75. *Berakhot* 17a.

76. This motif is common in the Psalms especially. See also Esther's prayers, *Berakhot* 32a, *Midrash Tehillim* 22:19, ed. Buber, p. 189; and Israel's prayer regarding sacrifices and the rebuilding of the Temple, Leviticus *Rabbah* 7:2.

77. See Lamentations *Rabbah* 5:21, but also *Midrash Tehillim* 70:1, ed. Buber, p. 321. Also *Midrash Tehillim* 85:3, ed. Buber, p. 372.

78. For a complete discussion of the concepts of sin and repentance, consult Adolph Buechler, *Studies in Sin and Atonement*, and Jakob J. Petuchowski, "The Concept of 'Teshuvah' in the Bible and the Talmud," *Judaism* 17 (Spring 1968): 175–185.

79. See above, note 59.

80. *Mekhilta*, Bahodesh, ed. Lauterbach, 2:271–272; *Avodah Zarah* 5a; Exodus *Rabbah* 32:1, 51:8; Leviticus *Rabbah* 18:3. God plans it this way, see Exodus *Rabbah* 41:7, 51:8.

81. David's death—*Shabbat* 30b. Joshua b. Levi tricks the Angel of Death only to be made by God to accept death—*Ketubot* 77b. See also the stories of R. Eleazar, R. Sheshet, R. Ashi, R. Hisda, and R. Hiyya—*Mo'ed Katan* 28a, and R. Nahman—*Baba Metzia* 86a.

82. Deuteronomy 3:24–28; also Numbers 27:12–14, Deuteronomy 32:48–52.

83. Genesis *Rabbah* 9:5.

84. Genesis *Rabbah* 9:8–11.

85. *Mekhilta*, Bahodesh, ed. Lauterbach, 2:271–272; *Avodah Zarah* 5a; *Ketubot* 77b, *Shabbat* 55b; Exodus *Rabbah* 38:2; Numbers *Rabbah* 19:11; *Sifré* Deuteronomy *Ha'azinu*, piska 339, ed. Finkelstein, p. 388.

86. See above, note 82, and Numbers *Rabbah* 19:10; *Shabbat* 55b.

87. At the Burning Bush—Leviticus *Rabbah* 11:6; Numbers *Rabbah* 21:15; Deuteronomy *Rabbah* 9:6–7; *Midrash Tehillim* 18:22, ed. Buber, p. 150. After Moses' first rejection by the Israelites—Exodus *Rabbah* 5:23, *Sanhedrin* 111a, *Tanhuma* Va'eira:1, pp. 71b–72a. At the Golden Calf—Deuteronomy *Rabbah* 7:10.

88. Deuteronomy *Rabbah* 11:9. This sort of exegesis is frequently used to prove God's justice in the long run. Jacob vows with *v'hayah* and God vows to bring the redemption with *v'hayah*—Genesis *Rabbah* 70:6. Judah saves Tamar from burning as a harlot, and God vows to save Judah's descendants from Nebuchadnezzar's furnace—*Sotah* 10b. God expels Adam with *eikhah* and later He expels Israel with *eikhah*—Genesis *Rabbah* 19:9. God utters "How long?" twice and Israel will utter it under each of the four kingdoms—Numbers *Rabbah* 16:22; *Midrash Tehillim* 13:1, p. 109. Israel wept without cause at the report of the spies; God will give them something real to weep about on that same date in the future (the Ninth of Av)—Numbers *Rabbah* 16:20; *Sotah* 35a.

90. Numbers *Rabbah* 19:13.

91. The angels protest in favor of Moses: *Sifré* Deuteronomy *Ha'azinu*, piska 339, ed. Finkelstein, p. 388; *Shabbat* 55b.

92. Deuteronomy *Rabbah* 11:10.
93. Deuteronomy *Rabbah* 11:9.
94. Deuteronomy *Rabbah* 11:10. Compare Moses' arguments here with those he uses in his attempt to gain entry into the Land. He argues based on God's mercy and graciousness—Deuteronomy *Rabbah* 2:1, 7. He argues based on God's breaking His oath and by His double standard toward Joseph and Moses—Deuteronomy *Rabbah* 2:8. He argues that not to enter the Land is a very great degradation for him—Deuteronomy *Rabbah* 2:8, 9:4; Numbers *Rabbah* 19:33; *Sifré* Deuteronomy Ha'azinu, piska 339, ed. Finkelstein, p. 388. He argues based on the precedent of the Golden Calf, using a *kal vahomeir* argument—*Sifré* Deuteronomy Va'ethanan, piska 27, ed. Finkelstein, pp. 41–42. He argues based on the precedent of his having already set foot on Gad's and Reuben's share of the Land (and by God's nature)—*Sifré* Numbers Pinhas, piska 134–135, ed. Horovitz, pp. 179–182. He appeals to enter as a private person, by an alternative route, in death if not in life—*Mekhilta*, Amalek, ed. Lauterbach, 2:151–154; *Sifré* Numbers Pinhas, piska 135, ed. Horovitz, pp. 181–182; *Sifré* Deuteronomy Ha'azinu, piska 341, ed. Finkelstein, p. 390.
95. Deuteronomy *Rabbah* 11:10; *Sifré* Deuteronomy Nitzavim, piska 305, ed. Finkelstein, pp. 326–327. Moses wants an honorable death like Aaron—Avot de Rabbi Natan A:12, ed. Schechter, pp. 49–50; he does not wish to be taken by death as a beast (see R. Sheshet—*Mo'ed Katan* 28a). Compare Moses' struggle with those of the other characters mentioned in note 81.
96. Deuteronomy *Rabbah* 11:10.
97. *Sotah* 13b. Compare this entire account with that of *Midrash Petirat Moshe*; see Peter S. Knobel, *Petirat Moshe: A Critical Edition and Translation* (Cincinnati: unpublished rabbinic thesis, 1969).
98. *Sifré* Deuteronomy Va'ethanan, piska 29, ed. Finkelstein, p. 46.
99. *Sotah* 13b.
100. *Sifré* Deuteronomy *Ha'azinu*, piska 307, ed. Finkelstein, p. 344.

NOTES TO CHAPTER 3

1. Isaiah 54:7–8.
2. Psalm 90:4.
3. For a full development of this, and many of the other issues raised in this chapter, particularly with regard to Lamentations *Rabbah*, consult Charles A. Kroloff, *The Effect of Suffering on the Concept of God in Lamentations Rabba* (Cincinnati: unpublished rabbinic thesis, 1960).

4. See the classic discussion on this view of suffering in *Sifré* Deuteronomy Va'ethanan, piska 32, ed. Finkelstein, pp. 55–58; also *Mekhilta*, Bahodesh, ed. Lauterbach, 2:277–282. Akiba learned this teaching from Nahum of Gamzu. Compare their two teachings: *Ta'anit* 21a and *Berakhot* 60b. This view of suffering is repeated in many places in the Talmud and Midrash. For the relationship of this submissive attitude toward suffering and its attitude towards protest, consult *Sifré* Deuteronomy Ha'azinu, piska 307, ed. Finkelstein, pp. 344–346. However, the connection between the two is by no means constant or even uniformly applied by the same teachers. See discussion of this view in Adolf Buechler, *Studies in Sin and Atonement*, pp. 150–211; and Arthur Marmorstein, *The Old Rabbinic Doctrine of God* (London: Oxford University Press, 1927), pp. 185–196.

5. Consult Jakob J. Petuchowski, *Theology and Poetry* (London: Routledge and Kegan Paul, 1978), p. 73.

6. Lamentations *Rabbah* 3:11; *Midrash Tehillim* 102:8; *Pesikta de Rav Kahana*, piska 16, ed. Buber, p. 126b; *Pesikta Rabbati*, piska 26, ed. Friedmann, pp. 131b–132a.

7. *Sifré* Deuteronomy *Ha'azinu*, piska 306, ed. Finkelstein, p. 330.

8. *Midrash Tehillim* 10:8.

9. *Berakhot* 32b. See also other arguments on similar motifs: Lamentations *Rabbah* 1:3; *Midrash Tehillim* 10:8; 13:1; 68:3; 146:9; *Pesikta de Rav Kahana* 17, ed. Buber, p. 134b, *Pesikta Rabbati* 31, ed. Friedmann, pp. 143b–144a.

10. *Pesikta Rabbati* 31, ed. Friedmann, pp. 143b–144a; also p. 142b; Exodus *Rabbah* 31:10.

11. *Midrash Tehillim* 137:8; Lamentations *Rabbah* 5:1.

12. *Midrash Tehillim* 10:4; Lamentations *Rabbah* 5:1.

13. Lamentations *Rabbah* 3:1. See *Avodah Zarah*, 2b for the legend to which Israel refers.

14. See Genesis *Rabbah* 49:10, where God rewards Abraham by allowing his descendants to question Him, too.

15. *Midrash Tehillim* 44:1. See also *Midrash Tehillim* 13:2; 42:8; 71:2,3,4; Lamentations *Rabbah* Proem 24; *Mekhilta*, Shirta, ed. Lauterbach, 2:66.

16. *Midrash Tehillim* 22:17; 119:32; Lamentations *Rabbah* 1:37.

17. *Pesikta Rabbati* 33, ed. Friedmann, p. 149b. See also Israel's argument based upon Exodus 22:21 and Psalm 9:19, in which she expects God to protect her as one of His wards, *Midrash Tehillim* 13:1.

18. *Midrash Tehillim* 13:1; Lamentations *Rabbah* 5:19. See also Samuel b. Nahmani's teaching in *Midrash Tehillim* 13:1 on God's justice and His mercy, and the view in Lamentations *Rabbah* 2:21 that God must compromise His justice—both similar to Abraham's aggadic

argument with God at Sodom and Gomorrah. Similarly, Israel asks that God be compassionate to them like Abraham and Jacob were, *Pesikta de Rav Kahana* 19, ed. Buber, p. 139a.

19. *Gittin* 58a.
20. *Midrash Tehillim* 44:2.
21. *Yoma* 69b; *Midrash Tehillim* 19:2.
22. Another equally daring liturgical midrash is that of the school of R. Ishmael in which the word *ba'eilim* in the phrase *mi khamokha ba'eilim* is rendered as *mi khamokha ba'ilmim* (among the dumb?). See *Mekhilta*, Shirta, ed. Lauterbach, 2:60; *Gittin* 56b; and the discussion of this passage in Petuchowski, *Theology and Poetry*, pp. 71–73. The *Mekhilta* passage would seem to support both interpretations suggested by Petuchowski, i.e., that God does willfully keep silent but that He will not remain so forever.
23. *Midrash Tehillim* 119:17.
24. Lamentations *Rabbah* Proem 24. The patriarchs are not always so inclined to defend Israel. While in *Menahot* 53b Abraham defends Israel, and in *Baba Metzia* 85b Elijah wakes the three Patriarchs separately lest they pray together and bring the Messiah, in another case, only Moses will defend Israel, Esther *Rabbati*, 7:18, ed. Lewin-Epstein, pp. 15b–16a; or in another case, only Isaac will defend them, *Shabbat* 89b. In the latter passage, Israel also prefers to be rebuked by God Himself rather than entrust that task to their Fathers. This reflects the often contradictory attitude of the Rabbis to the *zekhut avot.* See Marmorstein. *Doctrine of Merits.* David, Daniel, Jeremiah, and others also intervene on behalf of Israel in a number of midrashim, *Midrash Tehillim* 98:1; 109:1; 119:30,31; 137:7; *Pesikta Rabbati* 31, ed. Friedmann, pp. 144b–146a, to cite but a few examples.
25. Lamentations *Rabbah* 1:50; *Gittin* 57b.
26. It is this attitude, I believe, that inspired R. Akiba's teaching of submission to God's judgment. Like so many of the Rabbis, Akiba was forced to admit that God had done the deed, which could only lead him, like it or not, to assert that God was just in all that He did. No Rabbi seems to deny God this; only some, in their midrashim, do protest against the severity of the sentence.
27. *Pesikta Rabbati* 29–30, ed. Friedmann, pp. 138–141b; *Pesikta de Rav Kahana*, piska 16, ed. Buber, pp. 127b–128a.
28. *Pesikta Rabbati* 30, ed. Friedmann, p. 142a.
29. For more detail on Israel's sins, consult Kroloff, *Effect of Suffering*, pp. 7–18.
30. *Midrash Tehillim* 10:1,2; 13:1,2. See also *Rosh Hashanah* 31a–b.
31. *Berakhot* 32b; *Pesikta Rabbati* 31, ed. Friedmann, pp. 144b–145a; *Pesikta de Rav Kahana* piska 17, ed. Buber, p. 133b.

32. *Midrash Tehillim* 13:2; *Pesikta Rabbati* 31, ed. Friedmann, pp. 143b–144a.
33. *Pesikta Rabbati* 29–30, ed. Friedmann, pp. 138–141b; *Pesikta de Rav Kahana* 16, ed. Buber, p. 126b.
34. *Sifré* Deuteronomy Ha'azinu, piska 306, ed. Finkelstein, p. 330; *Midrash Tehillim* 10:8; *Pesikta Rabbati* 31, ed. Friedmann, pp. 143b–144a.
35. Lamentations *Rabbah* proem 24; *Pesikta de Rav Kahana* 17, ed. Buber, p. 134b; 19, p. 139a.
36. *Midrash Tehillim* 13:1.
37. *Menahot* 53b.
38. *Midrash Tehillim* 119:17, also the references to Job and Jerusalem, note 6 above.
39. *Mekhilta*, Shirta, ed. Lauterbach, 2:66; *Midrash Tehillim* 44:1; 71:2,3,4.
40. *Mekhilta*, Shirta, ed. Lauterbach, 2:60–61; Exodus *Rabbah* 15:17, 30:1; Numbers *Rabbah* 11:1; *Midrash Tehillim* 109:1.
41. *Mekhilta*, Pisha, ed. Lauterbach, 1:113–115; Shirta, 2:27; Amalek, 2:159–160; *Sifré* Numbers Beha'alotekha, piska 84, ed. Horovitz, pp. 81–83. Later references to this same motif include Exodus *Rabbah* 2:5,7; 15:12; Numbers *Rabbah* 2:2; *Midrash Tehillim* 20:1,3.
42. *Mekhilta*, Shirta, ed. Lauterbach, 2:41–42.
43. Lamentations *Rabbah* proem 24. See Kroloff, *Effect of Suffering*, pp. 49–66, for more detail on the limiting of God through empathy and anthropomorphism.
44. *Midrash Tehillim* 20:1; Exodus *Rabbah* 2:5.
45. Lamentations *Rabbah* proem 8, proem 24, 1:1, 1:45; *Pesikta Rabbati* 29, ed. Friedmann, pp. 136b–137a; *Midrash Tehillim* 121:3; *Pesikta de Rav Kahana* 15, ed. Buber, pp. 119b–120a.
46. *Midrash Tehillim* 121:3.
47. Ibid.
48. *Pesikta de Rav Kahana* 13, ed. Buber, p. 113b; Lamentations *Rabbah* proem 34, 1:32.
49. Lamentations *Rabbah* proem 24, 2:3; *Pesikta de Rav Kahana* 17, ed. Buber, p. 132a; *Midrash Tehillim* 98:1, 137:7; *Pesikta Rabbati* 31, ed. Friedmann, pp. 144b–145a.
50. *Pesikta Rabbati* 31, ed. Friedmann, p. 144b. Compare with the *Mekhilta* passage cited in note 42. See also *Midrash Tehillim* 59:5.
51. Exodus *Rabbah* 38:4. Also Leviticus *Rabbah* 7:3, *Menahot* 110a, and Abraham's law-court argument with God in *Ta'anit* 27b and *Megillah* 31b, in which God says that if one studies the sacrifices, He will account it as if one had offered a sacrifice. The destruction of the Temple constituted a serious break in Israel's relationship with God. In the Rabbis' own words a barrier between Israel and God came into

being following the destruction of the Temple, and only the Gate of Prayer (elsewhere, of Weeping, or of Mercy) remained open to Israel— Lamentations *Rabbah* 3:35; Deuteronomy *Rabbah* 2:12; *Berakhot* 32a–b, *Baba Metzia* 59a; *Midrash Tehillim* 4:3; 65:4. See David's intercession on behalf of the generation which has no king, prophet, priest, *urim* or *thumim*, only prayer—Leviticus *Rabbah* 30:3. See also the assertion that God still hears prayer in the post-Temple era— *Midrash Tehillim* 3:7; 4:1.

52. Numbers *Rabbah* 18:21, also *Midrash Tehillim* 25:3. Compare with the prayer of R. Sheshet, *Berakhot* 17a.

NOTES TO CHAPTER 4

1. Heinemann, *Prayer in the Talmud*, pp. 193–208, and Lee, *The Private Prayers of the Rabbis*, pp. 38–69, 159–163, have done work on the Rabbis' personal use of the law-court pattern of prayer. Lee in particular has contributed to the substantiation of Heinemann's claim that many of the Rabbis' thanksgiving and confessional prayers (some of which are found in the liturgy) have the form of the law-court pattern. The Rabbis' use of the pattern, as Heinemann says on p. 193, "belongs primarily to the area of private and nonobligatory prayers; for although such a prayer may frequently be recited by an individual on behalf of the congregation, it is never found in its pure form in statutory public worship."

2. R. Tsadok prayed: "My Father in Heaven! You have destroyed Your city and burned Your Temple. Now shall You sit and be calm and quiet?!" Tanna de be Eliahu, 28, ed. Friedmann, p. 149.

3. See Levi b. Sisi's prayer in *Pesikta de Rav Kahana* 25, ed. Buber, p. 165b, *Ta'anit* 3:66d and R. Eleazar's prayer in *Ta'anit* 4:68d.

4. Gamaliel's prayer—*Baba Metzia* 59b. See text in note 61.

5. Judah HaNasi's prayer—*Ketubot* 104a. Other examples include R. Sheshet's prayer on the occasion of his fast—*Berakhot* 17a, and R. Alexandri's prayer against the evil inclination and the exile—*Berakhot* 17a. For additional sources see Lee, *The Private Prayers of the Rabbis*, pp. 38–69.

6. Leviticus 26:18–20; Deuteronomy 11:13–17;· 28:22–24; Jeremiah 14:1–7,20; Amos 4:7–8; 1 Kings 8:35. *Mishnah Ta'anit* 1:1, 7.

7. The list of sins is quite inclusive, see *Ta'anit* 7b, 8b; Numbers *Rabbah* 8:4. For references regarding the gift of rain, see *Ta'anit* 7a, 8b; Genesis *Rabbah* 13:4,5,6; *Midrash Tehillim* 117:1.

8. Joel 1:14; 2:12–17. Also Jeremiah 14:7–9,12,19–22; and 1 Kings 8:35–38. Compare these with the psalms of lament—they are one of a kind.

See also 1 Samuel 7:5, 12:19–23; Judges 20:26 regarding fasts and assemblies.

9. 1 Kings 18:36–37.
10. Jeremiah 14:11–12, 15:1 and also Jeremiah's complaint regarding his inability to intercede—Jeremiah 15:10–12. The lament-prayer for rain found in Jeremiah 14:7–9,19–22 may either be Jeremiah's own words or the recorded words of the prayers of the priests. I would suggest the latter, while Jeremiah's words are the intervening section, verses 10–18.
11. Consult Adolph Buechler, *Types of Jewish-Palestinian Piety*, (London: Jews' College Publications, 1922), pp. 213–221 regarding the fast rituals and prayers of repentance; pp. 221–230 regarding the fast liturgies and doxologies; pp. 231–241 regarding the use of the *shofar*; and pp. 241–246 regarding the liturgy for the granting of rain. Consult also Heinemann, *Prayer in the Talmud*, pp. 108–111 regarding the fast liturgy and the use of the *shofar*; and pp. 144–155 regarding the use of litanies in the *Hallel*, *Hoshannot* and *Slihot*.
12. Buechler, *Types*, pp. 214–216, 219–221.
13. Buechler, *Types*, pp. 241–246.
14. *Ta'anit* 16a. Two other occasions where the use of the forceful law-court pattern is sanctioned in the liturgy are the prayer of the High Priest—*Sotah* 39a–b; Numbers *Rabbah* 11:4; and the prayer of the people following their giving of the tithes—Exodus *Rabbah* 41:1. Of course, the law-court-patterned confessional prayers, such as the mourner's prayer in *Berakhot* 19a, also were incorporated into the liturgy.
15. See the qualifications for such a person—*Ta'anit* 16a. Also Buechler, *Types*, pp. 200–201, 212–213, 255, 260–264.
16. *Ta'anit* 23a.
17. See Rashi on Par Hoda'ah and Buechler, *Types*, pp. 250–252.
18. *Ta'anit* 23a.
19. Other figures make use of the circle as well. Habakkuk is cited in the *Ta'anit* 23a account; see also *Targum* on Habakkuk 2:1 and *Midrash Tehillim* 7:17. Moses uses it in praying for Miriam's recovery, *Avot de Rabbi Natan* A:9, ed. Schechter, p. 41; and to delay his own death, Deuteronomy *Rabbah* 11:10. The oath is also used in conjunction with a Torah scroll. Thus Levi b. Sisi took hold of a Torah scroll, ascended the roof of a house, and exclaimed: "Master of the Universe! If I ever neglected a single word of this Torah, let the enemy enter, but if not, have them go." And they vanished.— *Pesikta de Rav Kahana* 25, ed. Buber, p. 165b.

In Jewish sources it is the oath, and not the circle that gives the power, and the oath's power derives from the individual's merit with

God. Consult Buechler, *Types*, note 2, pp. 246–247; and Heinemann, *Prayer in the Talmud*, note 11, pp. 206–207, for more on the use of the oath, the circle, and other devices to end a drought. Consult Sir James George Frazer, *The New Golden Bough*, ed. Theodor H. Gaster (New York: Criterion Books, 1959), pp. 38–53, for rainmaking techniques in other cultures and ages. While Buechler, in the reference cited immediately above, is correct in stating that Honi's act is unlike any other Frazer notes, there are great similarities in Israel's communal actions to end a drought and those done in other cultures. These include special dress, fasting, special acts, threatening prayers by the rainmaker, special processions, and the invoking (or use) of the dead.

20. *Ta'anit* 23b. Regarding Abba Hilkiah, see *Ta'anit* 23a–b.
21. *Ta'anit* 20a. See also Rabban Gamaliel's prayer in *Baba Metzia* 59b: "Master of the Universe! It is known to You that I did not act for my own honour nor for the honour of my father's house, but for Your honour that dissension not multiply in Israel"—and the storm abated.
22. *Ta'anit* 20a.
23. *Avot de Rabbi Natan* A:6, ed. Schechter, p. 32.
24. See the praise accorded to Hanina b. Dosa—*Berakhot* 17b, 61a; *Hagigah* 14a; *Sotah* 49b; *Ta'anit* 24a; *Sukkah* 51a, 53a.
25. *Yoma* 53b; *Ta'anit* 24b; *Sotah* 39a–b; Numbers *Rabbah* 11:4.
26. *Ta'anit* 24b; *Yoma* 53b. For other examples of Hanina b. Dosa's great deeds, see *Ta'anit* 24b–25a; *Berakhot* 34b.
27. Judah HaNasi, Nahman, Rabbah, Rab—*Ta'anit* 24a; Raba, Judah, Papa—*Ta'anit* 24b; Hama b. Hanina, Joshua b. Levi, Levi, Hiyya b. Luliani—*Ta'anit* 25a; Eliezar, Akiba, Judah HaNasi, Samuel HaKatan—*Ta'anit* 25b. Tanhuma—Leviticus *Rabbah* 34:14; Genesis *Rabbah* 33:3. For equally forceful use of the law-court pattern, though in other circumstances, see above, notes 2–5.
28. *Ta'anit* 25b.
29. *Ta'anit* 25a.
30. Leviticus *Rabbah* 34:14; Genesis *Rabbah* 33:3.
31. *Ta'anit* 25a.
32. *Ta'anit* 24b.
33. See *Ta'anit* 16a for the qualifications of the prayer leader. The Rabbis accepted the concept of special merit and recognized the ability of such an individual to bring rain; see R. Ammi's statement—*Ta'anit* 8a; also the success of R. Ilfa (Ilfi) over Rabbi, and the success of the unnamed reader over Rab—*Ta'anit* 24a; also the success of Honi and Hanina b. Dosa regarding the bringing of rain. See also note 43 regarding the special abilities of the *tzaddik*. However, much depended upon the repentance of the people—see the story of Joshua b.

Levi and the people of Hanina's town *Ta'anit* 3:66c; the remarks of
Eliezer and Samuel HaKatan *Ta'anit* 25b. In other instances, the
humbling of the intercessor brought on rain after all fasts and prayers had failed—see Judah HaNasi and R. Nahman, *Ta'anit* 24a;
R. Papa, *Ta'anit* 24b.

34. *Pesikta de Rav Kahana* 25, ed. Buber, p. 165b.
35. *Ta'anit* 25a; *Megillah* 22b. For Levi's prayer, see p. 92, and note 29.
36. *Berakhot* 31b–32a.
37. *Sukkah* 53a; *Ta'anit* 25a; *Megillah* 22b.
38. *Ta'anit* 24b. R. Jose also criticizes his son for troubling Heaven with
    a minor request and prays that his son die an early death. However,
    the stories that follow show R. Jose to be a harsh and heartless
    individual, see *Ta'anit* 24b.
39. See Buechler, *Types*, pp. 196–264; Heinemann, *Prayer in the Tal-
    mud*, pp. 200–202; David Daube, "Enfant Terrible," *Harvard Theo-
    logical Review* 68 (July–October 1975):371–376; Dov Noy, "Tefillat
    Hatamim Moridah Geshamim" *Mahanayim* 51 (1960):34–45; Louis
    Jacobs, "The Concept of Hasid in the Biblical and Rabbinic Litera-
    ture, "*Journal of Jewish Studies* 8:3–4(1957):143–154; Alexander
    Guttmann, "The Significance of Miracles for Talmudic Judaism,
    "*Studies in Rabbinic Judaism*, (New York: Ktav, 1976), pp. 47–90 for
    various analyses of this subject. Daube alone is highly critical of Honi
    and Hanina b. Dosa and disregards all references to their righteous-
    ness. The others do take note of their piety while recognizing the
    ambivalent attitude of the Rabbis to such prayers. Guttmann at-
    tempts to place the rabbinic reliance on miracles into the historical
    context of the Rabbis' struggle against Christianity.
40. Buechler, *Types*, pp. 199–201, 255. See the praise accorded Honi—
    Ta'anit 23a; Genesis *Rabbah* 13:7; *Ta'anit* 3:67a; and the praise
    according Hanina b. Dosa—notes 24 and 26.
41. Buechler, *Types*, pp. 200–201.
42. See *Ta'anit* 16a.
43. Honi—*Ta'anit* 23a; Hanina b. Dosa—*Baba Metzia* 106a; Jacob—
    Genesis *Rabbah* 79:3; Numbers *Rabbah* 14:4; *Pesikta Rabbati* 3, ed.
    Friedmann, p. 7b; *Pesikta Rabbati* 17, p. 85b; Amram—*Sotah* 12a;
    Moses—Exodus *Rabbah* 21:2, 43:1; Deuteronomy *Rabbah* 2:3;
    Numbers *Rabbah* 18:12; *Sifré* Numbers Beha'alotekha 105, ed. Horo-
    vitz, p. 104; *Pesikta Rabbati* 17, p. 85b; Elijah and Miciah—Numbers
    Rabbah 18:12; Judah HaNasi—*Ketubot* 103b; *Shabbat* 59b; the
    righteous in general—*Mo'ed Katan* 16b; *Sukkah* 14a.
44. *Ta'anit* 19a, 23a; *Berakhot* 19a.
45. *Ta'anit* 23a. Buechler, *Types*, pp. 249, 252–254.
46. *Ta'anit* 3:67a.

47. *Ta'anit* 23a.
48. Buechler, *Types*, pp. 246–247, 249.
49. Buechler, *Types*, pp. 249–252.
50. See Daube, "Enfant Terrible," p. 374, Jacobs, "Concept of Hasid," pp. 151–153, and Noy, *Tefillat Hatamim*, pp. 34–36, 40. This latter article also contains several good examples of law-court prayers for rain in later centuries; see in particular the prayer of the villager as told by the Lubavitcher Rebbe, p. 44, and the prayer of the man who threatens God that he will tear his *tzitzit* unless God sends rain, p. 45.
51. This analysis follows Buechler, *Types*, pp. 199–201, 203–204, 247–249.
52. *Berakhot* 34b.
53. See Buechler, *Types*, note 1, pp. 203–204.
54. *Ta'anit* 3:66c–d.
55. *Song of Songs Rabbati* 1:44, p. 29a.
56. See Samuel HaKatan's parable in *Ta'anit* 25b, also *Sifré* Deuteronomy *V'zot haberakhah*, 343, ed. Finkelstein, pp. 394–395 for the example of "proper prayer" provided by Moses, David, Solomon, and the prophets. See Heinemann's analysis, and source references for, the servant-before-the-master pattern, *Prayer in the Talmud*, pp. 202–204.
57. *Yoma* 53b; *Ta'anit* 24b.
58. Buechler, *Types*, p. 217.
59. *Berakhot* 19a, and Rashi ad. loc.
60. Daube, "Enfant Terrible," p. 372.
61. *Baba Metzia* 59ab. See also *Mo'ed Katan* 3:1, 81cd. This story ironically ends with a good law-court prayer *and* an acceptable miracle. Rabban Gamaliel, Eliezer's brother-in-law, who, as *Nasi*, was ultimately responsible for the ban, was traveling on a ship on the day R. Eliezer was banned. R. Gamaliel's ship was threatened by a huge wave and he recognized its source: so great was R. Eliezer's prestige that disasters (negative miracles) had spread around the world on that day. So R. Gamaliel arose and prayed:

> **Address:** Master of the Universe!
> **Defense/Petition:** You know full well that I have not acted for my honor, nor for the honor of my paternal home, but for Yours, so that differences may not multiply in Israel.
> **Divine Response:** At that, the raging sea subsided.

62. Guttmann, "Significance of Miracles," pp. 50–81.
63. *Berakhot* 60a. See also Guttmann "Significance of Miracles," p. 76 and references cited there; see also pp. 70, 87–90.

NOTES TO CHAPTER 5

1. See *Berakhot* 33b and *Megillah* 25a for these amoraic interpretations. See Arthur Marmorstein, *The Old Rabbinic Doctrine of God*, vol. 1 (London: Oxford University Press, 1927) pp. 205–206, for an interpretation of these amoraic statements.
2. Heinemann, *Prayer in the Talmud*, p. 201, suggests that the final line of the story, which states that Rabbah was only testing Abaye, is a later editorial emendation designed to harmonize the two conflicting views.
3. Genesis *Rabbah* 75:13.
4. Lamentations *Rabbah* Proem 24 (used by Moses), 1:37; *Midrash Tehillim* 22:17.
5. Leviticus *Rabbah* 27:11.
6. *Ta'anit* 16a.
7. *Hagigah* 14b–15a; *Hagigah* 2:1, 77b. Also Song of Songs *Rabbati* 1:4.
8. Marcus Jastrow, *A Dictionary of the Targumim, the Talmud Babli and Yerushalmi, and the Midrashic Literature* (New York: The Judaica Press, 1971), s.v. *pardes*.
9. Gershom G. Scholem, *Major Trends in Jewish Mysticism* (New York: Schocken Books, 1961), pp. 52–53; also his *Jewish Gnosticism, Merkabah Mysticism and Talmudic Tradition* (New York: Jewish Theological Seminary, 1965), p. 14. For more on *Pardes*, see his *Jewish Gnosticism*, p. 16.
10. Samson R. Levey, "The Best Kept Secret of the Rabbinic Tradition," *Judaism* 21 (Fall 1972):468.
11. Consult Levey, "The Best Kept Secret," pp. 456–462 for a summary of scholarly views regarding ben Zoma. Regarding Aher, consult *The Jewish Encyclopedia*, 1901 ed., s.v. "Elisha Ben Abuyah" by Louis Ginzberg.
12. See Scholem, *Major Trends*, p. 68; and *Jewish Gnosticism*, pp. 41, 43–55, for more on Metatron and his place in the Heavenly court. See *Sanhedrin* 38b, where a Jew and a heretic argue about the worship of Metatron. See Scholem, *Major Trends*, pp. 65–66, and note 24 to lecture II; also Marmorstein, *Background of the Haggadah*, pp. 6–7, for more on the Jewish form of Gnosticism. See Scholem, *Jewish Gnosticism*, addenda, p. 127 and note 6, for the meaning of Aher's cutting the saplings.
13. Ruth *Rabbah* 6:6, p. 73; Ecclesiastes *Rabbah* 7:18, p. 125.
14. *Hullin* 142a; *Kiddushin* 39b.
15. See Marmorstein, *Old Rabbinic Doctrine of God*, vol. 1, pp. 181–208.

16. *Sifré* Numbers Beha'alotekha 103, ed. Horovitz, pp. 101–102; Exodus *Rabbah* 45:5, 6; *Berakhot* 7a; *Midrash Tehillim* 25:6; *Avot de Rabbi Natan* A:25, ed. Schechter, p. 79; *Tanhuma, Ki tisa*, p. 124; *Tanhuma Buber, Ki tisa*, p. 116; *Tanhuma, Va'ethanan*, p. 101.
17. *Menahot* 29b.
18. For some of Aher's "political" crimes see *Hagigah* 2:1, 77b. Dr. Petuchowski has drawn my attention to a work in German which analyzes this question in some detail, Johann Maier, *Geschichte der Jüdischen Religion* (Berlin: Walter de Gruyter, 1972), pp. 209–211. Regarding the contradictory traditions about Aher, consult *Encyclopaedia Judaica*, 1972 ed., s.v. "Elisha Ben Avuyah" by Shmuel Safrai.
19. See Akiba's responses in the following situations:

    To the sick Eliezer—*Mekhilta, Bahodesh*, ed. Lauterbach, 2:277–282; *Sifré* Deuteronomy *Va'ethanan*, 32, ed. Finkelstein, pp. 57–58; *Sanhedrin* 101b.

    Upon seeing the Temple ruins—*Sifré* Deuteronomy 43, pp. 94–95.

    Regarding the "suffering of the Torah"—*Sanhedrin* 101a.

    Regarding suffering in general—*Sifré* Deuteronomy *Va'ethanan*, 32, pp. 55–56.

    Regarding divine justice in his own life—*Berakhot* 60b, 61b; *Berakhot* 9, 14b.

    For more detailed information regarding the views of Akiba, consult Buechler, *Studies in Sin and Atonement*, pp. 150–189; and Marmorstein, *The Old Rabbinic Doctrine of God*, vol. 1, pp. 185–208; and the many references contained in both. On another aspect of Akiba's thought, his use of anthropomorphisms to describe God, see Arthur Marmorstein, *Essays in Anthropomorphism* (London: Jew's College Publications, 1937).
20. Heinemann, *Prayer in the Talmud*, pp. 203–204, and sources quoted there.
21. *Berakhot* 5, 9c.
22. See Buechler, *Studies in Sin and Atonement*, pp. 163–189.
23. See Heinemann, *Prayer in the Talmud*, p. 205. The view that sufferings should be borne in love and patience does gain legitimacy and is incorporated into the liturgy. See for example, *Berakhot* 19a, 33b, 54a, 60b; *Megillah* 25a; *Pesahim* 50a and the mourner's *Tziduk Hadin* prayer.
24. Ruth *Rabbah* 6:6, p. 73; Ecclesiastes *Rabbah* 7:18, p. 125; *Hullin* 142a; *Kiddushin* 39b.

NOTES TO CHAPTER 6

1. See, for example, Deuteronomy 8:5; Psalm 94:11–12; Proverbs 3:11–12; Job 5:17–18; ben Sirach 18:11–14.
2. *Semahot* 8; *Midrash Tehillim* 26:2.
3. Ecclesiastes *Rabbah* 7:8; *Mekhilta, Beshalah*, ed. Lauterbach, 1:248; *Bahodesh*, 2:277–278; *Sifré* Deuteronomy, *Va'ethanan*, piska 32, ed. Finkelstein, pp. 55–56.
4. *Pesikta Rabbati* 47, ed. Friedmann, pp. 189b–190a.
5. *Mekhilta, Bahodesh*, 2:277–278; Deuteronomy *Rabbah* 2:4; *Midrash Tehillim* 11:4.
6. See Buechler, *Studies in Sin and Atonement*, pp. 163–189 and references cited there. See also note 13 to chapter 2.
7. Marmorstein, *The Old Rabbinic Doctrine of God*, vol. 1, pp. 188–190. See, for example, the responses of Hiyya b. Abba, Johanan, and Eleazar in *Berakhot* 5a.
8. See note 21 to chapter 2.
9. See notes 86 and 87 to chapter 2.
10. Hosea is punished for not disputing with God—*Pesahim* 87a–b, but Habakkuk argues and ends up repenting his rash words—*Midrash Tehillim* 7:17, *Midrash Tehillim* 90:7.
11. The term "statutory liturgy" refers to those basic prayers required for public worship, originally just the *Sh'ma* and its blessings, and the *Amidah*. It is meant, in this work, to include as well the later additions to the worship service.
12. Heinemann, *Prayer in the Talmud*, p. 205.
13. Heinemann, *Prayer in the Talmud*, pp. 205–206; Lee, *Private Prayers*, pp. 67–69.
14. *The Authorized Daily Prayer Book*, revised ed., Joseph Hertz, ed. and trans. (New York: Bloch Publishing, 1974), p. 129.
15. *Authorized Daily Prayer Book*, pp. 454–455.
16. Ibid., pp. 530–531.
17. *Prayer Book for Sabbath and Festivals*, trans. Philip Birnbaum (New York: Hebrew Publishing, 1964), p. 378.
18. *The Authorized Selichot for the Whole Year*, ed. and trans. Abraham Rosenfeld (New York: Judaica Press, 1978), p. 15 and many places.
19. The concluding prayer for the evening service of the Ninth of Av serves much the same function. Here prophetic verses are recited, in which God utters words of consolation and promises of redemption to His people. The verses both remind God of His promises and comfort the congregation with the divine pledge of redemption at the time of their greatest sorrow. *The Authorized Kinot for the Ninth of*

Av, ed. and trans. Abraham Rosenfeld (New York: Judaica Press, 1979), p. 39.

20. See, for example, Rosenfeld, *Selichot.* p. 7, 9, and many places. See also Abraham Millgram, *Jewish Worship*, (Philadelphia: Jewish Publication Society of America, 1971), pp. 228–230 and *Authorized Daily Prayer Book*, p. 187.

21. *Rosh Hashanah* 17b.

22. See "For on Your abundant mercies" in Rosenfeld, *Selichot*, p. 6 and many places.

23. Leviticus *Rabbah* 29:9; and parallel sources cited in note 22 to chapter 2.

24. *Prayer Book for Sabbath and Festivals*, p. 92.

25. *Authorized Daily Prayer Book*, pp. 882–883.

26. Rosenfeld, *Selichot*, p. 7 and many places.

27. Ibid. and many places.

28. This same argument motif is used following the chanting of *Kol Nidrei* on Yom Kippur eve. Here too is another example of God's words being quoted back to Him for Israel's benefit. Immediately after *Kol Nidrei*, God's words regarding the perpetual forgiveness for sins made unwittingly are recited (Numbers 15:26), to which is added Moses' argument from Numbers 14:19 (quite possibly meant to represent a plea for forgiveness of conscious sins). With both sorts of sins accounted for, God then assures the worshipers, "I have forgiven according to your word" (Numbers 14:20), as He had said previously to Moses.

29. *Authorized Daily Prayer Book*, pp. 168–187. For commentary on these prayers see Eli Munk, *The World of Prayer* 2 vols., vol. 1, trans. Henry Biberfeld and Leonard Oschry, vol. 2, trans. Gertrude Hirschler (New York: Philip Feldheim, 1961 and 1963), 1:161–170.

30. *Authorized Daily Prayer Book*, pp. 182–185. See Munk, *World of Prayer*, 1:176–178.

31. Rosenfeld, *Selichot*, pp. 178–179 and elsewhere.

32. Ibid., pp. 180–181 and elsewhere.

33. *Prayer Book for Sabbath and Festivals*, pp. 360–362.

34. If this is a correct understanding of the prayer, then a number of other prayers, all found in the various *Musaf* services, also advance a similar argument. For example, the *Rosh Hodesh Musaf* prayer "You formed," *Prayer Book for Sabbath and Festivals*, pp. 215–216, like "But on account of our sins" also combines a confession of sinfulness with a plea for redemption and restoration. Similarly, the inserts in the Rosh Hashanah *Amidah* ("And therefore set Your fear," "and therefore give honor," "and then the righteous," "and You will rule"), *Authorized Daily Prayer Book*, pp. 846–851, all suggest that for God

to rule supreme, recognized by all, He must first put the fear of God into the hearts of all humankind (even as Israel acknowledges His sovereignty), restore honor to His people, send the Messiah, and punish the wicked. Spelling out in detail the hope expressed in the second paragraph of the *aleinu*, "We therefore hope," these inserts tell God specifically what He must do in order to win universal acknowledgment of His sovereignty. Israel, of course, has a hidden agenda, for by helping God "clarify" what He needs to do, all of Israel's deepest and most heartfelt prayers are also answered. The Exile will end, Israel will be vindicated, her enemies punished, the Temple will be rebuilt, and the nations shall join with Israel in the worship of the one God.

NOTES TO CHAPTER 7

1. Jakob J. Petuchowski, *Theology and Poetry: Studies in the Medieval Piyyut* (London: Routledge & Kegan Paul, 1978), p. 11.
2. For a summary of the types of *piyyutim*, see A. Z. Idelsohn, *Jewish Liturgy and Its Development* (New York: Schocken Books, 1967), pp. 40–45; and T. Carmi, ed. and trans. *The Penguin Book of Hebrew Verse* (New York: Penguin Books, 1981), pp. 51–55.
3. Petuchowski, *Theology and Poetry*, pp. 14–15.
4. Ibid., p. 15.
5. For more information on the dispute over the inclusion of *piyyutim* in the worship service, see Petuchowski, *Theology and Poetry*, pp. 5–6, 16–17; and his *Prayerbook Reform in Europe* (New York: World Union for Progressive Judaism, 1968), pp. 28–30; Idelsohn, *Jewish Liturgy*, pp. 45–46; Eli Munk, *The World of Prayer*, 2:104–109.
6. Petuchowski, *Theology and Poetry*, p. 16; *Prayerbook Reform*, p. 29.
7. For a historical survey of the development of the *piyyutim*, see Shalom Spiegel, "On Medieval Hebrew Poetry," in Louis Finkelstein, ed. *The Jews: Their Religion and Culture*, 4th ed. (New York: Schocken Books, 1971), pp. 101–112; and T. Carmi, *Hebrew Verse*, pp. 14–39.
8. Petuchowski, *Theology and Poetry*, p. 15.
9. Petuchowski, *Prayerbook Reform*, p. 28.
10. Ibid., p. 24.
11. For more on *kinot* and *slihot*, see Idelsohn, *Jewish Liturgy*, pp. 249–256, 346–352; Munk, *World of Prayer*, 2:317–334; and Millgram, *Jewish Worship*, pp. 275–285.

   For the translations of the *slihot* and *kinot* found in this chapter, we have used, by and large, the versions by Rosenfeld, *The Authorized Selichot for the Whole Year* and *The Authorized Kinot for the Ninth for the Ninth of Av.* His translations have in most cases been modified slightly.

12. The most representative collection of stories and poems commemorating the various persecutions Jews have suffered through the ages is Shimon Bernfeld, *Sefer Hadema'ot (The Book of Tears)*, 3 vols. (Berlin: Eschkol Publishers, 1924–1926). For *piyyutim* focusing solely on medieval European persecutions, see A. M. Haberman, ed. *Sefer G'zeirot Ashkenaz V'Tzarfat* (Jerusalem: Tarshish Books, 1945); for *piyyutim* on the Eastern European persecutions of the seventeenth century, see C. J. Gurland, *Likorot Hag'zeirot Al Yisrael* (Przmsyl: Zupnik et al. 1887). For a brief survey of the medieval period and its impact on the prayer book, see Millgram, *Jewish Worship*, pp. 441–464. For a chronological portrayal of medieval suffering with many excerpts from the *piyyutim*, see Leopold Zunz, *The Suffering of the Jews in the Middle Ages*, trans. A. Loewy, rev. ed. George A. Kohut (New York: Bloch Publishers, 1907), reprinted in *Historical Views of Judaism: Four Selections* (New York: Arno Press, 1973). Consult Elliot M. Strom, *Theology in Crisis: Jewish Theodicy at the Time of the Crusades* (Cincinnati: unpublished rabbinic thesis, 1977), for a detailed survey of contemporaneous Jewish response to the massacres of the Crusades, including their use of the arguing with God motif. For a brief study of pogrom poetry in the late nineteenth and early twentieth centuries, see David G. Roskies, "The Pogrom Poem and the Literature of Destruction," *Notre Dame English Journal* XI (April 1979), and also his book *Against the Apocalypse: Responses to Catastrophe in Modern Jewish Culture* (Cambridge, MA: Harvard University Press, 1984). See also Alan Mintz, *Hurban: Responses to Catastrophe in Hebrew Literature* (New York: Columbia University Press, 1984), an excellent historical survey.

13. *Prayer Book for Sabbath and Festivals*, trans. Philip Birnbaum (New York: Hebrew Publishing, 1964), pp. 167–168.

14. The full text of Simeon bar Isaac bar Abun's poem "Hasten, my Beloved," in Hebrew and English, with notes and commentary, can be found in Petuchowski, *Theology and Poetry*, pp. 56–62.

15. *Prayer Book for Sabbath and Festivals*, pp. 167–168.

16. Ibid., pp. 165–166.

17. Ibid.

18. The full text of Isaac bar Shalom's poem "There is none like You among the dumb," in Hebrew and English, with notes and commentary, can be found in Petuchowski, *Theology and Poetry*, pp. 71–83.

19. Specifically the prayers "You have been the help of our fathers" and "Who is like You?," *Prayer Book for Sabbath and Festivals*, pp. 165–168.

20. See, for example, Spiegel's analysis of the two *piyyutim* in their liturgical context in Spiegel, "On Medieval Hebrew Poetry," pp. 96–97.

21. Isaac b. Judah ibn Ghiyyat (1038–1089), "I will go and return," in Rosenfeld, *Selichot*, pp. 253–254. See also references in note 89.

22. Ephraim of Bonn (1132–1200), "Woe is me if I speak," in Carmi, *Hebrew Verse*, pp. 384–385.

23. Kalonymous b. Judah (eleventh century), "O that my head were water," in Rosenfeld, *Kinot*, pp. 132–134. See also Moses b. Samuel b. Absalom (c. 1160), "Let it not seem little before You," in Rosenfeld, *Selichot*, pp. 120–121. Solomon b. Judah Habavli (c. 980), "We long for You," in Rosenfeld, *Selichot*, p. 48.

24. David b. Meshullam of Speyer (twelfth century), "O God, do not silence my blood," in Carmi, *Hebrew Verse*, pp. 374–375.

25. See the discussion of martyrdom in Jacob Katz, *Exclusiveness and Tolerance: Jewish-Gentile Relations in Medieval and Modern Times* (New York: Schocken Books, 1962), pp. 82–92.

26. Kalonymous b. Judah (eleventh century), "I said 'Look away from me,'" in Rosenfeld, *Kinot*, pp. 139–142. See also Saadya Gaon (892–942) "We beseech You, look," in Rosenfeld, *Selichot*, p. 176.

27. Eliezer b. Joel Halevi, in Bernfeld, *Sefer HaDema'ot*, 1, p. 209; quoted in Shalom Speigel, *The Last Trial*, trans. Judah Goldin (New York: Schocken Books, 1967), p. 21.

28. Anonymous (eleventh century), "I will speak out in the grief of my spirit," in Carmi, *Hebrew Verse*, pp. 372–373.

29. Kalonymous b. Judah, "I said 'Look away from me'" in Rosenfeld, *Kinot*, pp. 139–142. See also his poem "O that my head were water" in Rosenfeld, *Kinot*, pp. 132–134, where he compares the massacres to the destruction of the Temple and rationalizes mourning the martyrs on *Tisha b'Av*.

30. Ephraim of Bonn (1132–1200), "Woe is me if I speak," in Carmi, *Hebrew Verse*, pp. 384–385.

31. Solomon b. Judah Habavli (c. 980), "In the day of my anxiety I will call upon You," in Rosenfeld, *Selichot*, p. 100. See also poem cited in note 30.

32. Saadya Gaon, "May it be Your will . . . that this coming year be," in Rosenfeld, *Selichot*, pp. 170–172.

33. Kalonymous b. Judah, "I said 'Look away from me,'" in Rosenfeld, *Kinot*, pp. 139–142.

34. Anonymous (eleventh century) "I will speak out in the grief of my spirit," in Carmi, *Hebrew Verse*, pp. 372–373.

35. Joseph of Chartres (c. 1170), "God, lords other than You have ruled over us," in Rosenfeld, *Kinot*, pp. 168–170. See also the poem by Saadya Gaon, "We beseech You, look," in Rosenfeld, *Selichot*, p. 176.

36. David b. Meshullam of Speyer, "O God, do not silence my blood," in Carmi, *Hebrew Verse*, pp. 374–375.
37. Ephraim of Bonn, "I shall invoke the memory of my Fathers," in Carmi, *Hebrew Verse*, pp. 379–384. See also Jehoseph Ezovi (1270), "I will remember the days of old" (for the Ninth of Av) in Hermann Gollancz, *Translations from Hebrew and Aramaic* (London: Luzac & Co., 1908), pp. 151–160, which refers to the saving merit of the ten rabbinic martyrs of Roman times. An anonymous poem written at some point from the fourth to the early seventh century, "Aitan [Abraham] taught knowledge of You," in Carmi, *Hebrew Verse*, pp. 201–202, is based upon the original saving merit of Isaac's sacrifice.
38. Two poems by Eleazar Kallir (seventh century) paraphrase various portions of Proem 24 of Lamentations *Rabbah*—"Then when Jeremiah went," in Rosenfeld, *Kinot*, pp. 135–136, and "Then when [Israel] was in fullness of abundance," in the same, pp. 136–137.

Frequently, an appeal to the saving power of the merit of the Patriarchs is made precisely because Israel has no merit of her own with which to plead. Thus in the poem, "My eye pours out tears to God," by Joel b. Isaac Halevi (d. 1200), the Patriarchs are called upon to intercede upon Israel's behalf since Israel is constantly sinful and bereft of good deeds. Joel b. Isaac Halevi, "My soul pours out tears to God," in Rosenfeld, *Selichot*, pp. 143–144. See also Solomon ibn Gabirol (1021–1056), "Judge of all the earth," in Rosenfeld, *Selichot*, p. 164.

In other poems, a reference to the deeds of the Patriarchs—and to the *akeidah* in particular—is of sufficient weight so as to base one's entire petition on it. Thus the *akeidah* poem, "Though the pigeon offering has ceased," by Ephraim b. Isaac, states that although Israel no longer has sacrifices upon which to rely for forgiveness, she still has the *akeidah* to rely on. The merit of this singular deed was considered as everlasting as the Covenant itself. By referring to it in prayer, God must take note and have mercy on Isaac's children. Ephraim b. Isaac, "Though the pigeon offering has ceased," in Rosenfeld, *Selichot*, p. 204.

Similarly, in his poem, "Then on Mount Moriah," ibn Gabirol bases his petition on God's promise to Abraham that He would always remember the *akeidah* in Israel's favor. Solomon ibn Gabirol, "Then on Mount Moriah," in Rosenfeld, *Selichot*, p. 166.

Many of the *k'rovot* (*piyyutim* inserted among the first three benedictions of the *Amidah*) for Rosh Hashanah and Yom Kippur deal exclusively with the saving power of the merit of the Patriarchs, and especially with the *akeidah*. A number of *hoshannot* for *Sukkot* and *Hoshanah Rabba* link the merit of the Patriarchs with the merit of other righteous individuals, taking note of how God had acted on their behalf in their time of need.

39. Moses b. Samuel b. Absalom (c. 1160), "May it not seem little to You," in Rosenfeld, *Selichot*, pp. 120–121.

40. Saadya Gaon, "We beseech You, o Lord, . . . who keeps the Covenant," in Rosenfeld, *Selichot*, p. 175.

41. Joseph of Chartres, "God, lords other than You have ruled over us," in Rosenfeld, *Kinot*, pp. 168–170.

42. Judah Halevi (c. 1080–1145), "O Zion, will you not ask?" in Rosenfeld, *Kinot*, pp. 152–153.

43. Solomon ibn Gabirol, "The poor one sits in a strange land," in *Otzar Hatefillot* (Vilna: Rom, 1924), part 2, pp. 256–257; quoted in I. Zinberg, *A History of Jewish Literature*, 12 vols., ed. and trans. B. Martin, vols. 1–3 (Cleveland: Case-Western Reserve Press, 1962); vols. 4–12 (Cincinnati and New York: Hebrew Union College and Ktav, 1975), 1:51–52; and in Simon Dubnow, *History of the Jews*, 5 vols., trans. M. Spiegel (South Brunswick, NJ: Thomas Yoseloff, 1968–1973), 2:639.

    Many of ibn Gabirol's poems combine the complaint of Israel with the reassurance of God. See, for example, the following poems in *Selected Religious Poetry of Solomon ibn Gabirol*, trans. I. Zangwill (Philadelphia: Jewish Publication Society of America, 1924 and 1952): #18, "God and Israel," pp. 22–24; #19, "Reassurance: A Trialogue," pp. 25–27; #20, Duologue," pp. 28–29. For a further description of life in exile, see #21, "Establish peace," pp. 30–34.

44. Abraham ibn Ezra (1089–1164), "If my enemies speak evil of me," in Petuchowski, *Theology and Poetry*, pp. 131–134.

45. Moses ibn Ezra (1055–1138), "Faint of soul," quoted in Zinberg, *Jewish Literature*, 1:79. For full Hebrew text and alternative translation, see *Selected Hebrew Poems of Moses ibn Ezra*, trans. Solomon Solis Cohen (Philadelphia: Jewish Publication Society of America, 1934 and 1945), #47, pp. 113–114.

46. Ephraim of Bonn, "Woe is me if I speak," in Carmi, *Hebrew Verse*, pp. 384–385.

47. Moses b. Eleazar Hacohen (thirteenth century), quoted in Dubnow, *History* 3:169–170. For full text in Hebrew, see A. M. Haberman, *Sefer G'zeirot Ashkenaz V'Tzarfat*, pp. 220–222.

48. Solomon b. Menachem (c. 1360), "Thirteen are the Attributes," in Rosenfeld, *Selichot*, pp. 161–162. Verses from the psalms of lament occur frequently. See, for example, the following: Elijah b. Shemayah (1160), "I will call upon Your name," in Rosenfeld, *Selichot*, p. 46; Moses b. Samuel b. Absalom (c. 1160), "Let it not seem little before You," in Rosenfeld, *Selichot*, pp. 120–121; Gershom b. Judah (960–

1028), "Where are all Your wonders?" in Rosenfeld, *Selichot*, pp. 64–65; Ephraim b. Isaac of Regensburg (twelfth century), "Because my fathers trusted," in *Otzar Hatefillot*, part 2, pp. 110–111; quoted in Zinberg, *Jewish Literature* 2:28; Zevadyah (870), "There is no God besides You," in Rosenfeld, *Selichot*, pp. 198–199.

49. Gershom b. Judah (920–1028), "Where are all Your wonders?" in Rosenfeld, *Selichot*, pp. 64–65. See also Benjamin b. Samuel of Coutances (1050), "Where are Your jealousy and mighty deeds?" in Rosenfeld, *Selichot*, p. 28.

50. Benjamin b. Zerach (1050), "The virgin daughter of Judah," in Rosenfeld, *Selichot*, p. 102.

51. Gabriel b. Joshua Strassberg of Raisha (seventeenth century), "How can I lift my face?" quoted in Dubnow, *History* 4:48. For full text in Hebrew, see Bernfeld, *Sefer Hadema'ot* 3:179–184.

52. Isaac b. Shalom (twelfth century), "Who is like You among the dumb?" in Petuchowski, *Theology and Poetry*, pp. 74–80.

53. Kalonymous b. Judah, "O that my head were water," in Rosenfeld, *Kinot*, pp. 132–134.

54. Menachem b. Jacob (d. 1203), "Woe unto me," quoted in Zinberg, *Jewish Literature* 2:26. For full text in Hebrew, see Bernfeld, *Sefer Hadema'ot* 1:239–240. See also the poem by Isaac b. Shalom in the same, 1:217.

55. Elijah b. Shemayah, "I longed for You and hoped in You," in Rosenfeld, *Selichot*, p. 30.

56. Barukh of Magenza (Mainz) (c. 1150–1221), "A fire that devours fire," in Carmi, *Hebrew Verse*, pp. 386–387.

57. Zinberg, *Jewish Literature* 2:26.

58. Eleazar Kallir (seventh century), "Then when Jeremiah went," in Rosenfeld, *Kinot*, pp. 135–136. See also his poem, "Then when [Israel] was in full abundance," in Rosenfeld, *Kinot*, pp. 136–137.

59. See the following: Menachem b. Machir (eleventh century), "When a man rose up against us," in Rosenfeld, *Selichot*, pp. 355–356; Abraham ibn Ezra (1092–1167), "How long shall there be weeping in Zion?" in Rosenfeld, *Kinot*, pp. 38–39; Eleazar Kallir, "How can man alter that which was already done?" in Rosenfeld, *Kinot*, pp. 105–108; Asher Cohen (1583), "O Zion lament for your house," in Rosenfeld, *Kinot*, pp. 157–158.

60. Samuel b. Judah Hacohen (b. 1120), "Angels of Mercy, servants of the Most High," in Rosenfeld, *Selichot*, p. 377; Anonymous, "Leave me in silence that I may speak," in Rosenfeld, *Kinot*, pp. 127–128; Judah Halevi, "O Zion will you not ask?" in Rosenfeld, *Kinot*, pp. 152–153; Meir of Rothenburg (c. 1215–1293), "O [Law] consumed by fire ask," in Rosenfeld, *Kinot*, pp. 161–162; Meir b. Eleazar (c. 1200–1220), "O

Zion diadem of beauty," in Rosenfeld, *Kinot*, pp. 163–165. See also
note 38.

61. Meir b. Eleazar, "O Zion diadem of beauty" in Rosenfeld, *Kinot*,
pp. 163–165.

62. Eleazar Kallir, "Turn, if seated on the Throne of Judgment," in *Service of the Synagogue: New Year*, ed. and trans. Arthur Davis and
Herbert Adler, (New York: Hebrew Publishing Co., n.d.), pp. 143–144.

63. Amram Gaon (c. 821–875), "When Israel sinned in the wilderness," in
Rosenfeld, *Selichot*, p. 177.

64. See notes 13 and 21.

65. Anonymous, "He who answered," in Rosenfeld, *Selichot*, pp. 180–181,
and many places.

66. See also pre-*Kol Nidrei* poem by Hai Gaon, "Hear my voice," in *Prayers for the Day of Atonement According to the Custom of the Spanish
and Portuguese Jews*, ed. and trans. David de Sola Pool (New York:
Union of Sephardic Congregations, 1939), pp. 23–24; and Eleazar
Kallir, "As You saved Israel in Egypt," in Petuchowski, *Theology and
Poetry*, pp. 90–93.

67. These two argument motifs are joined explicitly in some litanies. The
litany, "The Merciful One will remember for us," for example, commences with the reader saying, "The Merciful One will remember for
us the Covenant of Abraham the beloved," and the congregation
responding, "For his sake He will forgive." Each succeeding line
corresponds to this pattern with only the particular ancestor cited
being different. The litany ends with a petition: "O Merciful One, turn
from Your great wrath that we may not return empty from Your
presence." Anonymous, "The Merciful One will remember for us," in
Rosenfeld, *Selichot*, p. 391.

   Similarly, the *Hoshana Rabba* litany, "Answer! Your faithful pour
out their hearts like water," recalls various ancestors and their deeds
with "for the sake of so-and-so" in a plea for rain. Eleazar Kallir,
"Answer the faithful," in *Sabbath and Festival Prayerbook*, ed. Morris Silverman (New York: Rabbinical Assembly of America & United
Synagogue of America, 1952), pp. 206–207. Each and every litany
displays its distinctive style of argument: an argument based on the
rhythmic piling-up of past precedents. It is a unique and ancient
form.

68. Eleazar Kallir, "How in Your wrath You hastened," in Rosenfeld, *Kinot*,
pp. 93–94. Another nonlitany to use past precedents is a *pizmon* (a
hymn with a refrain) for the Fast of Gedaliah entitled, "You taught the
way of repentence," by Benjamin b. Zerach (1050). This *piyyut* argues
that just as God has established repentance as a means of obtaining
forgiveness for biblical sinners, so too it should be effectual for the

present generation. Accompanying each biblical precedent (the demerit of the ancestors, so to speak) is the refrain, "Cause us to return to You, O Lord, and we shall return." Benjamin b. Zerach, "You have taught the way of repentance," in Rosenfeld, *Selichot*, pp. 202–203.

69. Eleazar Kallir, "Where is the saying of 'thus'?" in Rosenfeld, *Kinot*, pp. 109–110. Similarly, in another *kinah*, "Then when Jeremiah went," the poet (perhaps Kallir) has the Patriarchs in Heaven confront God with their past deeds and the as yet unfulfilled promises God had made to them. Eleazar Kallir, "Then when Jeremiah went," in Rosenfeld, *Kinot*, pp. 135–136. In a third *kinah*, "You have said," Kallir begins each verse by citing a divine promise or deed, and then asks why: "Why has such-and-such a misfortune happened to us?" Eleazar Kallir, "You have said," in Rosenfeld, *Kinot*, p. 122.

70. Anonymous, "These things I will remember." Full text may be found in *Service of the Synagogue: Day of Atonement*, part 2, pp. 178–181.

71. Isaac b. Judah ibn Ghiyyat (1035–1065), "You search and survey all things," in Rosenfeld, *Selichot*, p. 103.

72. Solomon ibn Gabirol, "Six years were decreed," in *Selected Religious Poetry of Solomon ibn Gabirol*, p. 12.

73. Judah Halevi, "My beloved, have You forgotten?" in *Yehuda Ha-Levi, Divan*, 4 vols, ed. Heinrich Brody (Berlin: Mekize Nirdamim, 1894–1930) 3:4.

74. Meir b. Eleazar, "O Zion, diadem of beauty," in Rosenfeld, *Kinot*, pp. 163–165.

75. Elchanan b. Isaac of Dampierre (c. 1184), "The wife of Your youth," in Rosenfeld, *Selichot*, p. 276.

76. Judah Halevi, "The day the depths were turned to dry land," in Petuchowski, *Theology and Poetry*, pp. 65–68.

77. See, for example, the following: Benjamin b. Zerach, "How shall we open our mouth before You?" in Rosenfeld, *Selichot*, p. 6; Solomon b. Judah Habavli (c. 980), "If I say," in Rosenfeld, *Selichot*, p. 84; Elijah b. Shemayah (1160), "O Lord, God of Israel, You are righteous," in Rosenfeld, *Selichot*, p. 280; Amittai b. Shephatayah (c. 890), "I remember, O God, and I groan," in Rosenfeld, *Selichot*, p. 318.

78. Kalonymous b. Judah, "O that my head were water," in Rosenfeld, *Kinot*, pp. 132–134. See also Eleazar Kallir, "Incline Your ear, O my God," in Rosenfeld, *Kinot*, pp. 124–125.

79. Anonymous (1196), "I weep bitterly," (for the 17th of Tammuz, from a Salonika Mahzor manuscript), quoted in Zinberg, *Jewish Literature* 2:27. For full text in Hebrew, see Bernfeld, *Sefer Hadema'ot* 1:250–254.

80. Ephraim b. Isaac of Regensburg, "Because my fathers trusted," quoted in Zinberg, *Jewish Literature* 2:28. For full text in Hebrew, see *Otzar Hatefillot*, part 2, pp. 110–111.

81. Kalonymous b. Judah, "I said, 'Look away from me,'" in Rosenfeld, *Kinot*, pp. 139–142.
82. Anonymous (eleventh century?), "The merciful Father," in *Prayer Book for Sabbath and Festivals*, pp. 201–202.
83. Menachem b. Jacob (d. 1203), "Sword, wherefore do you turn?" in Rosenfeld, *Kinot*, pp. 171–172.
84. Ephraim of Bonn (1132–1200), "Woe is me if I speak," in Carmi, *Hebrew Verse*, pp. 384–385.
85. Elijah b. Shemayah, "Abandon Your burning anger," in Rosenfeld, *Selichot*, pp. 257–258.
86. Elijah b. Shemayah, "I longed for You and hoped in You," in Rosenfeld, *Selichot*, p. 30.
87. Solomon b. Judah Habavli, "Your qualities are not like those of man," in Rosenfeld, *Selichot*, p. 82.
88. See, for example, Eleazar Kallir, "As You saved Israel in Egypt," in Petuchowski, *Theology and Poetry*, pp. 90–93.
89. Anonymous (thirteenth to sixteenth century), "Lord, how much longer will this separation . . . ," in Carmi, *Hebrew Verse*, pp. 443–445. Other *piyyutim* that utilize the love-marriage motif to describe the revelation-exile-redemption of Israel are Isaac b. Judah ibn Ghiyyat, "I will go and I will return," in Rosenfeld, *Selichot*, pp. 253–254; also his poems "O Lord, bring back" and "Do you know, my friends?" in Carmi, *Hebrew Verse*, p. 317 and pp. 318–319 respectively. See also Eleazar Kallir, "The mother of children," in Carmi, *Hebrew Verse*, pp. 223–224. See also note 43, which deals with ibn Gabirol's use of this motif.
90. Petuchowski, *Theology and Poetry*, p. 138.
91. Ibid., p. 139.

NOTES TO CHAPTER 8

1. Samuel H. Dresner, *Levi Yitzhak of Berditchev: Portrait of a Hasidic Master* (Bridgeport: Hartmore House, 1974), p. 77.
2. Ibid., p. 81.
3. Ibid., pp. 86–87.
4. Ibid., pp. 79–80.
5. Ibid., p. 80.
6. Ibid., p. 82. Another example of his humor is the following:

Address: Master of the World,
Argument: The sages and prophets of old speak of the covenant at Mount Sinai as a marriage between God and Israel. But what kind of

marriage is it? Israel brought great *Yihus* [nobility] to the marriage, for are we not the children of the Patriarchs, Abraham, Isaac and Jacob? But what *Yihus* did You bring, Lord? Who were Your ancestors? You brought wealth to the marriage—that was Your part of the bargain, as it is written of You, "Mine is the silver and Mine is the gold."
Petition: Therefore, Master of the World, open up Your vast treasure house for us, ease our dreadful needs, and act like the One to Whom all the world belongs! [p. 80]

7. Quoted in Immanuel Olsvanger, *Contentions With God* (Cape Town, South Africa: T. Maskew Miller, 1921), p. 20.
8. See, for example, the prayers of Israel of Rizhin in Elie Wiesel, *Souls on Fire* (New York: Summit Books, 1972), p. 158, and in Louis I. Newman, *Hasidic Anthology* (New York: Schocken Books, 1963), p. 248. With the Rizhiner one can never tell what is humor and what is hubris.
9. I. Ashkenazy, ed., *Otzroth Idisher Humor* (1929), quoted in Newman, *Hasidic Anthology*, p. 57.
10. For more examples of the use of humor and of argument by the common folk, see Immanuel Olsvanger, *Contentions With God*, pp. 24–25, 27–30.
11. See the story "Tevye Strikes It Rich" in Irving Howe and Ruth R. Wisse, eds., *The Best of Sholom Aleichem* (New York: Simon & Schuster, 1980), of which the following excerpt (p. 137) is typical (the original Hebrew prayers are in italics—the rest is pure Tevye):

Address: Master of the Universe,
Arguments and Petitions: What have I done to deserve all this? Am I or am I not a Jew like any other? Gevalt! *Re'eh-no b'onyenu,* See us in our affliction . . . take a good look at us poor folk slaving away and do something about it, because if You don't, who do You think will? *Refo'enu ve'nerofey,* Heal our wounds that we be whole . . . please concentrate on the healing because the wounds we already have. *Borekh oleynu,* Bless the fruits of this year . . . kindly arrange a good harvest of corn, wheat, and barley—although what good it will do me is more than I can say: does it make any difference to my horse, I ask you, if the oats I can't afford to buy it are expensive or cheap?
But God doesn't tell a man what He thinks, and a Jew had better believe that He knows what He's up to. *V'lamalshinim al tehi tikvo,* May the slanderers have no hope . . . those are the big shots who say there is no God. What wouldn't I give to see the look on their faces when they line up for Judgment Day! They'll pay with back interest for everything they've done, because God has a long memory, one doesn't play around with Him. No, what He wants is for us to be good, to beseech and cry out to Him. *Ov harakhamom,* merciful, loving Father! *Shma koleynu,* You

better listen to what we tell You! *Hus v'rakhem oleynu*, Pay a little
attention to my wife and children, the poor things are hungry! R'tseh,
Take decent care of Your people again, as once You did long ago in the
days of the Temple, when the Priests and the Levites sacrificed before
You . . . .

12. Dresner, *Levi Yitzhak*, p. 81.
13. I. Ewen, *Fun Rebe's Hauf* (1922), quoted in Newman, *Hasidic Anthology*, p. 58.
14. See Levi Yitzhak's use of the biblical laws regarding the orphan and of the talmudic laws regarding court procedure in Dresner, *Levi Yitzhak*, pp. 81–83.
15. Olsvanger, *Contentions*, p. 12. Erich Fromm in his book *You Shall Be As Gods* (Greenwich: Fawcett, 1966), pp. 20–25, makes much the same developmental argument.
16. Judah Rosenberg, ed., *Tifereth Maharal*, quoted in Newman, *Hasidic Anthology*, p. 56.
17. S. G. Rosenthal, *Hithgadluth HaZaddikim*, quoted in Newman, *Hasidic Anthology*, pp. 58–59. See also similar stories in Olsvanger, *Contentions*, pp. 22–23.
18. Dresner, *Levi Yitzhak*, pp. 80–81. A similar prayer is made by the Savraner, Moshe Zevi, in Israel Berger, *Esser Ataroth* (1910) quoted in Newman, *Hasidic Anthology*, p. 58.
19. Quoted in Israel M. Goldman, *Lifelong Learning Among Jews* (New York: Ktav, 1975), p. 302.
20. *Histalkut HaNefesh*, trans. Samuel Dresner, in Jack Riemer, ed., *Jewish Reflections on Death* (New York: Schocken Books, 1976), p. 24. See also a legend about Moshe Yehudah Leib, related by Levi Yitzhak, in which the former *tzaddik* redeems hosts of souls from Gehenna by use of a law-court pattern argument and his personal prestige (Dresner, *Levi Yitzhak*, pp. 54–59).
21. Dresner, *Levi Yitzhak*, p. 78.
22. Quoted in Chaim Potok, *The Promise* (New York: Alfred A. Knopf, 1969), p. 9.
23. Quoted in Ruth Rubin, *Voices of a People: The Story of Yiddish Folksong* (Philadelphia: Jewish Publication Society of America, 1979), pp. 202–203. Another early ballad, published in 1717, describes an attack against the Jews in Poznan and asks, "How could God have witnessed this,/Which has not happened since the times of the wicked tyrant Titus?" (Rubin, *Voices*, pp. 206–207.) For a detailed study of both Hebrew and Yiddish responses to catastrophe in the modern era, see Roskies, *Against the Apocalypse: Responses to Catastrophe in Modern Jewish Culture*. For a study focusing on mod-

ern Hebrew poetry alone, see Mintz, *Hurban: Responses to Catastrophe in Hebrew Literature.*

24. Quoted in Rubin, *Voices*, p. 373.
25. Quoted in Roskies, Diane K., and Roskies, David G., *The Shtetl Book* (New York: Ktav, 1975), pp. 95–96.
26. Hayyim Nahman Bialik, "On the Slaughter," in S. Y. Penueli, and A. Ukhmani, eds., *Anthology of Modern Hebrew Poetry*, 2 vols. (Jerusalem: Israel University's Press, 1966), p. 31.
27. Bialik, *Kol Kithbhe Hayyim Nahman Bialik* (1938), trans. and quoted in Petuchowski, *Theology and Poetry*, p. 51.
28. Petuchowski, *Theology and Poetry*, pp. 52–53.
29. "A Song of the Chelm Ghetto" in Lucy S. Davidowitz, ed., *The Holocaust: A Source Reader* (New York: Behrman House, 1976), pp. 177–178.
30. Irving Howe and Eliezer Greenberg, eds., *A Treasury of Yiddish Poetry* (New York: Holt, Rinehart and Winston, 1969), pp. 15–17.
31. Paul Celan, "Zürich, zum Storchen," in Howard Schwartz and Anthony Rudolf, eds., *Voices within the Ark: The Modern Jewish Poets* (New York: Avon Books, 1980), p. 941.
32. See Sidra De Koven Ezrahi, *By Words Alone: The Holocaust in Literature* (Chicago and London: The University of Chicago Press, 1980), pp. 103–107 for a brief discussion of Hebraic Holocaust poetry and fiction. See also Roskies, *Against the Apocalypse*, and Mintz, *Hurban.*
33. Friedrick Torberg, "Seder, 1944," in Schwartz and Rudolf, *Voices*, pp. 980–981.
34. Jacob Glatstein, "Without Jews," in Irving Howe and Eliezer Greenberg, eds., *A Treasury of Yiddish Poetry*, pp. 331–332.
35. Simcha Bunen Shayevitch, "Slaughter Town," in Joseph Leftwich, ed., *The Golden Peacock* (New York: Thomas Yoseloff, 1961), pp. 524–525.
36. H. Leivick, "The Accounting is Still Yours, Creator," in *In Treblinka Bin Ich Nit Geven* (*In Treblinka I Never Was*) (New York: The H. Leivick Jubilee Fund, through ZIKO Publishing House, 1945), p. 17.
37. Uri Zvi Greenberg, "A Jew Stands at the Gates of Tears," in Leftwich, *The Golden Peacock*, pp. 193–194.
38. Aaron Zeitlin, "I Believe," in Howe and Greenberg, *Treasury*, pp. 321–325.
39. Isaac Katzenelson, "Shlomo Jelichovski," in Leftwich, *The Golden Peacock*, pp. 519–523.
40. Uri Zvi Greenberg, "To God in Europe," in S. Y. Penueli and A. Ukhmani, eds., *Anthology of Modern Hebrew Poetry*, pp. 264–278.
41. Isaac Katzenelson, *The Song of the Murdered Jewish People*, trans. and ann. Noah H. Rosenbloom (Israel: Ghetto Fighters' House, Ltd.;

Hakibbutz HaMeuchad Publishing House, 1980), pp. 12–20. H. Leivick, in his poem, "I Hear a Voice," turns this image around and, joining the dead on the ground, allows them to sing through him, in Schwartz and Rudolf, *Voices*, pp. 300–301.

42. See, for example, Mordechai Husid, "The Cry of Generations," in Schwartz and Rudolf, *Voices*, pp. 278–279; Anna Margolin, "My Kin Talk," in *Voices*, pp. 314–315; and Moshe Yungman, "The Sacrifice," in *Voices*, p. 367.

43. Uri Zvi Greenberg, "To God in Europe," in Penueli and Ukhmani, *Anthology*, p. 275.

44. Isaac Katzenelson, *Song of the Murdered Jewish People*, pp. 52–55.

45. Ibid., p. 68.

46. Jacob Friedman, "Kol Nidrei," in Leftwich, *The Golden Peacock*, pp. 580–581.

47. Jacob Glatstein, "Holy Name," in Leftwich, *The Golden Peacock*, pp. 287–288.

48. Isaac Katzenelson, *Song of the Murdered Jewish People*, pp. 82–85.

49. Itzik Manger, "The Lovers of Israel in the Death Camp Belshitz," in Leftwich, *Golden Peacock*, p. 570.

50. See Eliezer Berkovits, *With God in Hell: Judaism in the Ghettos and Deathcamps* (New York: Sanhedrin Press, 1979), pp. 127–128, for further examples of lawsuits against God during the Holocaust. The poem by Jozef Wittlin, "On the Jewish Day of Judgment in the Year 1942 (5703)" (in Schwartz and Rudolf, *Voices*, pp. 1074–1075) has this motif as do several of Elie Wiesel's stories.

51. I. J. Segal, "Yiskor," in Leftwich, *Golden Peacock*, pp. 338–339.

52. Jacob Glatstein, "Dead Men Don't Praise God," in Ruth Whitman, ed. and trans., *The Selected Poems of Jacob Glatstein* (New York: October House, 1972), pp. 68–70.

53. Uri Zvi Greenberg, "To God in Europe," in Penueli and Ukhmani, *Anthology*, p. 267.

54. Kadia Molodowsky, "God of Mercy," in Howe and Greenberg, *Treasury*, pp. 289–290.

55. Uri Zvi Greenberg, "To God in Europe," in Penueli and Ukhmani, *Anthology*, p. 269.

56. Jacob Glatstein, "My Brother Refugee," in Whitman, *Selected Poems of Jacob Glatstein*, pp. 71–72. For two other intensely anthropomorphic God poems, see David Vogel "When I Was Growing Up," in Schwartz and Rudolf, *Voices*, pp. 209–210, and Uri Zvi Greenberg, "The Great Sad One," in *Voices*, pp. 93–94.

57. Jacob Glatstein, "The Beginning," in Howe and Greenberg, *Treasury*, pp. 335–337.

58. Itzik Manger, "A Dark Hand," in Schwartz and Rudolf, *Voices,* pp. 311–312.
59. Itzik Manger, "Like a Murderer," In Howe and Greenberg, *Treasury,* pp. 272–273.
60. David Shimoni, "From the Tales of a Sick Youth," in Penueli and Ukhmani, *Anthology,* pp. 149–153.
61. Elie Wiesel, *Night,* trans. Stella Rodway (New York: Avon Books, 1969), p. 43.
62. Wiesel, *Night,* p. 44.
63. Wiesel, *Night,* pp. 55–56. See also the episode of the death of the young boy by hanging, pp. 74–76, and Wiesel's arguing prayer, p. 78. For more examples of Wiesel's experience of theodicy, see *The Accident,* trans. Anne Borchardt (New York: Hill & Wang, 1962), pp. 97, 116; *The Town Beyond the Wall,* trans. Stephen Becker (New York: Atheneum, 1964), pp. 52–53, 114; *The Gates of the Forest,* trans. Frances Frenaye (New York: Holt, Rinehart & Winston, 1966), pp. 134, 190, 194; *Legends of Our Time* (New York: Holt, Rinehart & Winston, 1968), pp. 114, 127; *A Beggar in Jerusalem,* trans. Lily Edelman and Elie Wiesel (New York: Random House, 1970), p. 73; *A Jew Today,* trans. Marion Wiesel (New York: Random House, 1978), pp. 96–97.
64. Wiesel, *The Town Beyond the Wall,* pp. 149–151; *Dawn,* trans. Frances Frenaye (New York: Hill & Wang, 1961), p. 66.
65. Wiesel, *Night,* p. 76, also pp. 44, 78; *Dawn,* p. 61; *Gates of the Forest,* pp. 82–83, 129.
66. Wiesel, *Souls on Fire,* trans. Marion Wiesel (New York: Random House, 1972), and *Messengers of God,* trans. Marion Wiesel (New York: Random House, 1976), contain examples of arguing with God too numerous to document. See also these examples: *A Beggar in Jerusalem,* pp. 73–80; *The Oath,* trans. Marion Wiesel (New York: Random House, 1973), pp. 223–224; *A Jew Today,* pp. 125–127, 135–136.
67. Wiesel, *Ani Maamin: A Song Lost and Found Again,* trans. Marion Wiesel (New York: Random House, 1973), pp. 31–33. So numerous are the Patriarchs' arguments with God, we urge the reader to consult the entire work.
68. Wiesel, *Ani Maamin,* Abraham's arguments, pp. 37–41; Isaac's pp. 41–43; Jacob's, pp. 45–47.
69. Ibid., pp. 47–65.
70. Ibid., pp. 65–75.
71. Ibid., pp. 75–87.
72. Ibid., pp. 89–105.
73. Ibid., p. 105.
74. Wiesel, *The Town Beyond the Wall,* pp. 10, 135.

75. Wiesel, *Night*, p. 76; *Gates of the Forest*, p. 129.
76. Wiesel, *The Accident*, p. 32.
77. Wiesel, *Night*, p. 76; *Dawn*, p. 48; *Gates of the Forest*, p. 8.
78. Wiesel, *The Accident*, pp. 41–42; *The Town Beyond the Wall*, p. 10; *Gates of the Forest*, pp. 31–33, 225; *The Oath*, p. 80.
79. Wiesel, *Ani Maamin*, p. 105.
80. Wiesel, *Legends of Our Time*, p. 6; also Wiesel's comment at the top of the page. See also Elie Wiesel, *One Generation After*, trans. Lily Edelman and Elie Wiesel (New York: Random House, 1965), pp. 43, 165–167.
81. Wiesel, *Ani Maamin*, pp. 65–75.
82. Wiesel, *The Trial of God (As It Was Held on February 25, 1649 in Shamgorod)*, trans. Marion Wiesel (New York: Random House, 1979), p. 1.
83. Ibid., pp. 133–134.
84. Ibid., p. 134, also 54, 125.
85. Ibid., p. 156, also p. 133.
86. Ibid., p. 157, also p. 132.
87. Ibid., pp. 133–134.
88. See Emil L. Fackenheim, *God's Presence in History* (New York: New York University Press, 1970), p. 73; Eliezer Berkovitz, *Faith After the Holocaust* (New York: Ktav, 1973), p. 94; Irving Greenberg, "Judaism and Christianity After the Holocaust," *Journal of Ecumenical Studies* 12 (Fall 1975):533, 540; and Byron L. Sherwin's critique of the doctrine in B. Sherwin and S. Ament, *Encountering the Holocaust: An Interdisciplinary Study* (Chicago: Impact Press, 1979), pp. 409–412.

   An early modern precursor to this rejection of the on account of our sins doctrine was the poet Hayyim Nahman Bialik. In his poem "In the City of Slaughter," Bialik has God take the victims of the Kishinev pogrom to task for blaming themselves for their misfortune rather than abusing Heaven. For a translation of the pertinent section of Bialik's poem, and for a brief discussion of the rejection of this doctrine by Zionism and Reform Judaism, see Petuchowski, *Theology and Poetry*, pp. 50–53. See pp. 192–193.
89. Wiesel, *The Trial of God*, p. 156.
90. Ibid., p. 158.
91. For the words of prayer that Gregor wants to hear the Rebbe utter, see Wiesel, *Gates of the Forest*, p. 198.
92. Wiesel, *Gates of the Forest*, p. 197.
93. Ibid., p. 199.
94. Ibid., p. 198. Also, *One Generation After*, pp. 195–196.
95. Solomon ibn Verga, *Shebet Yehudah*, ed. M. Wiener (Hanover: C. Ruempler, 1856), ch. 52; and Wiesel's version of the story, *A Jew*

Today, p. 136. See also similar type of prayer in *Legends of our Time*, p. 6. This defiant response is also utilized in Zvi Kolitz's story, "Yossel Rakover's Appeal to God," in Albert H. Friedlander, ed., *Out of the Whirlwind* (New York: Union of American Hebrew Congregations, 1968), pp. 390–399.

96. Elie Wiesel, *Zalmen, or the Madness of God*, adapted by Marion Wiesel, based on translation by Nathan Edelman (New York: Random House, 1974), pp. 4–7, 55–57, 78–82. See also the remarks of the Rabbi in Safed, in Wiesel, *A Beggar in Jerusalem*, p. 116.

97. Wiesel, *Gates of the Forest*, pp. 21, 198.

98. Wiesel, *The Accident*, p. 42; *A Beggar in Jerusalem*, pp. 73–80; and *A Jew Today*, pp. 96–97, respectively.

99. Wiesel, *Legends of Our Time*, pp. 6, 32–38; *One Generation After*, pp. 186, 195–196; *Gates of the Forest*, p. 198; *A Beggar in Jerusalem*, pp. 116–117; *A Jew Today*, p. 163; and *Legends of Our Time*, pp. 6–7, 32–38; *A Jew Today*, pp. 96–97, respectively.

100. Wiesel, *Night*, pp. 78–79; *The Accident*, p. 42; *Legends of Our Time*, p. 6; *A Beggar in Jerusalem*, pp. 73–74; *A Jew Today*, p. 136; *The Trial of God*, p. 156; and *Legends of Our Time*, p. 6; *A Jew Today*, p. 130, respectively.

101. Wiesel, *A Jew Today*, p. 6.

102. Wiesel, *One Generation After*, pp. 167–173; *A Jew Today*, pp. 29–61.

103. Wiesel, *The Accident*, pp. 117–118.

104. Wiesel, *Zalmen*, p. 81. See also pp. 5, 57, 79–80.

105. Ibid., pp. 4–7, 55–57, 78–83.

106. These Teachers are Gyula in *the Accident*; Pedro in *The Town Beyond the Wall*; the father, the Stranger and the Rebbe in *The Gates of the Forest*; and Katriel and the Rabbi in *A Beggar in Jerusalem*. In Wiesel's earliest and most pessimistic novels, *Night* and *Dawn*, the absence of "the Teacher" signifies, no doubt, that Wiesel had yet to find a satisfactory—and satisfying—response to the Holocaust.

It is also significant to note the exchange of names between Teacher and student. In *Gates*, Gavriel gives his name to the Stranger, becomes Gregor, and later redeems his original name only by releasing the past and learning to live in the present. In *The Town*, Michael becomes Pedro for the mute, who in turn will become Michael for someone else. In *A Beggar*, David becomes Katriel's spiritual heir and lover/husband to Malka (if he was ever anyone other than Katriel to begin with) only by freeing himself from the past and his search for Katriel. Finally in *Zalmen*, the Rabbi becomes Zalmen when he acts, just as Zalmen later claimed that he had become the Rabbi (p. 155).

107. Wiesel, *The Oath*, p. 239. For the whole concept see pp. 236–243.
108. Wiesel, *The Oath*, p. 80.
109. Wiesel, *The Oath*, p. 138. See also Moshe's utterances during his raving, in which his mad dream for "hastening the end" first mingles with, and later overwhelms, his more lucid teaching on human responsibility, pp. 189–193, but pp. 190–191 in particular.

    For similar messages conveyed by the other Teachers, see *The Accident*, pp. 115–118; *The Town*, pp. 115, 118; and *Gates*, pp. 33, 178.
110. See Wiesel, *Town Beyond the Wall*, p. 115. Also see Wiesel, *Gates of the Forest*, for the story of Joseph di-la-Reina, whose pity for Satan's suffering caused him to be thwarted in his attempt to hasten the coming of the Messiah. The entire tale can be found in Nathan Ausubel, ed., *A Treasury of Jewish Folklore* (New York: Crown, 1948), pp. 206–215. See also Gregor's comment on the story: "I wouldn't have the coming of the Messiah depend upon our lack of generosity and pity, even towards Satan. I don't want salvation to come through fire, through cruelty, and through the sacrifices of others" (*Gates of the Forest*, pp. 18–19).
111. Wiesel, *One Generation After*, pp. 128, 166; *Legends of Our Time*, pp. 6, 180–181.
112. Wiesel, *A Jew Today*, pp. 166–167.
113. Ibid., pp. 165–167. Wiesel's use of argument with God as part of his attempt to address secular Jews marks him as a proto-humanist thinker. It is helpful to draw a parallel between Wiesel's and Erich Fromm's use of the same motif in the development of Wiesel's Jewishly-based humanism. For Wiesel, argument with God must ultimately lead to a suspension of the longed-for confrontation (since that depends on God's revealing Himself to us again) and a turning toward human activism as if God does not exist and everything depends on us. For Fromm, according to his work, *You Shall Be As Gods* (New York: Fawcett World Library, 1966), pp. 20–124, argument with God marks the transitional stage of God's constitutional sovereignty, midway between the earlier stage of divine absolutism and the later stage of human independence and autonomous activity.
114. Wiesel, *A Jew Today*, pp. 163–164.
115. Wiesel, *A Jew Today*, p. 6; *One Generation After*, pp. 166–167.
116. Wiesel, *One Generation After*, p. 167.
117. Wiesel, *One Generation After*, pp. 165–166; *The Accident*, p. 118.
118. Wiesel, *A Jew Today*, p. 164. Adin Steinsaltz makes a similar point, also linking quarreling with God in the fight against the "sin" of despair, in Lesley Hazleton, "The Improbable Rabbi," *Moment* 5 (July–August 1980):18.

119. Wiesel, *One Generation After*, pp. 167, 173–174.
120. David G. Roskies, "The Pogrom Poem and the Literature of Destruction," in *Notre Dame English Journal*, XI (April 1979), p. 109.
121. *Mahzor for Rosh Hashanah and Yom Kippur*, ed. Jules Harlow (New York: The Rabbinical Assembly, 1972), pp. 555–559; *Gates of Repentance: The New Union Prayerbook for the Days of Awe*, ed. Chaim Stern (New York: Central Conference of American Rabbis, 1978), pp. 429–442.
122. Howe and Greenberg, *Treasury*, pp. 52–53.
123. Pinchas Peli, "Where was God During the Holocaust," part 1, *Jerusalem Post*, International Edition (April 17–23, 1983), p. 12. Quoted in a different form in Samuel Hugo Bergman, *Faith and Reason: An Introduction to Modern Jewish Thought*, trans. and ed., Alfred Jospe (New York: Schocken Books, 1963), p. 149. The essay on Magnes, though brief, is worth reading for a glimpse into Magnes' approach to the problem of theodicy.

NOTES TO THE AFTERWORD

1. *The Passover Haggadah*, rev. ed., trans. and ed. Nahum N. Glatzer (New York: Schocken Books, 1969), pp. 30–31. For more on the selectivity of Jewish mythmaking, see my essay on the Haggadah cited in note 7 to chapter 1.
2. Yosef Hayim Yerushalmi, *Zakhor: Jewish History and Jewish Memory* (Seattle: University of Washington Press, 1982), p. 98.
3. Yerushalmi, *Zakhor*, p. 98.
4. Abraham Kaplan, "The Jewish Argument with God." *Commentary* 70 (October 1980): 47.
5. *Makkot* 24a; Maimonides, *Guide to the Perplexed*, II:33, and in many other sources.
6. *Hagigah* 1:7.
7. *Hullin* 5a.
8. *Berakhot* 13a.
9. These ideas are based on conversations with my teacher, Arthur Lagawier, and on his unpublished essay "Reflections on the Source of Jewish Ethics," April 1969.
10. Deuteronomy 29:29.
11. Exodus 33:18–23.
12. See, for example, Kaplan, *The Jewish Argument*; Erich Fromm, *You Shall Be As Gods*; Hans Jonas, *The Phenomena of Life: Toward a Philosophical Biology* (New York: Harper & Row, 1966); Arthur A.

Cohen, *The Tremendum: A Theological Interpretation of the Holocaust* (New York: Crossroad, 1981).

For an overview of the concept of a limited God and a brief review of its primary proponents' works, see Lawrence Englander, "Revelation From a Limited God: A Re-evaluation of Torah as Blueprint," *Journal of Reform Judaism* 35 (Spring 1988): 65–75.

13. Martin Buber, "In the Midst of History." In *Israel and the World* (New York: Schocken Books, 1963), p. 82.
14. Abraham Joshua Heschel, *Man's Quest for God,* quoted in Albert Friedlander, ed., *Out of the Whirlwind* (New York: Schocken Books, 1976), pp. 490–492.
15. Deuteronomy 30:11–20.

REFERENCES

Alter, R. (1981). *The Art of Biblical Narrative*. New York: Basic Books.
—— (1985). *The Art of Biblical Poetry*. New York: Basic Books.
—— (1977). *Defenses of the Imagination: Jewish Writers and Modern Historical Crisis*. Philadelphia: Jewish Publication Society of America.

The Apocrypha of the Old Testament (1957). Revised Standard Version. Camden, NJ: Thomas Nelson and Sons.

Avot de Rabbi Natan (1887). Ed. S. Schechter. Reprint, New York: Philipp Feldheim, 1967.

Ausubel, Nathan, ed. (1948). *A Treasury of Jewish Folklore*. New York: Crown.

Authorized Daily Prayer Book (1974). Rev. ed., ed. and trans. J. Hertz. New York: Bloch.

Authorized Kinot for the Ninth of Av (1979). Ed. and trans. A. Rosenfeld. New York: Judaica Press.

Authorized Selichot for the Whole Year (1978). Ed. and trans. A. Rosenfeld. New York: Judaica Press.

Balentine, S. E. (1983). *The Hidden God: The Hiding of the Face of God in the Old Testament*. London: Oxford University Press.

Baumer, F. L. (1960). *Religion and the Rise of Scepticism*. New York: Harcourt, Brace and World.

Bergman, S. H. (1961, 1963). *Faith and Reason: An Introduction to Modern Jewish Thought*, trans. and ed. A. Jospe. New York: Schocken Books.

Berkovits, E. (1973). *Faith After the Holocaust*. New York: Ktav Publishing House.
—— (1979). *With God in Hell: Judaism in the Ghettos and Death Camps*. New York: Sanhedrin Press.

Bialik, H. N. (1938). *Kol Kitve Hayyim Nahman Bialik*. Tel Aviv: Dvir.

Blank, S. H. (1948). The confessions of Jeremiah and the meaning of prayer. *HUCA* 21:331–354.
—— (1971). An effective literary device in Job 31. In *Prophetic Thought:*

Essays and Addresses, pp. 65–67. Cincinnati: Hebrew Union College Press.

—— (1961). *Jeremiah, Man and Prophet.* Cincinnati: Hebrew Union College Press.

—— (1971). Men against God, the Promethean element in biblical prayer. In *Prophetic Thought: Essays and Addresses*, pp. 91–101. Cincinnati: Hebrew Union College Press.

—— (1971). The prophet as paradigm. In *Prophetic Thought: Essays and Addresses*, pp. 23–34. Cincinnati: Hebrew Union College Press.

—— (1967). *Prophetic Faith in Isaiah.* Detroit: Wayne State University Press.

Braude, W. G., trans. (1959). *The Midrash on Psalms*, 2 vols. Yale Judaica Series, vol. 13. New Haven, CT: Yale University Press.

—— trans. (1968). *Pesikta Rabbati*, 2 vols. Yale Judaica Series, vol. 18. New Haven, CT: Yale University Press.

Braude, W. G., and Kapstein, I. J., trans. (1975). *Pesikta de-Rab Kahana.* Philadelphia: Jewish Publication Society of America.

Brichto, H. C. (1970). Images of man in the Bible. *CCAR Journal* 71:2–9.

Buber, M. (1963). *Israel and the World.* New York: Schocken Books.

—— *The Prophetic Faith.* New York: Macmillan, 1949; New York: Harper Torchbook, 1960.

Buechler, A. (1928). *Studies in Sin and Atonement in the Rabbinic Literature of the 1st Century* (Jews' College Publications no. 11). London: Oxford University Press.

—— (1922). *Types of Jewish-Palestinian Piety from 70 b.c.e. to 70 c.e.* (Jews' College Publications no. 8). London: Jews' College.

Cargas, H. J., ed. (1978). *Responses to Elie Wiesel.* New York: Persea Books.

Carmi, T., ed. and trans. (1981). *The Penguin Book of Hebrew Verse.* New York: Penguin Books.

Cohen, A., ed. (1975). *Everyman's Talmud.* New York: Schocken Books.

Cohen, A. A., ed. (1970). *Arguments and Doctrines: A Reader of Jewish Thinking in the Aftermath of the Holocaust.* New York: Harper & Row.

—— (1981). *The Tremendum: A Theological Interpretation of the Holocaust.* New York: Crossroad.

Cohen, N. (1983). The leap of Nachshon ben Amminadab: a rabbinic redemptive model. *Journal of Reform Judaism* 30:30–39.

Daube, D. (1975). Enfant terrible. *Harvard Theological Review* 68:331–376.

Davidowitz, L. S., ed. (1976). *The Holocaust: A Source Reader.* New York: Behrman House.

Davidson, B. (1970). *The Analytical Hebrew and Chaldee Lexicon.* Grand Rapids, MI: Zondervan.

De Lange, N. (1978). *Apocrypha: Jewish Literature of the Hellenistic Age.* New York: Viking Press.

Dresner, S. H. (1974). *Levi Yitzhak of Berditchev: Portrait of a Hasidic Master.* Bridgeport, CT: Hartmore House. Updated version published as *The World of a Hasidic Master: Levi Yitzhak of Berditchev.* New York: Shapolsky, 1986.

Dubnow, S. (1968–1973). *History of the Jews,* 5 vols., trans. M. Spiegel. South Brunswick, NJ: Thomas Yoseloff.

—— (1973). *History of the Jews in Russia and Poland,* trans. I. Friedlaender. New York: Ktav.

Eidelberg, S., ed. and trans. (1977). *The Jews and the Crusades: The Hebrew Chronicles of the First and Second Crusades.* Madison: University of Wisconsin Press.

Englander, L. A. (1988). Revelation from a limited God: re-evaluation of Torah as blueprint. *Journal of Reform Judaism* 35:65–75.

Epstein, I., ed. (1935–1948). *The Babylonian Talmud,* 34 vols. London: Soncino Press.

Ezrahi, S. DeK. (1980). *By Words Alone: The Holocaust in Literature.* Chicago: University of Chicago Press.

Fackenheim, E. L. (1970). *God's Presence in History.* New York: New York University Press.

Frazer, J. G., Sir (1959). *The New Golden Bough,* ed. T. H. Gaster. New York: Criterion Books.

Freedman, H., and Simon, M., eds. (1939). *Midrash Rabbah,* 10 vols. London: Soncino Press.

Friedlander, A. H., ed. (1968). *Out of the Whirlwind: A Reader of Holocaust Literature.* New York: Union of American Hebrew Congregations.

Fromm, E. (1966). *You Shall Be As Gods.* New York: Holt, Rinehart and Winston. New York: Fawcett Premier Books, 1969.

Garfiel, E. (1978). *Service of the Heart.* North Hollywood: Wilshire Books.

Gates of Repentance: The New Union Prayerbook for the Days of Awe, (1978), ed. and trans. C. Stern. New York: Central Conference of American Rabbis.

Gemser, B. (1955). The rîb—or controversy—pattern in Hebrew mentality. In *Supplement to Vetus Testamentum* (Vol. 3, *Wisdom in Israel and the Ancient Near East*), pp. 120–137. Leiden, Netherlands: E. J. Brill.

Ginzberg, L. (1901). Elisha Ben Abuyah. *Jewish Encyclopedia,* vol. 5, columns 137–140.

—— (1909–1938). *The Legends of the Jews,* 7 vols. Philadelphia: Jewish Publication Society of America.

Glatstein, J. (1972). *The Selected Poems of Jacob Glatstein,* ed. and trans. R. Whitman. New York: October House.

———— (1973). *Anthology of Holocaust Literature*, ed. I. Knox and S. Margoshes. New York: Atheneum.

Glatzer, N. N., ed. (1969). *The Dimensions of Job*. New York: Schocken Books.

———— (1978). The God of Job and the God of Abraham: Some talmudic-midrashic interpretations of the Book of Job. In *Essays on Jewish Thought*, pp. 93–108. Judaic Studies 8. University, AL: University of Alabama Press.

————, ed. (1946). *A Jewish Reader in Time and Eternity*. New York: Schocken Books; Schocken, 1961.

————, ed. (1969). *The Judaic Tradition*. Boston: Beacon Press.

———— (1978). "Knowest thou? . . ." notes on the Book of Job. In *Essays on Jewish Thought*, pp. 82–92. Judaic Studies 8. University, AL: University of Alabama Press.

Goldin, J., ed. *The Jewish Expression*. New Haven, CT: Yale University Press, 1976.

————, ed. (1957). *The Living Talmud: Wisdom of the Fathers*. New York: New American Library.

Goldman, I. M. (1975). *Lifelong Learning Among Jews*. New York: Ktav.

Goldsmith, R. H. (1963). The healing scourge. *Interpretation* 17:271–279.

Goldstein, D., ed. and trans. (1971). *The Jewish Poets of Spain*. New York: Penguin Books.

Gollancz, H. (1908). *Translations from the Hebrew and Aramaic*. London: Luzac & Co.

Greenberg, I. (1975). Judaism and Christianity after the Holocaust. *Journal of Ecumenical Studies* 12:521–551.

Gross, M. D. (1973). *Otzar HaAgadah*. Jerusalem: Mosad Harav Kook.

Gunkel, H. (1967). *The Psalms: A Form-Critical Introduction*, trans. T. H. Horner. Philadelphia: Fortress Press.

Guttmann, A. (1976). The significance of miracles for talmudic Judaism. In *Studies in Rabbinic Judaism*, pp. 47–90. New York: Ktav.

Guttmann, J. (1964). *Philosophies of Judaism*, trans. D. W. Silverman. New York: Holt, Rinehart and Winston. New York: Schocken, 1973.

HaLevi, Y. (1894–1930). *Divan*, 4 vols., ed. H. Brody. Berlin: Mekize Nirdamim.

Halkin, S. (1950). *Modern Hebrew Literature: Trends and Values*. New York: Schocken Books.

Hartman, D. (1985). *A Living Covenant: The Innovative Spirit in Traditional Judaism*. New York: Free Press.

Heinemann, J. (1967). *Prayer in the Talmud: Forms and Patterns*. Berlin: Walter de Gruyter.

Heinemann, J. J., with J. J. Petuchowski, eds. (1975). *Literature of the Synagogue*. New York: Behrman House.

Heller, J. (1985). *God Knows.* New York: Dell Publishing.

Herberg, W. (1959). *Judaism and Modern Man: An Interpretation of Jewish Religion.* New York and Philadelphia: Meridan Books and Jewish Publication Society of America.

Heschel, A. J. (1954). *Man's Quest for God.* New York: Charles Scribner's Sons.

——— (1973). *A Passion for Truth.* New York: Farrar, Straus & Giroux.

——— (1962). *The Prophets.* New York: Burning Bush Press.

——— (1962). *Theology of Ancient Judaism* (Hebrew, 2 vols.) London: Soncino Press.

Hoffman, L. A. (1987). *Beyond the Text: A Holistic Approach to Liturgy.* Bloomington: Indiana University Press.

Holladay, W. L. (1963). Jeremiah's lawsuit with God. *Interpretation* 17:280–287.

Holtz, B. W., ed. (1984). *Back to the Sources: Reading the Classic Jewish Texts.* New York and Philadelphia: Summit Books and Jewish Publication Society of America.

Howe, I., and Greenberg, E., eds. (1954). *A Treasury of Yiddish Stories.* New York: Viking Press.

———, eds. (1969). *A Treasury of Yiddish Poetry.* New York: Holt, Rinehart and Winston.

Howe, I., Greenberg, E., and Wisse, R. R., eds. (1980). *The Best of Sholom Aleichem.* New York: Simon & Schuster.

Howe, I., Greenberg, E., Wisse, R. R., and Shmeruk, K., eds. (1987). *The Penguin Book of Modern Yiddish Verse.* New York: Viking Penguin.

Huffmon, H. H. (1959). The covenant lawsuit in the Prophets. *Journal of Biblical Literature* 78:285–295.

Hyman, A. (1971). *Otzar Divrei Hacamim U'Pitgameihem.* Tel Aviv: Dvir.

ibn Verga, J. (1856). *Shebet Yehuda,* ed. and trans. M. Wiener. Hanover, FRG: C. Ruempler.

Idelsohn, A. Z. (1967). *Jewish Liturgy and its Development.* New York: Schocken Books.

Jacobs, L. (1957). The concept of hasid in the biblical and rabbinic literature. *Journal of Jewish Studies* 8:143–154.

——— (1973). *Hasidic Prayer.* New York: Schocken Books.

——— (1976). *Hasidic Thought.* New York: Behrman House.

——— (1973). *A Jewish Theology.* New York: Behrman House.

Jastrow, M. (1903). *Dictionary of the Targumim, the Talmud Babli and Yerushalmi, and the Midrashic Literature.* New York and London: Judaica Press and Luzac, 1971, 2 vols. in 1.

Joseph b. Joshua HaKohen (1971). *The Vale of Tears,* trans. H. S. May. The Hague: Nijhoff.

Kaplan, A. (1980). The Jewish argument with God. *Commentary* 70:43–47.

Karff, S. E. (1979). *Agada: The Language of Jewish Faith.* Cincinnati: Hebrew Union College Press.

Katz, J. (1962). *Exclusiveness and Tolerance: Jewish-Gentile Relations in Medieval and Modern Times.* New York: Schocken Books.

Katzenelson, I. (1980). *The Song of the Murdered Jewish People*, trans. and ann. N. H. Rosenbloom. Israel: Ghetto Fighters' House; HaKibbutz HaMeuchad Publishing.

Kaufman, Y. (1972). *The Religion of Israel*, trans. and ab. M. Greenberg. New York: Schocken Books.

Kaufmann, W. (1961). *The Faith of a Heretic.* Garden City, NY: Doubleday.

Kazantzakis, N. (1960). *The Saviors of God: Spiritual Exercises*, trans. K. Friar. New York: Simon & Schuster.

Kiner, E. D. (1965). Views of Job in the Midrash. Rabbinic thesis. Cincinnati: Hebrew Union College.

Knobel, P. S. (1969). *Petirat Moshe*: a critical edition and translation. Rabbinic thesis. Cincinnati: Hebrew Union College.

Kolitz, Z. (1982). *The Teacher: An Existential Approach to the Bible.* New York: Crossroad.

—— (1968). Yossel Rakover's appeal to God. In *Out of the Whirlwind*, ed. A. H. Friedlander. New York: Union of American Hebrew Congregations.

Kroloff, C. H. (1960). The effect of suffering on the concept of God in Lamentations *Rabbah.* Rabbinic thesis. Cincinnati: Hebrew Union College.

Lagawier, A. (1969). Reflections on the source of Jewish ethics. Unpublished.

Lao Tzu. *Tao Te Ching* (1963). Trans. D. C. Lau. New York: Penguin Books.

Laytner, A. H. (1981). Remnants of a dissenting tradition (in the Haggadah). *Conservative Judaism* 34:42–48.

Lee, B. G. (1970). The private prayers of the rabbis: aspects of their form and content. Rabbinic thesis. Cincinnati: Hebrew Union College.

Leftwich, J., ed. (1961). *The Golden Peacock.* New York: Thomas Yoseloff.

Leibowitz, N. (1976). *Studies in Bereshit, Shemot, Vayikra, Bamidbar, Devarim*, 6 vols., trans. A. Newman. Jerusalem: World Zionist Organization.

Leivick, H. (1945). *In Treblinka Bin Ich Nit Geven.* New York: H. Leivick Jubilee Fund, through ZIKO Publishing.

Levey, S. R. (1972). The best kept secret of the rabbinic tradition. *Judaism* 21:454–469.

Levinson-Labie, M. Z. (1938). "Hattahat Devarim K'lapei Ma'alah" (Hurling Words Against Heaven). In *Sefer HaShannah: The American Hebrew Yearbook*, pp. 113–127, ed. M. Ribolow. New York: Histadrut Haivrit BeAmerica.

Likorot HaGezeirot al Yisrael (1887), ed. C. J. Gurland. Przmsyl, Poland: Zupnik, Kholler, and Hammerschmidt.

Liptzin, S. (1985). *A History of Yiddish Literature.* Middle Village, NY: Jonathan David.

Madison, C. A. (1968). *Yiddish Literature: Its Scope and Major Writers.* New York: Frederick Ungar.

Mahzor for Rosh Hashanah and Yom Kippur (1972), ed. and trans. Jules Harlow. New York: Rabbinical Assembly of America.

Maier, J. (1972). *Geschichte der Juedischen Religion.* Berlin: Walter de Gruyter.

Marcus, J. R., ed. (1965). *The Jew in the Medieval World, A Source Book: 1351-1791.* New York: Harper & Row.

Marmorstein, A. (1950). The background of the haggadah. In *Studies in Jewish Theology*, pp. 1–71. London: Oxford University Press.

—— (1920). *The Doctrine of Merits in Old Rabbinic Literature* (Jews' College Publications no. 7). London: Jews' College Publications.

—— (1927–1937). *The Old Rabbinic Doctrine of God*, 2 vols. (Jews' College Publications, nos. 10, 14). Vol. 1: the names and attributes of God—vol. 2: essays in anthropomorphism. London: Oxford University Press.

Mechilta de-Rabbi Ishmael (1933), trans. J. Z. Lauterbach, 3 vols. Philadelphia: Jewish Publication Society of America; reprint 1976.

Midrash Rabbah (1960) 2 vols. Jerusalem: Lewin-Epstein.

Midrash Rabbah (1968), 11 vols., ed. M. Mirkin. Tel Aviv: Yavneh.

Midrash Tanhuma (1885), ed. S. Buber. Vilna: Rom.

Midrash Tanhuma (1953), ed. H. Zundel. Jerusalem: Lewin-Epstein.

Midrash Tehillim (1891), ed. S. Buber. Vilna: Rom, reprint, New York: Om Publishing, 1947.

Millgram, A. (1971). *Jewish Worship.* Philadelphia: Jewish Publication Society of America.

Mintz, A. (1984). *Hurban: Responses to Catastrophe in Hebrew Literature.* New York: Columbia University Press.

Montefiore, C. G. and Loewe, H., eds. (1974). *A Rabbinic Anthology.* New York: Schocken Books.

Moore, G. F. (1971). *Judaism in the First Centuries of the Christian Era: The Age of the Tannaim*, 2 vols. New York: Schocken Books.

Munk, E. (1961, 1963). *The World of Prayer*, 2 vols. Vol. 1, trans. H. Biberfeld and L. Oschry; vol. 2, trans. G. Hirschler. New York: Philip Feldheim.

Nathan H. (1983). *Abyss of Despair (Yeven Metzulah)*, trans A. Mesch. New Brunswick: Transaction Books.

Newman, L. I., trans. and ed. (1934). *The Hasidic Anthology.* New York: Charles Scribner's Sons. New York: Schocken, 1963.

Noy, D. (1960). "Tefillat HaTamim Morida Geshamim" (The Innocents' Prayer Brings Down Rain). *Mahanayim* 51:34–45.

Olsvanger, I. (1921). *Contentions With God: A Study in Jewish Folk-lore.* Cape Town, South Africa: T. Maskew Miller.

Orlinsky, H., ed. (1973). *Torah: The Five Books of Moses,* 2nd ed. Philadelphia: Jewish Publication Society of America.

Otzar HaTefilot (1924). Vilna: Rom.

Parkes, J. (1961). *The Conflict of the Church and the Synagogue: A Study in the Origins of Antisemitism.* New York: Meridian Books.

The Passover Haggadah (1969). Rev. ed., trans. and ed. N. N. Glatzer. New York: Schocken Books.

Patai, R. (1979). *The Messiah Texts: Jewish Legends of Three Thousand Years.* Detroit: Wayne State University Press.

Peli, P. (1983). Where was God during the Holocaust? *Jerusalem Post International Edition,* April 17–23 and April 24–May 1.

Penueli, S. Y, and Ukhmani, A., ed. and trans. (1966). *Anthology of Modern Hebrew Poetry,* 2 vols. Jerusalem: Israel University's Press.

Pesikta de Rav Kahanna (1868). Ed. S. Buber. Lyck, Poland: L. Silbermann; reprint, New York: Om Publishing, 1949.

Pesikta Rabbati (1880). Ed. M. Friedmann (M. Ish Shalom). Vienna: 1880 (self-published).

Petuchowski, J. J. (1968). The concept of "Teshuvah" in the Bible and Talmud. *Judaism* 17:175–185.

—— (1968). *Ever Since Sinai: A Modern View of Torah.* 2nd rev. ed. New York: Scribe.

—— (1968). *Prayerbook Reform in Europe.* New York: World Union for Progressive Judaism.

—— (1970). *Heirs of the Pharisees.* New York: Basic Books.

—— (1978). *Theology and Poetry: Studies in the Medieval Piyyut.* London: Routledge and Kegan Paul.

—— , ed. (1981). *Understanding Jewish Prayer.* New York: Ktav.

Plaut, G. W., ed. (1981). *The Torah: A Modern Commentary.* New York: Union of American Hebrew Congregations.

Potok, C. (1969). *The Promise.* New York: Alfred A. Knopf.

Prayer Book for Sabbath and Festivals (1964), ed. and trans. P. Birnbaum. New York: Hebrew Publishing.

Prayers for the Day of Atonement According to the Custom of the Spanish and Portuguese Jews (1939), ed. and trans. D. de Sola Pool. New York: Union of Sephardic Congregations.

Rabinovich, I. (1968). *Major Trends in Modern Hebrew Fiction,* trans. M. Roston. Chicago: University of Chicago Press.

Reuther, R. R. (1974). *Faith and Fratricide: The Theological Roots of Anti-Semitism.* New York: Seabury Press.

Riemer, J., ed. (1975). *Jewish Reflections on Death.* New York: Schocken Books.

Rosenfeld, A., and Greenberg, I., eds. (1978). *Confronting the Holocaust: The Impact of Elie Wiesel.* Bloomington: Indiana University Press.

Roskies, D. G. (1979). The pogrom poem and the literature of destruction. *Notre Dame English Journal* 11.

—— (1984). *Against the Apocalypse: Responses to Catastrophe in Modern Jewish Culture.* Cambridge, MA: Harvard University Press.

Roskies, D. K., and D. G. (1975). *The Shtetl Book.* New York: Ktav.

Rubenstein, R. L. (1966). *After Auschwitz: Radical Theology and Contemporary Judaism.* New York: Bobbs-Merrill.

Rubin, R. (1979). *Voices of a People: The Story of Yiddish Folksong.* Philadelphia: Jewish Publication Society of America.

Sabbath and Festival Prayerbook (1952), ed. and trans. M. Silverman. New York: Rabbinical Assembly of America & United Synagogue of America.

Safrai, S. (1972). Elisha Ben Avuyah. *Encyclopaedia Judaica,* vol. 6, cols. 668–670.

Sarna, N. M. (1966). *Understanding Genesis.* New York: Jewish Theological Seminary of America and McGraw-Hill.

—— (1986). *Exploring Exodus.* New York: Schocken Books.

Schechter, S. (1909). *Some Aspects of Rabbinic Theology.* New York: Macmillan.

Scholem, G. G. (1941). *Major Trends in Jewish Mysticism.* Jerusalem: Schocken Books; New York: Schocken, 1961.

—— (1965). *Jewish Gnosticism, Merkabah Mysticism and Talmudic Tradition.* New York: Jewish Theological Seminary Press.

Schulweis, H. M. (1964). Suffering and Evil. In *Great Jewish Ideas,* pp. 197–218, ed. A. E. Millgram. Clinton, MA: B'nai B'rith Department of Adult Jewish Education.

—— (1965). Man and God: The moral partnership. In *Jewish Heritage Reader,* pp. 118–121, ed. L. Edelman. New York: Taplinger Publishers.

Schwartz, H., and Rudolf, A., eds. (1980). *Voices Within the Ark: The Modern Jewish Poets.* New York: Avon Books.

Seder Eliahu Rabba and Seder Eliahu Zuta (Tanna d'be Eliahu) (1969), ed. M. Friedmann (M. Ish Shalom). Warsaw: Verlag Achiasaf, 1904; reprint, Jerusalem: Wahrmann Books.

Sefer Gezeirot Ashkenaz v'Zarfat (1945), ed. A. M. Haberman. Jerusalem: Tarshish Books.

Sefer HaDema'ot (1924–1926), 3 vols., ed. S. Bernfeld. Berlin: Eschkol Publishers.

Selected Hebrew Poems of Moses Ibn Ezra (1934 and 1945), trans. S. S. Cohen. Philadelphia: Jewish Publication Society of America.

Selected Poems of Jehudah Halevi (1924 and 1952), ed. H. Brody, trans. N. Salaman. Philadelphia: Jewish Publication Society of America.

Selected Religious Poetry of Solomon Ibn Gabirol (1924 and 1952), trans. I. Zangwill. Philadelphia: Jewish Publication Society of America.

Seltzer, R. M. (1980). *Jewish People, Jewish Thought: The Jewish Experience in History.* New York: Macmillan.

Service of the Synagogue: Day of Atonement, ed. and trans. A. Davis and H. Adler. New York: Hebrew Publishing, n.d.

Service of the Synagogue: New Year, ed. and trans. A. Davis and H. Adler. New York: Hebrew Publishing, n.d.

Sherwin, B. L., and Ament, S. G., eds. (1979) *Encountering the Holocaust: An Interdisciplinary Survey.* Chicago: Impact Press.

Shilo Prayer Book (1972), 6th ed. New York: Shilo Publishing House.

Sifré Deuteronomy (*Sifré d'be Rav*) (1939), ed. L. Finkelstein. Berlin: Juedischer Kulturband in Deutschland, 1935–1939; reprint, New York: Jewish Theological Seminary of America, 1969.

Sifré Numbers and *Sifré Zuta* (*Sifré d'be Rav*) (1927), ed. H. S. Horovitz. Leipzig: G. Fock, 1927; reprint, Jerusalem: Wahrmann Books, 1966.

Silver, D. J. (1982). *Images of Moses.* New York: Basic Books.

Spiegel, S. (1940). *The Last Trial,* trans. J. Goldin. New York: Jewish Theological Seminary of America; New York: Schocken, 1967.

—— (1971). On medieval Hebrew poetry. In *The Jews: Their Religion and Culture,* 4th ed., ed. L. Finkelstein. New York: Schocken Books.

Steinsaltz, A. (1976). *The Essential Talmud,* trans. C. Galdi. New York: Basic Books.

Strom, E. M. (1977). Theology in crisis: theodicy at the time of the crusades. Rabbinic thesis. Cincinnati: Hebrew Union College.

Talmud Bavli (1912). 12 vols. Vilna: Rom.

Talmud Yerushalmi (1866). Krotoshin: D. B. Monasch.

Tanakh: The Holy Scriptures (1988). Philadelphia: Jewish Publication Society of America.

Torah, Nevi'im, Ketuvim (*The Jerusalem Bible*) (1969). Jerusalem: Koren Publishers.

Tsevat, M. (1966). The meaning of the Book of Job. *HUCA* 37:73–106.

Twain, M. (1963). *Letters from the Earth,* ed. B. DeVoto. New York: Crest Books.

Ullendorf, E. (1966). Thought categories in the Hebrew Bible. In *Studies in Rationalism, Judaism and Universalism,* pp. 273–288, ed. R. Loewe. London: Routledge and Kegan Paul.

Urbach, E. E. (1975, 1979). *The Sages: Their Concepts and Beliefs,*

2 vols., trans. I. Abrahams. Jerusalem: Magnes Press, Hebrew University.

Usque, S. (1965). *Consolation for the Tribulations of Israel*, trans. and ed. M. A. Cohen. Philadelphia: Jewish Publication Society of America.

Weiser, A. (1976). *The Psalms: A Commentary*. Philadelphia: The Westminster Press.

Wels-Schon, G. (1968). *Portrait of Yahweh as a Young God, or How to Get Along With a God You Don't Necessarily Like But Can't Help Loving*. New York: Holt, Rinehart & Winston.

Westermann, C. (1965). *The Praise of God in the Psalms*, trans. K. R. Crim. Richmond, VA: John Knox Press.

—— (1974). The role of the lament in the theology of the Old Testament. *Interpretation* 28:20–38.

Whitman, R., ed. and trans. (1979). *An Anthology of Modern Yiddish Poetry*, 2nd ed. New York: Education Department of the Workmen's Circle.

Wiesel, E. (1961). *Dawn*, trans. F. Frenaye. New York: Hill & Wang.

—— (1962). *The Accident*, trans. A. Borchardt. New York: Hill & Wang.

—— (1964). *The Town Beyond the Wall*, trans. S. Becker. New York: Atheneum.

—— (1965). *One Generation After*, trans. L. Edelman and E. Wiesel. New York: Random House.

—— (1966). *The Gates of the Forest*, trans. F. Frenaye. New York: Holt, Rinehart & Winston.

—— (1968). *Legends of Our Time*. New York: Holt, Rinehart & Winston.

—— (1969). *Night*, trans. S. Rodway. New York: Avon Books.

—— (1970). *A Beggar in Jerusalem*, trans. L. Edelman and E. Wiesel. New York: Random House.

—— (1972). *Souls on Fire*, trans. M. Wiesel. New York: Random House.

—— (1973). *Ani Maamin: A Song Lost and Found Again*, trans. M. Wiesel. New York: Random House.

—— (1973). *The Oath*, trans. M. Wiesel. New York: Random House.

—— (1974). *Zalmen, or the Madness of God*, adapt. M. Wiesel, based on translation by N. Edelman. New York: Random House.

—— (1976). *Messengers of God*, trans. M. Wiesel. New York: Random House.

—— (1978). *A Jew Today*, trans. M. Wiesel. New York: Random House.

—— (1979). *The Trial of God (As It Was Held on February 25, 1649 in Shamgorod)*, trans. M. Wiesel. New York: Random House.

—— (1982). *Somewhere a Master*, trans. M. Wiesel. New York: Summit Books.

Yerushalmi, Y. H. (1982). *Zakhor: Jewish History and Jewish Memory*. Seattle: University of Washington Press.

Zeitlin, S. (1946). An historical study of the first canonization of the
    Hebrew liturgy. *Jewish Quarterly Review* 36:211–229.
—— (1961). The temple and worship. *Jewish Quarterly Review* n.s.
    51:208–241.
Zinberg, I. (1972, 1975). *A History of Jewish Literature*, 12 vols., ed. and
    trans. B. Martin. Vols. 1–3: Cleveland: Case Western Reserve Press. Vols.
    4–12: Cincinnati and New York: Hebrew Union College Press & Ktav.
Zohar: The Book of Enlightenment (1983), ed. and trans. D. Matt. New
    York: Paulist Press.
Zunz, L. (1907). *The Suffering of the Jews in the Middle Ages*, trans.
    A. Loewy. Rev. ed., G. A. Kohut. New York: Bloch Publishers; reprinted
    in *Historical Views of Judaism: Four Selections*. New York: Arno
    Press, 1973.

CREDITS

The author and publisher gratefully acknowledge the following for their permission to reprint material found in this book: From *The Holocaust: A Source Reader*, ed. L. Davidowitz. Copyright © 1976 by Behrman House. Reprinted by permission of Behrman House. From *The Golden Peacock*, ed. J. Leftwich. Copyright © 1971 by Thomas Yoseloff. Reprinted by permission of Tantivy Press. Copyright © 1986 Samuel H. Dresner from *World of a Hasidic Master: Levi Yitzhak of Berditchev*, Shapolsky Publishers, New York. Reprinted by permission of Shapolsky Brothers. From the *Hasidic Anthology*, trans. and ed. L. I. Newman. Copyright © 1963 by Schocken Books. Reprinted by permission of Jeremy Newman. From Diane K. and David G. Roskies, *The Shtetl Book*. Copyright © 1975 by Ktav. Reprinted by permission of Ktav. From *Authorized Selichot for the Whole Year* and *Authorized Kinot for the Ninth of Av*, ed. and trans. Abraham Rosenfeld. Copyright © 1974 and 1979 respectively by Judaica Press. Reprinted by permission of Judaica Press. From *A Treasury of Yiddish Poetry*, ed. Irving Howe and Eliezer Greenberg. Copyright © by Irving Howe and Eliezer Greenberg. Reprinted by permission of Henry Holt and Company, Inc. From *Selected Religious Poetry of Solomon ibn Gabirol*, trans. I. Zangwill, and Ruth Rubin, *Voices of a People: The Story of Yiddish Folksong*. Copyright © 1924, 1952 and 1979 respectively by The Jewish Publication Society of America. Reprinted by permission of the Jewish Publication Society of America. From *Voices within the Ark: The Modern Jewish Poets*, ed. Howard Schwartz and Anthony Rudolph. Copyright © by Avon Books. Reprinted by permission of Erna B. Rosenfeld, trans., and Joachim Neugroschell, trans. From Jakob J. Petuchowski, *Theology and Poetry: Studies in the Medieval Piyyut*. Copyright © 1978 by Oxford University Press. Reprinted by permission of the Littman Library of Jewish Civilization, published by Oxford University Press. From *The Penguin Book of Hebrew Verse*, ed. and trans. T. Carmi. Copyright © 1981 T. Carmi. Reprinted by permission of Penguin Books Ltd.

INDEX